NATO

NATO

From Cold War to Ukraine,
a History of the World's Most
Powerful Alliance

STEN RYNNING

YALE UNIVERSITY PRESS
NEW HAVEN AND LONDON

Copyright © 2024 Sten Rynning

All rights reserved. This book may not be reproduced in whole or in part, in any form (beyond that copying permitted by Sections 107 and 108 of the U.S. Copyright Law and except by reviewers for the public press) without written permission from the publishers.

All reasonable efforts have been made to provide accurate sources for all images that appear in this book. Any discrepancies or omissions will be rectified in future editions.

For information about this and other Yale University Press publications, please contact:
U.S. Office: sales.press@yale.edu   yalebooks.com
Europe Office: sales@yaleup.co.uk   yalebooks.co.uk

Set in Minion Pro by IDSUK (DataConnection) Ltd
Printed in Great Britain by TJ Books Limited, Padstow, Cornwall

Library of Congress Control Number: 2023952221

ISBN 978-0-300-27011-2

A catalogue record for this book is available from the British Library.

10 9 8 7 6 5 4 3 2 1

To Emil, Axel, and Clement—heroes of the future
To Anne—heroine of the present

Contents

Plates and Maps

10. Harlan Cleveland and Robert McNamara, 1966. Courtesy of NATO Archives.
11. Pierre Harmel and Joseph Luns, 1967. Courtesy of NATO Archives.
12. Manlio Brosio and Robert McNamara, 1965. Courtesy of NATO Archives.
13. Secretary General Joseph Luns receives US President Richard Nixon at NATO headquarters, 1974. Courtesy of NATO Archives.
14. President Jimmy Carter standing with West German Chancellor Helmut Schmidt, outside the White House, Washington, DC, 1979. U.S. News & World Report Magazine Photograph Collection, LC-U9-37702-A- 18, Library of Congress Prints and Photographs Division Washington, DC. 20540 USA.
15. General Bernard Rogers speaking at The Hague, 1983. Nationaal Archief, 932-4625.
16. President Ronald Reagan and President François Mitterrand at the G7 summit in Williamsburg, Virginia, 1983. National Archives, 276563663.
17. Politicians at the Brandenburg Gate opening, 1989. US Defense Imagery, DF-ST-91-03540.
18. President George H. Bush, Secretary of State James Baker, and NATO General Secretary Manfred Wörner, 1989. Courtesy of NATO Archives.
19. British Royal Engineers serving in NATO's stabilization force in Bosnia-Herzegovina, after 1995. Courtesy of NATO Archives.
20. President George W. Bush in the White House, 2001. National Archives, 5997259.
21. Spanish and US troops prepare to board a Chinook helicopter at Bala Murghab Forward Operating Base, Badghis province, northwestern Afghanistan, 2012. Courtesy of NATO Archives.
22. Prime Minister Silvio Berlusconi, President Vladimir Putin, and NATO Secretary General George Robertson at the NATO–Russia Council summit, Rome, 2002. Courtesy of NATO Archives.

Maps

Acknowledgments

This book is the fruit of the generosity shown to me by many people and institutions through decades of scholarship. Without it, I might have hesitated when Yale University Press editor Joanna Godfrey got in touch in early 2022 to talk about the idea of tracing the full historical trajectory of NATO and to get a book out in time for the alliance's seventy-fifth anniversary in April 2024. Instead, Jo's idea struck home. I knew from the moment we began our conversation that this was the book I had to write because, intellectually speaking, it was my destiny.

I am indebted to many individuals—scholars, diplomats, and decision-makers—who have taken the time to educate me about an alliance as historically rich and as politically complex as NATO. I owe a special thanks to Carsten Søndergaard who diligently read all draft chapters and engaged in many thoughtful discussions. Had he not chosen the path of diplomacy, Carsten would have made a wonderful scholar. Rasmus Mariager challenged me in my historical thinking, and we have now happily begun new NATO research adventures. For the many early-morning café meetings where we kept our book projects on the rails, I am grateful to Claire Yorke. I am grateful also to my editor, Jo, who read along and strove to keep me within bounds. For comments on the project and the idea of an aspirational alliance and on portions of the manuscript, I am thankful to Christilla Roederer, James Rogers, and Susan Colbourn, as well as the anonymous reviewers of both my book proposal and the full manuscript. Nicholas Nguyen and the team at NATO Archives were outstandingly helpful.

Researching and writing the manuscript proved to be an intense deep dive. Anne Ingemann Johansen was in every way a lifeline of intellectual and moral support, bringing oxygen to my submerged existence. My institution, the University of Southern Denmark, was an ideal home for immersed free thinking. Jens Ringsmose and Peter Møllgaard generously allowed me to let go of everything but the book. Marianne Holmer hosted me at the Danish Institute for Advanced Study where Sune Vork Steffensen and Francesco Sannino became interdisciplinary comrades in arms. Brent R. Clausen housed me during my California writing retreat. For all their support, I am truly grateful.

For shared insights and experiences in the course of researching the book, I am indebted to George Robertson, Jaap de Hoop Scheffer, James Everard, Ben Hodges, Alexander Vershbow, Stefano Stefanini, Ahmet Bülent Meriç, Ömer Sölendil, Levent Murat Burhan, Iskender Okyay, Haldun Yalçinkaya, Murat Aslan, Fatih Tayfur, Fatih Ceylan, and Zerrin Torun. Xenia Wickett generously offered me a connection. Julian Lindley-French has throughout offered me a stimulating and enriching home in the Alphen Group. Hüseyin Bagci went out of his way to offer me a most extraordinary stay at the Foreign Policy Institute and the Middle East Technical University in Ankara where Murat Demirel, Seyma Kalac, and Ilbey Coban kindly guided me.

I am thankful to other ports of call that during the making of the manuscript advanced my thinking on NATO. Tom Sauer hosted me at the University of Antwerp for a workshop on the European security order. Kate Hansen Bundt of the Norwegian Atlantic Treaty Association brought me to Oslo for an amazing Leangkollen Security Conference. Jörg Muth engaged me at the Baltic Defence College where Louis Wierenga and my ever-present friend Eoin McNamara joined us for a night of reflections. Henrik Larsen, an original thinker with a big heart, brought me to Zurich to speak at the Center for Security Studies at ETH Zurich and perhaps not least to see Vladimir Lenin's Swiss home, yet another marker of Europe's predisposition for high drama. The many good people of the NATO Defense College brought me to Rome several times during the writing of the book to lecture on the Senior Course. I have been to the college close to thirty times since 2012 when I began lecturing there, and it has consistently been both a magnificent host and a wonderful arena for security discussions with talented people of many nationalities. Outstanding diplomatic servants of Danish foreign policy likewise merit my sincere thanks, in particular Lone Dencker Wisborg, Jakob Henningsen, Morten V. Jacobsen, and Eva Marie Frida Barløse.

I would like also to thank people who through the years have been generous partners in my quest for insight. NATO has been fortunate to have a number of terrifically creative thinkers who ordinarily would be called civil servants but who in fact have been thought leaders and ambassadors of NATO as an open and engaged organization: Jamie Shea, Diego Ruiz-Palmer, Michael Rühle, Nicholas Williams, and Heinrich Brauss. If any set of people embody a "NATO spirit" of consultations, you are it. I would like to thank also my old mentor, Donald J. Puchala, who guided my thinking on ideas, international history, and the meaning people ascribe to political institutions. This book, this inquiry into NATO's "soul," really began decades ago with Don's probing questions on human thought and power. Don worked at the crossroads of humanities and social sciences, and so would my later comrade-in-arms, Jens Ringsmose. We ventured into the territory of NATO inquiry and never looked back. At one point, though, on a turbulent plane ride back from NATO headquarters, we were not so sure. That ride now lives forever. My sincere thanks also go to Jim Goldgeier, Theo Farrell, Terry Terriff, John R. Deni, Andrew Michta, and Stan Sloan for the friendship and intellectual exchanges offered through the years.

My sons, Emil, Axel, and Clement, have endured NATO throughout their childhood and now early manhood. Happily, they have emerged from the ordeal as vigorous, curious, and wonderful young men. At a time when a beleaguered European continent again calls on the leadership of a great generation, they are an inspiration and a source of hope. I am privileged to be their father. My mother, Ruth Rynning, has witnessed all events dealt with in this book, and she remains a loving pillar of strength in the family. My late father, Svend Erik

Rynning, attracted her from her native Norway to Denmark, and together they created a family exposed to transatlantic experiences and encouraged me to be curious about it all. This book is the fruit of all their devoted and caring parental labor. Anne Ingemann Johansen, my muse, braved the depths of NATO research and writing to tenderly insist that passion must have a say. I am so immensely grateful for her love and friendship.

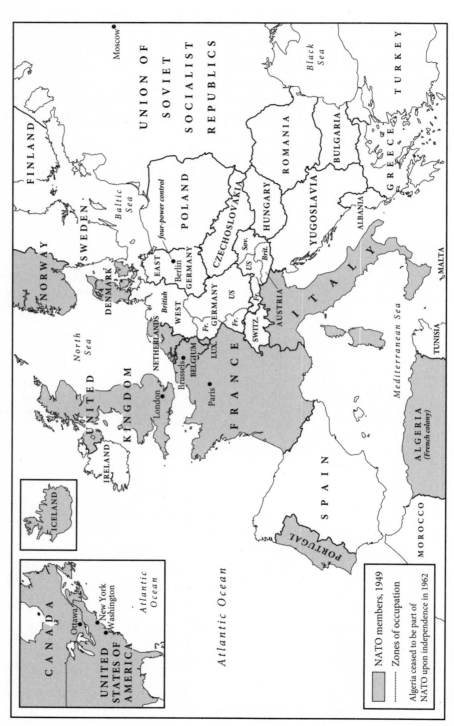

1. The NATO area in 1949.

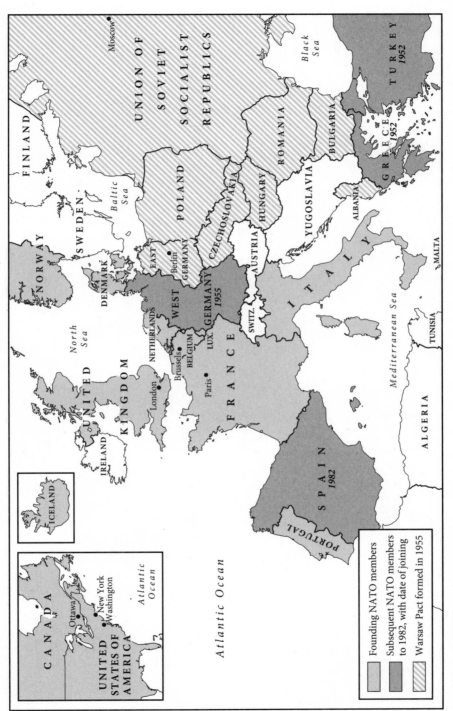

2. NATO Cold War enlargement.

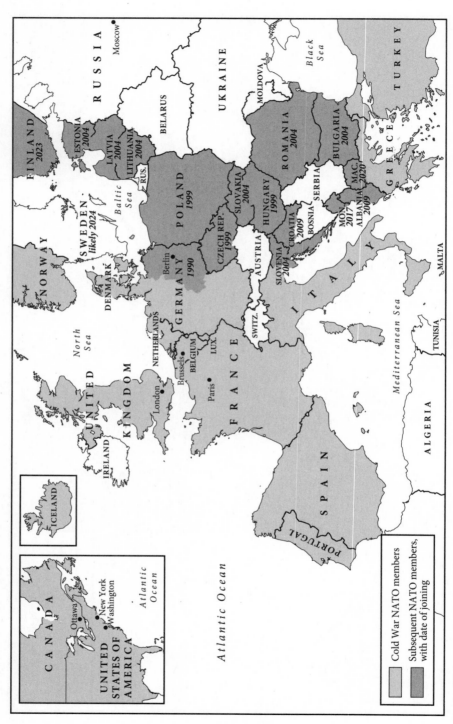

3. NATO post-Cold War enlargement.

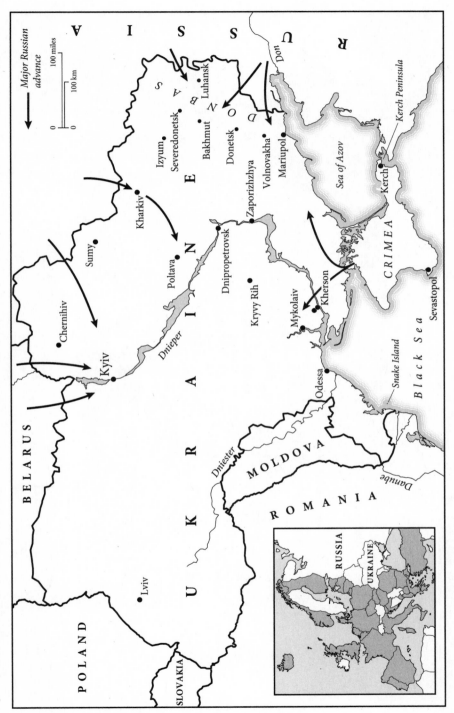

4. Russia's war in Ukraine and for Europe.

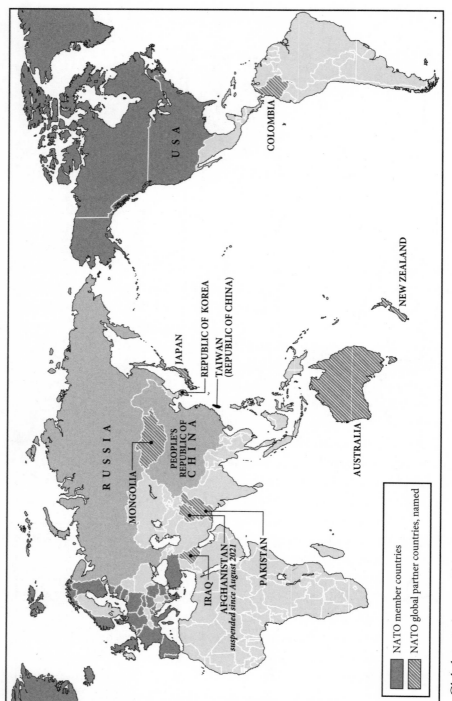

5. Global strategic competition.

The North Atlantic Treaty Organization

In February 2022, Russia's President Putin committed a "breach of civilization" when he unleashed a devastating war in an effort to remove Ukraine's right to exist independently.[1] In so doing, he brought NATO back to life as a defensive shield against external aggression. That was why NATO had been created back in 1949; but like everyone else, President Putin was aware of how in recent years the organization had lost its geopolitical mojo. US President Obama had dithered on NATO leadership, and then President Trump had sent a wrecking ball smashing into its diplomacy. Gloom set in on the European side, and French President Macron declared the alliance brain dead. To cap it all, in August 2021 the Taliban kicked NATO out of Afghanistan. Perhaps, therefore, by breaking Ukraine's statehood, President Putin could also break NATO.

Yet, for all his cunning, Putin remained one step behind the late Paul-Henri Spaak. A Belgian statesman who served as both prime minister and foreign minister of his country, he had been present at the birth of NATO, and in 1956 was appointed the organization's secretary general. Spaak had an intuitive feel for NATO's special character: no other alliance in history had had such a deep commitment to consultation among free countries; none had been likewise fueled by the desire to live in freedom and security. To distil this character into words, Spaak teamed up with André de Staercke, Belgium's ambassador to NATO who, impressively, would stay in post for twenty-six years. Spaak and de Staercke it was who gave NATO its motto, which drew on the history and staying power of the Roman empire: *Animus in consulendo liber*—"In consultation among free spirits."[2]

To seasoned leaders, NATO's motto is hard to miss. It was first written on the wall of the conference hall of NATO's Paris headquarters at Porte Dauphine, a building in the shape of an "A" (for alliance) which opened in 1959. It was then placed inside the main conference chamber of NATO's Brussels headquarters, both in the original headquarters of 1967 and in the new one of 2017. Following a quarrel with fellow NATO leaders over the Middle East, President Nixon once brutally told the allies that consultations were not "a legally binding obligation."[3] Nixon was right, but the point of NATO's character and the motto is not about legality: it is about the political nature of being free and in alliance. It is about how NATO's exercise of power is restrained because of the alliance's free spirits, and how the wisdom of free counsel makes for enduring power. And it is about how NATO, because of these qualities, continues to attract new member allies and partners.[4]

NATO's story is the exercise of power guided by free thinking. That is what this book is about. It is about how NATO was set up in 1949 to create peace for its community. It is about how this vision at times has been more than the NATO allies could handle. And it is about how NATO today must recalibrate its vision to encompass a new struggle for global order.

Why is NATO important?

NATO's vision of being free and allied contrasts with the Eurasian vision of President Vladimir Putin's Russia or the Sinocentric vision of President Xi Jinping's China. Essentially, NATO was and remains a testbed for the geopolitical relevance of Western values. What happens next to NATO is of concern to everyone.

NATO lies at the heart of Europe's security order. And that is no small matter. President Putin has effectively declared war on it, with the purpose of ultimately denying Ukraine the right to choose NATO, and NATO the right to choose Ukraine. Next to Russia stands

Xi Jinping's China. Their "no limits" friendship falls short of Chinese military assistance in the Ukraine war, but highlights the growing alignment of the two powers in opposition to the United States and NATO.[5] According to China, the war of attrition in Ukraine is a result not of Russia's attack, but of how NATO's "five consecutive rounds of eastward expansion" have violated "Russia's legitimate security demands."[6]

In the face of this assault on Europe's order, the NATO allies have had to go back to square one, so as to define their principles for order and provide the military muscle required to protect that order. NATO is the vehicle by which the Western allies—beginning with the United States, but involving all thirty-two countries—will invite Ukraine into an enhanced security partnership, and eventually into their alliance. It is a new order for NATO. And it is not just about Ukraine: it encompasses the entire NATO frontier—which, as a direct result of Russia's war, now includes Finland and soon Sweden. The allies must build up their military capacity to protect and defend this entire territory. Before Russia launched its war in February 2022, the allies did not really take this matter too seriously. Now they do. But forward defense—the ability to defend at the very frontier of NATO territory—requires enormous political-military effort, and it is around the table of the North Atlantic Council, NATO's decision-making chamber, that this effort will be shaped.

NATO allies have faced similar challenges before. But something has changed: power is no longer shifting in the West's favor—as it did in 1949 (when NATO was founded) or in 1990–91 (when the Soviet Union, NATO's Cold War adversary, disintegrated). China is the rising power, and it exudes the confidence of a rising power. The Western allies, by contrast, seem hesitant, unsure of how they can build a sustainable order in the face of adversity. They have provided considerable aid to Ukraine, but they have also restricted that aid in order to prevent an escalation. This pattern of significant but limited assistance comes after a decade of indecision. The bruising war on terror led the allies to seek to extricate themselves from wars in faraway countries, so as to carry out nation-building at home. Though their policy styles differed considerably, Presidents Obama and Trump shared this agenda. Other allied leaders likewise became introverted, expecting others to do the hard lifting for the NATO collective. And so, as China rose and Russia fulminated, NATO weakened.

Historically, the NATO allies have responded to international opportunity not with timidity, but with a degree of overconfidence. In 1949 they aimed high, as indeed they did again in 1990–91: in both instances they offered to "transform" international relations into something better. In the 1950s, this high-minded aspiration fueled a competition among the leading allies over the political spoils of leadership. Half a century later, it led the allies to undertake a vast and impossible mission to build a society for the Afghan government they had sponsored. The allies set up NATO to exercise power with restraint, but they have not always had the wisdom to do so. And there is a risk that the allies will once again bite off more than they can chew, only this time in a confrontation with Russia and China.

For Americans, NATO remains a critical resource of sustained international leadership. The alliance is a hub of growing attraction for allies and partners committed to the international order. When it has utilized NATO's complex multinational diplomacy, the United States has been able to win high-quality policy reflection, consensus, and resilient security commitments; whenever the country has ignored NATO consultations, it has typically suffered.[7] NATO helps the United States guide the exercise of power by free and pluralist counsel, and it helps US decision-makers mobilize greater force than the country could manage on its own.

For Europeans, NATO is just as important, but for different reasons. Europe has a wealth of nations and free counsel, but it cannot exercise power collectively. NATO—not the European Union (EU)—is where European allies can have multiple voices *and* exercise real military power alongside their American ally. At heart, Europe's peace is built on America's extended nuclear deterrent: to imagine Europe's strategic autonomy independent of that deterrent is to deny military reality. Russia's predilection for hard power is there to remind the European allies that if NATO did not exist, they would have to invent it.

What is NATO?

Like NATO's motto, NATO's founding document, the North Atlantic Treaty, builds on the relationship between the spirit of freedom and the staying power of political communities. The treaty itself is short, is written in plain language, and conveys a clear message that NATO seeks to exercise power in the service of a higher aspiration of freedom and peace. Aspiration is NATO's DNA.

The treaty refers to the twelve countries that signed the treaty on April 4, 1949, simply as "parties to this treaty." Tellingly, it is a far cry from the traditional language of European statecraft, which would have invoked high contracting parties, excellencies, extraordinary envoys, ambassadors, and so on. NATO was meant to be different. The alliance was for the people and communities of the North Atlantic area; it was not a classical tool of state power. It puts collective defense in the service of public betterment. Thus, it is committed to freedom, democracy, individual liberty, and the rule of law (preamble). It seeks to strengthen "free institutions," promote "conditions of stability and wellbeing," and "eliminate conflict" in international economic policies (Article 2). And it is open to expanding the alliance to "any other European state" in a position to further these values (Article 10).

Remarkably, the North Atlantic Treaty speaks of no evil. The allies were barely four years out of a world war that had been waged against an axis of revisionist powers—Germany, Italy, and Japan—and they were entering a Cold War with the communist Soviet Union. But at no point do the allies single out one or more threatening countries or menacing ideologies. Instead, the treaty aligns itself with the United Nations—the organization for world cooperation that came into being in 1945. The first sentence of the preamble reaffirms the values of the UN Charter. The allies promise not to act in a way that runs counter to the Charter (Article 1). They promise to exercise individual and collective self-defense in line with the Charter (Article 5). And they affirm that their treaty does not in any way affect the obligations and responsibilities established under the UN Charter (Article 7).

If inclusive and global security under the United Nations is the ultimate goal, NATO pursues it by protecting its own North Atlantic community from outside aggression. That is, NATO is about defense, but in the service of broader security aspirations. Articles 3–6 describe how this works. Article 3 commits every ally to a defense effort: in other words, the alliance is not a US dependency, but a collective effort. Article 4 offers every ally the right to seek allied support if it feels threatened: with this clause, the allies can put NATO on alert and flex its muscles to forestall an impending armed attack. Should such an attack occur, Article 5 commits all the allies to take action to restore and maintain the security of the North Atlantic area. Article 5's obligation of solidarity is clear and obvious, but it leaves it up to each ally to define the appropriate and necessary action. Article 6 defines the geography of this commitment: it covers armed attacks on allied territories in Europe and North America, as well as on allied forces, vessels, and aircraft in the North Atlantic area north of the Tropic of Cancer.

Political management and guidance are dealt with in two articles. Article 8 obliges the allies not to undertake any commitments or engagements that could conflict with the NATO treaty. Thus, if a European ally felt the need to make the EU a defense mechanism, that could well conflict with the NATO treaty. Likewise, the United States cannot enter into any bilateral agreement in the North Atlantic area—say, with Britain, Poland, or any other ally—that would take precedence over its NATO obligations. Article 9 describes how NATO should take decisions: it defines a permanent council—later the North Atlantic Council (NAC)—to consider all matters relevant to the treaty; this should have the capacity to meet promptly at any time. The Council, the treaty continues, must set up a defense committee to support it; and it may set up other subsidiary bodies. In due course, this provision led the allies to create a wider political-military arrangement that provided the "NAT" (North Atlantic Treaty) with a concluding "O" (organization).

Because the treaty was regarded as being in the service of freedom and peace, the allies felt no need to fix an expiration date. In principle, the treaty's duration is indefinite. However, the allies did build in both a review clause and an exit clause. Once the treaty had been in force for ten years, any ally might, in light of global or regional developments, call for a review of it (Article 12). In effect, the treaty has been revised only twice: on the accession of Greece and Turkey, and on the independence of Algeria from France. Both revisions concerned the territory to which the treaty referred. The exit clause stipulates that once the treaty has been in force for twenty years, any ally can withdraw from it with one year's notice (Article 13). No country has ever left NATO.

The North Atlantic Treaty was thus *geographically bounded*: its collective defense clause applied to the North Atlantic area, and prospective members had to be European. But it was also *politically unbounded*: allies can consult on any issue of global order, and they must consider all issues—not just military issues—that threaten their values, free institutions, and wellbeing. What this meant in practice was then up to NATO governments as they consulted and exercised power.

How to think about NATO

In December 1988, US Secretary of State George Shultz attended his final North Atlantic Council meeting. Having been present at such meetings since 1982, he had had a good innings, and his NATO colleagues wanted to show their appreciation. On behalf of their collective, Italian Foreign Minister Giulio Andreotti offered Shultz a gift, a small model train dubbed THE NATO TRAIN. In a subsequent letter of good wishes to Andreotti, Shultz explained how THE NATO TRAIN had become "a big hit" in Washington. He had taken it to a private meeting with President Reagan, who was "fascinated by it." "We ended up," wrote Shultz, "spending an inordinate amount of time playing with it."[8]

It is tempting to read into this type of anecdote how the NATO allies have a special bond: they offer each other gifts and play with them; they quarrel, but at the end of the day they patch things up— thanks to a unifying thread of political, economic, and private exchanges that extends across centuries. NATO leaders and officials regularly invoke this bond in the service of common values or a shared commitment to democracy. NATO's latest strategy speaks of "freedom and democracy," and in 2022 President Biden said it is simply the way of the world that every generation must "defeat democracy's mortal foes."[9]

Some analysts agree that the NATO allies benefit from a special bond. Shared values and a democratic willingness to compromise keep NATO on track, and institutional ties (i.e., NATO itself) help the democracies keep their values of compromise in focus.[10] It follows from this long view of embedded values that NATO is enduring, but must still adapt. Thus, if a global conflict erupts and threatens democracy, the alliance must build a "global security web," or even transform itself into a "global NATO."[11] It follows also that the NATO allies may have enduring values, yet still get their policies wrong: they fought too long and too hard in Afghanistan.[12] Yet despite this failure, NATO continues to operate on valiant ideas of freedom and democracy. And Russia's invasion of Ukraine in 2022 was but a stark reminder that democracy is worth fighting for.[13] The United States is in NATO to fight for freedom in Europe; the Europeans must increasingly realize that they should be ready to fight for it in the Indo-Pacific region.[14]

Not everyone agrees, though. Some analysts think that far from being valiant, NATO's liberal ideals are distortive, or even corruptive. That is, liberal ideals may cause policymakers to chase dreams and ignore the realities of power.[15] Some analysts claim that this is what happened in the case of NATO's enlargement. They believe that the Soviet (and later Russian) leaders got a raw deal at the end of the Cold War: NATO leaders promised them a spirit of cooperation, but instead expanded NATO.[16] In the end, this teed Russia and NATO up for conflict and, ultimately, an armed contest for influence, which is what came to be played out in Ukraine in 2022.[17] According to this line of reasoning, President Bush senior and President Clinton forgot that, in victory, the defeated adversary—Russia—should be treated with magnanimity.[18] If they wanted NATO to expand (which they did), they should have taken the process to its logical conclusion of including Russia.[19]

So why did the United States not do this? Essentially, some argue, because its political elite is a "Blob" that keeps doing the same thing.[20]

The literature mostly focuses on the Washington elite, but NATO supposedly works in the same way: as a band of multinational elites who fear public retribution for their costly security choices, and who band together in NATO to survive politically.[21] Some believe the problem is manageable and can be resolved through less self-absorbed leadership within NATO.[22] Others consider the problem so intractable that they want America to abandon NATO and leave the alliance to the Europeans.[23]

These critics have a point. Liberal values *can* lead to aspirational overreach.[24] But analysts tend to portray values as either inherently good or inherently bad. The debate is mostly conducted in black and white: there is little room for shades. But NATO is all about shades: it is about how free counsel can restrain power. NATO's history is not one of total success or resounding failure: it is a history of how free counsel is empowering, but hard to organize; and of how the exercise of power sometimes benefits from heeding sage counsel, but sometimes fails to listen. This is the history of NATO—and importantly it is forged at the level of NATO, rather than simply in one capital or another.

Critics who want the United States to "pull out" of Europe, or Europe to "liberate" itself from American tutelage—or who simply want to change the Euro-Atlantic order and make it more diverse or "multipolar"—sweep aside the historical evidence of NATO as a collective. Most see NATO as an American tool. But in their dislike of US policy, they overlook how important the alliance is as a forum for the building of partnerships: NATO is where US diplomats can get a sense of the lay of the land; where they can anticipate allied thinking; and where they can probe the repercussions for the US's wider interests before they push a particular policy. NATO is thus a place where European and Canadian ideas matter, and where continental experiences meet and sometimes merge.

Another critical point is the degree to which this debate lets Russia off the hook. If NATO is a runaway train of Western (American) expansion, then Russia's ideas and actions (such as its war on Ukraine) can be excused.[25] However, history shows that there has been plenty of scope for Russian ideas to make themselves heard, and that in Europe (as elsewhere) it takes two to tango. From the early 1990s, NATO began to change considerably: it grew noticeably softer, becoming politically more open and militarily less strong. Allied forces downsized and were retooled for security missions in faraway countries. There was no collective NATO military command structure or facilities planted on the territory of new allies. NATO also offered Russia a significant partnership. But in exchange for NATO's military weakening, Russia was meant to democratize. That was the deal, but the critics overlook this: they disregard the way in which Putin's Russia developed revanchist ideas, how it began to manipulate external conflicts to its own political ends, and how it sought the subjugation of smaller nations in a new policy of continental revision.[26]

To grasp NATO's evolution and endurance, to comprehend how it has weathered crisis after crisis and still prevailed, and to understand both why it stuck around after the Cold War ended and why it offered Russia partnership, rather than membership, we must look deep into NATO's idea—some might say its soul. An alliance is shaped by many things: geography, military power, the number of allies, the game of the adversary, and perhaps the fortunes of war. The premise of this book is that the sum of all this is intelligible only if we grasp the idea that inspires government and people to invest in power. To study power is to interpret the idea that motivates it.[27] To study NATO is to study the idea of the West and the will of political leaders to mold it into political order.[28] This book is therefore largely a political history: it will refer to military strategy, but its emphasis will be on politico-strategic debate within NATO.

Such an inquiry must begin inside NATO. In this book, NATO is not a facet of some mysterious outside force (whether global capitalism, US imperialism, or something else). Rather, and very straightforwardly, NATO is what the NATO allies decide and what the NATO-mandated diplomats or soldiers subsequently do. In terms of sources, the bedrock of the book will therefore be NATO archives, documents, and recorded statements. NATO archives are opened only after thirty years (and even then, only if the allied governments agree), which means that at some point the archived sources run dry. Nevertheless, there is a lot there, and I have had access to all declassified NATO archives. Of course, NATO decision-makers and officials also continue to make public statements, and in addition I have had the pleasure and privilege of speaking both on and off the record with many of them both specifically for this book and more generally over the course of my more than twenty years of research on NATO.

There is a lot outside NATO that goes into its decision-making. I rely on Lawrence Freedman, who, in his magisterial history of the United States and the Middle East, wrote: "I know of no better approach than to consider the available evidence in an effort to sort out the sequence of events and the influences on decisions."[29] In so doing, I stand on the shoulders of many gifted colleagues who have researched the historical drama of NATO. While the book's bibliography cannot do full justice to the richness of the field, it is a guide for the curious. That said, the book is also a book of novel interpretation—of NATO's pattern and what it means today. A few thoughts about this grander perspective are in order before the story begins.

NATO's future must not resemble its past

NATO's character has led to a certain recurring pattern in its history, in that the alliance has twice undergone a cycle of ambition and crisis. If NATO is to continue, this pattern must change, and change will require leadership.

NATO's character has emerged from two great ideational sources: Europe's history and its experience of war and peace; and America's experience of war and peace. There is little similarity between them: Europe has many states, has experienced many wars, and its states have historically sought to limit war by building alliances in order to balance power, and by using diplomatic finesse to adjust that balance; meanwhile North America has one dominant state (the United States), which has successfully fought wars to secure its continental peace, and which has then asserted the universal relevance of its values.[30] NATO leadership is about balancing and, at best, integrating these different continental experiences and ideas, in order to give the alliance direction.[31]

We can thus begin to trace NATO's historical pattern. It has had two moments of great ambition: in 1949, when the organization first came into being; and in 1990–91, when the Soviet adversary collapsed. Both moments of overweening ambition were followed by crises of power and confidence, which led the allies to search for pragmatic compromises to shore up their alliance. This pattern results from America's historical experience of aiming high—of going overseas not to balance power, but to build an Atlantic community within which *war would be inconceivable*. The pattern also results from Europe's legacy of contesting the practicality of grand ambition. In Europe, the reality of political pluralism churns ambition into pragmatism. And so, this is NATO: an alliance created to aim high, but destined to struggle with the practicality of aspiration.

The book is organized to demonstrate this pattern. *Part I* covers the early years of original and high aspiration. It brings us back to the years of the Second World War and the energy unleashed by the confrontation with the axis powers, and looks at how NATO was born both as a community of peace and as a bulwark against Soviet communism in the emerging Cold War. *Part II* covers the years of pragmatism and conservatism that set in once that initial wave of political aspiration had crash-landed on the altar of national interests. NATO persisted, but the alliance needed to rebalance its commitments. Effective consultations were high on the alliance's agenda, as it confronted a difficult and dangerous East–West arms race. If NATO made it through the turbulent 1970s and 1980s, it was because the will to live free and allied trumped any national desire to stand out or be exempted. *Part III* deals with NATO's return to great aspiration with the fall of the Berlin Wall and then of the Soviet Union. Europe's future should build on NATO, the allies agreed, and not develop in opposition to it. They then charted a course for a new alliance, with which they hoped a new Russia would reconcile. *Part IV* covers a decade of disillusionment and fatigue: Russia did not reconcile with NATO, and the allies went overboard in their efforts to build a new Afghanistan. Bereft of confidence and energy, the allies merely drifted, whereas Russia embarked on its campaign against Ukraine with the annexation of Crimea. Today, NATO is confronted by

Russia's major war effort and faces the challenge of rekindling the alliance's purpose without overreaching.

What this history means for the future is a classical, but difficult question.[32] The book argues that NATO must correct its trajectory: it cannot resume the pattern of boom (in aspiration) and bust (in trust and relationships). As other nations are seen to be on the rise—not just China, but many countries in the Global South—NATO leadership faces hard choices. This book suggests three lessons.

NATO must temper its aspirations with geopolitics. High aspirations centered on democracy versus dictatorship offer a compelling narrative, but can all too easily become another runaway ambition. Behind Russia there is China, and China is a global and multifaceted competitor. But NATO has a geography, and it should not go global. NATO is Atlantic: it links North America to Europe's order. Whatever the allies do on the question of China, NATO should stick to the underlying imperative of building a Europe that is attached to Western values and free of war. The primary challenge in this respect remains Russia. But China is present in and around Europe, and NATO should not neglect that presence. The NATO allies should also prepare for the contingency of war in Asia, and particularly for an attack on Taiwan. But at the end of the day, NATO's role is to secure Europe if or when the major allies divert forces to Asia. NATO's aspiration can have a global dimension, but its core must be Euro-Atlantic.

NATO must foster European leadership. The allies must not backslide (as they have twice done already), on the assumption that American leadership will sort out NATO's internal politics. Even when the United States was far and away the most powerful state in the global arena, Americanization was a risky strategy. US leaders, Congress included, do not want to do all the heavy lifting. Moreover, the European allies resent being told what to do. Today, with the rise of China and recurring budgetary debates in Washington, DC, such mutual resentments could get out of hand. To pre-empt this risk, the allies should build a real European pillar of defense and defense policy influence within NATO. Throughout the Cold War, the allies failed to build this pillar; after the Cold War, they moved it half out of NATO and into the European Union. But the reality is that European defense cannot take place outside NATO. A European pillar will require both increased European defense spending and also a political redistribution of influence.

NATO must think ahead. The allies, finally, should cease being so dependent on summit meetings of heads of state and government. As we shall see, summitry has become widespread over the past two decades. In theory, it is comforting: national leaders attract attention and make decisions. But summits also cause NATO to lose focus. Heads of state and government bring with them broad concerns, and they cannot be seen to fail. Thus, in order to help these summits along, NATO widens its gaze and toils to make the next summit a success. The end result is policy sprawl and short-termism. This trend needs to be reversed. NATO must revert to the long-term policy planning that it proved capable of during the Cold War. Heads of state and government should be involved less often in NATO, but should become better at setting a political-military direction for the organization and at recruiting the brightest and best to it.

As someone who came from a small country that had been overrun in the Second World War, whose command of English was poor, and who was a socialist, Paul-Henri Spaak on the face of it had no broad political appeal and was an unlikely originator of NATO's motto. But he was as dedicated to NATO as anybody, and he saw—perhaps more clearly than others—that NATO's commitment to free counsel in the exercise of power made it special. Hence the motto of "In consultation among free spirits."

In itself, it is amusing that Spaak should have chosen a Latin motto (*Animus in consulendo liber*) for an alliance led by the United States. In so doing, he of course symbolically wedded the language of the old world to the power of the new.[33] But perhaps his motives were more personal, reflecting an element of self-deprecation: referencing both a British fellow statesman whom he held in high regard and a dashing French-American actor of the times, Spaak used to remark that "I look like Winston Churchill and speak English like Charles Boyer, but I wish it was the other way around."[34]

PART I

A Grand Ambition Is Born: America's Alliance, 1939–65

1

America's Search for United Nations

Japan's attack on Pearl Harbor on the morning of December 7, 1941, was "the climax of a decade of international immorality." "Powerful and resourceful gangsters have banded together to make war upon the whole human race," broadcast President Roosevelt. The United States, together with other free peoples, was ready to fight for the right to live "in freedom and in common decency."[1] Four days later, Japan's co-conspirators, Germany and Italy, declared war on the United States.

The United States was now required both to prosecute a war that had been foisted on it and to devise a policy to create global order after the conflict. The United States was not an established world power before 1941, but the Second World War would make it one. With global power would come global responsibility, but to what end and by what means? The answers that President Roosevelt and his team would provide emerged from the particular and distinctively optimistic American experience, whereby peace truly was possible. This would rub against Europe's obsession with balances of power to limit and regulate war. The American way of combining ideals and power was both more global and more hopeful. As the US began to take control, so Europe's options for regional organization came to be severely constrained.

America's condition

In the 1940s, the question of US international leadership was not a new one, but it remained greatly contested. President Roosevelt's principal legacy was his ability to navigate not only the war, but also the contest of ideas at the heart of US foreign policy—and still to offer an architecture for US overseas engagement. It was not perfect, but from its foundations would emerge NATO.

Some twenty years earlier, on the heels of the Great War of 1914–18, President Wilson had sought to make the United States a cornerstone of global collective security. The League of Nations followed, but Wilson failed to secure the US Senate's ratification of the League's treaty. The country's international leadership role was thus postponed—hopefully for good, according to US isolationists, who held that the United States should stay out of Europe's wars and economic rivalry. In 1935 these political forces led Congress to pass the first of several neutrality acts that forbade US assistance to any party to war, whether victim or aggressor. The driving forces behind these acts did not vainly imagine that the United States could be cordoned off from the world: rather their ambition was to minimize entanglement in Europe's power politics and to promote a new age of cooperative international law and organization.[2]

How to balance these ideals and the reality of aggression by "powerful and resourceful gangsters" (in the president's words) was a challenge that fell to Roosevelt himself. He had been elected on a platform of domestic renewal, the New Deal, and did not favor international entanglement. However, the revisionism of Germany, Italy, and Japan and the weakness of the League of Nations pulled him into the ring. At first, he sought to modify Congress's neutrality acts to allow the president—himself—discretionary powers to assist victims of aggression. Ultimately, he would chart a course for US global engagement that far exceeded any past principle of neutrality.

Roosevelt's political condition was in fact a privileged one. To be sure, domestically he would have to sway public opinion, continue to win elections, and persuade Congress that some type of involvement would further US interests. This was, by any measure, a formidable task.[3] However, he was privileged by geography and US muscle power: the war would only take place overseas, and the United States could afford to offer itself as "the arsenal of democracy," as Roosevelt put it in December 1940.

Importantly, Roosevelt was also privileged in terms of the scope he had for political imagination. European and Asian belligerents found that the war permeated the very social and political fabric of their societies. For them, there could be no return to yesterday's peace. Even though the democracies of Europe won against Germany, Italy, and Japan, they would face continued social and political conflict motivated by the ideologies of liberalism, communism, and socialism. The United States was above this fray: it was some distance removed and was largely untainted by overseas ideological strife. It could imagine victory as an end that would lead to peace.[4] And peace for the United States meant a condition whereby it continued to navigate by its liberal compass and was not compelled to compete for strategic advantage. Peace implied scope for American ideas of improved global order.

The Atlantic Charter

In 1940–41, prior to the Japanese attack on Pearl Harbor, the United States was still at peace, while Britain was at war. In August 1941, the dramatic implications of this were on display in Placentia Bay, on the coast of Newfoundland, as the British battleship HMS *Prince of Wales* drew abreast of the US cruiser USS *Augusta*. The British battleship was camouflaged, its brass either painted or tarnished, and its decks worn and gray. In contrast, the US cruiser was spotless, with beautiful rubber steps, gleaming brass, and "pine-white woodwork."[5]

The two ships brought together British Prime Minister Churchill and US President Roosevelt. It was their first meeting. In traveling to Placentia Bay, Prime Minister Churchill hoped to secure President Roosevelt's commitment to take the United States into the war against the axis powers of Germany, Italy, and Japan. But that was not what President Roosevelt had in mind: he sought an agenda for American, not British, leadership, and he intended to unfold it at his own pace.

The meeting resulted in an Atlantic Charter that set out a grand and largely liberal vision for "a better future for the world." It foresaw a world where countries sought no aggrandizement, where people could choose the form of government under which they would live, and where countries would have equal access to trade and agree to abandon the use of force.

The backdrop for this statement of war aims—because that is really what the Charter was all about—was the urgency President Roosevelt felt to shape the war effort. Hitler's Germany had previously, in August 1939, ensured that the Soviet Union would stay out of the war by entering a pact with it, the Molotov–Ribbentrop Pact. The two countries had then partitioned Poland and parts of Eastern Europe. Germany next defeated France, the Benelux countries, Denmark, and Norway. In the ensuing battle for Britain, the best that Roosevelt could offer was US support so long as Britain promised to pay for it. This lend-lease scheme was in line with US neutrality law, but did not suit a hard-pressed Britain. When, on June 22, 1941, Hitler's Germany launched a major attack on the Soviet Union—Operation Barbarossa, named after the German Holy Roman Emperor Frederick I—the war seemingly shifted even further in Germany's favor.

At this point, the US State Department began reporting to the president that Britain and the Soviet Union were coordinating "peace commitments" in the Baltics, Eastern Europe, the Balkans, and the Middle East.[6] The reports raised concerns that Britain and the Soviet Union might define war aims that President Roosevelt could not support.[7] To pre-empt matters, Roosevelt dispatched a telegram to Churchill on July 14 regarding "unpleasant repercussions" in the United States, given certain "rumors regarding trades or deals which the British government is alleged to be making with some of the occupied nations." It was "much too early for any of us to make any commitments," continued Roosevelt. "I am inclined to think that an overall statement on your part would be useful at this time." He went on, "I could then back up your statement in very strong terms." Laconically, the president concluded, "There is no hurry about this but you might think it over."[8] Receiving no reply, Roosevelt was all the more determined to define war aims at their Placentia Bay meeting.

The ensuing Atlantic Charter proved a deft move on the part of President Roosevelt. With the Charter, he defined war aims that, given their liberal and aspirational character, could consolidate his domestic support base. He tied Prime Minister Churchill to the mast of Anglo-Saxon partnership and, in effect, US leadership. His vision left room for the Soviet Union, which was now engaged in an intense land war against German aggression, and which Roosevelt had already decided to assist with lend-lease arrangements. And he sketched the contours of a new post-war international system, leaving few in any doubt that he, more than any other leader, would construct it.

However, the Atlantic Charter was not a carefully thought-out grand strategy. It was an occasion on which Roosevelt seized control of the secrecy, drama, timing, and important actors that would enable him to shape public opinion.[9] Britain's leaders may at this time have had a better grasp of the geopolitics of the war; but Roosevelt at least saw clearly what it would take to create a "touchstone" of support for his policy.[10] In particular, he needed a vision that was coherent enough to inspire his own country, but sufficiently ambiguous to pre-empt isolationists' accusations that after the war there would likely be foreign entanglements. And for this, he needed time.

Roosevelt ingeniously asked Churchill to draft the statement of war aims. The suggestion sprang from the clash of interests between Britain and the United States over the issue of the British empire. At heart, the United States was opposed to the empire's unequal political relations and discriminatory trade practices. Roosevelt wanted to bend Britain to the different liberal vision that resonated in the United States, and to do so without damaging the relationship. He knew that Churchill would be attracted to the opportunity to define war commitments that applied also to the United States, and he wanted to use the discussions in Placentia Bay to tidy up the text.

Churchill's draft statement alluded to an "effective international organization" that would cast down Nazi tyranny forever and offer the world peace and security. This was too much of an entanglement for Roosevelt. The final wording of the Charter was therefore broader, invoking the hope that the use of force would be abandoned and, "pending the establishment of a wider and permanent system of general security," it declared the disarmament of aggressor nations "essential." Under Secretary of State Sumner Welles, who undertook the nitty-gritty of the negotiations with his British counterpart, Sir Alexander Cadogan, warned Roosevelt that isolationists at home would resist any provision that tied the United States to a mandatory policy of disarmament. It would be seen, Welles warned, as the United States having committed to war. Roosevelt brushed off this warning, however. The open-ended aspiration for general security coupled with political resolve was what he was looking for.[11]

Churchill was particularly touchy over the issue of free trade and Roosevelt's frank anticolonialism. This led to testy exchanges between the two leaders and several rounds of negotiations among their assistants.[12] In the end, in the appeal to free trade, Britain secured respect for "existing obligations" (i.e., the empire). It was a small concession. But with the personal rapport between the two political leaders, it raised Churchill's hopes that Britain could still shape affairs. However, the hope was not widely shared in London, and both the fate of the empire and the trustworthiness of the United States caused concern. Back in London, when Foreign Minister Anthony Eden first clapped eyes on the Atlantic Charter, he felt "that FDR [Roosevelt] has bowled the PM a very quick one."[13] Churchill knew of these reservations. Accordingly, he telegraphed Clement Attlee (leader of the War Cabinet in Churchill's absence), "It would be most imprudent on our part to raise unnecessary difficulties ... We must regard this as an interim and partial statement of war aims designed to reassure all countries of our righteous purpose and not the complete structure which we should build after victory."[14]

The inclusion of the Soviet Union in a new political order was another of Roosevelt's concerns. Recently assaulted by Germany, it had become a recipient of US lend-lease aid and was kept abreast of the Placentia Bay meeting. Inclusion was thus a priority; but questions of power and distrust would bedevil the intention. In September 1941, Ivan Maisky, Soviet ambassador to London, did commit his country, alongside other allied governments, to the ideals of the Atlantic Charter.[15] However, the fact that just months earlier Maisky had negotiated with Poland, under instructions from Moscow and assisted by London, stoked Roosevelt's anxiety. Maisky was clearly a front for the jealousies and ambitions inherent in Soviet power. The ambassador had an excellent grasp of this power and of the diplomatic scene, but that did not save his skin: he would be recalled to Moscow, sacked from the ministry, imprisoned and tortured by the intelligence services, and was about to be executed in 1953, when he was improbably spared by the death of Joseph Stalin.

Roosevelt would wrestle with the nature and reach of such Soviet power in his effort to set up a structure of peace. It would lead him to promote a United Nations organization and go to extraordinary lengths to woo Joseph Stalin into supporting it. When, finally, the Soviet Union proved too difficult for partnership, the hope and vision of the Atlantic Charter were transferred to the North Atlantic Pact. By then Britain was increasingly of secondary importance in the great-power entanglement. As an ominous sign of this decline, HMS *Prince of Wales*—on which Churchill had traveled to Placentia Bay— would be sunk just a few months later, on December 10, 1941, in an ill-fated attempt to intercept Japanese forces off Singapore. USS *Augusta*, the cruiser carrying Roosevelt, survived the war.

Globalism

Although it was Japan that attacked the United States on December 7, 1941, the Big Three of the United States, Britain, and the Soviet Union could readily agree that the focus for their global struggle was Germany. They reached agreement on this at the December 1941– January 1942 Arcadia conference in Washington, DC, where Roosevelt and Churchill met again, and where Ambassador Maxim Litvinov represented the Soviet Union.

"Notwithstanding the entry of Japan into the war," wrote the American and British chiefs of staff in their Arcadia grand strategy, "our view remains that Germany is still the prime enemy and her defeat is the key to victory."[16] Eventually this would lead to Operation Overlord, the June 1944 invasion of German-occupied Western Europe. But the interim planning was fraught with difficulties. Joseph Stalin continually pushed the allies to accelerate their invasion plans.

The US Army chief of staff, General George Marshall, likewise thought that the overriding priority must be the build-up for this invasion. If President Roosevelt nonetheless decided in favor of a North African campaign, Operation Torch of November 1942, it was because he wanted US forces to be engaged sooner rather than later, and because he wanted this engagement to take place in or around the European theater. Europe was where the great-power contest would be decided, and victory crafted.[17]

But what would come after victory? At Arcadia, the twelve signatories to the Atlantic Charter were joined by fourteen additional countries in issuing a declaration by "the United Nations"—a term coined by President Roosevelt two months previously. The declaration was simple, committing each signatory to the fight against the axis powers and not to conclude a separate peace. It was the political implications of this that raised the main issue.

Churchill had some ideas of his own. Invoking Europe's history, from 1940 onwards he sketched a plan for how a carefully designed balance of power could lead to concerted power and thus stability. The key was to amalgamate smaller nations into confederations, and then to join these confederations up with the great powers in a unifying Council of Europe. "In Europe," he remarked in March 1943, when setting out his post-war vision in a radio address, "lie most of the causes which have led to these two world wars." A Council of Europe should thus include the three great powers, a number of "confederations," as well as a "High Court" to adjudicate in disputes.[18] It would then represent the United Nations at a regional level. At the subsequent Trident conference in Washington, Churchill expanded his vision to include several councils—for Europe, Asia, and the Americas.[19]

This vision failed, and its failure left Winston Churchill in an uncomfortable secondary role throughout the Big Three meetings at Tehran (November 1943), Yalta (February 1945), and Potsdam (July–August 1945). Churchill did succeed in gaining American and Soviet support for the resurrection of France as a great power. For Churchill, as well as for Foreign Minister Eden, who was quite adamant on this point, Franco-British cooperation was key to Europe's future balance of power. For Roosevelt and Stalin, France was secondary, an occupied country riven by political strife. For General de Gaulle, head of the London-based Free French, France was obviously anything but secondary. American and Soviet skepticism, along with Anglo-American support for de Gaulle's rivals for leadership of the Free French in North Africa, François Darlan and Henri Giraud, would leave a lasting mark on his thinking.

Churchill's vision failed more generally because it contradicted Roosevelt's own vision, and because Churchill did not command total loyalty at home. It was a classical European vision, in the sense that it was regional and focused on the balance of great power. Roosevelt aimed for a global framework of cooperative politics that went beyond the balance of power. He was averse to America getting caught up in Old World politics. Instead, he sought a new order rooted in the Atlantic Charter and its capacity to unite nations. How to move this order beyond the balance of power was the tricky part.

Global institutions were part of the answer. Cordell Hull, Roosevelt's secretary of state, led the detailed work on these from early 1942 onward. Ultimately, it would lead to the creation of the United Nations in June 1945 and the associated institutions for monetary and financial cooperation, the International Monetary Fund and the International Bank for Reconstruction and Development (the World Bank). In 1945, some months after his resignation as secretary of state, Cordell Hull would receive the Nobel Peace Prize for this work.

The inclusion of the great powers in these institutions was another and more difficult part of the answer. Through 1942 and into 1943, Roosevelt hesitated: he had become attached to the idea of "four policemen" (the United States, Britain, the Soviet Union, and China) and did not want formal matters of law and organization to disrupt their cooperation. The experience of the League of Nations was instructive: strong on rules but weak on power, the League had succumbed to German revisionism. However, slowly but surely, Under Secretary of State Sumner Welles convinced Roosevelt that the four policemen and a global institution could be mutually reinforcing. The key was to formalize the decisive influence of the great powers and to set up a universal assembly, at which small countries could voice their concerns.

Roosevelt thus brushed aside Churchill's ideas at their May 1943 Trident meeting. Anthony Eden had, in fact, warned Churchill just two months earlier that the idea of regional councils should be dropped: there was a real risk that the concept would give "free ammunition" to American isolationists, who wanted nothing more than to sit back in their own regional council. Britain and Europe would then be on their own.[20] A close alliance between the United States and Britain, Eden thought, was fundamental.

The split between Churchill and Eden would also play out at the February 1945 Yalta conference. In front of American diplomats, Churchill argued for an alignment with Joseph Stalin on the issue of a great-power veto in the United Nations. Stalin wanted a firm and all-encompassing veto. Churchill agreed, seeing that this could serve his regional interests and the interests of the British empire. But Eden demurred, aligning himself with the American position that the veto should be limited to enforcement issues—and not extend to the peaceful settlement of disputes. Eden agreed with US diplomats that a strong veto could cause great-power cooperation to grind to a halt. He also shared the fear that it would engender strong protests from small countries. At Yalta, Eden went so far as to threaten to bring the issue to a vote in the House of Commons. However, Charles Bohlen of the US State Department was able to intervene, treating Churchill to generous food and drink and an explanation of the US position. Churchill then relented and offered his support for a limited veto.[21]

The Trident meeting of 1943 defines the point at which Roosevelt shifted from primarily courting Churchill to wooing the Soviet leader, Joseph Stalin.[22] Stalin was now the key player to get on board for a new global initiative. In October 1943, the effort paid off, in so far as Stalin allowed Foreign Minister Vyacheslav Molotov to sign the Four Nations Declaration, which promised the establishment of a "general international organization" for the "maintenance of international security and peace."[23] One month later, in Tehran, Stalin would confirm this commitment in a private conversation with Roosevelt.

Roosevelt's conversion of Stalin to a United Nations organization raises questions that ultimately reflect the constructive ambiguity of the US president's policy style. Did his embrace of great-power privilege within the United Nations amount to nothing more than regionalism by another name? Did Roosevelt's successful inclusion of China—then an ally of the United States—in the ranks of the great powers de facto represent balance-of-power politics American style? Was Roosevelt's persuasion of Stalin little more than old-style horse-trading, where the United States first (at both Tehran and Yalta) gave in to Soviet demands in Europe, and then (at Yalta) offered the Soviet Union excessive influence in China and Japan?[24] Roosevelt was sufficiently ambiguous on these points to convey ambition and aspiration, but there was no question that he understood that without power, aspiration was going nowhere.

Roosevelt's peculiar—some might say Machiavellian—policy style also extended to his inner arena of US policymaking. Cordell Hull, so useful to Roosevelt because of his connections to Congress, was too much of a full-throated globalist for Roosevelt's liking. Hull suffered not only from tuberculosis and diabetes, but also from his political marginalization in US decision-making. For the Big Three meeting in Tehran, Roosevelt simply left Hull at home. Sumner Welles knew better how to speak to Roosevelt's concerns over the issue of great powers, but lacked the political acumen to gain the president's trust. In the fall of 1943, Welles was felled by sex scandals. His replacement, Edward Stettinius, later Hull's successor, had to compete with James Byrnes for the role of presidential confidant. At Yalta, Byrnes seemed the closer of the two to Roosevelt, but the intimacy was manipulated: Roosevelt kept Byrnes out of decisive discussions and sent him home early to sell a partial and upbeat version of events to Congress and the US public.[25] When Roosevelt's Yalta deals with Stalin emerged, Byrnes—now secretary of state to President Truman—would be burdened by his association with a "Yalta myth."[26]

Still, for all his political machinations, Roosevelt did, in a unique way, attempt to reconcile power and globalism. He wanted to build on power, in order to move the world beyond bare power politics, and he was greatly inspired by America's experience. It was only after Roosevelt's death (April 1945) and after the failure of global cooperation that his peace ambitions were channeled into transatlantic cooperation.

Collective defense

Senator Arthur Vandenberg was among the great supporters of United Nations cooperation, but he was concerned about the reach of the great powers. Vandenberg wanted great-power cooperation, but not great-power interference and mischief. This concern led him to take the lead in crafting what became a key clause of the United Nations Charter, Article 51, on the right to collective defense. With this clause, Vandenberg wanted to protect cooperation not in Europe, but in Latin America. Having succeeded in gaining this right to collective defense, he joined his Senate colleagues in July 1945 in ratifying the Charter. Almost exactly three years later, as great-power mischief focused on Europe, Vandenberg crafted a Senate resolution that authorized the president to engage in collective defense in Europe. With this later resolution, Vandenberg etched his name into NATO history; but the genesis of the move was his abiding concern that the great powers should play by the rules.

Great powers often claim special rights, such as the ability to impose a veto on international decisions. And so it was at the February 1945 Yalta conference, where the Soviet leader Joseph Stalin favored a strong and comprehensive veto. At a plenary session, Churchill decided to relent and offer his support for the American position, which was to limit the veto. "I was terrified," Churchill's advisor Alexander Cadogan later confided, because "he does not know a thing about it."[27] But Churchill hit the mark, and after much haggling the three leaders struck a deal: the great powers—later the five permanent members of the UN Security Council—would have a veto on enforcement action. Procedural matters and recommendations on peaceful conflict settlement could then be decided by an affirmative vote.[28]

This Yalta deal provoked some anxiety both in Washington and across Latin America. Their shared (Western) hemisphere was exempt from European-style power politics, they agreed. To be sure, this exemption had started out as a singular US policy statement—the Monroe doctrine of 1823. It had also developed into a paternalistic relationship reminiscent of empire, especially under President Theodore Roosevelt's "big stick" policy of 1901–9. However, Franklin

Roosevelt (fifth cousin to Theodore) wanted a new beginning. In 1933, he placed Cordell Hull in charge of a "good neighbor" policy of non-intervention, reviving regional consultations that had blossomed in the late nineteenth century. Roosevelt bolstered this policy with reciprocal trade agreements and a somewhat lofty promise of New Deal reform across the hemisphere.[29] While far from a perfect community, the hemispheric countries wondered in 1945 whether the veto would enable outside powers to block regional enforcement measures. In short, whether it would open the hemisphere up to meddling and mischief.

On the heels of the Yalta conference, in Chapultepec Castle in Mexico City, hemispheric leaders and delegates met to address this issue, among others. They agreed to the transformation of their existing Pan-American Union into a more community-based Organization of American States that notably put the countries on a more equal footing. Highlighting this character further, they agreed in the Act of Chapultepec to the multilateral protection of hemispheric security. They declared aggression against any one of the signatories to be aggression against all. They also stated their intention of making this regional arrangement compatible with the emerging general international organization (the United Nations).[30]

Senator Vandenberg had about two months in which to deliver on this intention during the United Nations conference in San Francisco (April 25–June 26). The difficulty lay not only in the risk of a great-power veto on hemispheric enforcement, but also in the united Soviet, French, and British drive to have existing bilateral treaties of mutual defense exempted from the new United Nations obligations. These treaties were directed against Germany and Japan, and were thus hard to deny or to seek to alter: the San Francisco committee on regional arrangements granted the exemption in early May. Did this imply that there could be a regional exemption in Europe and Asia, but nowhere else? Vandenberg sought to deal with this uncertainty by having the UN Charter make explicit reference to the Act of Chapultepec, but in vain. He was thus faced with the "grave problem" of protecting "legitimate regional arrangements without destroying the over-all responsibility of united action through the United

Nations and without inviting the formation of a lot of dangerous new regional spheres of influence."[31] Thus, Vandenberg had to protect both the Americas and the principle of globalism.

The compromise that Vandenberg engineered became Article 51 of the UN Charter: the right to individual or collective self-defense if an armed attack occurs, and until the Security Council has taken the necessary measures to re-establish international peace and security. In 1949, Article 51 would form the bedrock for the North Atlantic Pact. However, in 1945, for Vandenberg and Secretary of State Stettinius, Article 51 was a means to a different end—namely, the securing of the hemispheric community. They therefore immediately called for a new hemispheric conference to turn the Act of Chapultepec into permanent treaty form.

There followed the September 1947 Rio Treaty, which was a collective defense arrangement for the Americas. The parties to the treaty condemned war and backed the UN Charter, albeit with the proviso that they endeavor to settle disputes themselves, before referring matters to the UN. They also agreed that "an armed attack by any State against an American State shall be considered as an attack against all the American States." In such an event, they undertook to assist in the exercise of the inherent right to self-defense contained in the Charter's Article 51.[32]

The Rio Treaty was more than a collective self-defense mechanism. European alliances had often been about collective self-defense, but this treaty was different: unlike in Europe, it represented a community that forswore war and sought to protect itself from power politics. It was an embryonic legal order that promised collective punishment for any violation of the peace. Unlike the UN Charter (and European practice), the Rio Treaty does not leave the definition of such violations to *ex post facto* discussion in, say, a security council. Instead, it defines peace and defines the violation—armed aggression—that will be punished. European movements had long debated such a communitarian and legal approach to war, but never managed to implement it politically. For European statesmen, war remained a breach of contract or of certain diplomatic rules of the road. Their response would involve resistance, balance-of-power politics, and demands for damages and reparations. In marked contrast, American states saw war as something they could outlaw, and they did.

The Rio Treaty's provisions for collective self-defense were of direct consequence to the North Atlantic Pact. What happened was in essence the planned and intended transfer of the principles and purposes of the Rio Treaty to the North Atlantic area.[33] Senator Vandenberg, who made this duplication of the hemispheric engagement possible in his 1948 Senate resolution, did not see a North Atlantic Pact as a departure from his international engagement and support for UN collective security. His June 1948 resolution is rich in references to the UN Charter, and lacks any sense of balanced power. Shortly after the making of the North Atlantic Treaty, in private correspondence, Vandenberg protested about any attempt to liken it to a military alliance: "In my humble opinion the North Atlantic Pact is *fundamentally* of an entirely different character. It is a *peace* Pact."[34]

Here was the answer to the aspiration harbored by various decision-makers and analysts in the Atlantic area: it was possible to strive for a new type of political community, but it would have to flow from the United States' sense of regional community within a global UN order. Its regional collective defense commitment tied in with a wider and global commitment to collective security. There is ample ambiguity between regional defense and global security, but the basic point is this: the Rio Treaty and the North Atlantic Pact were expressions of communities that aspired to a certain peace. This peace is compatible with global human ideals, as expressed in the UN Charter, but is fundamentally anchored in regional communities. Both the Rio Treaty and the North Atlantic Pact foresaw growth in their communities for this reason. Their peace was regional, but it could expand. The Atlantic Pact's Article 10 thus states that "any other European State in a position to further the principles of this Treaty and to contribute to the security of the North Atlantic area" may be invited to join the community, the pact.

This community-based approach to collective defense was intuitive to American leaders, but the translation to Europe promised to be difficult. Europe was steeped in balance-of-power thinking. In North America, US leaders could lean on Canadian leaders, who likewise thought in terms of community. However, Canada's conception of community was stronger and more ambitious. US leaders thus had to tread a fine line as they sought Europe's transformation. They wanted to go beyond the balance of power, but to stop short of Canada's full-blown Atlantic community. What this meant for Europe was the question.

Europe's cacophony

When John Hickerson, a founding father of the North Atlantic Pact, was told at one point that George Kennan, who fathered the idea of containment, considered him the State Department colleague with whom he had disagreed most, Hickerson's response was "Thank you."[35] The in-house struggle between these two bright officials is telling: not so much because Hickerson's idea of a North Atlantic Pact prevailed (allowing him to be gracious in reply to the observation of his conflict with Kennan), but rather because the struggle between them shows the policy uncertainty that followed from America's aspirations. The Americans engaged to build a new order; but in Europe, they wanted Europeans to lead. This meant they had to translate their thinking to Europe's political reality, and for this they had no grand design. The United Nations Charter and the Marshall Plan were grand and coherent, but the next steps in Europe were improvised. We shall consider the making of the North Atlantic Treaty in the next chapter. Here we look at the European cacophony that US and allied leaders had to deal with. It forced American officials to consider at least a holding measure until Europe's condition improved; and that became NATO.[36]

Germany was an obvious flash point, the power in Europe's midst that had ignited two world wars in just three decades and that was now divided into four zones of occupation. Kennan, a Germanophile, wanted the vanquished Germany to re-emerge as a unifier of Europe. This "third force" vision was an odd appeal to power (Germany) and transcendence (unification), and in 1948–49 it appalled many policy-makers. Walter Lippmann, a prominent columnist, aligned himself with Hickerson and his boss, Secretary of State Dean Acheson: the

West had to organize its own collective defense. But Lippmann parted company with Hickerson and Acheson in his embrace of balance-of-power politics: he wanted the Soviet Union to have its own sphere of influence, and he sought to neutralize Germany in Europe's midst.[37] Lippmann's vision was thus attuned to the global balance of power. In contrast, Hickerson and Acheson sought to build a Europe compatible with US ideas of cooperative security.

As this debate unfolded in the United States, Europeans—poverty-stricken and insecure—sought to maximize America's engagement. Its "empire" in Europe was perhaps by design early on, especially in the case of the Marshall Plan; but in the next few years it would be by invitation—i.e., led by European pleas and desires.[38] However, Europeans were simultaneously confronted by their own lack of political agreement. Just like Kennan, Lippmann, Hickerson, and Acheson, they struggled to come up with a solution to the challenge of German power. For now, Germany was down and out. But what happened next would have major consequences for their own security and for Europe's political order.

We know the outcome: Europe's order became based on Germany's division. Cooperation among the four occupying powers—the United States, Britain, France, and the Soviet Union—gradually broke down. The three Western powers, led by US thinking, then started to merge their three zones and to create a provisional West German state—the Federal Republic of Germany (FRG). It came into being in May 1949, one month after the North Atlantic Pact was signed. Its constitution was a provisional Basic Law, pending a clarification of Germany's unification (which would happen in 1990). Soon thereafter, in October 1949, the Soviet Union created an East German state, the German Democratic Republic (GDR). The four occupying powers retained the authority to decide on unification: the two Germanies were thus not fully sovereign. They defined the front line between East and West, retaining the potential both to bolster it by military force and to challenge it by political design. The German question thus remained at the heart of the Cold War.

For Western European countries, it was obviously important in the wake of the world war to construct an order that would lay the

German question to rest. Significantly, Britain—so prominent during the war—declined to act as leader in this. Clement Attlee of the Labour Party had gained the premiership in mid-July 1945—during the Potsdam great-power conference. In 1948, his foreign secretary, Ernest Bevin, fostered a first attempt at European defense cooperation, designed to secure US backing for an alliance relationship—the Western Union—and spoke of Europe's "spiritual union." But in essence, the Attlee government attached to its European policy the same two higher priorities that Churchill had pursued: Britain's global presence (the empire) and the special relationship (with the United States).[39] British leaders would speak highly of European unity, but did not conceive of Britain as being part of it. In 1950, addressing the new Council of Europe, Churchill spoke eloquently of a unified Europe; but in private remarks he clarified that "I meant it for them, not us."[40]

Continental federalists had extraordinarily high hopes for the Council of Europe, created in May 1949. However, their hopes for continental transformation were stillborn. A British counterproposal in January 1949 had undermined the momentum created by the grand founding conference in The Hague in May 1948. Britain ensured that the Council would work on the principle of unanimity and that it had no competence to deal with matters of defense. Paul-Henri Spaak, Belgian premier and foreign minister, brought both vision and experience to the Council's parliamentary assembly, which he chaired. Spaak would, in fact, also chair the first UN General Assembly and the assembly of the Organisation for European Economic Co-operation (OEEC), the organization set up to channel Marshall Aid into Europe. Spaak harbored federalist ideas and wanted to pursue them in the Council of Europe, he later wrote, but had to give priority to compromise, so as to avert a British exit.[41] This early shadow of a "Brexit" led the Council of Europe to become a "black hole," in Lawrence Kaplan's harsh assessment—"toothless and essentially meaningless."[42]

European disunity likewise characterized the OEEC, the offspring of Marshall Aid. Though Paul-Henri Spaak aligned himself with key US representatives—Paul Hoffman, Marshall Aid administrator, and Averell Harriman, special presidential aide to the program—he failed to move the British. Through 1948–49, Spaak and others responded to Secretary Marshall's original call for structural change in Europe. Aided by a special Committee of Nine, as well as US support, Spaak proposed endowing the OEEC with a strong political executive. However, Stafford Cripps and Ernest Bevin, the key British negotiators, outsmarted him. To counter creeping supranationalism, Cripps and Bevin mobilized Europe's small countries in their support and daringly sidelined Averell Harriman. Officially they wanted to create space for Britain's positive lead in Europe; unofficially they sought to prevent "the formation of an American bloc in the OEEC."[43]

Britain's choices thus mattered greatly during these years, even as its power was eroding. The country sought to build a special relationship with the United States to mask this decline; but still it mattered. Arguably, only in Churchill's own "Whig" version of history—where hindsight is allowed to distort events—is it possible to minimize the British decline by portraying it as a passing of the torch to another branch of the English-speaking peoples.[44] Decline did not mean that Britain did not have options (including the option of leadership). It had three key relationships: with the United States, the empire, and Europe. This multitude of relations offered scope for policy. Anthony Eden, a Conservative like Churchill, found both Churchill and Attlee too timid on Europe: he was focused on building relations with France.[45] And he wanted to invest more in the Hague process (the Council of Europe) and draw the fruits of its labor under the North Atlantic umbrella.[46] Eden's reading of history was that Britain should not place its fate entirely in the hands of the United States: it also needed to show leadership in Europe.

The irony is that Eden proved too timid on Europe: European leadership was there for the taking, but he was late to the game of engaging with it.[47] In the late 1940s, there was some excuse, as Eden was in opposition and the ball was in Attlee's court. But in the early to mid-1950s, he was prime minister. And as we shall see later, this is where Eden struggled to translate principle into practice. His timidity should also be explained with reference to key US policymakers who did not want European leadership to be a direct US responsibility. Like George Marshall—who in 1947 lent his name to the great US assistance program—they wanted the United States to be the midwife of Europe's own unitary effort. Some wanted to build Europe around Germany; others were less sure. In practice, the US search for options offered scope for British leaders and let them off the hook: they could choose not to lead Europe, and mostly they chose not to.

Britain's choice placed the onus on France. The country had emerged battered and bruised from the war: Germany had overrun it, and the French leadership had splintered in a type of civil war. General de Gaulle had been based in London, where he represented the Free French; but for much of the war, the main French authorities—all contested—were in Vichy, mainland France, and Algiers. In his struggle for recognition, de Gaulle developed a famously bad relationship with President Roosevelt, as well as with Churchill. He would be empowered by the great invasions of France in 1944—Operation Overlord in Normandy (June) and Operation Dragoon in Provence (August), becoming head of France's provisional government. But neither he nor any other French leader would be part of the great-power conferences in Tehran, Yalta, and Potsdam that shaped war strategy and post-war order. As we shall see in the next chapter, during the decisive "Pentagon talks" of April–May 1948 that teed up the North Atlantic Pact, France found itself excluded yet again.

By 1948, de Gaulle had resigned from his political positions in protest. In his view, France's new constitution—the Fourth Republic—was too timid on executive leadership. One of his closest collaborators, Georges Bidault, then took over. Bidault was a hero of the resistance: he had spent the war in mainland France and had become head of the National Council for Resistance in 1943, after its leader Jean Moulin had been betrayed and then captured by the German Gestapo. It is hard to overestimate Bidault's influence on post-war France: he helped found the Christian-democrat party that would contribute greatly to shaping the Fourth Republic, and he became both foreign and prime minister. It was on his watch that other towering figures such as Robert Schuman and Jean Monnet revolutionized ideas of European cooperation. Konrad Adenauer, the first chancellor of the new Germany, was likewise a Christian democrat, and their cooperation changed Europe.

But this was later, and their meeting of minds would be circumscribed by the difficulty for France in the late 1940s of moving into a leadership position. Germany was the issue. Twice in a lifetime Germany had wrecked France, and Bidault's primary focus was on permanently eradicating the cause of Prussian militarism. He wanted a new Germany to be heavily decentralized in a confederation, thus with no central political authority to speak of. He wanted the industrial powerhouse of the Saar region to become either French or independent. And in line with classical French balance-of-power policy, he supported de Gaulle in underwriting a Franco-Soviet Treaty of Alliance and Mutual Aid (December 1944).

For a new era, France was thus disposed to reinvent its balance-of-power policy, not to build a community of reconciled nations. This, along with France's sense of weakness and wartime humiliation, made the country a difficult partner before, during, and after the North Atlantic Treaty negotiations. Some of those involved spared no criticism of the French negotiating style and behavior.[48] But French negotiators had a point in insisting on a clarification of the continental engagement of Britain and the United States.[49] With the North Atlantic Treaty of April 1949, French leaders gained an iron-clad political commitment. But this commitment also, in a sense, merely raised new questions. As France struggled to get back on its feet after a devastating war, who would provide the military muscle to insure against German revanchism? Presumably the United States and Britain. But those countries had, from the French perspective, made a mess of the Council of Europe and the OEEC, and the North Atlantic Treaty was just that, a treaty. France was looking for tangible military support. One month after the signing of the North Atlantic Treaty, in May 1949, Western Germany was resurrected in the guise of the Federal Republic of Germany. As an occupying power, France assisted in this process, but the United States and Britain were in the vanguard; and their concern was not to keep Germany down, but to keep both German and Soviet revanchism out. For France, all this raised multiple questions regarding its own role in Europe. For the United States, it defined a test of the ideas it managed to impute into the North Atlantic Treaty, a process to which we turn next.

If we content ourselves with concluding that the Second World War mattered because it made the United States and the Soviet Union the masters of Europe's destiny, then we miss half the picture. It also mattered enormously that America's increased might also meant the rise of powerful ideas that were foreign to Western Europe. European leaders did not envisage the passing of Old World balance-of-power politics: to them, war was a fact of life, and the balance of power was the best means of regulating and minimizing it. World war was obviously catastrophic in Europe, too, and just as in the United States it nurtured progressive thinking. But in the political arena, realist pragmatism prevailed. Churchill supported community, but reserved a balance-of-power role for Britain. Bidault supported Christian Democracy, but wanted first to eradicate the root causes of German militarism. Europe's sense of community was, in effect, hostage to the balance of power.

The United States had the power to reject entanglement on Europe's terms. And it had ideas of hemispheric community to guide its search for a progression from balance-of-power politics to collective security. This search proceeded incrementally, moving with the diplomatic crises that ended in world war and Japan's attack on Pearl Harbor. And it continued past this point. American policymakers were not naïve: they grappled with contradictions between power and order, empire and equality, inclusion and exclusion. Roosevelt was more idealist when presenting his vision to the American public than when dealing with Joseph Stalin in Tehran or at Yalta. Roosevelt and other American policymakers were confronted with the same dilemmas and tensions as Europe was, and they recognized that.

Still, the basic point regarding the roots of transatlantic alliance making is that America's privileges led it to define a peace that Europe could not have fathered. The peace was global and it outlawed armed aggression. It seamlessly integrated regional collective defense—otherwise a key piece in balance-of-power politics—into a global collective security ambition. This peace was overwhelmingly American in character. Roosevelt enabled it by creating a framework of cooperation between the great powers—in effect, by bringing Britain into the fold and courting Stalin. His team enabled it by negotiating a UN Charter that balanced great-power privilege and small-state influence. And the hemisphere enabled it by insisting on its peculiar character as a zone of peace that differed from Europe's balance-of-power experience.

The paradox for the countries that were about to become America's peacetime allies was that they could appreciate America's vision, but could not easily translate it into practical policy. Europeans invited America's entanglement, but were steeped in a history of checking imperialism by balance-of-power politics. This balance of power may at points have been brutal; but the occasional reach for empire— spurred by Napoleon, Kaiser Wilhelm, or Adolf Hitler—was even more brutal. When European leaders in the wake of the Second World War confronted the American insistence on European community, their protestations got lost in translation. Community was not their experience, it was America's. There were thinkers and movements in Europe who reached for political transformation, but the reality of diverging national interests was depressingly familiar. Though hard to imagine once the guns fell silent, Europe's and America's experiences could only come together in an enduring collective defense framework that anchored America's leadership role in Europe.

2

The North Atlantic Treaty

On April 4, 1949, the representatives of twelve Atlantic nations came together in the US State Department's Auditorium, "a blue-domed chamber full of stone columns and golden ginger-bread," and committed to the principle that an attack on one should be regarded as an attack on all.[1] The North Atlantic Pact thus came into being.

NATO was, in a way, an afterthought. As we saw in Chapter 1, America's primary focus was on defining a certain peace and building it into a United Nations collective security vision. For US decision-makers, collective defense smacked of European-style balance-of-power politics. What they wanted was collective security, a more inclusive and cooperative world order. In the end, with relations with the Soviet Union deteriorating rapidly, they latched onto NATO as a collective defense pact. But it was not meant to be any ordinary defense pact: it was to promote cooperative order in Western Europe, the transatlantic area, and, if possible, the wider international arena. This was a peculiarly American vision. Europe could not have thought of making collective defense the handmaiden of general security, but America did.

The North Atlantic Pact was thus far from preordained. About a year and a half of intense and creative talks and negotiations were needed to overcome the differences in Atlantic outlooks. American diplomats had to define their own terms of engagement, which was complicated enough. European diplomats meanwhile learned to speak the language of American-style collective security, while tending to their own national interests. They wanted America in Europe—but to protect them, not transform them. The pact that came into being was thus loaded with energy: it promised peace, but deterred war; it promised transformation, but balanced power; it comprised a mere twelve countries, but left the door open. Enlargement of the pact's mission and membership was both possible and likely, but how it should happen, and whether it should be according to the logic of balanced power or cooperative security, were open and unresolved questions.

President Truman, of course, had a final word to say on the occasion of the signing ceremony: "Men with courage and vision can still determine their own destiny."[2] This upbeat vision of NATO being in charge of its own better future was also subtly incorporated into the dinner arrangements at the Carlton Hotel in Washington, DC, where some sixty-five guests were seated in honor of the treaty. The table was decorated with pink roses and pink snapdragons, blue irises, and white ferns—the colors of love and hope, trust, and peaceableness.

Entanglement

By signing the North Atlantic Treaty, the United States declared itself a European power and pulled together Europe's north (Norway, Iceland, and Denmark), its south (Italy and Portugal), and its west (Britain, France, and the Benelux countries), alongside Canada and itself. NATO as a single framework encompassing so many different countries was by no means a foregone conclusion, even as the Cold War intensified and Europe was seen to lack political initiative.

In a way, the idea of an Atlantic Pact crystallized in the middle of the Atlantic in December 1947, on board a ship carrying John D. Hickerson, director of the Office of European Affairs at the State Department, and John Foster Dulles, representative of Senator Arthur Vandenberg (chairman of the Senate Foreign Relations Committee), from London to New York. The context was a somber one, because the four-power Council of Foreign Ministers had just days earlier broken up in disagreement between, on the one hand, the Soviet

Union and, on the other, the United States, Britain, and France. The promise of East–West cooperation was giving way to confrontation. For European nations still emerging from the Second World War, the reality of combined hardship and fear was particularly grim.

Ernest Bevin, Britain's foreign secretary, had pleaded with US Secretary of State George Marshall for a common initiative. Bevin was not cut from the cloth of elite institutions such as Oxford or Cambridge University: he was a "massive, hulking, and dominant" figure out of the British trade union movement who would, on occasion, struggle with the "chemistry" between himself and the American leaders.[3] In London, on December 17, 1947, following the breakdown of the Council of Ministers, Bevin had a number of private meetings with the French and Canadian foreign ministers, and then also with Secretary Marshall. The latter meeting did not go particularly well. Marshall, John Hickerson would later recall, tended to be a "cold" and "sort of formal" person, and following his meeting with Bevin, the secretary of state asked Hickerson to iron out some issues. As Hickerson did so, he realized that the British were appealing for "future arrangements" between Britain, some Western European countries, and the United States and Canada. "Bevin didn't call it an Atlantic Pact. All that was worked out later on, but that was it."[4]

In mid-Atlantic, on his way home alongside John Foster Dulles, Hickerson became convinced that Bevin had it right and that his own boss, Secretary Marshall, was too limited in his outlook. Once back in Washington, in the afternoon of New Year's eve he sought out his director of Western European Affairs, Theodore C. Achilles. Hickerson and Achilles would later dispute whether his blunt declaration was aided by the intake of martinis (Hickerson's more sophisticated claim) or fish-house punch (Achilles' amused recollection), but either way he blurted out: "I don't care if entangling alliances have been considered worse than original sin since George Washington's time. We've got to have a peacetime military alliance with Western Europe. And we've got to get it ratified."[5]

Hickerson was referring to the September 1796 farewell speech of the first US president, George Washington. He admonished his country to steer clear of "permanent alliances," a principle that had resonated ever since. It did not imply, though, that the United States did not pursue its own interests; nor that it did not think about its power relative to other states. For the young country, the key challenge was sea power. No longer protected by the British flag, American merchant ships were vulnerable to piracy, and so Thomas Jefferson, the country's third president, launched bold military raids against the Barbary States of North Africa. When the Spanish empire in the Americas crumbled in the wake of the Napoleonic Wars, in December 1823 President Monroe put into words the doctrine that no European power should establish itself in the Americas. Never mind, then, that at this point the United States could not rival British naval power, and that Britain, not the United States, ruled the Atlantic. The point was that the United States thought about power to protect itself and to keep Europe at bay.

Secretary Marshall, Hickerson's boss, knew full well that even as US power grew, it remained critical for the government to be in full command of national policy. President Wilson had, on the eve of the First World War, sought to engage the United States in the transformation of Europe, via the League of Nations, but the Senate had not been on board, and isolationism followed. To engage, the administration needed to get Congress on board. Secretary Marshall did not father the idea of NATO; but on June 5, 1947, in a speech at Harvard University, he did sire the Marshall Plan, or rather the Economic Recovery Program for Europe. The idea was to offer European nations American capital and materials for economic reconstruction, but only on certain terms—not least of which was a requirement for European political cooperation. In short, Europe would have to change its ways—move beyond balance-of-power policy and earnestly cooperate. The idea led to the creation of the OEEC and sowed the seeds of further economic integration in Europe, but only once a security framework had been put in place.

Having launched his bold initiative, Marshall's next concern was to get it off the ground. Europeans could grumble about the enforcement of close cooperation, but take-off depended first and foremost on Congressional approval and funding. Congress had not resisted

President Truman when, on March 12, 1947, at a joint session of Congress, he had linked the security of the United States to the protection of democracy in Greece and Turkey. In fact, Congress promptly voted the financial funds to underwrite this "Truman doctrine." But Secretary Marshall's idea of a full-scale program to fund Europe's recovery was a grander policy program, with financial implications of a different magnitude.[6] Congress would need time to digest and shape the idea, before deciding on whether to fund it. It was only in April 1948 that Congress passed the Economic Cooperation Act that enabled the Marshall Plan. In the interim, Marshall knew better than to propose major initiatives that Congress would have to underwrite, including a defense pact with European nations.

British Foreign Secretary Bevin could, in the meantime, pursue his own thinking. Bevin is commonly seen as the fountainhead of the idea of a North Atlantic Pact. In his private conversations of December 17, 1947, including the difficult conversation with Marshall, he had sketched ideas for a "powerful consolidation of the West."[7] Though Bevin's thinking remained somewhat aloof or abstract, he ploughed on. On January 4, 1948, he informed the British cabinet of his view that the protection of Western civilization necessitated the creation of "some form of union in Western Europe, whether of a formal or informal character, backed by the Americas and the Dominions"— the latter being a reference to the British empire. On January 13, 1948, Bevin asked the British ambassadors in Washington and Paris to follow up on his private conversations of December, and on January 22, 1948, he took his view to British parliament and thus, in effect, the world.[8]

Gladwyn Jebb, who at the time advised Bevin, found it "a very clever speech."[9] This was because Bevin did not brutally demand the permanent involvement of the United States in Europe's security affairs, but rather issued a sufficiently ambiguous invitation for engagement. Jebb, one of Britain's most seasoned diplomats, had participated in the great conferences of the war, at Tehran, Yalta, and Potsdam, just as he had participated in the drafting of the UN Charter. Jebb knew that the United States would have to define its own terms of engagement. Bevin and others could nurture and encourage US

thinking, especially regarding the global vision of security cooperation that was so important in Washington; but—reflective of the
mature institutions George Washington had called for—America's
course of action would be defined by America's leaders.

The Soviet coup in Prague, Czechoslovakia, that unfolded through
February 1948 rattled Bevin's interlocutors into action. In France,
Prime Minister Robert Schuman and Foreign Minister Georges
Bidault supported greater defense efforts. In their view, the Soviet
Union was trouble; but the main threat remained Germany—a
neighbor that, over a thirty-year timespan, had twice imposed cata-
strophic war on France. In March 1947, Schuman and Bidault thus
took France alongside Britain into a bilateral pact explicitly directed
against Germany, the Dunkirk Treaty. It marked the beginning of
Western security cooperation—but only that, a beginning. In the
United States, Hickerson's superiors, Secretary Marshall and Under
Secretary Robert Lovett, insisted that Europeans would have to go
further if the United States were to consider supporting their efforts.
Prodded by the Americans, Bevin and Bidault overcame their differences and pulled their Benelux colleagues into an agreement: the
collective defense Brussels Treaty that they signed on March 17, 1948.

Foreign Minister Paul-Henri Spaak signed the Brussels Treaty on
behalf of Belgium, and he had early on spotted the essentials of the
matter. When Bevin approached him in early January to inform him
of the Dunkirk negotiations between Britain and France and to invite
him to consider his country's adherence to it, Spaak had been cool.
The Dunkirk Treaty was Western European and directed against
Germany. Spaak told Bevin that a defense pact was meaningless,
unless designed to protect against the Soviet Union and unless the
United States was included. He subsequently advised Theodore
Achilles and other US officials of the exchange, and was directed to
read the Rio Treaty for further inspiration.[10]

The Brussels Treaty promised action along the lines of the Rio
Treaty. In the case of an armed attack on one of the six signatory
countries, its Article 4 stipulated, the others would "afford the Party
so attacked all the military and other aid and assistance in their
power."[11] This was, in fact, a remarkably strong commitment that

nailed the countries' colors to the mast. The nature of such a commit-ment would bedevil the final phase of the Atlantic treaty negotia-tions. For now, though, the problem was that the Brussels Treaty allies had no military power to speak of. It immediately raised the question of whether the American leaders would associate the United States with the treaty. A twin-track approach was taken: one involved highly secretive talks between the core Anglo-American countries of the United States, Britain, and Canada; the other involved Congress, which would ultimately have to ratify a deal.[12]

The secretive talks took place deep inside the Pentagon and lasted for about ten days, from March 22. They soon produced a memo-randum, penned by the American representative, John Hickerson, but following close consultations with the Canadian and British teams led by, respectively, Lester Pearson, Under-secretary for External Affairs, and Lord Inverchapel, British ambassador to the United States. The memorandum proposed the enlargement of the Brussels Treaty to include Norway, Sweden, Denmark, Iceland, and Italy, and for the US president to extend an invitation to a conference on a security pact for the North Atlantic area.[13] The memorandum underwent some minor tweaks during the Pentagon talks, but its main conclusion remained that "there would be a treaty."[14] In other words, there would be a new treaty covering the North Atlantic area. This was clearly an ambitious step extending beyond a loose associa-tion of the United States with the Brussels Treaty.

The entire affair was kept secret, because the three Anglo-Saxon powers wanted to establish this framework before drawing others into it. France, a key driver of the Dunkirk and Brussels treaties, was not informed of the talks. Getting France on board would thus be a task. Oddly, Soviet leader Joseph Stalin was better informed than France, because his agent "Homer" sat on the British team. This was Donald Maclean, first secretary at the British embassy in Washington and a graduate of Cambridge University, where he was recruited by the notorious Kim Philby. Maclean evaded capture in May 1951 and was later made a KGB colonel.

The other track involved Congress and led to the so-called Vandenberg Resolution of June 11, 1948. It involved intensive negotiations between key people from the administration—as well as Lovett and Achilles, also Charles Bohlen, counsellor in the Department of State, and George Kennan, head of its Policy Planning Unit—and leading US senators, not least chairman of the Foreign Relations Committee, Arthur H. Vandenberg. Vandenberg had risen to this position in 1947, but he was an experienced political hand who had converted to internationalist US foreign policy. "In the spirit of anxious humility," Vandenberg informed the Senate in 1945, the critical conditions confronting the nation called for "the straightest, the plainest and the most courageous thinking of which we are capable." And in Vandenberg's eyes, such thinking necessitated a departure from isolationism and an embrace of internationalism. We saw in Chapter 1 how Vandenberg had become an acolyte of collective security policy and crafted the compromise that enabled regional collective defense organizations within the United Nations Charter. He thus spearheaded both collective security and post-war US bipartisan foreign policy.

In May and June 1948, Senator Vandenberg took bipartisanism one step further. He would support involvement, but only on specific terms: there could be no automatic commitment by the United States to collective defense; self-help had to precede mutual aid; and engagement must be in support of the United Nations Charter he had helped bring to life in San Francisco in 1945. The resolution of June 11, 1948, drafted under the supervision of later Secretary of State Dean Rusk (at the time director of the State Department's Office of United Nations Affairs), advised the US president to support the United Nations by associating the country with "such regional and other collective arrangements" as "affect its national security" and by "making clear its determination to exercise the right of individual or collective self-defense under [UN Charter] article 51."[15] It was thus from inside the UN Charter that Vandenberg saw an opportunity for an Atlantic defense pact.

Even as these two tracks ran their course, it was not a given that an Atlantic Pact would follow. There remained the considerable challenge of hammering out a draft pact in negotiations with invited countries, and then getting it ratified by them all. We shall consider this shortly. Inside the administration it was also not clear that the pact enjoyed support. Lovett was the central State Department senior figure, as Secretary Marshall was attending to other business, including an extended trip to Bogota, Colombia, in the late spring. Vandenberg thus turned to Lovett as he developed his thinking on "an American commitment to Europe."[16] Inside the State Department Lovett could count on Hickerson and Achilles to speak warmly in favor of a pact. But they were mid-level officials. Two of their superiors, Charles Bohlen and George Kennan, were opposed to it. Bohlen and Kennan were under no illusions about the Soviet Union: they considered it a "rival" that warranted a "long-term, patient but firm and vigilant containment" policy, as Kennan wrote in his spectacular "X Article" of 1947.[17] But they also believed that it was not in the US interest to contain the Soviet Union by military commitments. They instead focused on political and economic containment measures that dovetailed with the Marshall Aid.

Kennan was ultimately won over to the argument for an Atlantic treaty, and Canada's ambassador to Washington, Hume Wrong, would play a role in his conversion. On May 19, the day that the Senate Foreign Affairs Committee approved the Vandenberg Resolution, paving the way for the resolution's consideration by the full Senate, Wrong hosted Kennan for a lunch. Wrong carefully explained how anything less than a treaty would make it difficult for Canada to associate itself with Europe's defense. Given the proximity of Canada to the United States and Canadian sensibilities surrounding sovereignty, the likely outcome would be "a policy of Canadian aloofness." Naturally, as his country's representative, Wrong was skillfully exploiting Canadian thinking about an Atlantic community and its reluctance to find itself tightly embraced by the United States in the North American space—as we shall see below. Still, Wrong had a point. If the United States sought community efforts by other nations, it would have to step into the ring. Kennan professed to be much impressed and promised to think it over carefully.[18] His conversion to a defense pact was thus underway. Bohlen would hold out and not convert. However, he was removed from influence in September, when he was sent to Paris for three months to advise the US delegation to the UN General Assembly. "By the time he was back in Washington, it was too late for him to affect the course of events."[19]

One for all and all for one?

Formal negotiations over a North Atlantic Treaty ran from June 1948 to April 1949. It was not a smooth ride: political interests were multiple, and political calendars—especially the US presidential elections in November—mattered greatly.[20] Still, the negotiations delivered the defense pact foreseen during the Pentagon talks and baked into the Vandenberg Resolution.

There were three phases to the negotiations. A first set of exploratory talks ran until September 1948. They produced the same conclusion that the American, British, and Canadian officials had reached following their secretive talks: namely, that nothing short of an Atlantic Pact could satisfy the full set of North American and West European security interests and needs. A second round of talks then did very little except to keep the issue going through the US presidential elections of November, after which a draft treaty followed in short order. That concluded the second phase. The opening of the third phase awaited President Truman's inauguration and the appointment of his new team. Secretary Marshall and Under Secretary Lovett both stepped down (they would return in September 1950 as secretary of defense and deputy secretary of defense, respectively), and Dean Acheson took over as the new secretary of state. Come February 1949, the third phase opened. It concerned the fine print of the treaty, including its membership and obligations.

There is a telling point in how these negotiations unfolded that serves to underscore the contingency of the Atlantic Pact—it might never even have come about. The point is that the draft treaty was forged by mid-level career officials. Naturally, it is entirely to be expected that staff members prepare policy, and that the senior leadership becomes involved only in the final phase of the negotiations. However, through all the negotiations in 1948, the senior officials chose to remain aloof, as the writing on the wall was not clear: their president, Harry Truman, had such dismal approval ratings in mid-1948—in the range of 35–40 percent—that he seemed unlikely to win the November elections.[21] Truman's opponent in the election, Republican Thomas Dewey, had done surprisingly well against Franklin D. Roosevelt in 1944. In 1948, he was emboldened by Truman's poor performance.

Dewey was a moderate, but he was also of the party of Senator Robert Taft, a committed isolationist (or non-interventionist). How he would navigate his party's currents if elected president was an unknown. However, in one of the greatest upsets in US political history, Truman snatched victory from the jaws of defeat. Famously, the *Chicago Tribune* ran a headline on November 3, "Dewey Defeats Truman," but it was not to be. Truman had performed, in the words of the *New York Times*, a "miracle of electioneering."[22]

In this context of political uncertainty, a high-level ambassadorial committee led by Under Secretary Lovett, which was supposed to guide the negotiations through the summer and into the fall, mostly trod water. European ambassadors were dependent on US thinking, but Lovett could not commit for political reasons. A lower-level working party instead kicked into action. Its two key architects were John Hickerson and Theodore Achilles. Charles Bohlen, the Atlantic Pact skeptic, was part of the American team, but in September he was posted to Paris for other work. The working party became, as Achilles recalled it, "a real band of brothers"—the source of a "practically complete" North Atlantic Treaty, lifelong friendships, and a "NATO spirit" whereby people focus on making things work, rather than sticking to instructions from back home.[23] By September 1948, the working party had drafted a memorandum that set out areas of agreement and issues for further consideration.[24] It agreed that "no alternative" to a treaty "appears to meet the essential requirements" for security. That was the bottom line: no treaty equaled no security.

With Truman's election in November, it became clear that this bottom line had political backing at the highest American level. Senior people such as Acheson could and did take over. This was timely. The election loss had put the Republicans in a foul mood, and they were looking to challenge the foreign policy credentials of the Democrats.[25] In October 1949, they would get their chance, as Mao Zedong's communist forces took power in China—raising the question of who had "lost" the country. Before then, in February and March, it fell largely to Dean Acheson to guide the US Senate towards the Atlantic Treaty, which the working party had drafted after the election.

A drama of sorts involved Dean Acheson and Tom Connally. Dean Acheson was secretary of state and an experienced hand. He had been assistant secretary of state through the war years, a delegate to the Bretton Woods conference that designed the United Nations Charter, and Lovett's predecessor as Under Secretary of State. He was a committed internationalist, an emerging architect of containment, and the right person to handle Tom Connally's ire with the administration and the treaty. Connally was a Democratic senator from Texas who, in November 1949, took over the chairmanship of the Senate Foreign Relations Committee from Senator Vandenberg. Connally was of Truman's Democratic Party, but he had no intention of simply bowing to an initiative (the Atlantic Treaty) that bore the stamp of his rival Vandenberg (his June 1948 resolution). In addition to his jealousy of Vandenberg, Connally suspected that the Truman administration had been less than forthcoming with the Foreign Relations Committee.[26] For his part, Acheson suspected that Connally was simply not "a smart cookie."[27] A British observer felt that age had added to Connally's limitations, rather than his virtues (he was seventy-two at the time).[28]

The drama intensified on February 14, when on the Senate floor Connally claimed that the emerging treaty threatened to leave it to Europeans to decide on war for the United States. It was a dire and "decisive moment" for the Atlantic Pact.[29] If Connally's claim stood, it would mobilize the Senate against the treaty. Connally had earlier in February sought to change the draft treaty to omit reference to military action and to the concept that the allies were committed by an attack on any one of them. Connally's suggestions had "appalled" British Foreign Secretary Bevin. French Foreign Minister Schuman began to find the exercise "meaningless." Canada's Ambassador Hume Wrong was instructed to inform the US government that Canada might be "compelled" to decide that the treaty was not in the national interest.[30] Acheson had done his best to calm tempers and move negotiations forward, when Connally chose to bring the matter out into the open, onto the Senate floor.

The senator probably overplayed his hand. The press did not react favorably, and with strong support from soon-to-be allies, Dean Acheson could bring Vandenberg and Connally together to craft a compromise. The treaty's central collective defense clause (Article 5) thus fell into place. The clause opens with the statement that an attack on one ally shall be considered an attack on all. The clause then continues that each ally will take "such action as it deems necessary, including the use of armed force" to respond to the attack. Both the three-musketeers appeal and the reference to armed force pleased the future allies. However, the decision to send troops abroad clearly remained with the national authorities, Congress included, because of the reference to "as it deems necessary"—wording that the senators firmly held on to. Finally, the clause also caters to the reigning US concern at the time with collective security and the central role of the United Nations. It is explicit about the defensive nature of the alliance, in that its actions must "restore and maintain the security of the North Atlantic," and all allied measures taken in response to an attack must "immediately be reported to the Security Council" of the United Nations.

The contours of Europe in the treaty

France and Britain were the leading European countries in the negotiations, but they struggled in terms of both impact and coordination. Britain was better off, being so closely associated with the United States at almost every turn; but even then, Europe and the empire caused some friction.

France's position was initially set forth by the French ambassador, Henri Bonnet, in the ambassadorial committee. Bonnet made it clear that France did not favor a new Atlantic treaty. Instead, he sought ironclad American guarantees to France and the Brussels Treaty allies. In his view (and thus France's), Atlantic security should rest on two pillars—the Brussels Treaty and a US commitment to it. There should be no dilution by bringing in a multitude of other European countries. Bonnet was so belligerently insistent that at one point Canada's Lester Pearson and Britain's Gladwyn Jebb made direct appeals for greater flexibility to Bonnet's superiors, including Foreign Minister Robert Schuman.[31] In the course of the fall negotiations, France abandoned the two-pillar idea and turned to enlarging its own footprint within an Atlantic treaty framework.

British thinking was, from the outset, different and more elastic. Bevin's original ideas revolved around three mutually reinforcing circles: one for Europe (the Brussels Treaty), one for the British empire (or the dominions), and one for the Atlantic (committing the United States to Europe). There was obviously wiggle room between these circles, but there was also a notable red line: the empire gave Britain special status. It belonged to both the Brussels Treaty and an Atlantic treaty, but not fully to either European or Atlantic politics. The two-pillar framework sought by France—and also by George Kennan inside the State Department—implied no distinction between Britain and Europe, which appalled British officials.

Bonnet's British colleague in the ambassadorial committee, Oliver Franks, who had become ambassador to the United States in the stead of an "aging and erratic" Lord Inverchapel, explored Britain's inherent wiggle room with great flair.[32] A former professor of moral philosophy with a commanding personality, Franks bonded with his American and Canadian counterparts in "playful intellectuality," or what Lovett would term a new "Periclean age."[33] Such playfulness would ease the negotiations over national interests, but not remove the pains of compromise with regard to the empire. Obviously, it was out of the question to highlight the empire in the treaty, but the geographical extent of the treaty was an issue. For Britain, the problem lay not in the North Atlantic, but in the Mediterranean, which at the time Britain considered to be under its influence, as a gateway to the Middle and Far East.

Italy—an axis power in the Second World War—was thus a tricky issue to settle. At first, in mid-1948, France objected to Italy's inclusion, on the grounds that a two-pillar treaty had to deal only with the Brussels Treaty allies and then the United States. In around November 1948, when this two-pillar idea fell flat, France became a strong proponent of including Italy in an Atlantic treaty, because it offered a southern axis across the Mediterranean into French North Africa. Britain never really budged: Italy was a nuisance in an Atlantic framework, and potentially disruptive to Britain's ability to run its empire along the road through the Mediterranean and the Suez Canal to India.

Italian Prime Minister Alicde De Gasperi forced the issue on January 12, 1949, when he submitted Italy's application to join the Atlantic treaty negotiations. For De Gasperi, it was a matter of equal treatment and an occasion to leave behind the trauma of having joined a "pact of steel" with Hitler's Germany. It was also a matter of anchoring Italian politics in a Western context, as De Gasperi's Christian democrats faced sizeable socialist and communist parties sympathetic to Soviet ideology.

Hickerson was consistently in favor of Italy's inclusion, but his superiors (including Dean Acheson, once he came into office) asked the Brussels Treaty countries to give a lead on the matter. This caused a small crisis: British officials in both Washington and Brussels sought to maneuver the issue into a default position of excluding Italy—by offering to include Italy only if the United States wanted it, which they well knew was not the case. This provoked France and its ambassador, Bonnet, to, once again, disrupt matters. They "incensed" Acheson by linking Italy's membership to that of Norway,[34] and they insisted "with equal strength" and in contradiction to Achilles' heralded spirit of compromise that French Algeria should be included in the treaty.[35] However, on Italy, Bonnet and Acheson were in agreement. In March, Acheson had secured assurances from his Italian counterpart, Foreign Minister Sforza, that Italy would not bring colonial matters into treaty negotiations, and he gained President Truman's backing to invite Italy to join the treaty negotiations. Acheson then proceeded to issue this invitation without first informing the British, who regarded that as "American high-handedness."[36]

The geographical scope of the treaty played out differently in the North Atlantic. There were multiple national interests, but the US interests were so strong that everyone realized that they would prevail.[37] The US concern was with the logistics of transoceanic power projection. In 1949, a civilian flight from New York to London would make two stopovers—for instance, in Newfoundland (Canada) and Glasgow (Scotland)—on a journey that would take between sixteen and seventeen hours. To project power, the United States needed stepping-stone countries. The obvious ones were Denmark (which includes Greenland), Iceland, Norway, and, further to the south,

Portugal (which includes the Azores in mid-Atlantic). Theodore Achilles found the question of "considerable importance" in the fall 1948 negotiations. Britain did not object to the idea, but France was concerned about the geographical proximity of some of those stepping stones to the Soviet Union.

Moving into the spring negotiations, the decisive issue became one of how far the United States was willing to go to allay domestic concerns in the stepping-stone countries. In fact, it was prepared to go quite far. Iceland had no armed forces and was put under no obligation to develop them; Norway and Denmark were allowed to maintain a policy of not opening their territories up to allied bases during peace time; and Portugal was allowed to remain aloof from European politics, in keeping with its historic role as an Atlantic seaboard country and its mistrust of Franco-British scheming to acquire Portuguese colonies. But there was a limit: Sweden received no invitation, on account of its non-negotiable neutrality policy; and Ireland was taken off the list, because it insisted on linking a North Atlantic Pact to the issue of Irish unification, which would have been at the cost of British Northern Ireland.

As mentioned, France had developed a liking for a southern axis that pointed in the direction of its territories and interests in North Africa. The draft treaty submitted by the working party on Christmas Eve, December 24, 1948, contained no agreement on the inclusion or exclusion of French North Africa.[38] Through January and February 1949, the United States continued to drag its feet on the issue. Nonetheless France persisted, and by March it had succeeded in securing a reference to "the Algerian departments of France" in the treaty's Article 6, which defines the geographical area of collective defense obligations. It was a victory for France, but in retrospect a short-lived one: the treaty reference was deleted in 1962, when Algeria wrested its independence from France.

Canada's search for Atlantic community

The signing of the North Atlantic Treaty on April 4, 1949 produced the American commitment to Europe's defense that the Europeans had hoped for. This was a matter of military muscle, of course. But it was also a matter of all the allies committing to uphold "the freedom, common heritage and civilization of their peoples, founded on the principles of democracy, individual liberty and the rule of law"—as outlined in the treaty's preamble. Little importance was attached to this part of the treaty during the negotiations, Theodore Achilles would recall, but the common values were, he noted, "probably more responsible than anything else for the enduring quality of the Alliance."[39]

US leaders had been clear on their desire only to enter Europe on their own terms. There could be no US involvement in mere balance-of-power politics: the United States was in it to transform political relations and build a community. This was entirely in line with the treaty's preamble. What was less clear—and increasingly so over time—was the obligation this imposed on the United States. Secretary Marshall's aid program for Europe had committed the Europeans to come together. And we saw in the previous chapter how this had caused political headaches in Europe, where countries tended to pass the buck of leadership. In signing up to the North Atlantic Treaty, the US government was, to an extent, raising the expectation that it, too, would take part in this leadership.

A certain thaw in East–West relations immediately following the signing of the treaty created a degree of hopeful anticipation: if military confrontation abated, then perhaps the alliance could expand its remit to include widespread political and economic cooperation? This was no trivial matter, since the threat of upheaval was in part (and as George Kennan's containment thinking revealed) related to social and economic hardship—something that the Soviet Union could exploit to foment revolt. The direct Soviet threat diminished a week after the signing of the North Atlantic Treaty, when Moscow sent word to the US State Department that it was ready to discuss calling off the Berlin blockade. The Soviet Union had instigated the blockade in June 1948, terminating ground transport across eastern Germany in the hope that it would force the United States, Britain, and France to abandon their outposts in Berlin, located in the heart of the Soviet zone of control. However, the Western response was not to leave, but to run a demanding—but also hugely successful—airlift into western Berlin. This ceased in May 1949, once the Soviet Union had raised its blockade.

President Truman next ordered a reduction of almost a third in the US defense budget. This was not only on account of the improved Berlin situation: the key drivers were slow growth in the US economy and a looming federal budget deficit. Truman's move predictably led to anxiety among the allies.[40] But it also pointed to an opportunity to frame allied relations not merely in terms of US military assistance to Europe, but as a wide-ranging transatlantic union. In short, did the twelve-nation Atlantic alliance embody a transatlantic political community?

Disappointingly, it did not. That at least is the clear view of Canadian diplomat Escott Reid, who wrote of his "chief disappointment" about the Atlantic Pact's political provisions. They were "weaker than what I hoped for and what I believed were needed."[41] Reid had sought a treaty couched in the form of a constitution for a North Atlantic community, and thus a treaty written in the name of the people of this community. The alliance should logically have a North Atlantic parliament, and its treaty provisions for the promotion of economic, social, and democratic wellbeing should be as far-reaching as possible. Because Reid found such a community realistic only in the North Atlantic area, he firmly opposed the inclusion in the alliance of Portugal and Italy, just as he resisted the treaty's reference to France's Algerian departments.

The Atlantic treaty does contain provisions relating to some of Reid's concerns. In Article 2—commonly known as the "Canadian article"—the parties promise to strengthen their free institutions, to bring about a better understanding of the principles behind those institutions, and to generally promote stability and wellbeing, including through economic collaboration. But Reid regretted the inadequacy of this article. Canada had been right in believing that this treaty obligation could foster a community, but "where we failed," Reid later wrote, was in not getting further provisions into the treaty, after which all the allies neglected to make sufficient use of them.[42]

Dean Acheson frankly disagreed. Speaking to Hickerson and other US officials, Acheson called Article 2 "the pie in the sky article."

He did not want to commit the United States to a treaty provision that promised vast cooperation beyond the security sphere. Hickerson, who teamed up with Canadian Ambassador Hume Wrong to talk to Acheson, underscored how, in fact, "this involves no commitment." Later, he took the same message to the US Senate, which would have to ratify the treaty: "We had to talk with a Senate group explaining there was no commitment, that this was just aspirations and things, and they and Vandenberg bought it."[43]

Canada's drive for a community vision had struck a raw nerve in US domestic politics. Senator Vandenberg and other Republicans saw in such "welfare provisions" the political program of their domestic opponents, the Democrats. Meanwhile, the Democrats were divided over the related issue of civil rights. In fact, civil rights splintered the party—with Progressives and Dixiecrats going their separate ways. In principle, the North Atlantic Treaty and civil rights issues were two separate things; but through February 1949 the Senate held hearings on both issues. If the treaty's Article 2 became the door connecting these issues, Dean Acheson could face a united Republican-Democrat opposition, and he was clearly anxious to tread very carefully around the issue. Canada's Ambassador Wrong then stepped forward with an offer of a restrictive interpretation of Article 2: he suggested that the article could lead to new "obligations" only if the allies accepted them by "normal constitutional arrangements."[44] Canada thus gained Article 2, but at the cost of rendering it toothless.

This did not mean that Canada's efforts had been in vain. Article 2 would, in fact, become the lodestar for "Atlanticists"—diehard proponents of a deep and wide transatlantic community. The opportunity was there to be seized by them whenever they felt (as they later would) that the time was right.

Canada also inspired the creation of the alliance's decision-making body—today the North Atlantic Council, but in the treaty's Article 9 referred to merely as "a Council." In December 1948, as the ambassadorial committee and the working party prepared a draft treaty for final political negotiations, Ambassador Wrong succeeded in coaxing no less a person than US Under Secretary Lovett around to the view that the alliance needed a political organ as a forum for consultation on the many issues that would impact on it. Lovett and his team of advisors had an instinctive preference for minimal provisions on decision-making. Their approach was to ensure flexibility, to avoid any requirement for unanimity, and instead to foster a culture of consensus. That is, no government should be able to prevent collective action by the other allies; and conversely, the allies should not be able to force a government to take action against its will.[45] Lovett prevailed on the issue of consensus over unanimity, but he gave in on the matter of the Council. Ernest Bevin had been against any such council as well, but when Britain found itself isolated on the issue, he instructed Ambassador Franks to accept its inclusion in the treaty.[46]

A council with wide powers of consultation could, of course, become a tool for community building. The treaty outlines two pathways to consultations. Article 4 stipulates that the allies must consult whenever one of them is threatened. This is the clause of "mandatory" consultations: if one ally brings a threat to the table, the others are under an obligation to consult with that ally. It is built around a threat; and not coincidentally, it is the article preceding the three-musketeer clause, Article 5. There is also a less dramatic and wider consultation option set out in Article 9. This is where we find the Council and the alliance's "permissive" consultations: allied Council representatives—organized to be able to meet promptly at any time—are free to consider any issue relating to implementation of the treaty, be it regional or global, military or economic, acute or emergent.[47]

But while Canada succeeded in establishing a council, it had less success in linking it to community-by-consultation. The personal fate of Escott Reid essentially mirrors the failure of the enterprise. Early on, in the spring of 1948, Reid had been in good company: Prime Minister Mackenzie King, Secretary of State for External Affairs Louis St. Laurent, Under-secretary of State for External Affairs Lester Pearson, and Canadian Ambassador to the United States Hume Wrong all stood behind the priority of developing the non-military dimension of an Atlantic treaty. Reid himself was Deputy Under-secretary of State for External Affairs, reported to Pearson, and passed on instructions to Canada's lead negotiator, Ambassador Wrong. It was an impressive "Atlantic community" negotiating team.

But by April 1949, Reid's teammates had parted company with him, and his reputation was in tatters.

The other team members adapted to the resistance offered by other governments. But Reid, who had been a driving force behind the vision, found compromise difficult. His legacy as an original and important policy contributor would thus be tainted by "undeniable weaknesses" in terms of single-mindedness, arrogance, and self-serving recollections.[48] In his Atlantic treaty memoirs, he expresses regret: "I should have played my cards better," been less "feverish," and "should not have disclosed that my ambitions for the North Atlantic alliance were so far-reaching." Tellingly, having confessed his sins, Reid takes a final potshot at some teammates: Hume Wrong did not stand up for their ideas, while Lester Pearson, Reid's immediate superior, "liked to get away from his desk in Ottawa"—where, naturally, Reid would be beavering away.[49]

Reid had a clear vision for a community, but did not manage to build one; and so both his community idea and his career stalled. However, the failure was not absolute—at least not as far as the idea was concerned. Reid and his fellow travelers did succeed in energizing Canada's so-called counterweight strategy of offsetting US preponderance in North America.[50] An Atlantic Pact was perfect for the purpose. It was what Ambassador Wrong had in mind when he suggested to George Kennan that a bilateral deal between the United States and Europe would lead to Canadian "aloofness." Without a collective treaty framework, there would be no home for Canada and no "counterweight" to the United States, so that Canada's persistent "quest for some kind of balance of power" in North American affairs would have to take a new direction.[51]

Balance of power and community are typically considered opposites: you either embed power in a community, or you balance it. But Reid and the other Canadian officials were right to combine them in a North Atlantic Treaty because, of course, such a treaty would have to engender community by somehow building on the existing balances of power. Their frustrations arose from the fact that, on the issue of how this should be achieved, the solution could not be a Canadian one: it would ultimately have to be American.

Alliances are typically formed in response to the intensity and geography of external threats. And so it was with NATO. The Soviet Union created anxiety, especially in Western Europe countries worn down by world war. In 1947, the Soviet Union turned its back on the Marshall program and then the Council of Foreign Ministers. In 1948, it staged a coup in Czechoslovakia and blockaded Berlin. Winston Churchill had, in March 1946, spoken of an "iron curtain" descending across the continent; by 1948 it was clear to see. The Soviet Union's proximity to the European heartland contrasted with the geographical position of the United States, separated as it was from Europe by an ocean. So this was another cause of Western European anxiety and another reason for European leaders to invite the United States to become permanently engaged in Europe's affairs.

But there is a lot more to NATO than Soviet policy and Europe's geography. The Atlantic Pact was simple in wording and bold in outlook. It reflected the experience of the American heartland that nations based on open institutions and individual freedom are ultimately more powerful, and that communities of such nations must provide for their collective defense. Unlike regular alliances, which are mostly tools of statecraft to balance power, NATO was born with a popular dimension and a commitment to enlargement, should the organization's popularity and community grow. This is the meaning of the treaty's Article 10. NATO's door is open. Thus, it guards the perimeter of likeminded nations and aims to expand this perimeter to (in principle) all countries of the Euro-Atlantic area. NATO is thus a collective defense alliance with general security aspirations.

The remarkably rapid negotiation of the treaty owed much to the experience of wartime collaboration. Europe could not return to its past, the European leaders agreed: they needed the engagement of the United States. And the American leaders were casting around for original ways to engender change in Europe. President Truman's commitment to democracy in Greece and Turkey and Secretary Marshall's offer of an aid program in return for European cooperation set the wheels in motion. Through 1947 and early 1948, the Europeans sprang into action. British Foreign Secretary Bevin insisted on security ties across the Atlantic; French Foreign Minister Schuman drew attention to an urgent security crisis; and Belgian, Dutch, and Luxembourgian leaders joined them in signing the Brussels Treaty. The wartime Anglo-Saxon club then pulled together, as key American officials—from Hickerson through Lovett to Vandenberg—foresaw that American help for Europe had to involve a defense treaty relationship. The rest was a matter of negotiation. The serious talking began only in February 1949, once President Truman had been reelected and had assembled his new team. In a matter of weeks, the North Atlantic Pact was all set.

The next challenge for the allies was to bring alive the aspiration for community in a Europe that was increasingly marked by Cold War competition. This competition would emphasize NATO's character as a collective defense shield, but NATO's community vision for Europe remained fundamental and inescapable. It teed NATO up for a difficult balancing act that was suffused with political drama.

3

Aspiration Lost?
The Emergence
of Cold War NATO

"It was extremely doubtful whether the military spirit was dead," French Foreign Minister Robert Schuman bluntly told his North Atlantic Council colleagues in New York on September 17, 1950. Schuman was referring not to the newly founded Atlantic alliance, but to Germany, which twice in thirty years had committed aggression against France and the continent. Current West German leaders were trustworthy, Schuman conceded, but then continued, "there were men of good will under the Weimar Government, but this did not prevent the subsequent rise of Hitlerism."[1]

The rearmament of West Germany had become the first real headache of the Atlantic alliance right after its inception. The Cold War competition with the Soviet Union, the war launched by North Korea in June 1950, and communist China's direct intervention in that war in October 1950 provoked grave concern in the alliance: if communist countries were this aggressive, the allies needed greater military muscle also in Europe. But German rearmament was not a lightweight issue. The allies had fought imperial Germany up until 1945. A rearmed West Germany, even if detached from the GDR, could yet again hold the key to Europe's balance of power. To rearm West Germany and avoid this dire balance-of-power prospect, the allies had to integrate the country into a Western community. But whether that community should be mainly Atlantic or European, and how it should move forward, were questions that tore at the alliance.

By the mid-1960s, leadership issues had debilitated NATO, and it had lost its zeal. It had the appearance of a balance-of-power tool intended to keep the Soviet bloc at bay. Its aspirational promise of political transformation was left behind. The exhaustion stemmed from the inability of NATO leaders to define a community vision compatible with West German power and the wider national interests of the leading allies. The United States, Britain, and France saw themselves as global powers, not mere NATO allies, and they vied for nuclear control and political influence. They had had a vision, but had managed to exhaust it. They likewise drained the guardians of their collective alliance—NATO's secretary general and its supreme allied commander. In a triumph of ordinary alliance over aspirational community, both resigned in the early 1960s, fatigued and disillusioned.

Atlantic machinery

The North Atlantic Treaty was originally not supposed to involve any significant collective organization. It had a council provided for by the treaty, and then some inherited modest machinery from the Brussels Treaty, such as its regional planning groups. Its first Strategic Concept—in theory a plan for defending the alliance—was mostly an amalgamation of diverse geographies and limited military means.[2] The United States, Britain, and France had occupying forces in West Germany, but the alliance had neither integrated command nor forces.

Secretary of State Dean Acheson was clear in his desire for the alliance to remain slim, or, in his words, "effective" and "businesslike." Certainly, it would have to have a "machinery," by which he meant a political organ (the North Atlantic Council) and a military leadership (notably a Military Committee). However, as Acheson made clear during the first meeting of the North Atlantic Council, in September 1949, this machinery should be kept "as simple as possible." Unsurprisingly, the remaining eleven foreign ministers approved of the US approach in general terms. However, Canada's Lester Pearson, France's Robert Schuman, and Norway's Halvard Lange did raise the concern that Acheson's approach to the military organization might be somewhat restrictive. The Council thus agreed to support Acheson's principle of simplicity, but with the proviso that the Council could choose to expand the organization.[3]

This caveat proved fortuitous. In July 1950, one month after the outbreak of the Korean War, the newly formed North Atlantic Council of Deputies expressed unanimous support for the US decision to counter "Korean aggression." Prompt action in Korea, they continued, would act as a deterrent to aggression in other parts of the world, Europe included. And to achieve that properly, the allies had to build real defense muscle. "The time for theoretical long term planning has passed," they agreed.[4] With this, they effectively set in motion a build-up of the defense organization that would put the "O" into NATO. And they did it with such vigor that people largely ceased to use the abbreviation NAT (the North Atlantic Treaty).

The United States wasted no time in building up NATO. Its effort in the war in Korea—so far from Europe—showed the way: the US assembled a powerful multinational force, unified it around an integrated plan and command, and the United Nations gave the force its blessing. In short, that force had muscle, unity, and legitimacy. The Soviet Union oddly helped out by boycotting the United Nations Security Council (UNSC), objecting to the Western opposition to admitting communist China to the UN. The Western powers could thus adopt a UN mandate for the Korean force. And the US allies did their part: the Briton Gladwyn Jebb and the Frenchman Jean Chauvel, who crafted the UNSC resolution, deliberately left considerable scope for US command. "There is no real need for such machinery," replied Jebb, when asked about a Security Council committee to oversee operations.[5]

President Truman soon pushed his European allies to accept a US supreme commander in the alliance for the purpose of building muscle and unity. The first supreme commander was Dwight Eisenhower, who had commanded Western forces from D-Day, June 1944, to the end of the war. The second was Matthew Ridgway, who had held supreme command in Asia and a leadership role in the Korean War. Both were intimately familiar with the task of organizing multinational forces in support of US political priorities. The main difference between Korea and Europe lay in the "machinery." In

Korea, the United States needed a free hand to fight a war; in Europe, it needed machinery to mobilize, corral, and align European defense efforts for the purpose of deterring the Soviet Union. The diverse forces of the allies needed to be raised, trained, and integrated according to a collective defense plan and under unified command. Thus began NATO's introduction of skilled and forceful American generals to European defense planning, which continues to the present.

Eisenhower and Ridgway shaped things early on. They were as different as they were remarkable. Dwight Eisenhower was not only a skilled general, but an accomplished diplomat. He had famous differences of opinion with British General Bernard Montgomery in the Second World War campaign, and yet he cooperated smoothly with Montgomery as his deputy supreme commander in NATO. Together, they organized the core command, Allied Command Europe, as well as its headquarters (Supreme Headquarters Allied Powers Europe, SHAPE—an acronym that would soon become a household name in the NATO community). General Ridgway was equally highly respected as a soldier, but his candor could rub political authorities up the wrong way. Eisenhower knew this and offered Ridgway a "masterly" introduction—according to Ridgway's recollection—to the political level of the alliance: the characters and trustworthiness of NATO leaders.[6] Their supreme command handover was peculiar, taking place in a darkened bedroom, with Eisenhower propped up on pillows and wearing sunglasses because of some eye trouble. The dim setting was perhaps ideal, and certainly symbolic for the transmission of knowledge about their political masters.

By the time of the handover, May 1952, much had happened. The allies had done away with their original Medium Term Defense Plan and had agreed to a huge increase over three years—more than a doubling—of defense forces. They had also consented to an annual review of national defense plans, and they had established an elaborate military command structure whose commanders were subordinate to the NATO Military Committee.[7] Ridgway believed that both he and Eisenhower had come in at the right time: Eisenhower, the soldier-diplomat, to awaken the allies; and Ridgway, ever the soldier, to collect on their "IOUs" (I Owe You). Eisenhower had to build something on bare ground; Ridgway confronted the formidable task of making a vast and complex logistical structure work. Eisenhower could mobilize political goodwill by distributing stars (posts) in the command structure; in the name of command effectiveness, Ridgway had to oppose national desires for added stars and prestige.[8] General Ridgway's ability to deliver got noted and, once he was elected US president, Eisenhower recalled him to serve as US Army chief of staff.

NATO's military build-up—and with it an infusion of US military leadership and oversight—came about by clear political design. It was crafted at the highest levels of the US government and approved by President Truman in National Security Council policy 82 of September 11, 1950. It contained the "full package" of desired NAT reform: notably an integrated command and integrated force, substantial US forces stationed in Europe, and German rearmament. It signaled that "America had made up its mind."[9] It was also a sort of ultimatum issued to Canada and the European allies: they could either take the full package or risk a US decoupling from their defense.[10] The full package included notably a prospect foreseen by John McCloy, US high commissioner for Germany, well before the Korean War: namely, the need for a "genuine European army" to absorb and contain West German power.[11]

Acheson now changed tack from alliance simplicity to alliance build-up. In September 1950, from the North Atlantic Council (NAC) meeting in New York, the *New York Times* reported at first that "European circles" felt the United States was "risking Western European unity" by pushing so hard for West German rearmament.[12] But just days later, it reported the decision by the United States, France, and Britain to end the state of hostilities with West Germany and endow its government with diplomatic privileges—pending full agreement among the allies: they had smoothly agreed to let the Atlantic alliance study the issue of including German forces in the overall defense of Europe. But this was only the beginning of the issue, not the end. Ominously, the *New York Times* portrayed the New York agreement as both "the rebirth of Germany as a world power" and "a major success for the United States policy."[13] This prospect of

German resurrection guided by US interests was sure to provoke great anxiety in France.

Secretary of State Acheson steamrollered any such anxieties. He dealt with the allies at the September 1950 New York conference with "bare-knuckled tactics," "tried to lay down the law," and "dismissed their most fundamental concerns out of hand," and he did so deliberately.[14] However, Acheson could not fully push the US package through the Council. He secured the allies' agreement "in principle" to add West German forces to the collective defense, but he had to leave "the detailed arrangements" to be worked out.[15] A political process was required. Charles Spofford, the US ambassador (formally speaking, the deputy permanently attached to the NAC), would play a key role in resolving NATO's German issue, but not before France had had a major say in the affair.

Germany in the heart of Europe was not the only geographical concern of the allies. The Eastern Mediterranean, where Turkey and Greece controlled Soviet-bloc access from the Black Sea to the Mediterranean—through Turkey's Bosporus Strait and Greece's Aegean territorial waters—was unsettled. The two countries had been left out of the original alliance agreement partly because they did not really fit the "North Atlantic" bill (though Italy's inclusion showed how pragmatism could prevail) and partly because Britain hoped to set up a separate Middle Eastern defense organization to secure its imperial interests. Turkey and Greece were cool to this idea, though, and Britain was at pains to realize it. To pre-empt a Turkish–Greek dash for neutrality, the United States looked to NATO. Still, it took lengthy talks through 1950 and 1951—and an intricate command arrangement deal that had to navigate British interests in Egypt, French and Italian desires for high command, and Turkish and Greek insistence on coming under US command—before NATO reached agreement in September 1951.[16] It was all a "snake pit of troubles," Dean Acheson recalled, and to the very end it required "much private exhortation."[17] But the alliance did reach agreement, and on February 18, 1952 Turkey and Greece acceded to NATO.

Dean Acheson would also later reflect on the issue of German rearmament that had so strained the 1950 NAC conference.

Somewhat disingenuously, he blamed the misery on the Pentagon. He himself had laid down the law, but in retrospect he was "inclined to agree" that the full US policy package presented to the allies had been a "mistake."[18] What is certain is that the insistent US push in 1950 for the military build-up of NATO, including West German rearmament, kickstarted a frantic French search for alternative ways to contain and control West Germany's military resurrection. It proved a costly failure for the alliance.

The ill-coordinated process not only delayed West Germany's rearmament, but it also cemented distinctively different approaches for France and the United States to Germany and continental security. The United States wanted to draw West Germany into a partnership, with a promise of continental transformation. Absent such a promise, US diplomats believed, West Germans would fret about the prospects for German unification and would be tempted to sacrifice West German membership of the alliance to obtain it.[19] But the United States wanted to stand aside and let France build a political community. For France, it seemed that the United States was reducing French interests to Europe. But France had global interests, its leaders were convinced; they also had long memories, and well recalled how Roosevelt's vision of cooperating great powers—the four policemen—had left out France.

Europe's illusory community

France succeeded in taking charge of the question of German rearmament, but failed to deliver on the European Defense Community that it had in mind. The problem was that France, lacking the sheer muscle to simply control West Germany, had to opt for a degree of political integration that would tie the hands not only of West Germany, but also of France itself. The whole affair thus rubbed against French ideas of sovereignty and great-power status. On August 30, 1954, after much hesitation, the French National Assembly gave up on the project. NATO then became the solution. On October 23, all the allies signed accords paving the way for West Germany's NATO membership. On May 9, 1955, following national ratification by all the allies, West Germany took its seat at the North Atlantic Council table.

Among those to welcome West Germany were Alexandre Parodi, French ambassador to NATO. Parodi had a troubled history with Germany: he had fought in the resistance against German occupation, his brother René had died at the hands of the Gestapo in 1942, and Parodi himself narrowly escaped a similar fate in August 1944. After the war, he rose in the diplomatic service to become secretary general of the French Ministry of Foreign Affairs, where he encountered the cumbersome project of European defense. So troublesome was the experience that in 1954 he exclaimed to Prime Minister Pierre Mendès-France: you have been subjected to the "toughest pressure, the most openly combined and most indiscreet pressure I have seen exerted on a French government."[20] The principal source of this trouble was American.

It was not that President Eisenhower and Secretary of State John Foster Dulles were opposed to European community: quite the contrary, they regarded the initiative to be of critical importance. In fact, Eisenhower's long-term goal was to make Western Europe into a "third great power bloc."[21] But Eisenhower underestimated the difficulty of defining this Europe politically. Who would actually run Europe, and would it be in alignment with the United States and NATO? Perhaps urgency prevented Eisenhower and Dulles from thoroughly considering the difficulties—which, as we shall see later, led President Nixon and his security advisor, Henry Kissinger, to regret US encouragement of European unity. Urgency in the early 1950s stemmed from US nuclear policy and its need for a political twin—the European Defense Community. Eisenhower and Dulles had concluded that NATO's ambitious conventional force goals of 1952 were unattainable. They had also concluded that nuclear forces were more sustainable economically and more effective at deterring communist aggression. But they needed a conventional element to escape from a strategy that was solely reliant on nuclear weapons. German conventional rearmament was the answer, but the political solution to it was in French hands.

Eisenhower's urgency had also to do with domestic politics. He had both political opponents and budgetary concerns. He was under political fire from Senator Taft, a fellow Republican who had vainly sought the Republican nomination against Eisenhower. Senator Taft's criticism of overseas entanglements had lost none of its rancor. In addition, Eisenhower had promised to balance the federal budget, half of which went on defense. Eisenhower was caught between involvement and solvency, and to square the circle he crafted a new nuclear strategy. He started by revamping the military chain of command, appointing Admiral Radford as chairman of the joint chiefs of staff and bringing General Ridgway to Washington to run the army. He then directed the new military team to produce a "new look" blueprint of greater reliance on nuclear forces and the role of "massive offensive striking power."[22] This "new look" nuclear strategy was finalized in National Security Council document 162/2 of October 30, 1953. Before long, NATO would adopt its own version of this.[23]

That left the challenge of West Germany and European community. Two pathways opened up early on, in January–February 1951. First, in January, came NATO talks at Petersberg (outside Bonn), which were animated by the strong US push for German rearmament. Then, in February, French-led West European talks were held in Paris on the European Defense Community. The impetus behind the French-led track originated with Jean Monnet and French Foreign Minister Robert Schuman, who in mid-1950 fed French Prime Minister René Pleven a proposal for a defense community. Its appeal was its complementarity to the European Coal and Steel Community that Schuman was spearheading in parallel, and whose purpose it was to "make it plain that any war between France and Germany becomes not merely unthinkable, but materially impossible."[24] But could they agree on a common defense? Prime Minister Pleven seized the moment with such vigor that, in the course of 1951, NATO's Petersberg track folded. In May 1952, the countries of the Coal and Steel Community—France, Germany, Italy, the Netherlands, Belgium, and Luxembourg—signed a European Defense Community treaty.

Things then turned sour. Political reticence in France stalled the ratification project, and the renegotiations changed very little. In December 1953, John Foster Dulles felt obliged to dramatize the US position. He did so during an NAC meeting, at which he outlined the need for a "complete and organic" union in Europe. A failure on the part of the European allies to achieve this, Dulles continued ominously, "would compel an agonizing reappraisal of basic United States policy."[25] Through 1954, he orchestrated a politico-diplomatic campaign of such magnitude that Alexandre Parodi, as we have seen, felt compelled to sympathize with his prime minister.

And yet the French initiative collapsed. As it did so, British Foreign Secretary Eden and US Secretary of State Dulles began to jockey for influence. This involved a clash of vision and policy, which Eden largely won. However, he was helped by the fact that President Eisenhower and leading administration officials did not want to go up against British policy.[26] The "agonizing reappraisal" thus failed to materialize.

Both Dulles and Eden saw the key problem clearly: NATO membership alone could not solve the problem of West German rearmament. In NATO, all allies were equal: thus, once rearmed and inside the organization, West Germany could, in principle, abandon ship and seek German unification on its own terms—a risk that was made more real by a Soviet peace offensive in the wake of Stalin's death in March 1953. With the European Defense Community ship-wrecked, the question was thus whether there was an alternative set of ties that could bind West Germany. Dulles remained committed to European political integration and grew frustrated; Eden instead looked for a more classical intergovernmental solution.

What he proposed involved simultaneous West German member-ship of NATO and the Brussels Treaty. The latter was key. It would be converted from focusing on a German threat into a general framework for collective defense complementary to NATO. West Germany and Italy would be brought into it. And it would gain a general monitoring framework for verifying its members' commitment to agreed levels of armament. This reworked Brussels Treaty—renamed the Western European Union—would thus treat everyone equally, while in fact serving as a check on West German rearmament. Simultaneously, West Germany would unilaterally give up any claim to nuclear or other weapons of mass destruction, and the Western European Union authorities would have the right to review the list of weapons prohibited to West Germany. Eden's plan was greeted enthusiastically both in Europe and—once the Eisenhower administration had adjusted its sights—in Washington.[27] Nine of the key allies then met in London in late September and early October 1954 to thrash out a final agreement on generalized control over West European armaments (and, in fact, West German armaments), and on West Germany's NATO membership.[28]

Dulles may have had to give in on the ambition for Europe's integration, but he was not wrong in arguing that Europe's political aspirations would suffer. The new Western European Union was essentially a fig leaf of control. NATO was what mattered. This design—strong NATO, weak Europe—would draw the United States further into Europe, which Dulles and Eisenhower had always resisted. Baked into the 1954 deal was an offer by the United States—and Britain—to permanently station troops in Germany under NATO command. This framework reassured the European allies, but also gave them leeway to pursue their own national interests. And these did not add up to a coherent Europe.[29]

Britain and France, self-consciously global powers, looked beyond Europe. The Suez crisis of late 1956 followed. It saw Britain's Anthony Eden, France's Guy Mollet, and Israel's David Ben-Gurion conspire against Egyptian leader Gamal Abdel Nasser. Their plan was to punish Nasser for seeking control of the Suez Canal. But they failed, and instead further stoked the Arabist passion on which Nasser rode. They also fueled US anger, because President Eisenhower wanted the United States to engage the Middle East with Arab sentiment on its side. In December 1956, he forced the two European allies to retreat in disgrace. The effect on Britain and France was not to turn them into good disciples of NATO force posture, though. It was rather to channel their limited means into continued overseas interests, and then also national plans for nuclear arms: Britain to create a special US–British relationship, France to wrest influence from the two allies.

Chancellor Adenauer's West Germany thus joined an alliance that was fast making nuclear weapons the centerpiece of its politics. Predictably, Adenauer began to look for ways to gain nuclear influence. Neither West Germany's 1954 renunciation of nuclear weapons nor the fact that raising twelve full divisions of conscripted soldiers represented an overwhelming task was regarded as an obstacle here: what mattered was equality and influence, which for West Germany meant influence on Europe's strategic balance and the fate of the two Germanies. Of course, a mere decade after the world war, it did present a steep political challenge. In mid-1956, Adenauer informed his imposing and ambitious political ally Franz Josef Strauss, minister of atomic affairs, "as long as I am Chancellor, you will never be Minister for Defence."[30] Months later, in recognition of the challenge ahead of him, Adenauer pivoted and promoted Strauss to defense minister.

The Eisenhower administration toyed with different ideas for sharing nuclear technology and weapons with Britain, France, Italy, and West Germany. The United States was already committed to a nuclearized strategy, and the Eisenhower administration wanted to share nuclear capabilities with its allies, in order to build up a European force and ease the need for US engagement.[31] In 1957, the United States made a deal with Britain, whereby it would provide the UK with medium-range ballistic missiles. It sought to extend this program to the continent, by helping France and encouraging the European production of such missiles. It also involved West Germany in these talks and proposals. Chancellor Adenauer played along, but simultaneously explored nuclear options with France. Defense Minister Strauss worked to prepare the German army for a nuclear battlefield—that is, to make it smaller, more agile, and better equipped. In Strauss' view, the 1954 pledge to renounce nuclear arms was binding only so long as NATO was able to protect West Germany.[32]

This was the bind created by Eisenhower's policy: NATO was effectively Americanized and nuclearized, and yet he wanted it Europeanized. It begged the question: who was Europe? The European Defense Community had collapsed and the Western European Union was a fig leaf. Did the weakness of these frameworks suggest that it would be impossible to nuclearize *and* Europeanize NATO? Confronted with this difficulty, the Eisenhower administration increasingly sought to promote an integrated "NATO" solution, meaning it offered to furnish a NATO nuclear stockpile and share the keys with the organization.[33] But this then raised another question: who was NATO, if not the United States?

From Eisenhower's European aspiration emerged tensions between the NATO "machinery," France, and West Germany. NATO's supreme allied commander, General Lauris Norstad, had an answer to that question: he, the supreme commander, was NATO. He thus pushed the North Atlantic Council for more and better nuclear forces, to be placed directly under his authority.[34] Charles de Gaulle, who returned to political life in France in 1958, dismissed the whole business as two sides of the same coin: Norstad or Eisenhower—they were both American.[35] De Gaulle wanted a wholly French nuclear force. Chancellor Adenauer sympathized with his instinct, but also felt that it was too nationalist. Adenauer knew and feared that if nationalism afflicted West Germany, it would reawaken "the German question" and put at risk West Germany's anchoring in a Western alliance.

The irony for West Germany was thus that it had regained its sovereignty and become a NATO ally at the very time when NATO leaders were losing their sense of collective aspiration. If national interests ran rampant, West Germany would either be held hostage as a geopolitical prize, or it would regain its national voice, but in such a way that would wreck the very institution, NATO, that offered it stability and legitimacy. In this treacherous situation, someone needed to speak up for Atlantic cohesion and aspiration.

Atlanticism exhausted

General Norstad turned out to be the zenith in the supreme allied commander's claim to influence. Had he had his way, he could have become a voice of Atlanticism. But he did not. His reach for nuclear command influence followed logically from the strategic thinking of the Eisenhower administration, but this thinking was shifting by the late 1950s; and with the arrival of the Kennedy administration in January 1961, it changed entirely.

Political control was central to the Kennedy team. It sought notably to control the proliferation of nuclear weapons—obviously to the detriment of France—in order to establish deterrence and limit any war with the Soviet Union. The idea was to control war across non-nuclear and nuclear thresholds by targeting enemy forces instead of cities, supposedly encouraging enemy authorities to limit escalation before it reached the level of all-out nuclear war. Norstad derided these ideas. Escalation would be "explosive," he warned President Kennedy in October 1961.

Trouble was brewing in the spring of 1962, when Kennedy's secretary of defense, Robert McNamara, prepared to outline a new nuclear strategy. The NATO allies encountered it in May, in Athens, where McNamara laid out his thinking on the need for "a controlled and flexible nuclear response in the event that deterrence should fail."[36] Sensing that the allies did not appreciate the idea that war might be confined to Europe, or that their lot should be to invest in conventional forces complementary to US nuclear forces, McNamara and other US officials sought to rid themselves of Norstad. He had, they felt, moved too close to the European position: "I had the NATO votes, and they knew that," Norstad later observed, noting also how he understood the discomfort this represented to the Kennedy team.[37] In June 1962, Norstad was effectively fired.

The alternative place to look for an Atlantic voice was on the civilian side of NATO. Opportunely, the allies had, in December 1956, appointed Paul-Henri Spaak as NATO secretary general. A champion of both Atlantic cooperation and European unity, Spaak had variously, as prime minister and foreign minister of Belgium, been present at the creation of NATO, the Brussels Treaty, and the European Economic Community. Moving to NATO in May 1957 as secretary general, Spaak was sadly cognizant of the degree to which the allies were at odds politically.[38] And he almost fell victim to them, as his socialist convictions and background were a source of dislike among conservatives, including West Germany's Chancellor Adenauer. However, Spaak did become NATO's helmsman and was thus able to leverage his prime ministerial experience at the highest levels, akin to what the Dane Anders Fogh Rasmussen and the Norwegian Jens Stoltenberg would do again from 2009 on. In December 1957, Spaak thus, for the first time, gathered the North Atlantic Council at the level of heads of state and government. It was, observed the *New York Times*, an opportunity to "give a fresh sense of vitality to the Atlantic alliance."[39]

Yet, in 1961, a few months ahead of General Norstad's forced resignation, Spaak retired disillusioned and worn out by political division among the allies. He had wanted to turn matters around for NATO by encouraging the development of a broad NATO community. He had in mind complementing NATO's existing politico-military command machinery with extensive political consultations and economic cooperation. The rationale was nothing less than civilizational: in pitting the "Christian civilization" against the "Communist civilization," the Cold War challenged Western nations to safeguard their most sacred heritage, namely society organized in "respect for the individual."[40] If the allies were worth their salt, Spaak ventured, they would match the Soviet Union not only in military might, but also in economic and political acumen.

At a time when the Soviet Union was seeking to coerce the allies on Berlin, the alliance thus had at its organizational helm a strong spokesperson—in fact, an entrepreneur—for their comprehensive community. He pulled the major allies—otherwise inclined to focus on their own diplomacy vis-à-vis each other and the Soviet Union—into extensive discussions in the NAC. For sure, Spaak felt, the big allies merited "positions of leadership," but not to the point where they could "authorize alliance policy."[41] Spaak's frank and involved leadership counterbalanced the tendency of the United States, Britain, and France to deal with the Berlin crisis as a matter of privilege—flowing from their size and their status as former occupying powers. West Germany likewise looked to this exclusive club of big allies (as opposed to all allies), because of its power to recognize East Germany: if the big allies offered this recognition, West Germany would be confronted with a cemented division of Germany into two states—something that it did not desire. It was thus "thanks largely to Spaak" that NATO-wide consultations on these thorny issues continued through 1958–59.[42]

The NATO allies had, in fact, willingly sought such an entrepreneurial secretary general. In 1956, reacting to the painful discord of the Suez crisis, but also the failure of the European Defense Community, the allies sought to correct a political-military imbalance inside the alliance. The military leg had grown strong; the political leg was weak. This asymmetry had been an issue from the outset. At the moment of creation, in April 1949, the allies had ministers meet in the North Atlantic Council to run political affairs. A year later, in May 1950, they provided for a first upgrade, with the establishment of the North Atlantic Council of Deputies, or ambassadors, located in London, to run alliance affairs on a day-to-day basis. But the deputies represented only the foreign ministers, not the full governments, and they had limited leadership muscle. They had no secretariat to speak of, and one of the deputies double-hatted as chairman of the Council. Thus, in February 1952 the allies once again upgraded the civilian side. The deputies were transformed into permanent representatives, supported by national delegations, and were geared up to take decisions at a moment's notice. They simultaneously created the post of secretary general and a single integrated international secretariat. And they moved the whole lot into a permanent headquarters in Paris—at first to an interim location in the Palais de Chaillot overlooking the Eiffel Tower, and then to Porte Dauphine, in a new headquarters building in the shape of an "A" (for alliance).

With the secretary general backed by an international staff, the allies gave the organization as a whole "a spokesperson of its own at the Council table."[43] At first, though, it was a limited voice. Lord Ismay—Churchill's chief military advisor during the war—took up the post after Oliver Franks, Britain's ambassador to Washington, had declined the offer.[44] Ismay had to go about the tedious task of setting up an organization and assisting diplomats in establishing practices of consultation. One thorny issue was the question of whether the allies should consult broadly on any political matter that might affect the alliance. It was not a given. The schism between the treaty's clause for emergency consultations in the case of looming threats (Article 4) and its provision for a broad political forum (Article 9) came into full play. For Canada's Lester Pearson and others convinced of the need for an Atlantic community, Article 9 was where the allies had to focus their attention.

Ismay had to tread carefully, though, given the embryonic nature of his office and the political divisions among the allies. In his NATO memoirs, he recalled how he and the international staff were "conscious of being, in a very real sense, the trustees of the Atlantic Community."[45] Still, Ismay, the staff, and the North Atlantic Council were entirely disregarded by Britain and France in the Suez affair of 1956. The episode ultimately brought about a clash between these two allies and the United States that took place not in NATO, but in the UN Security Council. The fraying of relations and the complete disregard for NATO left Ismay disillusioned and ready to resign. In the end, close friends managed to persuade him "to grin and bear it."[46]

The affair ripped open issues of Atlantic community that especially Canada had put on the table in 1948–49. The Truman team had rejected Canada's comprehensive vision of an Atlantic community and had chosen a path of building a European community, though within an Atlantic framework. But that community had then faltered. Where that left the Atlantic framework or community was the question. Central in answering it was Canada's Lester Pearson. As Secretary of State for External Affairs at the time, Pearson had early on, in 1951–52, spearheaded thinking on how to extend and embed political consultations among the allies. In a February 1952 report submitted to the North Atlantic Council on behalf of the five-nation Committee on the North Atlantic Community, Pearson highlighted the need for more extensive political consultations on any issue impacting on the Atlantic community. The committee thus looked beyond the strict geographical confines of the North Atlantic. It also encouraged the allies to enhance the type of non-military cooperation that Canada had inserted into Article 2 of the treaty. The allies approved of the report, but did not follow through. The key problem, as during 1948–49, was that no ally—and especially not the major allies, the United States and Britain—was ready to afford the alliance a role in limiting its freedom of action.[47]

Pearson would gain another opportunity to press the issue. Reacting to their own limited success in coordinating foreign policy, as well as to Soviet offerings of so-called peaceful coexistence, the allies in May 1956 asked Pearson to serve alongside two fellow foreign ministers,

Norway's Halvard Lange and Italy's Gaetano Martino, in a Committee on Non-Military Cooperation, also known as the Committee of Three or, more poetically, the "Three Wise Men." Secretary of State Dulles had been so enthusiastic about exploring Article 2 cooperation that he was ready to consider changing NATO's structure, perhaps to set up a whole new Atlantic council to deal with political problems.[48] Cautionary voices in the US government reminded him of the risk that NATO could be pulled under UN Security Council authority as one of its "regional arrangements," though, and Dulles thus pulled back.

The Committee of Three spearheaded important thinking on NATO political reform. In line with Dulles' brief flirtation with ideas of structural reform, the three ministers held back on any big change to the machinery. Their objective was instead to change allied diplomatic practice. They recommended an obligation on the part of the allies to inform the NAC of developments that would significantly affect the alliance; this included a duty for one country to consult its allies (as far as possible) prior to the adoption of any national policy that could have an impact on NATO. They also advised the allies to extend their cooperation beyond the politico-military realm to economic matters. Finally, they stressed the need to enhance the role of the secretary general who, they recommended, should preside over the Council and have greater leeway in promoting and directing political consultations.[49]

The message from the Three Wise Men "could not have been clearer," noted Lawrence Kaplan, a NATO historian; but the results were nonetheless "mixed."[50] John Milloy, a NATO scholar, put the point more bluntly: "By the end of 1957, there was no question that the Committee of Three process had been a failure."[51] The big allies—not represented on the committee—had colonial possessions and global interests that caused them to hesitate before committing to an obligation to consult. John Foster Dulles did not want to tie US hands; Christian Pineau of France disliked the idea of having the secretary general evaluate allies' record of consultations—a principle to which Spaak seemed particularly committed; and Britain's Selwyn Lloyd wondered whether it made sense to speak of an obligation to consult so long as the term "common interest" remained unclear.[52] It was certainly not lost on the allies that these three countries were the very ones that clashed over the Suez affair, which erupted a month prior to NATO's approval of the Three Wise Men's report. The *New York Times* caught wind of the reticence of the big allies to accept an obligation to consult, and reported in December 1956 how "Dulles rules out consulting NATO in time of stress." Favoring extensive NATO consultations only "in times of relative tranquility," Dulles was in effect capping the effort to make NATO as strong politically as it was militarily.[53]

In light of these political reservations, it is not surprising that NATO's first secretary general, Lord Ismay, had "little impact" on the organization's broader strategic vision.[54] Instead, Ismay teed things up for his successor, Paul-Henri Spaak, in that he built respect for the office and helped the allies overcome the shock of Suez.[55] However, as we have seen, Spaak would exhaust his energy and enthusiasm within just four years as NATO secretary general. The culmination came in 1960, when he sought to chart a long-term plan for NATO. The rationale was sound enough, and originated with US Secretary of State Christian Herter: because the North Atlantic Treaty provided for the allies to be able to withdraw from the alliance with one year's notice after twenty years (i.e., in 1969), it made sense to think in terms of long-term vigor. Spaak used the occasion to expand on the themes contained in the Committee of Three report: namely greater political consultations and enhanced economic cooperation.

He circulated his thinking to the allies in mid-1960, and in December tabled them for a North Atlantic Council decision. That session was "particularly disappointing," Spaak recalled: "I was supported by no one."[56] A few months later, he was gone. Spaak's departure signaled that "the forces of nationalism that separated the members of the alliance were greater than those of the personality that sought to unite them."[57]

Americanization

Did the building of a European community imply that NATO would have to be mostly a traditional alliance—that it managed power, while Europe aspired to overcome power's divisive effects? And if the

European community failed, as it did in 1954, did that mean that NATO had to develop into a full-fledged political-economic community?

By around 1960, the allies had no common answer to these questions. Instead, they had a number of national projects rubbing against each other. France's President de Gaulle had returned to political office in 1958 and soon promoted a new organization of political leadership. Offering a global view of politics and conflict, de Gaulle submitted a memorandum to President Eisenhower and Prime Minister Macmillan arguing that NATO was no longer an adequate format for the political and strategic leadership of the free world. Instead, de Gaulle suggested the organization of a tripartite leadership structure, wherein the United States, Britain, and France could run policy in distinct theaters (the Arctic, the Pacific, the Atlantic, and the Indian Ocean).[58] Eisenhower and Macmillan did not buy into the idea, but the affront to NATO was palpable. Spaak, laboring to realize the community vision of the Committee of Three, found the memorandum "detestable."[59]

Britain did at one point try to put a wider community initiative on track, but it ultimately lacked financial means and political leverage. The British initiative coincided with the Committee of Three and came in the wake of another and successful British idea, namely the design for West German rearmament. Wedding the Brussels Treaty and NATO, Prime Minister Eden had seen, was a way to move Atlantic cooperation forward. In 1956, Britain's foreign secretary, Selwyn Lloyd, proposed a next step—in fact, a "grand design" that would create a European caucus within a reinforced NATO. But the notion was stillborn, a "total failure."[60] Britain simply lacked support among its European allies: budgetary problems had led the country to unilaterally withdraw forces from West Germany, in spite of the 1954 deal to keep them there; it had not joined in the negotiations on a European common market; and it had ignored NATO when intervening in Suez.

British diplomacy thus turned to the priority of securing US support for a British nuclear deterrent, a wholly national priority. This Britain managed by cleverly pursuing the promise of assistance made by President Eisenhower and then, at a critical moment in

1962, securing President Kennedy's support for supplying Polaris missiles for Britain's submarine nuclear deterrent. President Kennedy found the entire deal (which, of course, he had agreed to) so unsettling (because it ran counter to his overall strategy of centralized nuclear control) that he commissioned a study of it. This showed how alliance politics could disrupt a carefully laid-out design for central control. The study was sobering, but also not helpful in furthering US control. As Kennedy lamented to his national security advisor, McGeorge Bundy, "I don't know who the hell I can show this to."[61]

By the early 1960s, therefore, Britain had secured its national nuclear deterrent, and France was developing one (it detonated its first nuclear device in the Sahara Desert in February 1960). The United States offered a strategy of centralized nuclear control—that is, American control—but had to bow to the reality of two additional nuclear forces in the alliance. A schism thus evolved between alliance theory (centralized control) and great-power practice (national control). The situation resembled President de Gaulle's vision of a triumvirate—of three nuclear powers—except that leadership was not coordinated, but contested. And this contest would stabilize only in March 1966, when de Gaulle informed President Lyndon Johnson of France's decision to withdraw from NATO integrated military command—the "machinery" that NATO had built since the early 1950s and had not managed to balance politically.

De Gaulle's decision to loosen France's military ties to NATO emerged gradually and, in a sense, followed from the US–British rejection of his 1958 memorandum. In March 1959, France withdrew its Mediterranean fleet from NATO's command, and in June 1963 its Atlantic fleet. In parallel, as France extricated itself in 1962 from the Algerian War, which led to Algeria's independence and the deletion in the North Atlantic Treaty of the reference to "the Algerian departments of France," its homebound troops were put under national, not NATO command.

In reaction to the nuclear alignment of the United States and Britain, de Gaulle also tried to energize European cooperation. He first sought a new design for the European Economic Community, then appealed to Franco-German reconciliation. But like Eden in

1956, de Gaulle in 1962–63 found that years of great-power priority failed to give him much leeway with small allies and partners. They successfully resisted change to their Economic Community. West German Chancellor Adenauer played along to a degree, and in January 1963 signed a Franco-German treaty of friendship, also known as the Elysée Treaty. But unlike de Gaulle's, Adenauer's intent was not one of geopolitical revision: it was instead the protection of NATO and the continued engagement of France in the Western ring. For some time, President de Gaulle probed Adenauer and his successor, Ludwig Erhard. In the end, he resigned himself to national action.[62] France's withdrawal from the integrated command followed.

In the course of all these events, something essential escaped the notice of the senior leadership of the allies, and perhaps especially the US leaders. This was the cumulative effect on the alliance of seemingly distinct, and sometimes small, policy adjustments. They drove the alliance from aspirational promise to exhausted balance-of-power politics. How so? Partly it was nuclear policy. Nuclear weapons permitted the United States to extend deterrence to Europe—to keep the Soviet Union out. But should these weapons be shared with the allies? This was tricky, and by the time the Kennedy administration finally said "no," it was too late. Britain and France were nuclear powers (in the making), and other allies saw right through the Kennedy and Johnson administrations' efforts to organize "sharing" under US "control" in a "Multilateral Force." Harlan Cleveland was, in 1965, posted to Paris as NATO ambassador partly to kill the "multilateral farce"—as the affair became known—softly. There should be no "embarrassing funeral," Cleveland recalled. The whole affair was to be "quietly forgotten."[63]

But nuclear politics was not the whole story: community politics mattered, too. As we have seen, Presidents Truman and Eisenhower did not want a full-fledged Atlantic community, preferring the creation of a European community within an Atlantic framework. President Truman and his team thus encouraged the French lead in the European Defense Community project. Likewise, they brought Greece and Turkey into NATO in 1952, as the British attempt to organize Eastern Mediterranean security relations increasingly faltered (and would end dismally with the Suez intervention of 1956). The extension of NATO to Turkey—and thus to the doorstep of the Middle East—followed from US global interests and the principle that the alliance was a US-led framework, within which European cooperation could deepen. Put differently, the inclusion of Greece and Turkey in NATO would not have made sense if the idea was to transform the alliance into a political community.

The price for cultivating community politics somewhere other than NATO—perhaps within an Atlantic "framework," but still apart from NATO itself—was the narrowing of the organization to a military instrument that the United States would inevitably dominate. Successive French governments caused the European Defense Community—which was outside NATO and was intended to build European defense muscle in support of transatlantic cooperation— to unravel; and yet the result of this European failure was not NATO's broadening, but rather its constriction. It involved an effort by continental leaders to kickstart community building through economic means and outside NATO—first in 1951, with coal and steel, and then in 1957, with a wider economic community, forerunner to the present European Union. It also involved the Eisenhower administration, which was content to primarily build NATO's military muscle. The administration supported genuine political consultations in the organization, but ultimately wanted US freedom of action and greater European cohesion. In nuclear matters, it thus supported a partial transfer of leadership from the United States to Europe, where Britain and France openly vied for nuclear control. When the Kennedy administration backtracked on this, the genie was out of the bottle.

The organization of a political and economic initiative outside the Atlantic partnership introduced an element of transatlantic competition. Naturally, when the Eisenhower administration supported the upgrading of the OEEC (the old Marshall Aid framework), the idea was to nip such competition in the bud and ensure Western Europe's adherence to wider Atlantic cooperation. In 1960, the OEEC was upgraded into the Organisation for Economic Co-operation and Development (OECD). But all this was still a bet that NATO could thrive on strategic and military issues alone.

An intense Cold War competition added to the credibility of this bet: everyone needed NATO. But even then, the overwhelming US advantage in strategic and military affairs would almost inevitably come to pose a long-term threat to NATO's legitimacy: a skewed alliance would cause law makers and the various publics to question its fairness: in the United States, law makers would demand greater efforts on the part of the allies; in Europe, they would demand to be included in strategic decision-making. And everyone would more or less overtly threaten some sort of sanction if fairness was denied.

Alliance leaders such as Lester Pearson and Paul-Henri Spaak were central to alliance affairs in this period, because they so clearly perceived the risk of a narrow, US-dominated alliance. Going in this direction could introduce an element of competition in the overall Atlantic partnership and risk public support for a security deal that, over time, would not seem entirely fair. Thus, their struggle was to breathe life into the alliance's community vision and its Article 2 commitment to policies of stability, wellbeing, and economic collaboration.

"If fear goes," Pearson pondered in a retrospective article on NATO's ten-year anniversary, "will NATO break up?"[64] The point of introducing Article 2 into the treaty framework, which Canada insisted on, was precisely to advance beyond this question: to move NATO further on from the normal condition of alliances—that they are based on external threats. Article 2 offered community, but it was also a mere guide, Pearson cautioned. It must be put to work in the day-to-day politics of the alliance. Spaak was of a similar persuasion. He fought the separation of security and economic cooperation—the parallel existence of NATO and the OECD; and he fought the tendency of the great powers to consult or act outside the alliance framework. Spaak would, at times, thought-provokingly ask US representatives to choose between the United Nations and NATO. What he had in mind, of course, was the privileged position of the United States in the UN Security Council and how it possibly led the United States to pay less attention to NATO. In effect, he was pinpointing a cleavage between Roosevelt's vision of cooperating policemen in the Security Council and Truman's vision of a cooperating Western alliance. Senator Vandenberg had wanted both to be part of an overall aspiration for cooperative international affairs. Spaak was telling him and others that they had to choose.

Pearson and Spaak give us an important insight into durable alliances: namely, that power alone is not enough. Durability emerges from shared ideas. Pearson and Spaak asked the allies to temper their global policies and national impulses to suit the regional alliance. Since no one in NATO listened, Spaak left the building. He returned to Belgian politics, only to find that his Socialist Party also failed to listen. In June 1966, when the Belgian government of Paul Vanden Boeynants sought parliamentary approval to host NATO's military headquarters (SHAPE) that France no longer wanted, the Socialist Party voted against. Spaak and his close friend Antoine Spinoy were the only two socialist deputies to dissent in NATO's favor. Helping secure a new home for NATO was Spaak's final act: "I left the parliamentary chamber discreetly, without saying goodbye to anyone. I knew I was not coming back."[65]

PART II

Retreat to Pragmatism: Nato Muddles Through, 1966–89

4

Losing Its Luster
NATO without Atlanticism

If the citizens of Wavre, a small Belgian city just southwest of the capital, Brussels, felt that history had dealt them a poor hand, it would not be without some justification. In June 1815, the town hosted a spectacular battle between the French and the Prussian armies; but because a bigger battle was fought next door, at Waterloo, very few people remember Wavre. In 1966, NATO was about to offer Wavre a second chance. French President de Gaulle had asked the organization's military installations to vacate France, and NATO's supreme allied commander, General Lemnitzer, had set his sights on the small city as the new home for his strategic headquarters, SHAPE.[1] Wavre apparently had everything that was required nearby: an airfield, labor supply, and the capital, Brussels. Except that it did not have political backing. At the insistence of the Belgian authorities, and in opposition to the pleas of General Lemnitzer, SHAPE headquarters were instead located in an economically depressed area, just outside the insignificant village of Casteau, not far from Mons, at the time more than an hour's drive from Brussels.[2] Wavre would remain on history's sidelines.

It had become NATO's fate to seek to contain resurgent nationalism without a unifying Atlanticist aspiration. Following the bruising power struggle within NATO in the late 1950s and through the 1960s, no one seriously imagined that NATO would be the forum where the allies would coordinate global issues of war and peace, such as in

Vietnam, or economic and financial policy. The relationship between NATO and these other, wider issues thus grew troublesome. If the alliance did not deal with them, did that mean it would be marginalized? If the superpowers after the Cuban missile crisis of 1962 were entering a period of live-and-let-live—also known as détente—did that mean that NATO should have a say in détente? These were not trivial questions. Rather, they went to the heart of Europe's political order.

To weather it all, the allies turned to pragmatism. And it served them well, for a little while. New compromises were found to sort out the situation created by France's military withdrawal, to close the chapter of nuclear doctrinal debate, and to invest in a forward-looking political doctrine. But NATO had become boxed into an unsustainably narrow military role in northeastern Europe: France was out militarily, West Germany was increasingly inspired by its own Ostpolitik approach to East–West dialogue, and the United States was preoccupied in China and Vietnam. NATO's need for new scope and broadened leadership was plain for all to see;[3] but the debate was bitter. Henry Kissinger, special assistant for national security affairs to the US president, complained that "the single worst mistake of the postwar period was to encourage European unity."[4] By contrast, Michel Jobert, France's foreign minister—a man sometimes dubbed the French Kissinger, but certainly no ally of the American—had no qualms about telling Kissinger face to face that US policy was a "Yalta of peace"—a superpower scheme to diplomatically carve up the world to Europe's detriment.[5] In the absence of Atlanticism, the allies discovered, NATO could all too easily lose its luster.

Nuclear pragmatism

The need for less drama followed from Charles de Gaulle's decision to pull France out of NATO's military command. The allies had to withdraw all NATO installations from France; and though France offered to maintain the alliance's political headquarters in Paris, they were in no mood to grant France this honor. The headquarters were slated to move to Brussels. But the allies had to keep an eye on the Atlantic Treaty's Article 13, which states that, after twenty years, "any Party may cease to be a Party one year after its notice of denunciation." And the twenty-year anniversary was right around the corner, in 1969. Continued allied division risked permanent fragmentation, therefore, and so the allies went about searching for pragmatic solutions to two thorny issues: nuclear strategy and East–West dialogue. This section considers military strategy; the next turns to East–West dialogue.

In mid-December 1967, the NATO defense ministers approved the alliance's new "flexible response" military strategy, also known as MC14-3, with MC referring to NATO's Military Committee, where national defense chiefs review and finalize military strategy. The MC14-3 strategy was well crafted and would last through to the end of the Cold War. In essence, it replaced the threat of "massive retaliation" with more dynamic and "flexible" responses. The former threat was one of great punishment: if the Soviet Union took over West Berlin, it risked its own existence. However, increases in Soviet nuclear capabilities meant that it could retaliate in kind, and so the threat of great punishment over local transgressions simply lost its credibility. Would Washington really risk Chicago for Berlin? NATO's answer was "flexibility"—the threat that NATO would "defeat aggression" by raising—and "where possible" controlling—the scope and intensity of combat.[6] This was thus a strategy of both denial (NATO would fight to stop advancing Soviet forces) and punishment (it might choose to escalate and, ultimately, choose to strike Soviet territory with nuclear weapons).

A senior NATO planner was enthusiastic about the change. Before, the alliance had "the bluff of massive retaliation." Now, "we ... have a new strategy."[7] And he had a point. In the 1960s, President Kennedy and Secretary of Defense Robert McNamara had pushed hard in this direction of flexible response strategy. The move had begun under President Eisenhower, but what was strategically compelling in Washington looked quite different to Paris. President de Gaulle blocked all strategic revision, because the American design implied added US nuclear control and, de Gaulle maintained, a subservient conventional force role for Europeans. Also, it would remain a staple of French strategic thinking that massive retaliation is a better and more credible way of deterring aggression. And so, for about a decade,

NATO lived with a proclaimed strategy of massive retaliation that the United States no longer believed in.

With France's decision to step outside the military command, the allies could finally move ahead and endorse a "flexible response" strategy. France no longer sat on the Military Committee that prepared military strategy. The allies also closed the Washington, DC branch of the Military Committee—the Standing Group, which represented only the United States, Britain, and France. Instead, they created a new defense political forum, the Defence Planning Committee (DPC), where ministers could meet without France to direct defense affairs. France remained, naturally, on the overarching North Atlantic Council.[8]

But French concerns were not the only obstacle to NATO consensus. As important was West Germany's preoccupation with its own frontline status and all the vulnerability that it involved. Seeking to embrace US thinking on "flexibility," but also limiting it, West Germany's defense minister, Kai-Uwe von Hassel, wrote in 1965 that "the concept of flexible response . . . must not be interpreted to mean that the so-called atomic threshold can be raised unduly high."[9] His worry was that full flexibility could mean a prolonged and regionally confined conventional war that would leave Germany devastated. To deter it, he wanted nuclear forces to be at the forefront. Hassel had in mind a variety of "atomic demolition mines, nuclear air defense weapons and, if need be, nuclear battlefield weapons" ready for use in the early phase of any war.[10]

"I cannot endorse the German concept in its entirety," US Secretary of Defense McNamara wrote in a Pentagon memorandum, after a meeting with Hassel and the German chief of staff, General Heinrich Trettner.[11] The West German concept was based essentially on what McNamara wanted to avoid: a very low threshold for the use of nuclear weapons, with the decision to use them being integrated into the military command. The US and German positions also differed on how much trust to place in the military command: Germany wanted to delegate command of nuclear weapons down into the military chain of command; the United States wanted to restrict it to the highest political level in Washington. Oddly, and in a twist of irony,

Germany then got embroiled in a case of military insubordination that cost General Trettner his job. He would be the last chief of staff in West Germany to have attained the rank of general during the Second World War. But it was not this record that cost him his job, nor nuclear weapons: it was his support for a widespread military revolt against a spectacularly unsafe military aircraft, the Starfighter. Hassel saw it as a case of insubordination, and out went Trettner. In backing Hassel, Chancellor Erhard reportedly regretted that Trettner had not had the guts to confront him about the matter "between two whiskeys at one of the many state parties in Bonn."[12]

It was an odd comment, considering the weighty implications of nuclear control down the chain of command, and NATO strategy could not be dealt with "between two whiskeys." McNamara had to think differently in the pursuit of allied acceptance of centralized US control. In the end, it led to a new type of nuclear consultation mechanism, NATO's Nuclear Planning Group (NPG). The genesis of this was the Kennedy administration's attempt from 1961 to shift the allies away from a strategy of massive retaliation. By 1963, it had led NATO's chain of command to draft a "strategic appraisal" that suggested a more flexible approach. However, the appraisal raised a difficult political question: if the United States favored a flexible response, but France was against it, which side would West Germany support?[13]

Chancellor Adenauer did not slam any doors shut; though inevitably, with France's departure from the military command, West Germany would have to engage with US-led strategy. First, Adenauer early on, in 1963, offered some support for France's idea of a European atomic force, though mostly to offset NATO momentum.[14] In parallel, he backed the US scheme for a NATO multinational nuclear force that would leave the decision to launch weapons with the US president, but at least offered the European allies a visible role in staffing and exercising a nuclear force. Ultimately, it was a tortuous scheme that met an unremarkable end in 1965. By this point, it was unclear how the allies could draw West Germany into a strategic framework that both delayed the threat of nuclear weapons and reduced the risk of limited war on German territory.

NATO's NPG, along with the flexible response strategy, became the answer. The NPG offered a new approach: instead of focusing on political control—which, the multinational force experience showed, could not be shared—it was all about confidential consultations. These would serve to educate the allies on nuclear issues and promised that, with experience and insight, the allies could gain real influence over US nuclear deliberations. The allies sealed this deal in December 1966. In April 1967, the NPG met for the first time; it has been in service ever since.

Secretary General Dirk Stikker, Paul-Henri Spaak's successor, had in early 1962 spotted the need for such added (nuclear) consultations.[15] However, the idea did not gain traction until Defense Secretary McNamara's realization in 1965 that the multinational force idea needed to be quietly shelved. In its stead, he undertook consultations in a select ministerial committee, a subgroup of which would deal with nuclear issues. This subgroup became the NPG. It was a turn to pragmatism, in the sense that it left behind the highly symbolic search for control with nuclear weapons in favor of consultations, the purpose of which was to fill in all the blanks in an elastic strategy (i.e., flexible response). In an editorial, the *New York Times* lauded the turn as a step out of a nuclear "morass" and a way to effectively offer European allies "a seat on Washington's National Security Council."[16]

Naturally, pragmatism prevailed in part because President de Gaulle decided to take his principled opposition outside the integrated command. But pragmatism resulted also from a leadership decision to embrace it. McNamara pursued the consultation idea with such extraordinary "drive and energy" that the European allies "were impressed," according to US ambassador to NATO, Harlan Cleveland.[17] Cleveland may not have been a neutral observer, but McNamara's drive was real. Equally important was the decision of leaders in Britain and West Germany to fill the gap left by France. As new (DPC and NPG) and reworked (MC) institutional mechanisms for allied consultation and planning were being set up, informal and intensive trilateral discussions among the three countries of the United States, Great Britain, and West Germany became the "most important" means for overcoming the crisis of nuclear diplomacy and strategy.[18]

Political pragmatism

It was not only in the nuclear domain that West Germany was gaining influence. On the wider political scene of East–West relations, too, the country was at the center of developments. The question was whether it was gaining a level of national political confidence that could upset allied relations, especially in a new era of East–West dialogue. This era is often said to begin in the wake of the prolonged Berlin crisis, which resulted in the building of the Berlin Wall (August 1961) and the Cuban missile crisis (October 1962). Chancellor Adenauer resigned from office in October 1963, creating an opening for successors with new political appetites. He had always navigated by the principle of West German integration into Western institutions. A number of factors—the denial of nuclear control, the prospect of limited war on German territory, a deep-seated longing for German unification—might cause his successor to refashion the country's national interest. "Views differ on how dangerous a revival of nationalism among the free Germans may become," wrote Richard Lowenthal, a professor, in 1966, but "there is little dispute that such a revival is under way."[19]

Conservative Kurt Kiesinger formed a grand coalition in West Germany in December 1966, bringing the Social Democrats, led by Willy Brandt, into government. Brandt, later the architect of the German détente policy of Ostpolitik, became vice-chancellor and foreign minister. A concern of this government was its ability to exercise greater control over West Germany's destiny in the context of East–West relations. They were particularly concerned that East–West cooperation—when viewed from Washington and Moscow—meant greater superpower control, and that such control would not necessarily benefit German interests. For instance, the superpowers were busy negotiating a nuclear Non-Proliferation Treaty (NPT) (signed in 1968) that would deny non-nuclear states such as West Germany access to this powerful weapon. Moreover, in the interests of superpower stability, they might seek to permanently freeze the geopolitical status quo—including Germany's partition. On the eve of Kiesinger's first visit to Washington, Cyrus Sulzberger, an American reporter, felt that German concerns over these issues had reached a point where the US public should be made aware of the Kiesinger government's "anti-Americanism."[20]

West German leaders saw trouble in the East, as well as the West. The Soviet Union was busy trying to force the Kiesinger government onto the back foot. It sought West Germany's recognition of its eastern counterpart, the GDR. With its Hallstein doctrine of 1955, West Germany had refused to open diplomatic relations with countries that recognized the GDR, all for the purpose of maintaining the option of German unification. Now the Soviet Union wanted to force a West German diplomatic retreat and launch open-ended talks that could sow further Western discord. West Germany's leadership might appeal to France, normally its go-to partner in European affairs, but France's single-minded pursuit of its national interests only added to West Germany's sense of relative isolation. In NATO, France was leaving the integrated command; in the European Economic Community, it had run a so-called empty-chair policy to force its preferences on its partners; and in all-European matters it preferred to bypass Bonn in the pursuit of direct dialogue with Moscow.

Gerhard Schröder (no relation to the later chancellor of Germany) came to embody the search for power politics, German-style. He served as foreign minister in the conservative Erhard cabinet (1963–66), before becoming defense minister in Kiesinger's grand coalition (1966–69). Conditions allowed Schröder to "seize almost full control of the Federal Republic's European policy" under Erhard, and he was ready to "provoke controversies, unmask the French politics and take maximum advantage" of a situation "highly unfavourable to France."[21] Before taking on de Gaulle, Schröder teamed up with his Italian counterpart, Attilio Piccioni, to demand the Europeanization of NATO's multilateral force. The United States easily rejected the demand, but it left a distinct sense among the allies that Schröder did not mind throwing West Germany's weight around.[22]

Schröder moved one step down the ladder in Kiesinger's cabinet, and perhaps he had overreached himself in the confrontation with France over the "empty-chair" policy. But Kiesinger and Foreign

Minister Brandt were ready to take over, and their efforts involved a degree of confrontation with the Johnson administration, balanced by, perhaps, renewed partnership with France. President Johnson and his advisors were worried. For their part, Kiesinger and Brandt were anxious about Johnson's ability to steadfastly steer East–West relations. They felt he might be tempted to strike a deal with the Soviet Union in Europe, in order to gain relief in Asia, where the Vietnam War was raging. Kiesinger and Brandt thus pushed for dialogue on a properly fashioned allied policy. The US ambassador to NATO, Harlan Cleveland, would later write that Kiesinger went too far, too fast, and was too German. In a communication to the West German ambassador to Washington, Secretary of State Dean Rusk described the situation as a "ticking time bomb."[23]

Knowing that détente and East–West dialogue could derail alliance relations, the allies in December 1966 agreed to let Pierre Harmel, the Belgian foreign minister (and a former prime minister), run a one-year study of "the future tasks" of the alliance. In pitching his idea to Eugene Rostow, US Under Secretary of State for Political Affairs, Harmel said he worried about NATO's longevity and its spirit of consultation.[24] He also had a domestic agenda, of course, which was to create local support for the move of NATO headquarters and infrastructure to Belgium. In the bigger scheme of things, the decision by the allies to go with Harmel's idea was important and anticipatory. They knew NATO would soon reach the ripe old age of twenty, at which point (as already mentioned) the treaty allowed for the withdrawal of individual allies. The Soviet Union was encouraging such withdrawal thoughts, for sure. And there was internal turbulence. By endorsing a study of "future tasks," the allies were effectively stating that NATO did have a future. The question was how to anticipate it.

Pierre Harmel proved a safe pair of hands. His final report, a mere seventeen paragraphs, did much to defuse the "ticking time bomb" that Rusk had observed with dread. Part of Harmel's secret was his choice of a pragmatic approach, even if he personally had strong convictions. He was a Europeanist and wanted Europe to overcome its historic divisions; yet he was also a transatlanticist. He was cut from the cloth of centrist politics—Christian Democracy—where progress is made by consultation and compromise. His centrist experience and sensibility proved timely and appropriate for NATO. In fact, his report had such a flavor of common sense that NATO Secretary General Manlio Brosio subsequently argued that "There is nothing spectacular in it, nothing unforeseen."[25] But this was salesmanship, and history belies the modesty. The Harmel report has become a lasting doctrine, among other things guiding NATO through the war in Ukraine that Russia began in 2022.

The Harmel report notably made the fundamental and lasting point that NATO's "first function" is to "maintain adequate strength and political solidarity to deter aggression." This first function was essential to the creation of a climate of stability and confidence, the report underscored. In such a climate, it continued, NATO can carry out its "second function," to pursue a more stable relationship with adversaries.[26] With this, Pierre Harmel made two critical and enduring points: that a changed or new Europe would have to build on NATO, and that NATO would contribute to change first and foremost by maintaining its collective defense capacity. Détente—or, by extension, the end of the Cold War—could not be an experimental leap into a progressive future, Harmel warned. It had to be carefully crafted, based on "realistic measures." "The relaxation of tensions is not the final goal but is part of a long-term process to promote better relations and to foster a European settlement."[27]

The report also made an important contribution to defining the relationship between the NATO area and the world outside this area. It first established that "the North Atlantic Treaty area cannot be considered in isolation from the rest of the world." It then allowed for diplomatic flexibility, in that "Allies or such of them as wish to do so will also continue to consult on ... problems without commitment and as the case may demand ... in accordance with established usage." In other words, it was legitimate for some allies to consider outside conflicts (such as war in the Middle East) to be a NATO concern. It was equally legitimate for some allies to coordinate in a war effort (such as in Vietnam), whereas other allies resisted any involvement. In short, NATO allies should consult, but need not be blocked by the lack of consensus on conflicts outside NATO's treaty area. This suited

President Johnson on Vietnam, but he would still have to consult widely to manage allied unease. Rostow would recall that no paragraph of the report "required more strenuous drafting and negotiation, some at extremely high levels."[28]

Naturally, Pierre Harmel did not labor on his own. He was flanked by two key assistants, Étienne Davignon (who reappears below as a promoter of European foreign policy cooperation) and André de Staercke, Belgium's long-serving NATO ambassador. Key allies were with him as well, as were Secretary General Brosio, to whom the North Atlantic Council had formally handed the study process. They set up four subgroups, of which the first and the third were particularly important. Subgroup I, led by John Watson of Britain and Karl Schutz of West Germany, dealt with East–West relations. Subgroup III, led by Foy Kohler of the United States, examined general defense policy. Their combined work on the détente–defense balance generated the core ideas for the Harmel report, not least the desire to further East–West stabilization without putting at risk the collective defense character of NATO. It was, of course, both symbolically and practically significant that these subgroup rapporteurs should have represented the three leading allies, after France's decision to part company with the military command.

The two other subgroups (II and IV) are noteworthy mostly for what they did not achieve. Subgroup II was led by Paul-Henri Spaak, who, for the moment, was back in the NATO game, though in a private capacity, as rapporteur. Spaak's group were to examine allied relations. Subgroup IV, led by Dutch Professor Constantijn Leopold Patijn, examined NATO relations with other countries. Among these two groups was plenty of potential for enlarging NATO's remit in terms of consultations on global issues, be they the Vietnam War or the stability of financial institutions. But to go down this path would be to reinvoke the Atlanticist option that Paul-Henri Spaak, as NATO secretary general, had valiantly but vainly promoted, and political conditions were no longer ripe for such an Atlantic community initiative. Revealingly, Paul-Henri Spaak would end up mostly arguing with the French representatives, criticizing them for undermining both NATO and the European Communities as collective institutions.

Unsurprisingly, Spaak's efforts were not well received in Paris. The same could be said of Professor Patijn's report, which likewise foresaw the need for an enhanced and more vigorous alliance in global affairs. Patijn was well connected in Dutch politics and sat in the Consultative Assembly of the Council of Europe; but in crafting the subgroup report he was perhaps guided more by academic rigor than political acumen.

Eugene Rostow lauded Pierre Harmel as "invaluable." Harmel had brought to the table a "high-minded" and "effective" style that furnished NATO with a "practical, tangible program intended to create peace."[29] But Rostow was a player as well, especially in the latter phase of the study, when the subgroups were wrapping up and the political game of writing the overall conclusions began. France was not pleased, in part because the exercise gave both defense and détente to NATO—where de Gaulle had seen détente as falling outside NATO's remit, in part because it suggested a wider consultation role for NATO. Harmel and Brosio would continually struggle with the format of the report to bridge positions and garner consensus.[30]

In November 1967, Rostow engineered a breakthrough in discussions with the French foreign minister, Maurice Couve de Murville. The two had discussed the project thoroughly in the preparatory phases, and they built on a friendship that extended back to 1943 and Algiers, Rostow recalled.[31] Now, in late 1967, they searched for a consensus formula. In essence, they agreed to distinguish between the overall report and the subgroup reports, which were of limited political significance.[32] With assiduous support from various allied representatives, as well as Brosio and Harmel, they reached agreement ahead of their mid-December 1967 deadline: the overall report, which France supported, was published; the subgroup reports, which France did not support, were not.[33]

The Harmel study was at one and the same time a precursor to a larger vision of what NATO could become and a pragmatic framework for taking one step at a time. Harmel knew that he could not, and should not, attempt to recreate a vision like Atlanticism—because such grand ideas divided the allies. Instead, he derived potentially wide-ranging principles for cohesion, and then left it to the allies to make the best of it. It was a subtle and cleverly crafted balance between vision and pragmatism, and it carried the day. Unbeknownst to them, the allies were thus preparing for the challenge posed by Willy Brandt's powerful ideas of East–West reconciliation. When, in December 1966, NATO kicked off the Harmel study, the *New York Times* found the "most striking and most applauded figure of the meeting" to be Willy Brandt, the "youthful-looking and self-assured" foreign minister of West Germany.[34] In October 1969, Brandt became West German chancellor. Could his high aspirations and youthful energy be fitted within NATO's newfound framework of pragmatism?

Pragmatism at work

Willy Brandt's West Germany made remarkable headway in East–West relations in just a few years. It began with two treaties of recognition and cooperation with the Soviet Union, in August 1970, and then in December with Poland. The outreach had to begin with Moscow, quite naturally; but Poland was an important follow-on interlocutor, because of potential territorial conflicts over its western border along the Oder-Neisse river. It was clear at the end of the Second World War that Poland's territory would be moved westward—to reward the Soviet Union and punish Germany. But the western frontier was a subject of dispute between Stalin (who wanted to push it further westwards) and Roosevelt and Churchill (who wanted a less offensive move in order to quell the potential for German revisionism). They did not manage to settle the issue at their Yalta conference in February 1945, and by the time they met again in Potsdam, with Truman replacing Roosevelt, Stalin had settled the facts on the ground. Unsurprisingly, the communist German Democratic Republic recognized the border in 1950 to ensure that the theme of German revisionism would be associated with West Germany.

Brandt settled this revisionist potential by recognizing the border and thus Poland's acquisition of some 40,000 square miles of pre-war German territory. During his December 1970 visit to Poland, he also atoned for Germany's recent war crimes. In front of the memorial to the victims of the Warsaw Ghetto, he dramatically dropped to his knees, remaining there a full minute before he rose heavily, with the edge of his mouth trembling.[35] And this was only the beginning. In

December 1972, on behalf of West Germany he signed a Basic Treaty of mutual recognition with East Germany, enabling both countries to become members of the United Nations. One year later, he signed a treaty with Czechoslovakia, recognizing the border and abandoning claims to the territory from which 3 million Germans had been expelled after the war.

With a few strokes, Brandt thus discarded the guiding idea, the Hallstein doctrine, in West German policy that there was just one Germany. He recognized two German states, even if the nation was one. As for the nation, he limited its aspirations by offering West Germany's recognition of its eastern frontiers. All of this was remarkable and a potentially serious challenge to the United States, Britain, and France—the victorious powers from the Second World War, who, along with the Soviet Union, formally remained in control of the German question. Agreement among these three countries and the Soviet Union was a prerequisite for the German Basic Treaty of 1972: and the four countries delivered. In September 1971, they agreed to a quadripartite treaty securing Western access to West Berlin. They thus settled the question that had been at the heart of Nikita Khrushchev's Berlin challenge of 1958, and the Cold War would not again witness a Berlin crisis. Still, it remained possible that West Germany was setting in motion political changes that would uproot Western cooperation, not least West Germany's relative subordination, and create a new and untested political space in Central Europe.

Henry Kissinger recalls how at the outset Brandt did not fully convince the White House. The fear was that the Soviet Union would "manipulate" and disrupt President Nixon's search for a "more active strategy" to manage the nuclear stalemate of the Cold War.[36] And all this because a player like Brandt might be able to insert his country in unexpected ways into the strategic triangle of the United States, the Soviet Union, and China. President Nixon was blunt in his off-the-record remarks. Referring to Brandt in mid-1971, he said, "Good God, this, if that's all Germany's hope is, then Germany ain't got much future." Nixon preferred his "friends," Adenauer's Christian democrats, to the newcomer Willy Brandt: "I don't want to hurt our friends by catering to that son-of-a-bitch."[37]

Yet Nixon would end up catering to Brandt, and this for a couple of reasons that involve also NATO. The Brandt team deliberately appealed to US leadership and anchored Ostpolitik in the Atlantic. They did not go solo. Willy Brandt early on dispatched his confidant, Egon Bahr, to the White House to assure it of tight coordination and to establish a secret backchannel of communication. Brandt sought to anchor Ostpolitik in the West, and he kept his word, Kissinger notes. Brandt also signaled his willingness to go slow on Ostpolitik, soothing Nixon and Kissinger's anxiety of uncontrolled change. Brandt could not cause Nixon and Kissinger to love his Ostpolitik, but he managed to convince them of a common interest.

NATO contributed in two related ways: it embedded political anxieties in both North America and Europe in a common policy framework, and it gave direction to this policy in the dialogue with the Soviet Union. In short, NATO reassured and steered. Without it, détente anxieties could have caused political ripples of great consequence for Europe's balance of power. European leaders, Brandt included, trod carefully in public, because they sought to safeguard the transatlantic link; but the fear was real.

A player as central as NATO Secretary General Manlio Brosio confided to his diary his fears that the United States was giving in on the German question. Especially the conclusion of the 1968 Non-Proliferation Treaty in 1968 seemed to Brosio a sign of "a return to Potsdam"—whereby the superpowers would make a deal to keep Germany down (i.e., non-nuclear). On this, Brosio's "views diverged widely from those of the US," and they would torment him during the negotiations leading up the Harmel conclusions.[38] The Harmel doctrine notably left open the question of who should fashion the second component, détente. If détente policies were not tightly coordinated, Brosio foresaw, then divergent national visions could tear into NATO. For a little while, the alliance had some success in this regard.

The Soviet Union pushed NATO in the direction of unity with its brutal and unexpected intervention in August 1968 to destroy political reforms—the Prague Spring—in Czechoslovakia. In a display of raw power, the Soviet leadership manhandled the country's leader Alexander Dubček and his close advisors and took control (Dubček survived the ordeal, but ended up an inspector of the Czechoslovak forestry administration). The NATO allies reacted by bringing forward their ministerial meeting (from December to November 1968), by condemning the intervention, and by declaring their alliance to be "of indefinite duration." The Prague intervention thus effectively ended any speculation regarding the dissolution of NATO on its twentieth anniversary. Even France fell into line—though with a statement added to the communiqué that "the French Government considers that the Alliance must continue as long as it appears to be necessary."[39]

The Soviet intervention forced the NATO allies to focus on their corporate or collective interest in a European security conference, which the Soviet Union had pushed for since the mid-1960s, and to which some allies were warming. The NPT had not involved such a NATO corporate interest, and hence it had caused Brosio's political headache. In terms of defining their collective interests, the allies were thus making progress. But it was not straightforward. Nixon and Kissinger remained skeptical of both the conference and Brandt's Ostpolitik, but also saw an interest in allied coordination.

Nixon and Kissinger would latch onto an idea that Britain had originally inserted into the Harmel discussions: namely, to pursue "balanced force reductions" between East and West.[40] The beauty of the idea was not only its appeal to Western publics eager for more cooperation and less confrontation, but also its ability to keep NATO focused on military tangibles. Nixon and Kissinger wanted a hardnosed policy that did not let the Soviet Union, which had superior conventional power, off the hook. They also needed a foil for domestic critics, such as Senator Mansfield, who sought unilateral US force withdrawals from Europe. By linking the status of US forces to what became talks between East and West on Mutual and Balanced Force Reductions (MBFR), Nixon sought to keep NATO together and tie the hands of Mansfield and other domestic critics.

Europe's side of this equation was simple in theory: the European allies would agree to make MBFR a precondition for a continental security conference, and in return they could take the lead on defining policy on this security conference. In practice, a diversity of interests complicated matters. For Brandt, the MBFR talks were important, because they could lead to a security conference—a major political objective for Brandt. For French President Pompidou (elected in June 1969 after de Gaulle's resignation), the MBFR talks were essentially unnecessary, and perhaps even a nuisance: continental political change was the point, and the talks risked cementing an order made up of NATO and the Warsaw Pact. For the new (Conservative) British Prime Minister Edward Heath, both the MBFR talks and the security conference were risky, given Britain's interests: securing both NATO's viability and Britain's entry into the European Communities (agreed in 1972, to take effect in January 1973). Britain could not afford to offend either France or West Germany.

Britain's Denis Healey, the Defence Secretary in the Labour government between 1964 and 1970, had had some success in organizing a European initiative inside NATO, a so-called Eurogroup, to beef up Europe's conventional defense and ensure Atlantic harmony on politico-strategic issues.[41] Healey had at first set up "Euro-dinners" among most NATO defense ministers and parallel "Euro-teas" among the associated permanent representatives (NATO ambassadors).[42] The impact of this Eurogroup on national defense budgets and collective armaments cooperation through the 1970s was "solid, if unspectacular."[43] Yet its political spinoff effects should not be underestimated. At first (and this was Healey's primary motivation), it helped commit the European allies to maintaining conventional force levels in support of the flexible response strategy.[44] Later, under his successor, Lord Carrington, in the early 1970s—and in conditions of economic and financial uncertainty—the Eurogroup helped prevent uncontrolled conventional force reductions, which was of benefit to both NATO's MBFR policy and to President Nixon in his domestic political battles. The experience would ultimately help prepare Lord Carrington for his 1984 appointment as NATO secretary general.

The wider security conference was more challenging. In essence, six European countries—the members of the European Communities (France, West Germany, Italy, and the Benelux countries)—launched a separate foreign policy initiative in 1969–70 to set up a "political

Europe," and policy on the East–West security conference got sucked into it. The point of the initiative was really to build the political muscle of the European Communities before offering Britain entry. This was best done, they believed, by building political cooperation around the European Communities' shared commitment to human rights and democracy. Such was the 1970 conclusion of a study undertaken by the political director of the Belgian Ministry of Foreign Affairs, Étienne Davignon—wingman of Pierre Harmel during the NATO study. Davignon is today regarded as the founding father of the European Union's foreign policy dimension.[45] He in effect drove the six to associate human rights policy with the European security conference. For Kissinger, this was fluffy; but for the six European allies, it was a "separate and more humane identity" that bolstered both the communities that Britain was seeking to join and their search for continental stability.[46]

This European identity quickly became part and parcel of NATO's diplomacy. As the six met in November 1970 to endorse the Davignon conclusions, Belgian Foreign Minister Pierre Harmel appealed for new European thinking on the East–West security situation. The intervention prompted the six to decide that their discussion had to continue on the margins of the following month's NATO ministerial meeting.[47] The neat division of labor imagined by Nixon and Kissinger—that NATO would do hard-nosed MBFR, while the Europeans would do fluffy security talks—thus got caught up in a political drive to define Western Europe's identity. Things quickly got complicated, and the NATO allies failed to define an overarching coordinated policy for both MBFR and the East–West security conference. Instead, frustrations grew—to the point where Kissinger demeaned European unity (as we saw above) as the "single worst mistake of the postwar period."

Discord

At the heart of the ensuing discord was the relationship between the great powers and the way in which it affected Europe. President Nixon had spectacularly visited Chairman Mao in Beijing, in

February 1972, an opening to a major communist power that gave Nixon leverage in the relationship with Leonid Brezhnev's Soviet Union. US–Soviet dialogue was advancing, with both Strategic Arms Limitation Talks (SALT) and talks on anti-ballistic missile (ABM) defenses, designed to stabilize relations around principles of mutual vulnerability. The two leaders were preparing to meet to sign both the SALT and the ABM deals, and did so during President Nixon's visit to Moscow in May 1972.

During the first plenary session of the summit, Nixon told his Soviet counterparts, including party leader Brezhnev and the Soviet premier, Aleksei Kosygin, that they could work together because the two sides both had a firm idea of their interests. Nixon stressed his own "long-cherished and solid reputation as a hard-line anti-Communist," which evoked a perceptible grin from the otherwise pained and dour Kosygin. "As if we didn't know," his face seemed to be saying.[48] Undeterred, Nixon continued to berate the "mushy sentimentality" that, allegedly, characterized much détente thinking.[49] The purpose of the summit was thus in a way psychological—to create superpower confidence and trust on the basis of coordinated hard-core security interests.

Confidence and trust inside NATO went into a simultaneous nosedive, though. The North Atlantic Council had, through 1971, wrestled with an overall approach to both MBFR and a security conference, but had been unable to agree. In April–May 1972, the allies returned to the matter, with quite a few of them, including West Germany and some of the smaller allies, desirous of tying MBFR to the security conference, for the sake of an integrated approach to European security. They were thus attached to some of the principles that Nixon would characterize as "mushy sentimentality."

The United States was against any such integrated approach, and at a NATO DPC meeting on May 24, Secretary of State William Rogers set out the case for maintaining two separate tracks—MBFR and a security conference. This was fully in line with NATO consultations: divergent interests and a search for compromise. What broke the mold, though, was Henry Kissinger's simultaneous summit preparatory trip to Moscow, where he agreed with the Soviet leaders to begin MBFR talks and let exploratory talks on a security conference run at their own pace on a different track. Kissinger left the allies in the dark, and they would awkwardly learn of the Moscow deal during their May NATO meeting.[50]

The Italian diplomat attached to NATO, E. Bettini, had earlier in the North Atlantic Council eloquently and forcefully set out the case against precisely such a twin-track position. It would divide the alliance, he argued. The problem was the MBFR's confinement to Central Europe: this meant that not all the allies would be equally relevant to it. (He had a point: the subsequent MBFR exploratory talks would be led by only seven allies: the United States, Britain, Canada, West Germany, and the Benelux countries.) MBFR would thus create a "fringe" status in the alliance, geographically as well as politically. "It was," continued Bettini, "bound to have a negative effect on alliance solidarity." The ambassadors from Greece, Turkey, Denmark, Norway, the Netherlands, and Belgium supported Bettini's criticism.[51]

Secretary of State Rogers, when reporting to the North Atlantic Council on the Moscow summit, would sidestep this criticism: "The interests of the Alliance had been taken into account during the talks, particularly with regard to MBFR." On the wider security conference, "the Soviet position had changed very little," and the Soviet representatives had made "no reaction" to the US proposals.[52] The summit thus apparently confirmed to President Nixon what he had learned on a trip to Europe in 1967, when an (unnamed) Belgian interlocutor had confided in him: détente "is like the Virgin Birth. I accept it, but I don't believe it."[53]

One result of this turn of events, "many diplomats" expected, would be an acceleration of progress in European political cooperation—the foreign policy coordination flowing from the Davignon report of 1970.[54] And so it came to pass: European coordination grew. It was partly driven by the two separate security tracks, where preparatory talks on the security conference began in Helsinki in November 1972, and preparatory MBFR talks commenced in Vienna in January 1973. But it was also helped along by wider trade and economic issues, where President Nixon's decision to let the dollar float sparked a hunt for new measures of equity and burden sharing. By early 1973, as

Britain entered the European Communities, European leaders were contemplating a common "float" of their currencies. This would enhance their unified voice in financial and economic matters, but it rubbed against Nixon and Kissinger's sense of fairness. In March 1973, Kissinger advised Nixon that the Europeans needed to be told that "the party is over." Some days later, Nixon penned a message to Kissinger stating, "European unity will not be in our interest."[55]

Thus began some fourteen months of tortuous diplomacy to bring the allies to a new agreement. Henry Kissinger gave the lead in April 1973, in a speech calling for a "Year of Europe" and the launching of a new Atlantic Charter.[56] By June 1974, at their twenty-fifth anniversary summit in Ottawa, Canada, the allies were able to issue a Declaration on Atlantic Relations, in which they looked to the future with confidence and conviction.[57]

The road to Ottawa had been exceptionally rocky, though, and Kissinger's speech had set the tone. It drew a distinction between European "regional" and US "global" interests, which were not "automatically identical." It identified Europe as a "strong competitor," building a "closed trading system." It suggested new linkages between defense and economic issues, to be hammered out in a new Atlantic Charter. And it sought a new trilateral political and trading order, built on relations between the United States and Canada, Europe, and Japan. All this had been woven by Kissinger into his speech without either consultation with the allies or due policy process in the national security bureaucracy in Washington. It followed from Kissinger's preference for personal initiative; and it backfired.

British Prime Minister Edward Heath felt betrayed. He had taken his country into the European Communities and thus the "common market," a British objective for some fifteen years; but instead of reaping the benefits, he struggled and in February 1974 was voted out of office. Heath's common-market triumph had effectively been taken hostage by Nixon and Kissinger's cajoling of Europe and France's vehement opposition to Kissinger's speech. Heath's loyalties then divided. On the one hand, and while he had maintained privileged bilateral contacts with Kissinger on a broad range of transatlantic issues, he now had to respect the desire of his European Communities partners to manage economic and financial issues in a dialogue with the US. On the other hand, he had to manage the wrath this provoked in Washington, where especially Kissinger (Nixon being increasingly caught up in the Watergate affair) railed against European coordination outside transatlantic consultations.[58] Kissinger lamented that Britain had failed to raise Europe to its own level, and had instead allowed itself to slide to the level of Europe. For his part, Heath complained that the United States would never "ask for 'A Year of China' without consulting the Chinese but ... had done that in the case of Europe."[59]

Things went from bad to worse in the fall of 1973 and the spring of 1974. The October War between Israel on the one hand, and Egypt and Syria on the other prompted the crisis. US forces were put on nuclear alert to counter a possible Soviet intervention, but the alert had not been coordinated with the European allies. Quite a few of them, heavily dependent on Arab oil as they were, responded by refusing US planes access to facilities or airspace as they undertook an airlift to Israel. Moreover, the allies mobilized European political cooperation to create a distinct Middle Eastern policy that was favorable to Arab political concerns, as well as their own oil dependency. In the spring, though, as he undertook shuttle diplomacy to unlock Israeli–Arab hostility, Kissinger demonstrated leverage that the Europeans did not have. He and French Foreign Minister Jobert entered a hectic political race to win hearts and minds in the region; inevitably, France could not win this contest.[60]

But nor could Kissinger: the battle of political wills had gone too far. The linkage between defense (NATO) and trade (the European Communities) that Kissinger had sought escaped him. By the spring of 1974, it was clear that there would be two declarations coming out of the "Year of Europe," one anchored in NATO and the other in the European Communities. Moreover, France had by then provided a key draft for negotiation in NATO over what would become the Declaration on Atlantic Relations.[61] Later, this draft would pass into creative hands in London—and would ultimately pass through so many hands that its "parenthood" could be interpreted in the most politically convenient way.[62]

Diplomatic craftsmanship and political exhaustion eventually brought the allies to consensus. It involved a change of gallery in Britain, West Germany, and France. In Britain, the Labour government formed in early 1974 by Harold Wilson began "to restore the partnership," Kissinger would later recall.[63] Shortly thereafter, in early April, French President Pompidou succumbed to blood cancer and passed away. His Gaullist party, for which Michel Jobert lined up behind Jacques Chaban-Delmas to contest the elections, finished a paltry third in the first round of voting. Pompidou's successor, Valéry Giscard d'Estaing, came from the liberal political current in French politics and sought change. Concurrently, in early May, Willy Brandt resigned his chancellorship in West Germany, following the revelation that a close advisor of his, Günter Guillaume, was an East German spy. Brandt's Social Democratic successor, Helmut Schmidt, held strong transatlantic convictions and was less attached to Brandt's Ostpolitik.

NATO's Ottawa Declaration—the Declaration on Atlantic Relations—was adopted in June 1974 to mark the alliance's twenty-fifth anniversary. It spoke to all sides in the debate: it recognized Europe's military contribution in terms of conventional forces (three-quarters of the combined strength) and the part played by British and French nuclear forces in "the overall deterrence" of the alliance. Simultaneously, it obliged the European allies to contribute to the common defense, whether via the European Communities or individually. And finally, it established the "indispensable" contribution of US nuclear forces, as well as the "irreplaceable" role of US and Canadian forces in Europe.

With the Declaration on Atlantic Relations the allies had rescued their alliance after bruising discord. Richard Nixon had, from the outset, identified his presidency with the rhythm of history, which he claimed favored Asia. "We should assist but we should not dictate," Nixon had stated in 1969 in Guam, portending a shift in power and a reduced reliance on the United States within the alliance.[64] Ultimately, NATO weathered this leadership challenge, and the 1974 declaration was symbolic of the alliance's political resilience.

But it was a close call. The 1974 summit marked NATO's twenty-fifth anniversary, and it was only the second time that NATO heads of state and government had gathered. Yet it lasted a mere two hours. President Nixon was visibly a declining political force, who labored in the shadows of Watergate impeachment hearings. The allies showed little respect: French President Giscard d'Estaing stayed home in Paris to host the shah of Iran. Nixon, feeling belittled, refused to receive d'Estaing's stand-in, Premier Jacques Chirac. European leaders meanwhile found a "backdoor way" during the summit to hold separate talks on economic matters. When President Nixon offered an evening reception at the American embassy, most of the alliance leaders failed to show up. Dutch Premier Joop den Uyl was quite blunt: he had no time for the American president, because he needed to return to watch a soccer match between the Netherlands and Argentina.[65]

Pearson and Spaak had, in their own way, foreseen the trouble. An alliance bereft of shared vision would all too easily succumb to the dissent of political diversity. President Nixon was a visionary statesman, a prophet of transformed global politics. In place of bipolar Cold War and militarized confrontation, he sought three-cornered diplomacy, opening up relations to China to enable it. But Nixon's vision also caused him to be impatient and harsh with NATO and his European allies. Kissinger's Year of Europe was infused with this spirit, relegating Europe to regional affairs, overshadowed by global US priorities. It was prophecy bereft of solid alliance politics. The same, of course, can be said of French President de Gaulle's attempt to unseat NATO.

That NATO weathered these years is testament to the importance of having an alliance machinery that captures and magnifies a commitment to pragmatic compromise. The late 1960s were a high point. The allies agreed to new machinery—the DPC and the NPG—and they committed to a strategy of principled pragmatism—the Harmel doctrine. That all three innovations continue to this day is evidence of their political worth and of the ingenuity that was originally invested in them. This was the NATO of foreign and defense ministers at its best. There were quarrels among the chiefs, but the ministers—supported by permanent staff in the headquarters—found solutions to carry NATO through.

The early 1970s is the story of how this NATO—the alliance of foreign and defense ministers—could only do so much. If the chiefs believe that "mushy sentimentality" has infected the alliance (in President Nixon's memorable words), then policy pragmatism must operate within the confines of political conflict. This is why NATO had to settle for two separate tracks to East–West cooperation: the MBFR track and the security conference track. NATO was mostly invested in the former, because that is what the United States wanted. The irony is that the MBFR ran into the sand, whereas the security conference of August 1975 resulted in the Helsinki Final Act and the creation of a political, social, and economic wedge into Eastern bloc affairs, the Conference on Security and Cooperation in Europe (CSCE). It also resulted in the formation of a European foreign policy "identity" that stood apart. There was nothing in this identity that conflicted with the tenets of the Harmel doctrine, but it was placed outside of NATO and partially in opposition to the United States. This was resilient NATO, but also a NATO of wrecked Atlanticism—an alliance engulfed by disputes over its politico-military character.

5

Conserving NATO
The Dual-Track Decision

It had been a "successful meeting of extraordinary importance," concluded US Secretary of State Cyrus R. Vance in mid-December 1979.[1] He was referring to a NATO decision to threaten the deployment of 108 Pershing II ballistic missiles and 464 Gryphon cruise missiles, all nuclear armed, by 1983 if the Soviet Union did not withdraw some of its newest nuclear forces. Most of these missiles would be deployed in West Germany—all the Pershing II missiles and about a quarter of the cruise missiles, with the remaining going to Britain and Italy, and then also possibly to Belgium and the Netherlands.

Vance's general approach as one of President Carter's primary foreign policy advisors would be "patience. Patience. Patience."[2] And while bringing NATO to consensus did require that quality, the pervasive mood in Europe was for urgency, not patience. European leaders, fearing a Soviet advantage in hardball nuclear politics, felt that patience might end up decoupling Europe's defense from that of North America. They saw it as a matter of urgency that President Carter exercise leadership in nuclear strategy. Urgency was also a matter of tending to their public opinion, which mostly did not want the reinforcement of extended US nuclear deterrence. In the end, and ironically, some of them had to plead not for urgency, but for patience. Belgian Foreign Minister Henri Simonet said that his country could accept new NATO missiles only after six months. Dutch Foreign Minister Chris van der Klaauw upped the ante, declaring that the

Netherlands could accept them only after two full years. Both were hoping that Soviet restraint would obviate the need for NATO deployments.

What the NATO allies were being pulled into now was a type of "liar's poker," with nuclear stability at stake: the interests involved and the world views were that different.[3] In this, Vance's patient style, his abhorrence of concept-driven thinking, and his lawyerly approach to issues did not encourage his boss, President Carter, to take charge. Instead it raised concerns in Washington and in allied capitals that Team Carter was too dovish. It sowed dissent within the team, where national security advisor, Zbigniew Brzezinski—who "debated like he played tennis—to win and to win all the time"—took it upon himself to counter Vance.[4] And in the end, it paralyzed especially the European leg of the alliance, where anxiety metamorphosed into conservatism. The allies had no eye for Europe's transformation: the preservation of NATO had become their ambition.

Strategic affairs and transatlantic unrest

The Gerald Ford presidency was unexpected, caused by Richard Nixon's sudden resignation in 1974 in the aftermath of the Watergate scandal; but its embroilment in strategic nuclear negotiations with the Soviet Union was entirely predictable. The superpower deal of 1972, SALT I, was remarkable, in that it was the fruit of superpower collaboration; but the deal had only limited the rough numbers of ballistic missiles. Moreover, it was set to expire in 1977. In late November 1974, President Ford and the Soviet leader, Leonid Brezhnev, met in Vladivostok to outline a new deal, whereby they limited a wider range of delivery vehicles and the number of warheads they could carry. This new deal, SALT II, would need refinement, and then (notably) ratification; but it promised to carry superpower détente into the 1980s.

From an allied perspective, SALT II brought both good news and bad. The good news was the continuation of East–West dialogue and stability. The Conference on Security and Co-operation in Europe (CSCE) Final Act of 1975 had captured popular hopes for a world that had moved back from the brink of nuclear war. The CSCE did not deal with hard security, though. The closest it came was its so-called confidence-building measures, which were norms and rules related to the timely announcement of military exercises. Hard security thus remained in the hands of the superpowers (strategic nuclear issues) and their alliances (MBFR and conventional force negotiations). The bad news was that SALT (I and II), in creating a balance of big guns among the superpowers, suggested that the superpowers might want to settle tests of force at a lower level of conflict. That is, in Europe, where the Soviet bloc had a numerical advantage. SALT thus stabilized superpower relations, but exacerbated European anxieties.

Flexible strategy was how the United States sought to deal with this tension. Secretary of Defense James Schlesinger would, in 1973–74, become associated with a doctrine that no longer threatened blunt strikes on Soviet cities, but which built on a "structure of nuclear attack options ... at levels well below those of massive attacks."[5] Though Schlesinger lent his name to the doctrine, the shift from a counter-value (targeting Soviet cities) to a counter-force (targeting a variety of Soviet forces) strategy had been in the making since the early 1960s. More significant than the name attached to the doctrine was the need for new and refined nuclear weapons: US ballistic missiles had to be more accurate; the yield of warheads (the destruction they delivered) had to be variable; and new capabilities, such as long-range cruise missiles, were needed to deliver the accurate and controllable impact presumed by the strategy.

The fact of the matter was that the alliance was in no condition to deliver on flexible deterrence. This was partly because the existing US nuclear arsenal in Europe was dated. Surface-to-surface missiles (Honest Johns), surface-to-air missiles (Nike Hercules), and manually placed mines were easy to locate, difficult to move, and of such short range that they no longer impressed Soviet decision-makers. Partly this was because the Soviet Union was proceeding apace with its own nuclear force modernization, beginning to replace old SS-4 and SS-5 missiles with the new SS-20. Soviet decision-making on SS-20 may have been driven by its own military-industrial complex, rather than East–West balances.[6] But for NATO, the problem remained that it did not have the forces to control escalation. The situation eroded NATO's flexible response strategy, as well as the coupling of Europe's defense to that of North America.

The SS-20s were problematic in several ways. They were highly mobile, of long range, and most of them had multiple nuclear warheads. They could not reach the United States or Canada, but they threatened the whole of European NATO. Moreover, their long range allowed them to remain within Soviet territory, which for NATO meant that any attempt to destroy the missiles would involve an attack not on the territory of the USSR's Warsaw Pact allies in Eastern Europe, but on the home territory of the Soviet Union. The SS-20s were thus double trouble:[7] they outgunned NATO at the intermediate steps on the escalation ladder, where NATO sought flexibility; and they denied NATO flexibility in terms of geographical targets. To compound matters, Soviet escalatory dominance was reinforced by its new strategic bomber aircraft—the "Backfire"—which could penetrate NATO airspace at very low altitude. But the backbone of concern related to the SS-20s and the likelihood that Washington might not dare to strike at Soviet territory in the name of Europe's defense.

Soviet negotiators inside the SALT II talks ingeniously argued that US forward-based systems were problematic. That is, US nuclear weapons stationed on European soil were allegedly particularly threatening to the Soviet Union, meaning that the Soviet leaders would limit their massive advantage in intercontinental missiles only if America's leaders dialed down its forward-deployed forces. The Soviet negotiators thus obviously sought to trade a superpower deal for transatlantic decoupling. Of course, the American negotiators spotted this, and they knew they needed to invest in new kit, from cruise missiles to refined ballistic missiles. But the temptation built into SALT II talks was for the United States to place all the new kit either on US soil or on US vessels and planes circling Europe.[8] Because this would partly decouple US forces from the soil of the allies, the mere temptation fed European anxieties even further.

Jimmy Carter thus had important nuclear decisions to make when he acceded to the presidency in January 1977. He was immediately confronted with a pending decision to either upgrade US land-based nuclear forces in Europe (the Honest Johns and Nike Hercules) or, alternatively, to enhance US nuclear forces at sea.[9] It was a decision pregnant with political impact. To manage it, the new president had to navigate two conditions. First, he would have to step forward and offer leadership on nuclear issues. The nuclear challenge could not be managed solely through the usual channel of nuclear consultations in NATO's NPG: the president needed to lead from the front.

The second, and related, condition was a growing perception in Europe that the United States was retrenching in world affairs, and this at a moment of growing complexity. The sense of retrenchment flowed from the Watergate scandal that had felled President Nixon, the US retreat from Vietnam (many would say loss), and the turbulence in monetary, financial, and trade affairs that had followed from the end of the Gold Standard (the Bretton Woods system) in 1971. West German Chancellor Helmut Schmidt, who had won parliamentary elections shortly before President Carter's election, saw the "world economic situation" as a real and pressing threat not only to industrialized nations, but also to the Atlantic alliance.[10]

President Carter could not hope to pull all this under a broadened NATO. The divide between the Nixon doctrine and Europe's "identity" had confirmed what the decline of Atlanticism had established: namely, that NATO was stuck in a politico-military role. The six largest industrialized economies—the United States, Britain, France, West Germany, Italy, and Japan—had instead inaugurated an informal leadership structure to deal with monetary and financial matters—so-called G6 summits, the first of which was held in November 1975. President Carter's transatlantic leadership challenge was to bring all this together.

Uncertain leadership

President Carter's first trip to Europe took place in May 1977, as he headed to London to attend both a G7 summit and then a North Atlantic Council meeting. Ahead of the trip, Carter's assistant for national security, Zbigniew Brzezinski, prepared a memorandum setting out a conceptual framework for the Carter presidency's "four-year foreign policy goals."[11]

Brzezinski intended to define the "basic concept" of the presidency, rather than produce a long paper reflective of national security bureaucracy negotiations. In thinking big, Brzezinski rejected "updated Atlanticism," which smacked of yesterday's international order. He was in search of something new. Brzezinski had been the first director of the Trilateral Commission, a private—if wealthy and influential—organization founded in 1973 to advise on growing interdependence between North America, Europe, and Asia.[12] Trilateralism, which anticipated a more pluralistic world order, offered a sense of direction. However, the concept was insufficiently developed to guide government policy. What the presidency needed, therefore, was "a broad architectural process" to define a policy suited for a new international system.[13]

President Carter approached the London summits in this spirit, seeking to establish partnerships for change. He had early on launched the idea of turning the planned NAC meeting into an "Atlantic summit." This more grandiose title suggested greater coordination and partnership. It was not immediately to the liking of French President Giscard d'Estaing or West German Chancellor Schmidt. The two had established close coordination on monetary and financial policy, and both worried that the new US president would be what he had claimed to be during his election campaign: strong on human rights and critical of nuclear policy.[14] President Carter was agile, though. He finished his intervention at the NATO meeting with a reference to French writer and aviator, Antoine de Saint-Exupéry: "the noblest task of mankind is to unite mankind." "In that spirit," the president continued, "I am confident that we will succeed."[15] His European trip was subsequently heralded as a "triumph," and West Germany's foreign minister, Hans-Dietrich Genscher, was overheard whispering to US Secretary of the Treasury Michael Blumenthal, "Now, I see why your President was elected."[16]

Hans-Dietrich Genscher and his boss, Chancellor Schmidt, would worry, though, and would become key drivers of a European effort to change nuclear perceptions in Washington. What they wanted was not the outsourcing of nuclear decisions from Washington to Brussels (NATO), but the right kind of US leadership. What this meant was political, of course; but the West German position as a frontline state in the Western defense posture mattered enormously: Germany could not be singled out in allied planning—and nor, of course, could it be sacrificed. It was a matter of both the national interest and highly sensitive domestic politics. Schmidt's Social Democratic Party (SPD) was divided between an Ostpolitik-wing, carrying the torch of Brandt (and led by Brandt's confidant, Egon Bahr), and a realist wing that was determined to correct transatlantic and East–West strategic imbalances. Helmut Schmidt belonged on this latter wing.

Hans-Dietrich Genscher was both part of Schmidt's political strength and a political headache. He was not of Schmidt's SDP, but rather of the Free Democratic Party (FDP), and Schmidt had made him foreign minister in 1974 to enable a governing coalition. But the FDP was no easy partner. Prior to 1969 it had supported a conservative government, but had then switched political sides. It was also in two minds on the big issues: it supported both détente and confrontation; it wanted to work with the Soviet Union, but did not trust it; it wanted West Germany to speak up, but not in a way that would inflame neighbors' memories of Germany's troubled past. Genscher was heir to this complex and seesaw-style political tradition, and he made ruling hard.[17]

Early on, Schmidt and Genscher acted in tandem to adjust the transatlantic strategic compass. West German leaders had, for several years, urged balance at all force levels—not only at the strategic level of SALT; and now, as Carter came to London, Schmidt homed in on the critical "intermediate" missile range, to which the SS-20 belonged. The strategic (intercontinental) level was at stalemate, he argued, and conventional MBFR negotiations were going nowhere. Thus, he continued, the alliance must be more aggressive in thinking about the link between new-theater nuclear weapons and arms control. President Carter's focus lay elsewhere, though, and mostly with the conventional balance of forces, which, in the words of Secretary of Defense Harold Brown, "required even more immediate attention than the strategic nuclear balance." The Americans thus pushed for

NATO's adoption of a long-term defense program (LTDP) that would raise European defense expenditure. Neither Brown nor Carter addressed the intermediate-range nuclear level that so concerned Schmidt.[18] As a sop, though, NATO leaders committed one of the LTDP task forces to an examination of tactical nuclear forces.

Nuclear issues then erupted into the public domain, and Genscher took to the trenches, worrying about "American perfidy" that posed a threat to the attachment of Germans to NATO.[19] Several things provoked this outburst. For one, the European allies—not just West Germany—worried that Carter was ready to restrict NATO cruise missile options in negotiations with the Soviet Union, by either limiting their range or restricting ground and sea versions of them.[20] But the real drama lay elsewhere. First, in June, the *Washington Post* ran a big story about advanced US work on an enhanced radiation weapon (ERW) or neutron bomb, whose smaller blast would reduce collateral damage, while its enhanced radiation would incapacitate more enemy troops. The neutron bomb was reasonable from the perspective of refining strike options, but the politics of enhancing nuclear radiation in Central Europe played very poorly with the German and European publics. Provokingly, Soviet leader Brezhnev penned letters to all NATO allies inviting them to reject ERW deployment. The final straw was the July leak of Presidential Study Memorandum No. 10 (PRM-10). It was submitted to President Carter by his advisor, Brzezinski. Observing the same dearth of conventional force depth as the LTDP, PRM-10 suggested a "stalemate" strategy, whereby NATO would absorb a Soviet attack by ceding part of Europe—notably West Germany—before digging in and striking back. In short, it considered West Germany partly expendable.

Helmut Schmidt was growing impatient. He had made three or four fruitless attempts in private conversation to persuade President Carter to take seriously the "Euro-missile" gap. But to no avail. And it was not just the president: in Washington generally, in 1977 there was simply "no strong constituency" favoring the deployment of new nuclear weapons in Europe.[21] In late October 1977, Schmidt thus went public. In a widely noted speech at the London-based International Institute for Strategic Studies (IISS), Schmidt essentially raised the same points as he had at the May NATO meeting: there was a gap, and he wanted US leadership to include "Euro-missiles" in the SALT II negotiations. Only now he did so in public. The speech was delivered in somewhat cautious language, Schmidt recalled, though its message was "quite clear" to the experts in the room. "There was a dinner afterwards," Schmidt continued, "and I was much more clearer [sic] at that dinner, even somewhat insulting as regards the American hesitance."[22]

NATO's NPG had, earlier in October, decided to upgrade the LTDP task force dealing with theater nuclear weapons to a high-level group (HLG). This would raise political awareness and draw in senior people from the capitals. Its chair was David McGiffert, US assistant secretary of defense for international security affairs. The HLG ran seven meetings in total into the fall of 1979, homing in on long-range theater nuclear forces, which is where the East–West gap was. But while helpful, the HLG was still not sufficient. The key problem was at the senior leadership level, where Schmidt "remained untrusting of President Carter's ability to take account of European interests."[23]

Matters did not improve until mid-1978, and it would take a major political crisis to get there. The issue was the "neutron bomb" (ERW). The weapon was so controversial in the public domain that the allies jostled to share the burden—or to avoid having the blame pinned on them. Schmidt again objected, this time to US suggestions that the decision on whether to produce the ERW should be made collectively in NATO. It was, Schmidt felt, a Carter ploy to reduce pressure from his left flank in Congress.[24] Meanwhile, Schmidt's own left flank, led by Egon Bahr, was busy rejecting the ERW and mobilizing public opinion against both the weapon and Schmidt.[25]

A standoff ensued. President Carter wanted to hold his production decision until the allied leaders requested ERW deployment, while the allied leaders wanted to delay their request until Carter made his ERW production decision. In early 1978, the allies then agreed a three-pronged formula for moving forward collectively. It involved a US production decision, a European deployment request, and then finally an offer to the Soviet Union to trade the weapon in an arms control deal. The alliance had an agreement. Unexpectedly, President Carter then hesitated and canceled the ERW altogether.

It was not clear what had provoked his decision. The president's team—including his security advisor, Brzezinski, and the secretaries of state and defense, Cyrus Vance and Harold Brown—were in alignment on the issue, and the president's name "had been invoked heavily" to build the NATO consensus, recalls Vance.[26] For months he had led intensive NATO consultations, and by March 1978 he had succeeded in engineering consensus on the three-pronged path forward. Concretely, he had agreed with his foreign ministerial colleagues that the United States would introduce a neutron bomb proposal in the North Atlantic Council, where West Germany would offer its support, and where the matter would then go into so-called silence procedure—a standard NATO measure to obtain political consensus.[27] But when the president saw the final decision memorandum of March 18, he backed down; Vance, normally a diplomat of great patience, grew exasperated.

The deal unraveled because—not trusting his volatile allies—President Carter veered away from it to a policy of again wanting West Germany first to demand the weapon. Cyrus Vance had to carry this message, which canceled the NATO procedure, to the allies. Schmidt was at first "restrained but deeply upset," and he had Genscher rush to Washington to "restate the German position." Genscher recalls how, at the Washington meeting, he argued against Carter's perception of European volatility: the allies were firmly behind the NATO resolution, Genscher argued; he continued to ask the president to which volatile Europeans he was referring. Carter's reply, "Chancellor Kreisky," amused no one. Vance had to lean over to the president: "Austria isn't a member of NATO." "Maybe not," Genscher reports Carter saying, but "in any case, he's a Social Democrat."[28] Carter dug in, justifying his decision as "proper" and "logical," and a result of European timidity.[29] To Schmidt, though, it was "a personal humiliation" and "an ignominious snub" to West Germany.[30] In Vance's assessment, the president simply did not appreciate "the enormous damage" the decision inflicted on his prestige and leadership.[31]

Some weeks later, the allied heads of state and government gathered in Washington for a NATO meeting. Chancellor Schmidt again expressed his own growing concern about the imbalance in medium-range weapons. President Carter recognized both the "tremendous explosive capability" of the new Soviet SS-20s and how at present there was no means by which NATO could induce the Soviet Union to constrain their deployment. However, the president left the next steps open. Britain's Prime Minister James Callaghan spoke first at the opening session; but like his colleagues, he had no ready recipe for moving forward at a time of acute tension.[32] Callaghan called for intensified NATO consultations. But consultations in hard times required leadership. Carter was a man of "deep moral convictions," Callaghan later noted respectfully, but he "had a manifest dislike of horse-trading."[33] And it was horse-trading that was now required to untie NATO's nuclear knot.

Framework consensus

Horse-trading would take place on the French island of Guadeloupe in the Caribbean in January 1979. Four leaders came together: President Carter, President Giscard d'Estaing, Chancellor Schmidt, and Prime Minister Callaghan. The host, President Giscard d'Estaing, decreed informality. There would be no formal record keeping and no declarations. Just "simple, plain, and direct" talks, Giscard said. Given the informality and the location, it became billed as the "swimsuit summit." True to European form, Chancellor Schmidt jokingly justified the participation of top-level staffers with the prospect of rainy weather. In that case, "we'd need those people to manipulate the umbrellas."[34]

The road to Guadeloupe had been bumpy, and the "swimsuit summit" would prove decisive, but not miraculously so. A further year of diplomatic footwork would in fact be required to bring NATO to consensus. A change of pace in US leadership contributed to the early momentum: in June 1978, as a direct response to the ERW debacle, President Carter issued PRM-38, which directed his national security staff to devise a new policy on "intermediate" nuclear forces. Something had to give, if the allies were to avoid a repeat of the ERW drama. Security advisor Brzezinski now took a lead role in crafting policy on the issue, which he hitherto had not.[35] By September, a decision was taking shape, which was that the status quo had to give: the United States could not deal with the European strategic landscape merely from the perspective of strategic arms talks (SALT II) and conventional force talks (MBFR). It would have to address the "gap" between battlefield and strategic nuclear weapons. How it should do so was the tricky part.

Brzezinski and his staff recommended an "integrated approach" to nuclear modernization and arms control. This had the virtue of communicating to several publics: in broad strokes it aligned US policy with Chancellor Schmidt's IISS speech, reassuring the European allies, while signaling to the Soviet leaders that the control of NATO policy through the manipulation of Western public opinion—something the Soviets had very deliberately sought in the neutron bomb affair—was out of their reach.[36] The relationship between the two parts of the approach—nuclear modernization and arms control—was left open, though. And so, questions followed. Did the policy imply that weapons' modernization would depend on arms control talks—which Soviet negotiators were experts at dragging out? Or inversely, that modernization had to happen even at the risk of stalled arms control talks, which public opinion might resist? Moreover, should the entire issue of "intermediate" nuclear modernization be uploaded to the strategic talks between the superpowers, and if so, how could the allies shape those talks?

Chancellor Schmidt felt that the issue was urgent, and he was against rolling it all into SALT II agreement and ratification. Domestically, to satisfy the Ostpolitik constituency, Schmidt needed arms control. But his personal conviction was on the side of force modernization, and under no circumstances could modernization be allowed to stall. British Prime Minister Callaghan was less enthusiastic than Schmidt about coupling force modernization to arms control, but he fully shared Schmidt's determination to modernize, and he was as concerned as the chancellor about the leadership offered by President Carter.[37] This meeting of minds—Schmidt and Callaghan were also both center-left social democrats/Labour—underpinned German and British coordination inside the HLG, NATO's working group. Their diplomats saw eye to eye on the need to reinforce European NATO with US long-range theater nuclear weapons that could strike into Soviet territory. Only thus, they believed, could deterrence be upheld. American diplomats inside the HLG meanwhile supported another option further down the ladder of escalation. The purpose remained deterrence, but the Americans wanted more shorter-range weapons to create a more effective fighting capability in Central Europe.

Through the spring of 1978, "the United States was wholly unprepared for any outcome other than support for" this shorter-range option.[38] When, by the early fall, the United States announced its PRM-38 emphasis on modernization and arms control, British diplomats wondered whether the American side really had its eyes on the SALT superpower negotiations and sought to "divide and rule" the alliance.[39] The paper trail indicates a degree of ambivalence on the US side. It did in fact commit to the deployment of long-range nuclear forces (modernization), which is what Britain and West Germany wanted. But it did not commit to "any course of action" for how modernization could take place in the context of ongoing arms control. This was as far as the thinking went at a NAC meeting on November 20, 1978.[40] Disturbingly, it resembled the ERW affair: the allies were not sure they all wanted the same thing, and they were hedging their positions. The Guadeloupe summit was held to offer leadership and to prevent another descent into allied upheaval.

The summit was a success, in that it generated a framework agreement among the top leaders. They notably agreed to the existence of a "gap," just as they agreed to an integrated "two-track" approach to it, though they left it to subordinates to hammer out what this meant. They also agreed that West Germany should not be the only ally to host new modernized nuclear forces. This point had in fact provoked a tense debate early on: President Carter thought he again was witnessing European reluctance to lead; Chancellor Schmidt thought West Germany was being singled out, which he wanted to avoid at all costs; and President Giscard d'Estaing and Prime Minister Callaghan poured oil on troubled waters.[41] The outcome in the end was a boon for Chancellor Schmidt's balanced approach. However, President Carter tied nuclear modernization and arms control to a prospective

SALT III, meaning that to get to a deal, Schmidt and Callaghan had to publicly support SALT II. It implied a reversal of positions for the two leaders, as well as backing for President Carter in his domestic struggle to obtain Senate ratification of SALT II.

The leaders also reached an understanding that within the twin-track approach, nuclear modernization was not something to be traded away for a promise of arms control. Mere Soviet talk could not and should not inhibit NATO action. The Guadeloupe host, President Giscard d'Estaing proved quite firm on this. Giscard's approach appealed to British Prime Minister Callaghan, who did not want to make modernization contingent on arms control. For Chancellor Schmidt, who had to sign up to this firm French line, the summit meant a domestic realignment. In effect, in Guadeloupe, he took one step away from his party's Ostpolitik wing, led by Egon Bahr, and moved closer to Foreign Minister Genscher, who was quite skeptical of Soviet intentions.[42] This adjustment would later become a major political headache for Schmidt.

The leaders managed to get to this level of agreement in a relaxed atmosphere, where their wives joined them for dinner on the first evening. They would otherwise jog, swim, play tennis, and even sail a small dinghy. They all spoke English and dressed in relaxed clothing. Their business meetings took place in a thatched hut, with only the sound of the sea to distract them. Greek mythology sometimes confronts heroes with a perilous voyage past Scylla (a six-headed monster) and Charybdis (a whirlpool); but at this summit there would be just a Scylla—and a hospitable one to boot. This was the British frigate HMS *Scylla*, on which Prime Minister Callaghan hosted President Carter for a reception. It was yet another Anglo-American naval meeting off the coast of the American continent; but it was no Placentia Bay, and the outcome was no Atlantic Charter. Instead, in Captain Jake Backus' quarters, Carter and Callaghan "retold old stories."[43]

The contrast to Placentia Bay is striking, in that in 1977 the allies simply were not at a point of strong collective confidence and sense of direction. The modest purpose of their meeting was to avoid a political train wreck, and then to communicate conviviality and harmony. The four leaders made a concerted attempt on the final day to talk up agreement as they met with several hundred reporters. They dressed in business suits for the occasion, but their advisors, hovering in the background, remained in shorts and polo shirts.

As the four leaders jetted home—in an indication that Guadeloupe had not been all relaxation, Schmidt would make a two-day stopover in the Bahamas for some rest—the question remained what Guadeloupe meant for the Atlantic alliance. It was good news, naturally, that the principal allies had come together to set a direction on a thorny issue. There was work to do, not least in hammering out the specifics of the two-track approach; but NATO had a machinery for this purpose. The more thought-provoking question concerned the wider implication of this informal summit in restrained format. Was this an informal directorate of Atlantic strategic affairs? Was it the kind of directorate that President Eisenhower and Prime Minister Macmillan had rejected when it was proposed by President de Gaulle in 1958? If so, it would represent a stunning turning of the tables in the alliance's internal diplomacy.

It was not to be, though. The summit would not be reproduced, and it remains in the history books as a one-off allied crisis-aversion measure. NATO thus did not go down the path of the European Communities, where in 1974, the summits of heads of state and government were formalized in the creation of the European Council—a type of super-decision-making body imposed on top of the Council of Ministers. This owed much to the liking of President Giscard d'Estaing for summitry. He thus invested in the G6 summit format, and French officials indicated that the Guadeloupe encounter was a precedent "they expect to be repeated from time to time."[44] But though he hosted the Guadeloupe summit, Giscard d'Estaing had not been the driver behind it: that was Chancellor Schmidt, and he had had Zbigniew Brzezinski present the idea to President Carter for his approval. Asking Giscard to host the summit was a deft political move on the part of Schmidt, because it gave France a role in nuclear negotiations. France was outside NATO's integrated command; it was not on the DPC or the Military Committee; it opposed the logic of flexible response; and it considered its minimal nuclear force to be exempt from arms control negotiations. Getting France on board was important for alliance cohesion and was, from the West German perspective, a measure of balance vis-à-vis the two established nuclear powers, the United States and Britain.

However, for all Schmidt's ingenuity, the summit was no panacea. In nuclear matters, France was not an easy partner. Giscard d'Estaing did not publicly engage in defense of the Guadeloupe "two-track" approach (and later NATO's dual-track policy), because he did not want France's nuclear force to be drawn into nuclear arms negotiations. Moreover, the entire two-track issue and Schmidt's high profile on it de facto bestowed a prominent nuclear role on West Germany, which Paris was not willing to grant.[45] In addition, Italy was left out of the summit, to its great chagrin.[46] In the preparatory phase of the summit, Brzezinski was only too happy to convey the impression that Italy's omission was due to West German planning.

The smaller allies were likewise alert and sensitive to the nuclear issue. The Netherlands and Belgium were particularly vulnerable, because they hosted US nuclear weapons on their territory—like Italy—and had strong popular movements protesting nuclear modernization. By insisting so firmly during the summit that West Germany should not be singled out, Schmidt was in effect arguing that one or all three allies—Italy, the Netherlands, and Belgium—should host modernized nuclear forces. As these forces should be able to strike at Soviet territory, following the long-range option pushed by West Germany and Britain, Schmidt was also in effect asking them to take on a new and more prominent nuclear role. This modernization track also grated on the political sensibilities of other smaller allies not in line to host modernized nuclear forces, but very committed to arms control.[47]

Schmidt's summit efforts thus in effect made domestic life more difficult for a number of allied governments. For them, Guadeloupe was long on great-power summitry and short on allied oxygen.

Transatlantic consensus, barely

James Callaghan did not get to enjoy the fruits of Atlantic summitry for long. He returned to a country beset by economic crisis and social unrest, and in early May 1979 he lost the general election to Margaret Thatcher, leader of the Conservative Party. Britain would now be governed by a woman whose Euro-skepticism and liking for the special bond with the United States were readily apparent, and whose Germanophobia would become more visible over time. "During my lifetime most of the problems the word has faced have come ... from mainland Europe," she would write at the turn of the century, "and the solutions from outside it."[48]

Prime Minister Thatcher's conviction that détente had led the Western alliance into a position of weakness drove her to focus on nuclear force modernization. She thus contributed to "the solution," going by her later observation. She would almost immediately clash with Chancellor Schmidt and President Giscard d'Estaing over European Communities budgets, but she would work closely, especially with Chancellor Schmidt, to get NATO to a consensus on nuclear modernization. When the Soviet Union invaded Afghanistan in December 1979, just days after NATO's double-track decision, the two would again cooperate closely to ensure that the combined pressures of twin-track implementation and Afghanistan sanctions did not cause Western Europe to "fall apart."[49]

Domestic fractures were by now visible in all allied countries. The shift from détente to incipient confrontation tested popular sentiment, generated significant anti-nuclear movements, and worsened conditions for political leadership. Chancellor Schmidt returned from Guadeloupe to a country where arms control animated large segments of public opinion, as well as his own party. In Guadeloupe, Schmidt had leaned in the direction of nuclear modernization, albeit within an integrated approach. Back home, he began to shore up the arms control dimension. Schmidt remained invested in nuclear modernization, but he was shifting emphasis. This move affected debates within NATO's HLG, and thus inside the NATO machinery. American and British diplomats were not enthusiastic about granting equal status to force modernization and arms control, but they also understood the need for arms control initiatives. Thus, following trilateral talks between the two and West Germany, they submitted to NATO the idea of setting up a separate arms control track, a special group (SG) to drive arms control policy. The NATO allies concurred, and the SG began deliberations in April 1979, under the chairmanship of US State Department officials—first Leslie Gelb, then Reginald Bartholomew.

In NATO there were now two policy tracks: the HLG considering nuclear force modernization, and the SG considering arms control. The SG track was largely a product of Schmidt's thinking and political needs—but not entirely so: the Dutch had contributed to the initiative, and the Netherlands, along with Belgium, Denmark, and Norway, engaged with it energetically. They sought an arms control-centric policy where force modernization was secondary, to be traded in an arms control deal.[50] As part of this, they sought to link force modernization and both SALT II and SALT III, hoping to generate broad arms control momentum and forestall the deployment of new NATO weapons. The Guadeloupe summit—where these allies had not been present—had called for an integrated approach, but these smaller allies now wanted "integration" to mean "sequencing": arms control first, and then possible force modernization. But sequencing had been built into the failed ERW policy. And it had failed because it allowed allies to take different positions, waiting for others to assume leadership.

The Carter administration was not hostile to the arms control track, but it could not afford a rerun of the ERW affair. US officials thus sought to privilege force modernization and make arms control a complementary component to it. In other words, they wanted the full alliance to demand new nuclear weapons for Europe and to avoid the worst-case scenario, whereby the United States would drive nuclear modernization, while the European allies took the lead on arms control. US officials were not ready to offer to trade away potentially new long-range intermediate nuclear weapons for the full retreat of Soviet SS-20s.[51] This "zero-zero" option required trust in Soviet political will. For as long as the Soviet Union had SS-20s deployed and NATO only had plans, the Soviet negotiators could manipulate issues, including the SALT III negotiations, without end. The domestic pressure to forgo nuclear modernization would become untenable. This could be the case in Europe, but also in the United

States, where Congress did not want to fund weapons for allies who shied away from political leadership, and where the president did not want to look isolated and weak.

By April–May 1979, NATO's dual-track policy began to take final shape, as the allies turned their backs on the ERW experience. Sequencing was thus out, and a commitment to rapid NATO decision-making was in. In Homestead, Florida, in late April, NATO's NPG directed the HLG to begin to wrap up its studies of nuclear modernization. The allies wanted a decision by the end of the year, meaning that the study on long-range nuclear force modernization had to be completed by mid-fall to allow for political approval. President Carter and Chancellor Schmidt converged in their view that NATO had to make a *simultaneous* commitment to force modernization and an offer of arms control. Forces would be modernized, and East–West talks would begin. The distinct point was that the Soviet Union would not be able to delay force modernization by dragging out talks. Moreover, it was not set in stone—indeed, not written anywhere—that successful talks would result in "zero-zero." An arms control deal could thus entail the permanent deployment of some, though not all, modernized nuclear forces.

This clarified outlook set the stage for a US policy drive.[52] In May, Carter approved a US roadmap for getting to a NATO dual-track decision. In June, he took the idea of sea-based missiles off the table, arguing that they made it easy for some allies to evade their responsibilities to station modernized weapons on their territory. In July, he presented a deployment program whereby Pershing II ballistic missiles would be stationed in West Germany and Gryphon cruise missiles in West Germany, Britain, Italy, the Netherlands, and Belgium. In September, a joint HGL-SG meeting accepted the deployment plan with a small amendment (some of the missiles bound for West Germany now went to Britain) and approved the arms control negotiation principles. NATO was getting close to a decision.

However, tensions related to domestic vulnerabilities and political disagreements over leadership continued. President Carter had initially not wanted to get too involved. In March, he instructed his key advisors that "We should be firm & supportive, but not 'take over' the lead nor become a supplicant."[53] The secretaries of state and defense, Cyrus Vance and Harold Brown, saw how this presidential reluctance could all too easily reproduce the ERW affair. They thus advised Carter that he had to take the lead, and he did so with the US roadmap in May. And he intended to offer further leadership in June, when he met Soviet General Secretary Brezhnev at a Vienna summit to finalize SALT II. But the summit brought more turbulence. Brezhnev notably did not commit to negotiate SALT III, likely because he saw that the US Senate, which had to ratify SALT II, would demand changes to the existing treaty. Even as he signed the treaty, Brezhnev anticipated further SALT II negotiations.[54] This implied uncertainty, which was bad enough. But far worse, as Chancellor Schmidt discovered, was that in Vienna President Carter failed even to bring up the "intermediate" missile issue so tightly coupled to SALT III. The omission "shocked" the chancellor.[55]

Tense debate followed at the joint HLG-SG meeting in September. West German officials wanted language to the effect that a zero-zero option remained possible, which might fast-track disarmament. US officials were squarely opposed, not wanting to weaken the commitment to modernization. The meeting fudged the language in the ensuing Integrated Decision Document, leaving it to political negotiations to sort out.

Continuing tensions among key allies made life harder for the rest of the alliance. The Netherlands became the weakest link.[56] Its coalition was exceptionally fragile—with a narrow majority and a governing party (Prime Minister Andreas van Agt's Christian democrats) that was the outcome of a recent merger of three formerly independent parties. Its public opinion was decidedly anti-nuclear and pro-détente. At an NPG meeting in The Hague on November 12–13, 1979, the allies were supposed to tee up a decision for December; but the Dutch government was simply not in a position to commit. Prior to the meeting, President Carter had sought to assist, offering to pull a thousand old US nuclear warheads out of Europe, but to no avail. In the end, the best the van Agt government could do was to offer a "commitment to commit," meaning that it would not oppose a NATO decision, but nor could it commit there and then to deployment. It needed a further delay, which became the two-year delay announced in December.

NATO's formal dual-track decision of December 12 spurred Soviet advances in the "intermediate" range of forces, both the SS-20 and the Backfire bomber. The alliance labeled these a direct threat to Western Europe and a potential threat to strategic stability, and thus to the NATO deterrence strategy. It announced the decision to modernize NATO forces, referring to the Pershing II and Gryphon missiles. It confirmed the US offer to withdraw a thousand older nuclear warheads from Europe, which was also to say that NATO's reliance upon nuclear weapons would not increase. And it encouraged arms control efforts that upheld "the principle of equality" between the sides—language reflecting the "Basic Principles of Relations" established by the superpowers in May 1972. Finally, NATO emphasized the "parallel and complementary" nature of its two tracks, meaning that force modernization plans would "be examined in light of concrete results" reached through arms negotiations.[57] The zero-zero option was thus not mentioned explicitly. NATO would instead take its cue from Soviet behavior.

It was, all things considered, a "successful meeting of extraordinary importance," as Secretary of State Vance would subsequently state. But consensus only barely held. The Netherlands postponed its decision for two years, and Belgium for one. Neither Denmark nor Norway would accept new weapons on its territory. President Carter and Chancellor Schmidt had offered leadership, but had also wavered at critical moments.

Through the 1970s, NATO moved from East–West détente to incipient renewed confrontation. Détente, the allies came to realize, did not cancel lethal arms races; it merely channeled them. And they came to realize that their concern with strategic and conventional weapons had left a gap at the intermediate level, which was hugely problematic for their strategic theory of controlled flexible response. Filling the gap required leadership. It was always going to be hard because of the intricate details of nuclear weapons and balances, and the high political stakes involved. Outside events and domestic expectations conspired to make it even harder.

President Carter almost instinctively recognized the challenge. When he learned that the Soviet Union had moved into Afghanistan, he exclaimed, "There goes SALT III."[58] East–West cooperation was not the only victim. Carter's presidency would go, too, as Ronald Reagan took advantage of Soviet moves and Iran's hostage taking of US diplomats to paint him as weak. The bigger story here is how the allies failed to anticipate how the high hopes of détente could backfire once East–West cooperation stalled or went into reverse. Inevitably, it would provoke a domestic backlash, and simultaneous setbacks elsewhere would test the alliance.[59] The fervor of domestic politics had become an alliance liability.

In the United States, Carter faced not only stiff opposition in the presidential race (hardly a surprise), but also a widespread campaign to tarnish his foreign policy credentials. It was not about fringe politics: one of the leading members of the Committee on the Present Danger, which railed against the president, was none other than NATO's former supreme commander, General Andrew Goodpaster. In West Germany, Schmidt succumbed to domestic turbulence. "Socialists scratched your face," charged one opponent, Rainer Barzel, who claimed that Schmidt's effort to placate the left wing of his party had mortally wounded his chancellorship and West Germany's traditional policy of Western alignment.[60] And he had a point. The left wing pulled Schmidt from the political center, causing Foreign Minister Genscher's liberal Free Democratic Party to abandon him in 1982, thus facilitating the rise of conservative leader Helmut Kohl.

These are just a few illustrations of the domestic trouble; there are many more. They help explain why, by the late 1970s, NATO had become a conservative alliance. The allies could, at best, hope to preserve NATO, not, as once was the case, to transform Europe. And the challenge of preservation was considerable, as the leadership and destinies of Carter, Schmidt, Giscard d'Estaing, and Callaghan demonstrate. By 1982, all of them were gone. But their efforts to work together in NATO were critical, and NATO's ability to pull its allies together in consensus-building talks was equally crucial. NATO enabled these leaders to be true "statesmen," according to Henry Kissinger's categorization of leadership—i.e., leaders who manipulate circumstances in order not to be overwhelmed by them.[61] They preserved NATO, and they sought the NATO they knew their societies would sustain. Had they not fought these battles, the outcome for NATO could have been far worse.

Prudence or Prophecy?
NATO Confronts New Aspirations

He was an unlikely prophet, Lech Wałęsa. A Polish electrician fired for union activity at the Gdansk shipyard, a temporary worker with a responsibility to raise his eight children, Wałęsa was set to become yet another victim of state security surveillance and repression. Yet he persisted in his quest for social and political rights. In 1981, Wałęsa was condemned by Army General Jaruzelski, who had seized power in Poland and imposed martial law. Undaunted, he persisted to gain the Nobel Peace Prize in 1983 and to inspire a slow-moving and, in the end, irresistible political revolution. It would bring democracy to Poland and, in 1999, Poland into NATO.

During the Cold War, Lech Wałęsa's Poland was in the camp of the opponent, the Warsaw Pact, but the country was still hugely important symbolically to NATO. Britain and France had declared war on Hitler's Germany in 1939 to safeguard Poland. The United States and Britain tried but were unable to protect an independent Poland during the war conferences with Stalin's Soviet Union. If the Yalta summit of February 1945 had produced a "myth," it was surely the one that Poland would be okay. It would not; it was instead swallowed up by the communist sphere. Lech Wałęsa thus saw in Yalta a source of national bitterness; but he also saw more than that. Yalta had at least preserved a Polish state and country, meaning the country had survived. Future generations could change it for the better. Wałęsa prophesied that the time for change had now come. Poland was about to move from the shadows into the light.[1]

For NATO, Lech Wałęsa and his movement, Solidarity, raised difficult questions. How could the allies support Solidarity—which prophesied change—and yet maintain the alliance's carefully constructed compromise on defense and détente? The drama of the dual-track decision had not subsided. NATO's policy was defense first, then détente. But Lech Wałęsa dreamed of big change, and Western publics were restless. Could the NATO allies stick to their dual-track guns, or would circumstances lead them into new pursuits? "I was appalled," writes Margaret Thatcher, Britain's prime minister, with respect to NATO affairs at this time. If anything, it offered "a lesson in how not to conduct alliance business."[2] NATO did pull through, and it did contribute critically to the peaceful conclusion to the Cold War. However, prophecy was no longer NATO's strong suit. By the time the Cold War ended, it was curiously bereft of a collective aspiration for a continent in transition.

NATO's playbook of prudence

The NATO allies supported political change in Poland, but sought to deter Soviet intervention by keeping a low profile. That is, with NATO out of the big picture, Soviet leaders would intervene at the risk of mobilizing Polish opinion against itself.[3] A NATO expert group had been encouraged by the February 1981 promotion of General Jaruzelski to the post of prime minister. It was, they assessed, a sign that the Polish leaders had persuaded the Soviet leaders to allow them to find an internal solution to their problems.[4] In response, NATO deplored a "sustained campaign" by Soviet authorities to deny Polish sovereignty and instead addressed demands for reasonable reform and dialogue directly to the Polish government.[5]

This low profile was guided by prudence; but it was also testing for Western leaders eager to stand up to communist repression. US Secretary of State Alexander Haig was one of them. At the meeting which led to NATO's formal position, Haig told his allied colleagues that the time had come to make a stand. The American expectation was clear: a failure by the Polish government to commit to genuine reform should have consequences. Worryingly, a few gestures by the Polish government, what Haig labeled "artificial progress," had succeeded in convincing "some" allies that no action might be needed. However, for NATO, "it was essential to succeed during the day; otherwise, the result would only be to add a Western failure to an Eastern failure." "Should the Allies fail to agree," Haig continued ominously, "the United States would act alone."[6]

Haig's frank intervention at the closed NAC meeting shows how NATO's position was a compromise between allied hawks and doves. Compromises are common in NATO, of course. But the situation in the early 1980s was exceptionally fragile, given the level of public protest engendered by the dual-track decision and the resulting inclination of European leaders to get on with East–West business. Cognizant of this delicacy, as well as the emerging crisis in Poland, NATO had in December 1980 established a playbook of prudence. It outlined "political measures" NATO could decide to take, depending on the gravity of a Soviet intervention in Poland. It notably did not include economic sanctions. These would be subject to "careful preparation" and "consultation" with other organizations, such as the OECD and the European Economic Community (EEC), and with due consideration of West Germany's "special economic relationship" with East Germany.[7]

Alexander Haig's intervention in January 1982—threatening unilateral US action—simply ignored this playbook. And this was just one step in a wider US effort to move the needle of alliance policy. The sum total was a heavy-handedness on the part of the United States that ultimately "appalled" Margaret Thatcher. The starting shot came in July 1981 at a G7 summit of the seven leading industrial countries, where President Reagan urged allies and partners to curtail the transfer of advanced technology to the Soviet Union and generally limit trade with the Warsaw Pact countries. All this was obviously outside the NATO playbook, and it risked pitting NATO leaders against their own publics' expectations of East–West détente. "The United States used to represent protection from risk," an unnamed French official remarked to the New York Times, but "now you represent protection and risk."[8]

Matters escalated after the imposition of martial law in Poland, in December 1981. A planned gas pipeline between the Soviet Yamal Peninsula in Siberia and West Germany became a flash point. The United States had long been critical of this project, which followed from détente policy and was intended to supply gas not only to West Germany, but also to France, Italy, Austria, the Netherlands, and Belgium. Italy, Britain, France, and West Germany were designated suppliers of a range of pipeline components (pumping stations, steel pipes, turbines, etc.). In a first reaction to Poland's martial law, in December, the United States imposed its own sanctions (denying the export of goods and technology from the United States). As sanctions go, this was not unusual; but considering the playbook commitment to allied consultations, it brought "palpable discomfort" to diplomats from the countries involved.[9] Six months later, in June 1982, the United States upped the ante with sanctions of extraterritorial reach, banning the sale to the Soviet Union of oil and gas equipment produced by foreign subsidiaries of US companies or under license from US companies. These sanctions "blindsided" the allies, Britain included.[10] Margaret Thatcher "condemned" the decision, noting among other things how it sat poorly with the Reagan administration's simultaneous decision to renew US grain sales to the Soviet Union.[11]

By November 18, 1982, the sanctions game was up. The Reagan administration turned the page by simply lifting its pipeline sanctions. They had achieved very little in terms of shaping Polish or Soviet government behavior. In contrast, they had seriously disrupted alliance diplomacy. Taking the sanctions off the table helped restore a semblance of allied unity. The question was then what would come next. There was no roadmap: the Reagan administration had essentially improvised its Eastern bloc policy through 1981–82. It had followed an ideological script and not a considered policy that built on allied consultation. In short, and in the words of Reagan advisor and later ambassador to the Soviet Union, Jack Matlock, Team Reagan had been "maladroit" in managing NATO.[12]

By happenstance (the administration denied any link), US pipeline sanctions were withdrawn the day after the Soviet Union announced a change of leadership. Leonid Brezhnev had passed away and Yuri Andropov, hitherto chief of the intelligence service, the KGB, assumed command. Leadership change was a political opportunity, of course, and so NATO leaders needed to contemplate it. As it turned out, opportunities would keep coming: Andropov would last a little less than a year and a half, before he, too, died. His replacement, Konstantin Chernenko, lasted just one year. In March 1985, Andropov's protégé, Mikhail Gorbachev, acceded to Soviet supreme command. NATO leaders could not know it in November 1982, but they knew that they were looking at change and needed to redefine their level of ambition.

Southern discomfort

NATO's prudence would be reinforced by events along its so-called southern flank, from the Persian Gulf to the Iberian Peninsula. There were various factors at play. NATO allies were not keen on being sucked into the regional conflict unleashed by the Iranian revolution, but they also did not want this theater of conflict to disrupt European affairs. Meanwhile, southern-flank politics brought a test of democracy to NATO. It would in some ways resemble the Polish crisis: would—and should—NATO go all out in supporting democracy, or should it give preference to stability? NATO's answer would again largely favor stability, or the prudent path to democracy.

NATO's southern flank was central to the alliance's Cold War mission of containing the Soviet Union, but in an indirect and difficult way. The British and French track record of imperialism had stoked Arab nationalism and tempted Arab nationalists to side with the West's adversary, the Soviet Union. Sandwiched between British and French designs and Arab anger, President Eisenhower had asserted US leadership in the region. He promised to protect Middle Eastern governments threatened by communist aggression, and he intervened in Lebanon in 1958 to make the point. NATO, hurt by the Suez debacle of 1956 and the splendid lack of allied consultations, drew back. It agreed to keep developments in the Middle East under "continuing observation," but also to deal primarily with threats "to the security of the NATO area."[13]

143

The fallout of the Iranian revolution fundamentally disrupted this NATO policy. In an early response to the revolution, President Carter established a new expeditionary force (a Rapid Deployment Force, RDF) to underpin his newfound doctrine of protecting the Persian Gulf against aggression. This soon implicated NATO. The RDF would suck forces from the US European command, and the Carter administration wanted Europeans to put up more forces—to backfill—in the event of a US drawdown in Europe. In addition, US Congress expected the European allies to contribute to the defense of the Gulf. The United States brought this issue into NATO through 1980, but the European allies "responded by completely stonewalling the issue."[14] They wanted no involvement, and some, such as France, resisted any notion of a NATO concept of global security that would tie French hands in Africa and the Middle East. This problem was not new—it had caused headaches for the Three Wise Men in 1956 and for Pierre Harmel in 1967—but the allies now needed to address it in the shadow of Iran's revolution and war between Iran and Iraq, which broke out in September 1980.

Following more than two years of extensive in-house consultations, the allies agreed in June 1982 to sharing "an interest in peace and security in other regions of the world." The agreement involved a willingness to consult in general and to facilitate action by allies "in a position" to act. Force compensation (backfilling) proved more difficult and required another six months of negotiation.[15] Still, by the end of 1982, the allies had their policy: consult, facilitate, compensate. It defined a new line along NATO's southern flank: a prudent policy of indirect out-of-area support intended to keep NATO free of unwanted entanglements.

It is important to note what this new policy was not. It was not an agreement to move towards a global security concept for NATO. Japan did exert a pull in this direction: it was represented in the G7, and it worried that NATO's dual-track policy might cause the Soviet Union to move its missiles eastward, closer to Japan. But one ally in particular held back: France. It had its own interests in Africa, the Middle East, and the Pacific, and it feared that a coordination of G7 and NATO policy would unduly tie its hands. French President

François Mitterrand thus went up against President Reagan, Prime Minister Thatcher, Prime Minister Trudeau, and Prime Minister Nakasone in March 1983, when, at a G7 summit in Williamsburg, Virginia, they sought precisely such coordination. In a "rude political battle," Mitterrand agreed to the invocation of "indivisible" security interests, but refused any reference to NATO.[16]

Nor was the policy prophetic in character. It was not guided by a righteous vision that implied the dislocation of current arrangements. The Atlantic Treaty spoke of freedom, and NATO's historical legacy was aspirational; but in the early 1980s, stability and equilibrium took precedence. NATO could, to an extent, dodge the bullet of democracy-versus-stability by arguing that the Persian Gulf was too geographically distant and too remote politically for NATO to consider democracy promotion there. The best it could do was to support measures of stabilization. However, closer to home, two leaders, Kenan Evren and Felipe González, pulled NATO full throttle into the dilemma of prioritizing either democracy or stability.

General Kenan Evren was chief of staff of the Turkish armed forces when, in September 1980, he staged a coup d'état and installed a military government in Turkey. He justified this with reference to extensive domestic instability and political violence, and promised to restore civilian rule. He then took his time doing so. Elections were held in November 1983, but only once the military had done its best to restructure the political system: it ran a referendum in 1982 that secured the approval of a new constitution and, by constitutional fiat, the military's role as arbiters of Turkish politics. Only then did it hold elections; but still, and just to make its point, it renewed martial law until well into 1984.

NATO's official line was mostly conservative, playing to the tune of stability more than democracy. A NATO spokesperson defined the military intervention in political affairs as "strictly an internal matter," emphasizing that a "strong, stable and violence-free Turkey" remained vital to the alliance. This was a NATO recipe for skirting the domestic issues of a member state—inherently a sensitive matter. But it was also a way of containing allied disagreement. European governments appealed for sanction; the United States for patience.[17] In a December

1981 letter to his German counterpart, Hans-Dietrich Genscher, Haig pleaded with "all friends of Turkey" to support the return of the country to stable democracy "in a reasonable timeframe."[18] To punish Turkey, Haig later explained, is to "court the danger of further deterioration" in the capabilities of a key ally.[19]

Haig had an eye to Greek–Turkish relations. Greece, which had entered NATO alongside Turkey, had experienced seven years of military rule in 1967–74. Its military rulers had brandished their anti-communist credentials, and it took patient footwork, led by Dutch Foreign Minister Max van der Stoel, for NATO to articulate a criticism of a key ally's domestic politics.[20] As always, Greece and Turkey were key allies that controlled Soviet access to the Mediterranean. NATO could not afford to estrange them. Matters worsened in July–August 1974, when war broke out between those two countries over Cyprus. Conflict between two allies was bad enough. But in addition, the war caused Greece to withdraw from NATO's integrated command structure. This happened as the military junta collapsed and the new regime, the Third Hellenic Republic, blamed NATO for supporting first Greece's military dictatorship, and then Turkey in its invasion of Cyprus, leading to the division of the island.

Alexander Haig wanted Greece back in NATO's command structure, and Turkish General Evren cleverly played to this desire. Turkey since 1974 had no intention of letting Greece back in without concessions in their bilateral Aegean Sea disputes; Greece had no intention of making any such concessions. There was deadlock. In return for Haig's *sotto voce* approach to his military dictatorship, in September 1980 General Evren offered to let Greece back into NATO. However, Evren could not be seen to be giving up on Turkish interests in the Aegean Sea, and so Haig gave him a "soldier's promise" that Aegean negotiations would continue. But what neither Evren nor Haig foresaw was that Andreas Papandreou and the PASOK movement would gain power in Greece in 1981. Seeing Turkish aggression and NATO support for it, Papandreou adopted an aloof policy of "equidistance."[21] It made both Evren and Haig look weak, and it nurtured NATO's policy gap between democratic values and security interests.

Felipe González exploited this gap to maintain Spain in NATO on exclusive terms. González was leader of the Socialist Party (PSOE) and, impressively, prime minister of Spain for fourteen years (1982–96). The reason for his NATO skepticism was the historical connection between NATO and the Franco dictatorship in Spain, which had come to an end with Francisco Franco's death in November 1975. The historical connection was indirect and resided in a bilateral US–Spanish agreement of 1953, routinely renewed, that allowed US forces access to Spanish ports and airfields. Spain offered NATO operational depth, even as most European allies were skeptical of the de facto alignment between the United States and Franco's Spain.

González came to power in October 1982, some five months after Franco's successors had secured the country's accession to NATO. He pragmatically shed his outright opposition to NATO membership, choosing instead to make the most of defining terms of engagement. Above all, considering the history of military dictatorships in Portugal, Spain, Greece, and Turkey, González did not want Spain's NATO membership to empower the military's voice in political affairs. Alarmingly, Spanish officers had staged a coup in February 1981. The coup had failed, but it highlighted the urgency of keeping the military down. In late 1982, González thus froze negotiations on Spain's military integration in NATO. He demanded an "à la carte" membership: no nuclear weapons on Spanish territory, no military integration, and fewer US troops in Spain.[22] Negotiations would be lengthy but, importantly, were undertaken in good spirit. In 1986, Spain gained its deal.

The Spaniards "knew all too well" how important freedom was to the human spirit, US Secretary of State George Shultz later wrote. He went on that it reinforced US "efforts to make freedom a centerpiece in our diplomacy."[23] But freedom was not consistently a centerpiece either in US diplomacy, or in NATO policy. In some countries, the military was a threat to democracy, and political change could awaken that threat. NATO allies were not in agreement on priorities, and searched for a balance between stability and political change. They tended to appeal to democracy while privileging stability. It made for a careful—some would say conservative—approach to political change and to the promotion of democracy and freedom. President Reagan was about to severely test this prudent heritage.

America's mixed signals

President Reagan prophesied change—so strong was his belief that communism was "a form of insanity" running counter to human nature. But Reagan was also an inherently complex political figure who possessed a curious mix of commitment and compromise. A common broad-brush interpretation of his foreign policy is that he started out as an ideologue, who mid-way turned to pragmatism, striking deals that helped end the Cold War peacefully.[24] But this neat distinction does not help us understand the competing impulses within the administration and how the allies struggled to interpret them. Reagan would ultimately side with the pragmatism of deal making, but he did so because of a grand vision of a world beyond nuclear weapons. The consistency of Reagan's vision, and the consistent difficulty of gauging its policy influence, defined another challenge for the NATO allies.

President Reagan brought in a fair number of hardline conservatives—mostly drawn from the Committee on the Present Danger—who had opposed not only President Carter's policy, but notably also that of President Nixon and his advisor, Henry Kissinger. These past leaders had been all too eager to strike deals with the Soviet Union, the Reagan conservatives insisted. What mattered was competition. Richard Allen, Reagan's security advisor, Richard Pipes, serving under Allen, William Casey, CIA director, Jeane Kirkpatrick, UN ambassador, and Richard Perle, assistant secretary of defense, were of this persuasion. Other central players who were anti-communist but pragmatic in their choice of ways and means offered a balance. James Baker, White House chief of staff, George Bush, vice president, Caspar Weinberger, secretary of defense, and Alexander Haig, secretary of state, were among them. In sum, Reagan's was a diverse foreign policy team.

President Reagan did not lean in to give it direction. He was better at vision than at the management of his national security bureaucracy.[25] He had his own ideas and was thus not staff-driven, but he was certainly staff-dependent.[26] Such an approach carries risks. Ultimately, it led to the Iran-Contra Scandal, where White House privateers traded arms for hostages, almost bringing down the Reagan presidency. Alexander Haig professed to have foreseen these risks. The problem began "on Inauguration Day," when President Reagan did not establish a structured foreign policy process, Haig later argued, continuing, "What begins in uncertainty nearly always ends in chaos."[27] What Haig omitted is how it was he who, on Inauguration Day, swept into the Oval Office with a draft directive for President Reagan to sign, promising to make Haig the head of crisis management. "That didn't go down real well with a lot of people," recalled James Baker, Reagan's chief of staff.[28] And so, chaos did ensue.

A year and a half later, in mid-1982, Haig was forced to resign. Disunity and a lack of presidential direction were at the bottom of this, though that is not to absolve Haig of personal responsibility (he famously and controversially claimed to be in control after the March 1981 assassination attempt on President Reagan). He sought to set policy on some big issues, but struggled. In April 1982, he mediated between the British government and the Argentine military junta, which had occupied the British Falkland Islands. However, Haig's mission was met with skepticism in London, where Margaret Thatcher was not keen on compromise, preferring the restoration of British sovereignty. And at home, the mission was opposed outright by administration hardliners, such as Jeane Kirkpatrick, who looked more favorably on Argentina, given its track record of supporting US anti-communist policy. It was with pointed irony that Prime Minister Thatcher later noted the coincidence on April 2 of the Argentine Falklands invasion and the gala dinner given in Kirkpatrick's honor by the Argentine UN ambassador.[29] Haig called his failed Falklands diplomacy his "Waterloo"—a collapsed peace effort that allowed "detractors" in the White House to mount "their final onslaught on my authority in foreign affairs."[30]

The lack of day-to-day leadership meant that priorities did not guide policy; instead, they were contested grounds in the struggle to shape policy. For NATO, the Falklands turmoil showed how the United States had unsettled priorities between the Americas and Europe—in fact, the two peace communities to which it had committed in the late 1940s. Back then, and fully in line with US history, the Americas had come first. In 1982, Kirkpatrick wanted the Americas to come first yet again, but Haig, Thatcher, and others thought Kirkpatrick was getting US values wrong. Britain was a democracy, Argentina a dictatorship, and the Cold War required an engagement with democratic values. From Ronald Reagan's ideological streak, one could surmise that the president would side with the right values. But in the early days of the administration, there was no such clarity. This much was visible in two affairs of direct concern to NATO.

The first concerned the negotiation position of allies on the dual track. Here, President Reagan opted for a "zero" policy, whereby the United States would seek the elimination of Soviet intermediate-range missiles, in return for the non-deployment of its own Pershing II and Gryphon missiles. President Reagan rolled out his zero vision in a speech on November 18, 1981, leaving allies and observers uncertain. By making steep demands (zero), was the president catering to his domestic political base, hoping to pin the blame for failed negotiations on the Soviet Union?[31] Or was he cleverly appealing to the desire of Western publics' for disarmament and détente?[32] These questions lingered, because the Reagan administration did not get its ducks in a row and could not communicate a clear intent.

President Reagan's inner circle was divided on the matter. Secretary of Defense Caspar Weinberger and his assistant secretary, Richard Perle, took it upon themselves to articulate a tough policy—which became the "zero" policy. Alexander Haig, secretary of state, in contrast wanted a "zero plus" policy: the purpose of the "plus" was to leave scope for negotiation with the Soviet Union, and, crucially, to cater to the allies' fear of decoupling. In short, "zero plus" would leave some US nuclear weapons in Europe. "We wouldn't want [a full zero] even if we could have it," Haig argued.[33] However, President Reagan wanted it, because zero had a power of its own. It was easy to communicate and ideal for political messaging.

Zero complicated US NATO policy, though. With a zero solution at the intermediate step on NATO's ladder of escalation, was the United States not opening a gap in NATO's strategy of flexible response? Was this not the transatlantic decoupling that Helmut Schmidt had warned against since the mid-1970s? Moreover, by pushing an intermediate-level zero, the United States would have to define the lower boundary of zero: should it apply also to tactical (short-range) nuclear weapons? Haig had strongly counseled against this idea, because it would generate an even greater degree of transatlantic decoupling; and in this instance, Reagan had accepted Haig's argument. Zero thus applied to the intermediate level only. But this merely raised new trouble. Because if NATO kept its stack of smaller tactical nuclear weapons, then presumably they should be fit for purpose: they should be modernized. And the prospect of tactical nuclear modernization promised to pull NATO through the same type of drama as the 1979 dual-track decision.

The allies worried about these issues, and then also about the superior level of strategic nuclear weapons. This was superpower territory, of course. As presidential candidate, Reagan had spoken out against SALT II—a "fatally flawed" deal, he had said.[34] But did the president intend to move to a counter-force nuclear doctrine that—in the view of the allies—could render war more likely (weaken deterrence) and accelerate the arms race? The United States had sought to develop counter-force options for more than a decade, and the allies knew this. But the Reagan administration was adding a competitive edge to counter-force, in that it went on the offensive in order to check Soviet advantage. The Soviet Union had a wealth of big, heavy, land-based missiles equipped with multiple high-precision warheads. It was the kind of force that could take out most of the US nuclear force in a surprise attack. Sure, the US would still have submarine forces, but their missiles were relatively limited in number and in precision: they had only a retaliatory potential, and a successful Soviet surprise attack could deter their use. The Reagan administration was steadfast in its demand that the Soviet Union either reduce its inventory of big missiles or switch to submarine missiles, like the US. And if the Soviet Union was not prepared to do this, the administration wanted Congress to fund large, land-based (MX) missiles for the United States.

This was complicated and obviously potentially destabilizing. When President Reagan rolled out his strategic policy thinking in the spring of 1982, the full implications of the issue might even have escaped the president himself.[35] It also left the allies wondering what to make of the strategic level, now that the intermediate level seemed potentially destined for zero. And most importantly, it left the allies to wonder at the strategic direction of US Cold War policy as a whole. Was the administration improvising, or was it guided by an underlying policy design?

President Reagan sought to quell all such concerns in January 1983, when he issued National Security Decision Directive 75 (NSDD 75)—a "threefold strategy" toward the Soviet Union. Here was the big picture, the full and integrated set of US priorities. They were to contain and over time reverse Soviet expansionism; to promote, within the narrow limits available, a more pluralistic Soviet system; and to negotiate agreements on the basis of strict reciprocity and mutual interest.[36] But uncertainty soon found its way into Reagan's strategy. Was it a firm strategy of opposition to communist expansion, and therefore an invitation to strike deals in honor of stability?[37] Or was it a strategy to *reverse* the Soviet sphere of influence and ultimately to win the Cold War?[38] These questions defined a big-picture version of the stability-versus-democracy conundrum that NATO had already encountered in its engagement with Lech Wałęsa, Kenan Evren, and Felipe González. The staffer who penned NSDD 75, Richard Pipes, was known for his distinctively critical view of East–West coexistence. Since Soviet institutions at their core built on different concepts and principles than Western institutions, in the long run, Pipes argued, one side had to win. Democracy, not stability, was the point. But was this President Reagan's intent, and would he channel it into NATO?

Breaking the nuclear mold

President Reagan captured headlines in March 1983, when, in a nationally televised speech, he charted a path for breaking out "of a future that relies solely on offensive retaliation for our security." He imagined US capabilities able to "intercept and destroy strategic ballistic missiles before they reached" US or allied soil.[39] This vision—later the Strategic Defense Initiative (SDI)—had not been subject to

NATO consultations. It also ran contrary to the advice of the White House Science Council. Upon learning of it, mere days ahead of the presidential speech, the president's science advisor, Jay Keyworth, was "surprised, shocked, even stunned."[40] Secretary of State Shultz "had no idea that anything regarding strategic defense was imminent."[41] Surprise was thus widespread, and the political desirability and military feasibility of the proposed shift from strategic offense to defense would cause allies headaches, but not immediately. NATO's focus in 1983 was elsewhere.

NATO was entering the key testing ground of the dual-track decision, namely final political clearance and then deployment. West Germany was always at the front line of the issue. Helmut Schmidt had lost office because he lost first control of his party, the SPD, and then the trust of his governing partner, Hans-Dietrich Genscher's FDP. The SPD was turning against the dual-track decision; the FDP supported it. The government fell in October 1982, and general elections followed in March 1983. On losing these elections, the SPD proceeded to vote against missile deployments. Its party leader, Helmut Schmidt, did not, though: Genscher was thus right when he wrote in his memoirs that, as chancellor, Schmidt would side with his party, though at heart he agreed with Genscher.[42] On November 22, the Bundestag's conservative-liberal majority—the Christian Democratic Union (CDU) and the FDP—approved a final dual-track resolution and enabled the deployment, the next day, of the first US missiles.

This struggle for dual-track implementation involved a meeting of Franco-German minds that was politically surprising and of some consequence for NATO. It was politically surprising because it brought together a boisterous conservative West German chancellor and a refined socialist French president. The political persuasions of Helmut Kohl and François Mitterrand were truly different. Mitterrand entered office in 1981 with a determination to change the country's fundamental economic and social institutions. He governed in alliance with the French communists, and his domestic program displayed all the hunger for political influence that more than twenty years of opposition had generated. In contrast, Helmut Kohl was a man of business and institutional pragmatism.

Both leaders were also unlikely crafters of NATO nuclear policy. West Germany, of course, did not possess nuclear weapons. France, which did, did not put its nuclear force under NATO command (and nor did Britain). Its nuclear force was strictly intended to secure the survival of France, and thus France (like Britain) refused any involvement of its nuclear force in superpower nuclear arms control talks. Yet it was these two leaders who would spearhead the allies' continued and robust support for the dual-track framework: no gaps in the ladder of escalation; no Western disarmament without Eastern disarmament.

President Mitterrand made the decisive opening move in January 1983, when he addressed the Bundestag on the occasion of the twentieth anniversary of the Elysée Treaty. It was a dramatic moment, where a socialist president, whose country stood outside NATO's dual-track decision, and who domestically was committed to upheaval, made a plea for Atlantic cohesion and balanced power. Nuclear weapons defined this balance, Mitterrand argued. Balanced power had enabled détente and the Helsinki agreement, and balanced power now depended on the "solidarity" and "determination of Atlantic alliance members."[43] In other words, Europe and NATO needed West German conservative-liberal determination to prevail over socialist opposition. In a likely accurate assessment, Hubert Védrine, Mitterrand's diplomatic advisor (and later French foreign minister), wrote that in the wake of the speech, Helmut Schmidt was "bitterly satisfied": he had made the case for nuclear balance all along, only to have his own party, the SPD, turn on him.[44] Now in opposition, he could witness a French socialist (Mitterrand) team up with a German conservative (Kohl) in the search for balance.

Mitterrand's message carried "great weight" and marked a "turning point" in West Germany's political discussions, Genscher found. The message carried into the G7 summit in Williamsburg, in March 1983, where, as mentioned, Mitterrand struggled to separate global and shared security interests from NATO policy. France proved more restrictive than West Germany, and it did not want Japan and NATO to develop institutional ties, which West Germany supported.[45] Still, and as Genscher underscores, the fact that France, as well as Japan, agreed to give the G7 a security dimension, and to turn it to Soviet missile deployments, was another great service to the dual-track framework: no détente without balanced power.[46]

NATO thus turned to balancing power—that is, implementing the dual-track deployments. There had been arms talks in Geneva on both intermediate and strategic forces, but these had gone nowhere. When NATO started deploying its dual-track missiles, the Soviet Union simply slammed the door shut on the Geneva talks, hoping to turn up the heat on NATO. If there was a high point in the renewed Cold War, in the tense East–West relationship that developed after the failure of détente, this was it. Late 1983 and most of 1984 were marked by high tension and low hope. It was another test for embattled European governments committed to dual-track deployments, but confronted by public discontent.

The allies thus searched for an initiative to "burnish NATO's credentials as a champion of dialogue."[47] It was defined by and then handed to the Belgian foreign minister, Leo Tindemans, who, in the spirit of his fellow countryman, Pierre Harmel, agreed to undertake "a thorough appraisal of East–West relations with a view to achieving a more constructive East–West dialogue." Tindemans stepped up as a service to the alliance, but also for reasons of domestic politics. This was entirely like Harmel, who had needed a balanced framework to render his country hospitable to NATO's headquarters as it sought to move from Paris to Brussels. For Tindemans, the balanced framework was needed to advance Belgium's difficult politics on the dual-track decision.

NATO's study ran from December 1983 to May 1984, when it resulted in the alliance's Washington Statement on East–West Relations. This essentially reaffirmed the Harmel approach, though it did replace "détente"—a concept pregnant with past failures—with "dialogue."[48] NATO's recipe was now defense and dialogue, which amounted to slightly newer wine in old bottles. This was simple enough, but NATO's commitment to dialogue was about to be tested. The Soviet leaders realized through 1984 that NATO was sticking to its dual-track guns, and that President Reagan might well win the presidential elections in November 1984. They thus had to deal with both. A thaw began, albeit very carefully. By early 1985, shortly before Soviet leader Konstantin Chernenko passed away and Mikhail Gorbachev took command, the two superpower foreign ministers, George Shultz and Andrei Gromyko, agreed to resume arms talks, though now with double linkage: intermediate missile talks should be linked to strategic arms reduction talks, and these talks should be linked to talks on weapons in space (also known as Star Wars) and thus Reagan's SDI vision (which the Soviet Union feared would become a reality). These linkages were inherently unwieldy—much too complicated to allow for a deal, but it was a way to get negotiations started.[49]

The big-umbrella approach—pulling everything under one cover—made for a dynamic East–West dialogue and test of ideas through 1985 and into 1986. Free-floating ideas might seem to define creative diplomatic opportunities, but they are in fact often disconcerting because of the ample space they leave for propaganda—the parading of new ideas that have not been subject to consultation. This was NATO's reality when confronted with Soviet leader Mikhail Gorbachev's whirlwind of proposals to, variously, greatly reduce the number of nuclear weapons, eliminate all of them in phases, shelve all weapons in outer space (SDI), and reduce conventional forces.[50] Some of it was real political intent, some just propaganda, and part of it was Gorbachev's way of telling his Soviet constituencies that "times they are a-changin'."

NATO weathered the avalanche of ideas by consistently supporting arms initiatives that were concrete, verifiable, and balanced. All of it had to be conducted with respect to NATO's strategy of flexible and controlled nuclear responses. There could be no gap on the ladder of escalation, and balance remained a precondition for dialogue (détente). Lord Carrington, NATO secretary general (1984–88), summed it up eloquently in his memoirs. Arms control must be undertaken with "caution." Stability was king. Every step of the way one must balance political desirability with the "continuing requirements of deterrence." Negotiators must understand strength and balance at all force levels. Political chiefs must understand enough of it to resist the temptation to gamble.[51]

The October 11–12, 1986, summit in Reykjavik, Iceland, between President Reagan and Soviet leader Gorbachev broke this mold entirely. They were prophets of change who, for a brief moment, had a meeting of minds. Perhaps they did not gamble, but they came close. The two leaders agreed to eliminate all intercontinental ballistic missiles (the backbone of strategic nuclear forces)—an agenda of which the allies had been informed beforehand. They also agreed to eliminate all intermediate-range nuclear forces—of which allies were not aware. The superpowers thus proposed to leap into a deal that, by and large, would confine the nuclear standoff to Europe. In the end, though, the two leaders walked away empty-handed. The deal-breaker was the SDI—Reagan's vision of a shift from deterrence to defense. Gorbachev wanted SDI to be restricted to lab tests; Reagan wanted to be able to test systems in space. Reagan offered to never deploy SDI if the Soviet Union eliminated its ballistic missiles; but it was not an offer Gorbachev could trust.

Prophecy restrained

The Reykjavik summit had defined a grand ambition to leap into a future of strategic defense, rather than offense, and with far fewer nuclear weapons. It was truly aspirational. It also failed. The two superpower leaders were visibly downbeat when they walked out to confront the press, with each arguing that a historic opportunity had been missed because of his counterpart's ultimate timidity. They then "withdrew" to their capitals to "shape perceptions of what happened" and "to await the world's verdict."[52]

"In truth, the world was not ready for Ronald Reagan's boldness," Secretary of State George Shultz later wrote, in his own effort to shape perceptions. But, he continued, the summit had still been an achievement. It had allowed Reagan to set out a compelling vision, and it had, with striking success, brought out Soviet positions that had not previously been clear. Post-summit diplomacy was able to move forward, to separate issues previously pulled under one umbrella, and to bring these issues to successful conclusions. Shultz flew to NATO headquarters to brief his allies on these summit outcomes; and allegedly "their reaction was positive."[53]

However, this was not the full story. Referring to the small wooden Hofdi (Höfði) House in which the summit took place, a French official remarked, "You should not allow two men to negotiate on a Saturday night in a haunted house." He specifically reacted to what Shultz had explained at NATO headquarters: namely, that the almost-deal on strategic zero would have to involve both France's and Britain's nuclear weapons. The leaders of those two countries were not amused. More broadly, the allies were struck by the unexpected superpower embrace of intermediate zero—the dual-track zero that Haig had resisted, and which the allies wanted to remain a "zero plus." General Bernard Rogers, US supreme allied commander for Europe, reportedly angrily expressed his misgivings to Secretary of Defense Caspar Weinberger. Other allied leaders and officials worried at the ease with which the alliance leader had swept away the logic of their flexible response strategy—to which they had committed, against popular opinion and in the name of alliance solidarity. To them, Reagan's boldness put at risk both NATO strategic cohesion and the political fortunes of NATO governments.[54]

Reagan's aspiration was causing rifts within the alliance. At heart, these were about the extent to which the president's aspiration was collective or national. Reagan argued that his proposals and thinking would reinforce the Western alliance as a whole. Fewer nuclear weapons, combined with improvements in conventional force maneuvers and deep strikes (captured in NATO's Follow-On Forces Attack doctrine of 1984) would leave the alliance in a better *warfighting condition* than before, the argument ran.[55] The counterargument, which echoed widely in Europe, was that Reagan's strategic outlook was by and large American.[56] NATO deterrence continued, in the view of most allies, to rest on the *escalatory power* of US nuclear weapons, not conventional warfighting or a futuristic strategic defense in space. The risk for President Reagan and his advisors was that, if they did not convince Europeans of their point of view, the allies might be tempted to go and look outside NATO for a security arrangement—and possibly even consider the idea of striking a deal of their own with the Soviet Union.[57]

Gorbachev cleverly played into this. In the spring of 1987, he proposed a big "zero," which would take out not only all intermediate-range missiles on both sides, but also short-range nuclear missiles. It had tremendous public appeal, but it would also leave a big hole in NATO's escalatory architecture. West Germany, as always, considering its frontline status, was in the eye of the storm. A weakened NATO architecture could enhance the risk of war confined to just the German space (East and West Germany). After all, the Soviet bloc remained superior in conventional numbers. Conversely, fewer nuclear weapons might be indicative of the true détente that had escaped both East and West in the 1970s. Perhaps it was worth betting on political change. West German Defense Minister Manfred Wörner was not a man for political betting. He wanted to retain escalatory coherence as much as possible. The big zero thus had to be limited. West German Foreign Minister Hans-Dietrich Genscher, by contrast, was ready to bet on change. He supported a big zero and had no clear ideas for restoring NATO deterrence: political change would carry the day. Chancellor Kohl sought to straddle these positions, while considering the interests of his allies. Allied and especially US patience was wearing thin when Chancellor Kohl finally agreed to a big zero, but with certain exemptions.[58]

The European allies then stepped outside NATO to emphasize their own view of things. It was a reaction to the US desire to move forward with a big zero, the deal-making of the Reykjavik summit, and the reigning US belief that everything would be okay because of the country's superior warfighting capabilities. On October 27, 1987, the allies issued their Hague Platform on European Security Interests. It was an odd document: although it was a Western European Union (WEU) document, the WEU had been dormant since it had facilitated West Germany's entry into NATO in 1955; it spoke of Europe, but was really about NATO; and it welcomed change, but sought above all to consolidate allied (nuclear) deterrence. It thus represented the escalatory school of thought. "Only the nuclear element … can confront the aggressor with an unacceptable risk," the WEU member states (European allies) argued. Fully in line with NATO orthodoxy, this involved support for a "substantial presence of US conventional and nuclear forces" in Europe. And, as agreed in NATO's 1974 Ottawa Declaration, and in a clear counter to Reagan and Shultz's thinking in Reykjavik, the independent nuclear forces of France and Britain "contribute to overall deterrence." Change was welcome, but it must be consistent with "the strategic unity of the Alliance."[59]

With all this, the allies were set to support an intermediate-range deal with Gorbachev and the Soviet Union. The deal—the Intermediate-Range Nuclear Forces (INF) treaty—dealt with land-based weapons with a range of between 500 and 5,500 km. This range defined the size of the big zero. Mikhail Gorbachev and Ronald Reagan signed the treaty in Washington in December 1987. With a stroke of the pen, they abolished no fewer than 2,611 land-based intermediate-range missiles and their nuclear warheads (1,752 Soviet and 859 American). The signatories could not choose to redeploy these weapons: the treaty demanded their destruction, and verification and inspection procedures were in place to ensure it. It was Gorbachev's first visit to the United States, and in fact the first visit by a Soviet leader to the United States for a full fourteen years. The INF treaty was remarkable, and it was in its own way a remarkable victory for NATO's 1979 dual-track decision to stand firm in the expectation of improved East–West dialogue.

The next challenge for the allies was the "strategic unity of the Alliance" in a theater where land-based weapons had a range of only up to 500km. How could flexible response defense and deterrence be upheld? West German opinion was swinging in the direction of entirely scrapping NATO's limited arsenal of small nuclear weapons (with a range of less than 500km). On this question, Chancellor Kohl began aligning with Foreign Minister Genscher. However, President Reagan wanted short-range nuclear modernization (to deter by warfighting capability), meaning the upgrading of older Lance missiles (with a range of up to 150km) to a capability closer to the 500km range. Britain, France, and the Netherlands likewise supported modernization, though to maintain nuclear deterrence by escalation. Through 1988, these leaders pushed for modernization, and Kohl and Genscher were in the eye of the storm. Genscher was particularly adamant in his opposition to modernization. He thought West Germany was wrongfully being subjected to a "loyalty test." He had been foreign minister since 1974, but the Lance modernization affair became "the most difficult period to date of my foreign ministry."[60] President Reagan—and from January 1989, President Bush—knew that, if pushed too hard, Genscher might switch horses and bring the SPD back to power. That would not only cancel Lance modernization, but might lead West

Germany to renounce nuclear weapons altogether. If that happened, US Congress could have been provoked to redeploy significant numbers of troops out of Europe, putting NATO at risk.[61]

Time made the difference, and time was not on Gorbachev's side. The Soviet leader ingeniously put forth limited disarmament proposals that exacerbated NATO's in-house problems; but his political pace and focus would increasingly be determined by domestic issues. In mid- to late 1988, in a radical attempt to recast his power base, Gorbachev terminated the communist monopoly on political power and took up the chairmanship of the national legislature. In 1990, he completed the shift away from communism by running for—and gaining—the presidency of the Soviet Union. This extraordinary shift in domestic power was ultimately in vain: the Soviet Union ceased to exist on December 31, 1991. But it was Gorbachev's strategy for political renewal and survival, and to pursue it, he needed a change of pace internationally. In December 1988, Gorbachev thus announced significant Warsaw Pact conventional force reductions. The initiative transformed the otherwise moribund MBFR talks into geographically broadened conventional arms talks. It also took the sting out of NATO's Lance modernization disagreement. After a winter of rough diplomacy, the Lance modernizers relented.[62] Finally, on May 30, 1989, NATO allies agreed to simply defer the issue—to kick the can down the road. "We can now exploit fully the potential of arms control as an agent of change," they declared.[63] A treaty on Conventional Armed Forces in Europe (CFE) followed in November 1990. By then, the rationale for returning to the issue of Lance modernization had evaporated, along with the Cold War.

The day after NATO's summit of May 30, 1989, held in Brussels, President Bush traveled to Mainz, West Germany. There, he spoke of aspiration. Of how NATO had wanted the human spirit to blossom, and of how the chill of the Cold War had prevented it from doing so. "But the passion for freedom cannot be denied forever. The world has waited long enough," Bush stated. "The time is right. Let Europe be whole and free." This had been NATO's original aspiration back in

1949; and though much had changed in the intervening four decades, NATO's centrality had not. A Europe whole and free, Bush declared, is now "the new mission of NATO."[64]

The late 1980s thus defined a point where NATO could relocate its exceptional condition: a collective defense alliance committed to general security principles. By performing collective defense, the primary task of the Harmel doctrine, NATO could open the door to continental reconciliation, the doctrine's secondary task. This is where NATO had begun, but then lost its way. The decline of Atlanticism, the uneasy relationship between European integration and transatlantic cooperation, the competing high hopes of détente, President Reagan's bold but ill-coordinated vision of a world transformed, and European allies' efforts to tie the president to the fundamentals of NATO defense and dialogue—all this had subjected NATO's original aspiration of freedom to the wear and tear of everyday alliance politics. President Reagan was prophetic, envisaging a world free of nuclear weapons and free of communist repression, which set him apart from European leaders. Reagan was open to great and sudden change; Thatcher, Mitterrand, Kohl, and colleagues preferred piecemeal change. Reagan sought to overcome deterrence and the strategic balance; European leaders sought to manage it.

Like Reagan, Lech Wałęsa would discover that prophecy wears. By 1989, Wałęsa had gained international stature and was in negotiations with a failed communist regime to secure a stable transition to democracy. But aggressive young workers—like the Wałęsa of his youth—challenged him with audacious and impatient aspirations.[65] They did not want to wait. Could Wałęsa, in the interests of stability and order, make them? In this regard, the predicaments facing Wałęsa and NATO were now similar. As the energy of continental change was being unleashed, NATO had to reconcile a vision of freedom—of a continent whole and free—with geopolitical interests and managed change. The decline of the Soviet Union and its Warsaw Pact made freedom possible, but it also created high hopes and a potential for radical reaction. NATO allies needed to set a compass and guide events; but to do so, they first had to clarify NATO's own worn and torn aspiration of continental cooperation.

PART III

Return of Great Ambition: How Nato Grew Big and Soft, 1989–2011

7

NATO's Search for New Atlanticism beyond the Cold War

In May 1989, Greek Prime Minister Papandreou traveled to Brussels to celebrate the alliance's fortieth anniversary, accompanied by his new companion and, to his embarrassment, also by his estranged wife, who wanted to lend her name and voice to critique of NATO at a so-called shadow NATO summit. Perhaps to his relief, Papandreou was far from the only beleaguered NATO leader. Italian Prime Minister Ciriaco De Mita and Foreign Minister Giulio Andreotti traveled together, but were at each other's throats. Within two months, Andreotti had succeeded De Mita. Chancellor Kohl and Foreign Minister Genscher were likewise caught up in domestic rivalry and symbolically stayed at separate hotels in Brussels.[1] British Prime Minister Margaret Thatcher was simply short on trust. She did not trust Britain's continental partners on the issue of nuclear modernization. Nor did she trust her foreign secretary, Geoffrey Howe, and the two traveled separately to Brussels. Within two months, Thatcher had sacked Howe. His "clarity of purpose and analysis had dimmed," Thatcher later wrote.[2] His "romantic longing for Britain to become part of some grandiose European consensus," his "misty Europeanism," would "bring us all no end of trouble."[3]

Despite all these difficulties, at their May 1989 meeting the NATO leaders succeeded in setting a new and forward-looking policy on NATO nuclear modernization and East–West dialogue and disarmament. But NATO's leaders were about to find that this agenda of controlled change would be overwhelmed by political upheaval in the Eastern bloc. Great risks were involved. If the Soviet Union descended into angry revisionism or simply political chaos, nuclear conflict could follow. Moreover, the implosion of East Germany brought into focus the issue of German unification. Any German decision to seek unity on terms that implied neutrality or looser alliance bonds could return Europe to old questions of balanced power. If that happened, the United States might recast entirely the transatlantic bargain.

But that did not happen. Instead, Germany united inside NATO and the allies committed to New Atlanticism. They also offered NATO as a vehicle for continental reconciliation. It was not the tired collective of leaders that drove this process: it was US President Bush and German Chancellor Kohl. Bush and Kohl saw a way to integrate the two principles of collective defense and general security. In their view, New Atlanticism started with the defense of the Atlantic community, but also offered everyone a place within a continental order. Bush and Kohl's starting point, NATO, was Truman's. But their aspiration for continental reconciliation was Rooseveltian in ambition. Their vision was audacious, made by a few but intended for the many. As such, and to borrow from Thatcher, it had a "misty" quality to it. Still, by July 1990, it had become NATO's collective aspiration for post-Cold War order. By December 31, 1991, when the Soviet Union folded and disappeared, it had become the defining vision for a new Europe.

NATO tries to catch up

The NATO allies had not entered 1989 in a stellar condition. Soviet leader Mikhail Gorbachev had, with skill, captured the public imagination in Western countries. In December 1988, he had boldly announced large and unilateral Soviet conventional force reductions. In January 1989, he extended the dynamic to nuclear levels, as he announced the withdrawal of two dozen short-range missile launchers and proposed coordinated nuclear reductions. NATO, committed to short-range nuclear modernization, looked sluggish and indecisive.

Nuclear modernization was such a sore issue for the allies because NATO needed nuclear weapons to uphold a military balance, the Soviet bloc being superior in terms of conventional forces. By the spring of 1989, NATO's agreement to modernize its small nuclear weapons was unraveling. Chancellor Kohl was under considerable domestic pressure to set modernization aside in favor of disarmament (force reductions), and he seemed ready to buckle. Meanwhile, US Congress was tempted to demand iron-clad deployment commitments from the NATO allies before funding nuclear modernization.[4] To pre-empt political damage, NATO defense ministers reached agreement on April 20, 1989, to postpone a modernization decision until after 1990. However, less than a day later, "Bonn dropped a bombshell": the Kohl–Genscher coalition voted to support immediate—and thus without delay, which was not NATO's position—East–West negotiations on short-range nuclear reductions. It was an attempt at "manipulation," thought Brent Scowcroft, Bush's security advisor. President Bush was annoyed: "I thought it an example of how *not* to conduct alliance business."[5]

President Bush needed to restore US leadership, and NATO's May 1989 summit was the occasion to do so.[6] The key NATO leader Bush needed to move was Prime Minister Margaret Thatcher, an adamant critic of sacrificing defense for a promise of disarmament. As leader of an independent nuclear power, she believed in modernized and effective nuclear deterrence. Nor was she in favor of reducing NATO aircraft, so central to NATO's nuclear mission. France's President Mitterrand shared these concerns, but was less centrally placed in NATO's nuclear deliberations, given France's 1966 departure from the integrated command. In the end, they both supported Bush's policy thinking, which guided the May summit. But Thatcher's support was not granted easily. She "frostily" received US envoys Robert Gates and Lawrence Eagleburger, dispatched to London to explain the policy (President Bush would later write how he "never found she warmed to humor").[7] In contrast, Helmut Kohl was receptive to Bush's policy: Gates and Eagleburger met with Kohl and his national security team on the patio of Kohl's official residence overlooking the Rhine. Enthusiasm prevailed on several fronts. "There was a plate of cakes on the table," Robert Gates recalled, "and Kohl devoured nearly the entire thing—challenged only by Eagleburger."[8]

NATO's new policy, adopted in May 1989, was to demand equality at lower levels of armament ("equal ceilings").[9] In essence, the alliance offered to forgo its nuclear modernization, if the Soviet Union would agree to equal conventional force ceilings. By implication, the Soviet Union would have to make the biggest conventional force reductions.[10] This looked skewed, but the purpose was to enable NATO concessions. For one, NATO offered to introduce equal cuts (15 percent) to all types of military aircraft. The Soviet Union had long demanded the inclusion of aircraft in disarmament talks, but NATO had resisted on grounds of their importance to NATO strategy. NATO also offered to suspend its nuclear modernization program for its tactical level Lance missiles for three years, until 1992. And as a final arrow in NATO's quiver, it suggested the two sides pick up the pace of negotiations. In fact, it challenged the Soviet Union and its allies to "join us in accelerating efforts to sign and implement an agreement."[11]

The 1989 NATO summit successfully reconfigured the alliance's defense-disarmament policy and gave the organization renewed political momentum. It was also an important moment of US–German alignment. President Bush began to see West Germany as a partner in leadership. On his trip to West Germany following the summit, he spoke in Mainz of a "Europe whole and free," as we saw in Chapter 6. Jim Baker, US secretary of state, established a close relationship with Hans-Dietrich Genscher.[12] A political axis was forming, and it would come to fruition especially in the spring of 1990 to enable German unification inside NATO.

Shifting sands

The US–German axis had formed around yesterday's issue—disarmament in dialogue with the Soviet Union—and would soon be faced with rapid and sometimes uncontrolled political change in Germany, Eastern Europe, and inside the Soviet Union. In the run-up to the May 1989 summit, a NATO expert group had advised the

North Atlantic Council that Mikhail Gorbachev remained a man of the future, though the sand was shifting. Regionalism and nationalism, it noted, was robbing the political center, Moscow, of power, and Gorbachev's best bet was to move into "the position of arbiter."[13] The sands were indeed shifting. The day prior to the report's submission, May 2, 1989, Hungary began to dismantle its barbed-wire fence on the border with Austria. Hungary still had border controls, and it still repatriated East German citizens seeking to flee. But the hour of major change was approaching, and its center of gravity would become East Germany—the one Eastern bloc country whose only justification was communist doctrine. Other Eastern bloc countries could turn to national history for their justification: East Germany had only an increasingly bankrupt doctrine to lean on.

Soviet leader Gorbachev visited West Germany in June 1989, some three weeks after the American president. Kohl and Gorbachev issued a Bonn Declaration that did not foresee unification—it was too early for that—but which spoke of jointly building a better future. It was an "exceptionally important document," in the words of Chancellor Kohl's spokesman, because it endorsed political change.[14] Only then did Gorbachev visit East Germany, in early October. He gloomily warned Erich Honecker and other East German leaders that "life punishes those who come too late."[15] Within two weeks, desperate colleagues had forced Honecker to resign; but his successor, Egon Krenz, a longtime wingman of Honecker's, predictably had no ability to steer events. Honecker fled to the Soviet Union, but was later returned to a unified Germany for trial; finally, suffering with a terminal illness, he went into exile in Chile. He died in May 1994, but did outlive his state: East Germany was politically terminated in October 1990.

As Honecker fell from power, in October and November 1989, events unfolded too fast for political control. Symbolic of this was the decision that prompted the fall of the Berlin Wall on the night of November 9, 1989. There was no decision to open the Wall. Instead, there was a mangled East German attempt to introduce new travel regulations. Günter Schabowski, a member of East Germany's inner core, the Politburo, fumbled a reply to a journalist regarding these regulations, indicating that anyone could now leave. And so, they did.

Soviet Foreign Minister Eduard Shevardnadze had two days previously refused to get involved in these travel regulations and, in effect, the threatened stability of the East German state. The Soviet masters were leaving the East German leadership to its fate, and its fate was to succumb.

Clearly, NATO's policy of "equal armament ceilings" was inadequate for the magnitude of events. The US–German axis would, in time, react and chart a new course. But the passions it would have to navigate were intense and politically explosive. French President Mitterrand had ideas of his own, as he hastily assembled the twelve European Communities leaders for an informal dinner in Paris on November 18.[16] At the dinner, British Prime Minister Thatcher made it clear that she saw no question of changing Europe's borders, in effect denying the prospect of German unification. Chancellor Kohl drily replied that ever since 1970 NATO had endorsed the ambition of German unification, to which Thatcher retorted that it "happened then because nobody believed it would ever take place." It did not bode well for the next steps of alliance cooperation.[17]

Contested ideas

For a moment it appeared that alliance cooperation might break down entirely over the issue of German unification. The specter of German *Alleingang*—of Germany going it alone—was evoked by Chancellor Kohl's ten-point program, which he presented on November 28, 1989.[18]

Kohl wanted to gain control of a situation in flux; but critically, he launched his program in grand solitude. The Kohl advisor Horst Teltschik was pleased: "We achieved our goal. The chancellor seized the leadership role in the German question."[19] But this was mostly true in relation to Kohl's closest competitor at home, Foreign Minister Genscher, the junior partner in the governing coalition. Internationally, Chancellor Kohl's seizure of leadership caused ripples. In the United States, President Bush, National Security Advisor Scowcroft and Secretary of State Baker all expressed their surprise and concern.[20] Kohl's program would soon be overtaken by events—he foresaw a long-term rapprochement of the two German states in a type of confederation—but that was not the point in late November. What mattered was the surprise and boldness of Kohl's maneuver and how it confronted Western leaders with a fork in the road.

On the one hand, they could allow for Germany's unification within a *new* continental collective security order. It would notably consist of a grand concert of power, where the United States, Britain, France, and the Soviet Union would cooperate to quell the historical fears that a unified Germany could evoke. All European governments would be included, but the major powers would have special responsibilities. This principled path resembled Franklin D. Roosevelt's vision of granting "policemen" a special status in a collective security organization. Soviet leader Gorbachev was drawn to this vision, and so were Genscher and other Western leaders.

On the other hand, they could build Europe based on its proven and *trusted foundations*, meaning maintaining NATO as a cornerstone of transatlantic cooperation. By pulling a united Germany into its midst, NATO would offer itself as the guarantor of continued community building. True, the community was Western, but NATO was purely defensive, adhered to the UN Charter, and could build dialogue and partnership with the former Warsaw Pact countries, including the Soviet Union (Russia from December 1991).[21] This principled path resembled the policy of President Truman, in that it placed collective defense (NATO) at the heart of order, while seeking to promote general security measures on top of this foundation.

President Bush and his national security team favored the second option, but it took them some time to flesh out their position. They did not fully align until the latter half of February 1990. By then, President Bush had been in office for more than a year. Did Team Bush in fact hesitate?[22] It certainly felt that President Reagan had been a bit too quick to declare an end to the Cold War, not fully considering all the geopolitical implications.[23] The Bush administration had also responded with timidity to the Chinese suppression of the Tiananmen Square protests in mid-1989, betting on longer-term relations with the Beijing government, rather than political change. As with the NATO arms control initiative of May 1989, Bush pursued policies that, under normal circumstances, would be prudent and statesmanlike, but that in 1989 all too easily seemed out of touch. Team Bush thus needed a forward-looking policy for a continent in transition. Eventually, it would chart the path for NATO's transformation, a legacy that rings to the present day. But, beginning in November, it would need about three months to define the parameters of its thinking.

Mikhail Gorbachev had long spoken of a common European home—a metaphor for a collective security organization to succeed NATO and the Warsaw Pact. In early December 1989, he sensed an opportunity to develop the point further, suggesting a revival of quadripartite meetings of the four Second World War victorious allied powers. The point was obviously to let these four powers somehow be the arbiters of German events. Not willing to deny the Soviet Union the formal right to call such a quadripartite meeting, the United States, Britain, and France agreed to hold one in Berlin on December 11. By then it had become clear that Gorbachev's drive for new thinking could provoke ill will among the NATO allies. At a NATO meeting on December 4, President Bush sought a compromise formula to cater both to Germany's hope for unification and to the worry of some allies that things were spinning out of control. The compromise—of endorsing political change, but with due regard for the role and responsibilities of the allied powers—provoked Giulio Andreotti (now Italian prime minister) to warn that self-determination could cause things to get out of hand. Chancellor Kohl responded furiously, but Thatcher leaned in to support Andreotti.[24] Days later, she would take her concerns into the European Council, where plans for European union were under way. "Twice we've beaten the Germans," she exclaimed, "and now here they are again."[25]

President Mitterrand of France was likewise concerned about shifting power, but he wanted a stronger Europe, not a stronger NATO. In mid-November, he told Gorbachev that France sought "to avoid any kind of disruption" and did not foresee the changing of borders (i.e., unification).[26] Three weeks later, Mitterrand told Gorbachev that the French position was to privilege European integration. "The Americans are not telling the complete truth, including

1. The US Navy destroyer USS *McDougal* transferring US President Franklin D. Roosevelt to the large and imposing Royal Navy battleship HMS *Prince of Wales* during the Atlantic Charter conference in Placentia Bay, August 1941. Roosevelt and British Prime Minister Winston Churchill agreed at the conference to a forward-looking Atlantic Charter. The Charter defined common war aims but also ensured that a future international order would be American, not British.

2. Leaders of Britain, the United States, and the Soviet Union at the July–August 1945 Potsdam conference. A few years later, British Foreign Secretary Ernest Bevin (back row, second from left) would be the first to voice the need for an Atlantic treaty.

3. President Harry S. Truman displays the North Atlantic Treaty. Senator Tom Connally, standing in the center, to the left of Secretary of State Dean Acheson, had in the spring of 1949 threatened to derail the defense pact on grounds of national sovereignty concerns. Acheson, however, averted the threat. Acheson later said of Connally that the senator was simply not a "smart cookie."

4. The Korean War of 1950 convinced allies of the need to add military muscle. US General Matthew Ridgway (right) came to NATO from Korea and assumed supreme command. Ridgway was a tough leader, cracking allied heads to acquire military force. General Eisenhower, who preceded Ridgway in the position, would later make Ridgway US Army chief of staff.

5. On the occasion of West Germany's entry into NATO: from right to left, John Foster Dulles, Anthony Eden, Konrad Adenauer, and Pierre Mendès-France. With the effort to secure West German rearmament via a European Defense Community failing, Eden masterminded the path to West Germany's NATO membership in 1955—a mere decade after the Second World War.

6. NATO in 1952 gained a secretary general to run its budding organization and to help advance political agreement. British Lord Hastings Ismay (left) founded the office (in 1952–57) and famously said that NATO's purpose was to keep the Americans in, the Germans down, and the Russians out. His successor, Paul-Henri Spaak (1957–61, right), sought to inspire a wide-ranging Atlantic Community but failed to bring allied rivals to agreement.

7. André de Staercke had an impressive run as Belgium's ambassador to NATO: a full twenty-six years (1950–76). He created NATO's motto—*Animus in consulendo liber*, "In consultation among free spirits"—along with Paul-Henri Spaak, glimpsed in the framed photograph behind Staercke.

8. West German Chancellor Konrad Adenauer defined a policy of strong Western engagement for Germany, implying that German unification could not happen at the expense of NATO. NATO allies remained concerned, though, that new German leaders might make a dash for German unity and fracture NATO. Whatever NATO did to stabilize the continent, it had to cater to the underlying German desire for change.

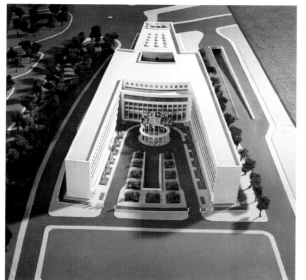

9. French President Charles de Gaulle asked NATO in 1966 to leave French territory, a decision following years of French frustrations with France's limited influence relative to the United States and Britain. France remained an ally, but NATO had to pack its bags. NATO staff thus had only a few short years to enjoy the new Paris headquarters at Porte Dauphine—a new building in the shape of an "A" (for alliance).

10. US Ambassador to NATO Harlan Cleveland (left), with US Secretary of Defense Robert McNamara, searched for new ways to enhance consultation inside NATO to satisfy allied demands for influence while retaining US-led nuclear strategy. Cleveland was posted to NATO in 1965 to kill the idea of a nuclear "Multilateral Force." In the end, NATO instead agreed to a "flexible response" strategy and a consultative Nuclear Planning Group.

11. With diverging allied designs for East–West stability and, in addition, public protests over the Vietnam War, NATO allies needed a new prescription for combining defense and dialogue. Belgian Foreign Minister Pierre Harmel (left) spearheaded a formula henceforth known as the Harmel doctrine. Harmel is seen in the photo with the later NATO Secretary General Joseph Luns (1971–84).

12. Manlio Brosio (left) would as NATO secretary general (1964–71) worry about the resilience of NATO consultations. His fear was that the great powers would tackle the major issues relating to nuclear weapons and East–West dialogue on their own, at the risk of eroding NATO solidarity. Brosio is seen here in dialogue with US Secretary of Defense Robert McNamara.

13. Secretary General Joseph Luns (left) receives US President Richard Nixon at NATO headquarters in 1974. To the right of Nixon is his national security advisor, Henry Kissinger. In the background is the "NATO Star," symbolizing the bond between Europe and North America. Nixon was not always sure of the bond, however. He disdained European left-of-center politics, at one point referring to West German leader and Social Democrat Willy Brandt as "that son-of-a-bitch." In the end, Brandt and Nixon coordinated policy effectively.

14. West German Chancellor Helmut Schmidt (right) strongly believed that the East–West nuclear balance had to be maintained at all levels, and he did not trust that President Jimmy Carter (left) would take into account European interests. Schmidt's call for more "Euro-missiles" was notably made at a speech in October 1977. At a dinner afterwards, Schmidt recalled, "I was much more clearer [sic] at that dinner, even somewhat insulting as regards the American hesitance."

15. NATO's 1979 decision to match Soviet nuclear missile deployments was designed to promote arms negotiations, but proved unpopular. It left allied governments with limited desire to invest in conventional forces. It was again up to a determined military leadership to insist on credible force options and to define new and smarter ways of deterring Soviet forces. Supreme Commander Bernard Rogers did just that.

16. At an economic summit in Williamsburg in 1983, French President François Mitterrand went against any reference to NATO in the context of global security concerns. US President Reagan and other leaders sought a coordinated global approach but had to bow to the French sense of geography. In the picture, Reagan and Mitterrand (seated center, facing the camera) are engaged in informal talks at the meeting.

17. West German Chancellor Helmut Kohl (center, looking to his right) took control of German unification in 1989–90. His decision to firmly anchor a unified Germany in NATO was crucial to the New Atlanticism of the 1990s. It also ensured that NATO enlargement eastwards would become a major issue. New Atlanticism rubbed against a competing vision of outreach to Russia championed by Kohl's Foreign Minister Hans-Dietrich Genscher (center, in overcoat: symbolically, here, Kohl turns his back on him).

18. A jovial moment between US President George H. Bush (center), Secretary of State James Baker (left), and NATO Secretary General Manfred Wörner (right). However, when in late 1989–early 1990 Baker backed Genscher's idea that a united Germany would not be a full and unconditional member of NATO, Wörner worked behind the scenes to counter him. President Bush did not support the idea either, and Baker dropped it.

19. A new NATO for a new Europe. British engineering troops serving in NATO's stabilization force in Bosnia-Herzegovina build a bridge to reopen the country. Russian troops also served in the NATO mission, and NATO and Russia in 1997, in their Founding Act, agreed that they were no longer adversaries.

20. The terrorist attacks of September 11, 2001 and the ensuing war on terror shook NATO in a fundamental way. President George W. Bush—here back in the White House on the day of the attacks—went into action without NATO, even after NATO activated its three-musketeer clause of collective defense. NATO was seemingly at risk of withering as a European peace project while the United States and selected partners got on with global order challenges.

21. NATO committed in 2002–3 to taking charge of a stabilization force in Afghanistan. It would become a massive and bloody operation, stretching NATO forces and diplomacy. In the photograph, Spanish and US troops prepare to board a Chinook helicopter at Bala Murghab Forward Operating Base, Badghis province, northwestern Afghanistan.

22. Russia and NATO were divided on the Kosovo intervention of 1999. However, the global fight against terrorism brought the parties together again—for a while. "All the old nonsense about only talking about the Balkans went away," NATO Secretary General George Robertson (right) recalled in an interview. Italian Prime Minister Silvio Berlusconi (left) hosted a summit in 2002 that resulted in the creation of a NATO–Russia Council and broad cooperation.

23. Dmitry Rogozin (center), Russia's NATO envoy in 2008–11, came to symbolize the fraught NATO–Russia relationship. Upon his arrival at NATO headquarters, he offered NATO Secretary General Jaap de Hoop Scheffer a large wooden ax. "I have come to bury the hatchet," Rogozin smilingly told a skeptical Scheffer. He is flanked here by Russian Foreign Minister Sergei Lavrov (left) and Scheffer (right).

24. Italian President Giorgio Napolitano (right) kept his country close to NATO during the troubled Libya intervention of 2011. Napolitano was a communist by political persuasion but also a convinced Atlanticist. He kept three photographs on the desk in his office: one of his grandchildren, one of Queen Elizabeth, and one of himself with President Obama.

25. President Donald Trump (right) was a wrecking ball smashing into NATO's diplomacy, coming close in 2018 to pulling the United States out of the alliance. After that, allied leaders gave up on summitry with him. NATO Secretary General Jens Stoltenberg (left) garnered praise for his constant efforts to explain to Trump the merits of NATO. Here, the president appears decidedly unconvinced. To Stoltenberg's side is US Secretary of State Mike Pompeo.

26. US General Curtis Scaparrotti (right) was struck by NATO's lack of consensus on Russia and the absence of a unified military strategy when he became supreme allied commander in 2016. In cooperation with British Air Chief Marshal Stuart Peach (left) and other allied chiefs of staff, Scaparrotti drove the creation of a new NATO military strategy worth its name.

27. In August 2021, Afghanistan's Taliban kicked out the remaining international forces propping up the country's government. In a chaotic exit and a clear defeat, NATO folded its training mission. Learning lessons and rethinking NATO crisis management policy both remain a headache.

28. Russia's brutal attack on Ukraine in February 2022 shifted the parameters of NATO diplomacy. NATO allies had reacted timidly to Russia's 2014 seizure of Crimea but now mobilized in Ukraine's support. Here, Ukrainian President Volodymyr Zelenskyy speaks to allied leaders—from the left, Spanish Prime Minister Pedro Sánchez, Turkish President Recep Erdoğan, UK Prime Minister Boris Johnson, US President Joe Biden, and NATO Secretary General Jens Stoltenberg. However, two years into the war, allied leaders had yet to define a path to NATO membership for Ukraine.

29. NATO leaders do not want the alliance to be directly involved in the war in Ukraine, but they do want NATO to be a strong bulwark against further Russian expansion. Troops must be able to move eastwards—here, French troops debark in Romania. And friends can join the alliance—with Finland and soon Sweden bringing the alliance up to a full thirty-two members. NATO was founded in 1949 by twelve allies. No nation has quit the alliance.

on the German issue," he offered.[27] Mitterrand thus set about a search for a design that would favor Western European integration, while offering hope for Eastern Europe. His thinking creatively drew on French and European history, but it was also very much his thinking: it surprised both his close advisors and, more alarmingly, France's close allies.[28] Mitterrand presented his thinking, a grand design for a European confederation, in his New Year's Eve speech on December 31, 1989. For a moment, his idea aligned with both Gorbachev's search for a collective security blueprint and Thatcher's skepticism about German unification and leadership. But Mitterrand, like Thatcher, would find that the failure to fully grasp the American and German desire for a unified Germany inside a revitalized NATO in the end meant his political marginalization.[29]

A shaky start to New Atlanticism

As events unfolded, US Secretary of State James Baker would come to symbolize the ambiguity of US policy in late 1989 and early 1990. He was present at the creation of "New Atlanticism"—a term chosen by his staff in preparation for President Bush's Malta summit with Mikhail Gorbachev on December 2–3, and then the NATO summit on December 4. New Atlanticism foresaw a unified Germany inside NATO and the European Communities, just as it foresaw the inter-locking of Western institutions (NATO, the European Communities) and the grand CSCE—the old intercontinental forum for East–West détente talks. This was option 2: a collective defense community at the core, overlaid with general security measures. Baker followed this script in December, speaking of "transforming" NATO for a new era of cooperation. NATO would no longer primarily be a military bulwark, Baker stated, but "an appealing model of international relations"—a vision of cooperation, open borders, and reconciliation.[30]

The ambiguity in the American position stemmed from the dual desires to support Chancellor Kohl and to consolidate Gorbachev's reforms. President Bush would outwardly avoid any sign of triumphalism, catering to Gorbachev, but inwardly investing in Kohl. "I don't want to give you a headline," Bush retorted to a journalist probing the president's timid appearance after the Malta summit with Gorbachev.[31] He then flew to Brussels and met with Kohl ahead of the December 4 NATO meeting. That evening, in a private setting, he gave Kohl "a green light" to move ahead on unification.[32] But outwardly, Team USA continued to lend a hand to Gorbachev. James Baker thus participated in the Berlin quadripartite meeting on December 11. He made his pitch for option 2, but the very nature of the quadripartite meeting—reserved only for the four allied powers— played to Gorbachev's favored option 1. In addition, after the meeting, Baker held an unannounced meeting with East German premier Hans Modrow, which could be interpreted as an effort to slow Kohl down. Baker would subsequently write a letter of apology to Kohl.[33]

The ambiguity continued into January and February 1990. President Bush's State of the Union address of January 31 contained no direct reference to German unification, but instead carried a bold proposal for further conventional force reductions in Europe.[34] The allies had been consulted on the proposal, naturally, but Bush clearly focused on superpower relations. He wanted both to support Gorbachev and to encourage further Soviet reforms. This superpower sensibility was a cue for Secretary Baker, as he prepared to meet with Gorbachev in Moscow on February 9 for what would be a much-noted, some might say notorious, meeting.

But first, between Bush's State of the Union address and his Moscow meeting, Baker met with German Foreign Minister Genscher, who had come to Washington to explain a speech he had made on January 31 in parallel with President Bush's address. "What NATO must do," Genscher had ventured, "is state unequivocally that whatever happens in the Warsaw Pact there will be no expansion of NATO territory eastward." NATO could remain as an alliance, Genscher signaled, but the future belonged to the intercontinental and inclusive CSCE. In short, Genscher was aligning his country with option 1.

At his meeting with Gorbachev, Baker would famously (or notoriously) pick up Genscher's formulation on the limits to NATO expansion. He suggested to Gorbachev that if the Soviet leader permitted German unification to go forward and allowed for continued German membership of NATO, then NATO's jurisdiction would not move eastward. "Not one inch," he offered. And the offer included the new German territories of the former GDR. The two statesmen parted with the understanding that any expansion of the "zone of NATO" was unacceptable.[35] But neither the offer nor the mutual understanding was put in writing, leaving it open to dispute how solid the Soviet–American understanding was, and whether it applied simply to German territory or in fact to all of Eastern Europe.[36]

The next day, February 10, as Baker departed, Kohl appeared in Moscow. Meeting with Kohl, Gorbachev now gave his green light to German unification. It was a major breakthrough for the Kohl team. With Gorbachev's concession, unification was sure to become a political reality. The team was "inwardly jubilant," even as it outwardly sought to keep a lid on the enthusiasm.[37] On the question of what German unification would mean for NATO, Kohl had some scope for maneuver, and the United States had created it. Baker made sure to have notes from his meeting with Gorbachev forwarded to Kohl; but the two did not actually meet on the tarmac in Moscow—as both wanted to avoid any hint of collusion on Gorbachev's home turf. But they thus also missed an opportunity to coordinate. Kohl could have informed Baker that he had received a note the day before from President Bush, informing him of a revised US position: namely, that at best the former GDR territory could gain a "special military status" in a transition period. After that period, which would allow Soviet troops time to leave in an orderly fashion, the whole of Germany would have to become NATO territory. An almost freak coincidence of schedules—Baker's departure from Moscow and Kohl's arrival— thus made it possible for Kohl to hold two US policy positions in his hand. Baker was brought up to speed on the president's thinking just hours after his Moscow departure, in Sofia, Bulgaria; but by then the damage had been done. Kohl had a choice, and he took the option that best catered to Gorbachev's sensibilities, namely Baker's. He was then quick to pocket Gorbachev's green light to unification at an impromptu press conference in Moscow.

The US course correction communicated by Bush had formed in Washington as the consequences of Genscher's visit and thinking settled in. NATO Secretary General Manfred Wörner had become an outspoken behind-the-scenes critic of Genscher's vision. In Wörner's view, it was nonsensical to offer NATO protection for only half a country. If a united Germany was in, then the NATO guarantee had to apply to the whole of the territory. The inverse—an incomplete NATO assurance—would limit German sovereignty and corrode NATO. The same point of view was forming in Washington, where Wörner made the rounds. As this unfolded, Baker was already on his lengthy European tour. He carried with him the old view, while the Bush team was forming a new one.

Once both Baker and Kohl had been in Moscow, the US position clarified and would not again waver. Henceforth, the United States insisted that a united Germany had the right to be free to choose NATO membership, and that—beyond a transitional period—membership must be without reservations. However, in late 1989 and early 1990, Baker and Kohl had, in their own ways, contributed to an unclear and incomplete Western position on German unification and NATO's future.[38] Analysts agree that Baker's "not one inch" idea did not amount to a promise or a deal that Soviet leaders could pocket; but they do disagree about its implications. Did it unduly raise Soviet expectations? Was it a mistake to do so?[39] Baker never conceded a mistake, and his memoirs skirt around the issue.[40] As a skilled lawyer, he soon walked back his message by clarifying its implications—how "not one inch" in fact referred not to NATO enlargement, but to the stationing of NATO troops on former GDR soil. Robert Gates, deputy national security advisor, put a positive spin on the affair: Baker's "reassurances led Gorbachev further toward accepting a unified Germany without giving him a pretext to say no."[41] Gates' boss, Brent Scowcroft, was more scathing—not because he felt that Baker had given Gorbachev a deal, but because he had lacked sufficient foresight to appreciate that, by going with Genscher's formulation, he had created problems for NATO.[42]

Meanwhile, the Soviet side was in such disarray that Western leaders had time to recover. Gorbachev and his foreign minister, Shevardnadze, did not trust the old Soviet troop of German experts: they may have been real experts on German affairs, but they were also die-hard communists. Gorbachev and Shevardnadze sidelined these experts in their search for renewal and room for maneuver. And all along they were confronted daily with an avalanche of problems, most of which were domestic in character. The sum of it was a severely limited leadership capacity. As Gorbachev failed to get the "not one inch" offer in writing, the ground slipped under option 1. It enabled a determined drive to establish the New Atlanticism of option 2.

American–German alignment

In the end, NATO would, in July, promise both alliance continuity and political transformation. To get there—to get from the Baker–Kohl meetings in Moscow in February to the alliance summit in July—President Bush and Chancellor Kohl drove the train. They first established their own alignment, next persuaded Gorbachev, and then finally persuaded the allies. The end result was an alliance commitment to regenerated cooperation, or New Atlanticism, but it came about essentially because of an American–German alignment at the highest level.

Political control by the chiefs became abundantly clear during a planned foreign ministerial meeting in Ottawa, Canada, on February 11–13, which was intended to advance East–West agreement on surveillance flights ("open skies"). The meeting would endorse a formula ("2+4"), whereby the four allied powers agreed with the two Germanies on a diplomatic format for unification talks. The formula of "2+4" granted primary responsibility to the two Germanies—because "2" came first. However, the "4" was an acknowledgment of the role and responsibilities of the four allied powers. It was a nod to the quadripartite format that figured so prominently in Gorbachev's option 1 thinking. But this nod might also be viewed as an opening that proponents of option 1—Gorbachev, Genscher, and others—could exploit to sidetrack option 2, meaning NATO. This became a concern among Bush's advisors, and so they had the president intervene, in effect to keep the foreign ministers—Genscher and Baker—on a tight leash.

In an odd diplomatic maneuver, as they were about to sign the 2+4 deal, Baker informed Genscher that Bush was unsure of Kohl's commitment to the deal. Awkwardly, they sat together in a room waiting for a green light from Kohl, who was on the phone with Bush. "It was a new experience to me," Genscher later wrote, and "it was to remain the only one of its kind."[43] Genscher pretended not to be insulted, but the slight was difficult to ignore. And Genscher would lash out. NATO foreign ministers were present in Ottawa for the "open skies" agreement, but most of them were ill-informed of the 2+4 deal.[44] When they gathered in NATO format for a brief introduction to 2+4, Genscher struck. The victims were the Italian and Dutch foreign ministers, who dared to suggest that German unification had external implications that concerned all NATO members, not simply the 2+4 countries. Genscher pointedly and dramatically asked his NATO colleagues, "Are you among the Four Powers responsible for Germany? Are you one of the two German states? You are neither."[45]

Genscher's denigration of his NATO colleagues would reverberate at a Bush–Kohl meeting in Camp David on February 24, 1990. President Bush primarily used this meeting to get Chancellor Kohl fully on board the NATO policy. "Full German membership is linked to our ability to sustain US troops in Europe," Bush made clear. "You must understand that."[46] Kohl offered his assurances. Next, it was important to assuage other alliance leaders. Britain's Margaret Thatcher feared "the ghosts of the past," but would be reassured by Germany's NATO membership: "we must bend over backwards to consult" her, Bush affirmed. And Germany had to be completely on board, he continued. "I hate to think of another France in NATO."

Moreover, it was important to slow-walk the 2+4 talks, Bush said to Kohl: "we don't want the Soviets to use this mechanism as an instrument to force you to create the Germany they might want." And finally, there was Genscher, who remarkably had not been invited to Camp David (his US counterpart, Baker, was present). Genscher "offended Italy, and some of the other guys" at the NATO meeting, Bush stated. Kohl acknowledged this. "I wasn't in Ottawa, but I had to take some of the consequences of Genscher's act. And I didn't like it." He attributed Genscher's behavior to domestic politics, where "everyone is confused but me." He then offered to stand firm with President Bush on the unified-Germany-in-NATO policy, singling out several allies of concern: Italy, France, Denmark, Norway, the Netherlands, and

Britain.[47] By the end of their time together, the two leaders had had a meeting of minds and had agreed on a course of action.

Persuasion

President Bush phoned Mikhail Gorbachev to inform him of the principal Camp David decisions, including, naturally, the decision that a united Germany should become a full NATO member. At this point the idea of the territory of East Germany somehow not being covered by NATO—the "not one inch" idea—had been clearly dispelled.[48] But Gorbachev still had leverage. There were 400,000 Soviet troops stationed in East Germany, and the Soviet Union remained a formidable nuclear power. Among Gorbachev's options were equivalence in troop drawdown, meaning he could insist that US forces would have to leave Europe, as Soviet forces left Eastern Europe. He could insist on neutrality guarantees for the whole of Eastern Europe, thereby favoring an all-European order built on a continued East–West distinction. In short, he could still make moves to derail option 2 and promote option 1. In the phone conversation, Gorbachev did not commit one way or the other. Therefore, to succeed with New Atlanticism, President Bush had work to do. Gorbachev needed additional persuasion, and so did recalcitrant allies.

Following extensive consultations with the allies, in early May Bush called for a July NATO summit. He placed this summit in the context of "a new Age of Freedom," calling on NATO to conduct a "wideranging NATO strategy review for the transformed Europe of the 1990s."[49] And he defined the agenda of change in broad brushstrokes: NATO's political dimension should be upgraded, its conventional and nuclear force dimensions reduced, and its contribution to all-European reconciliation enhanced.

Secretary Baker was scheduled to go to Moscow in mid-May, and Gorbachev was due to visit Bush in Washington at the end of the month. Ahead of these meetings, Bush and Kohl engaged in another round of confidential deliberations—this time with both Baker and Genscher present. They confirmed their exceptional spirit of cooperation and agreed that if Gorbachev resisted German unification in NATO, they should appeal to the Helsinki principle (embodied in the CSCE) that all sovereign nations have a right to choose their alliance membership.[50] This approach would prove decisive at the Bush–Gorbachev Washington meeting.

In Moscow, on May 16–19, Baker offered Gorbachev both political and military assurances, but Gorbachev had soured. His stated opposition to full NATO membership for a unified Germany had security advisor Scowcroft wonder whether he meant it, or merely was channeling conservative unhappiness.[51] The Washington summit on May 31 would demonstrate that it was mostly the latter. In Washington, Bush pulled Gorbachev away from his suggestion that a unified Germany could become a member of both NATO and the Warsaw Pact. Bush then highlighted the Helsinki principle of sovereign choice, and suggested that a unified Germany should be able to choose for itself. Gorbachev shrugged his shoulders and said, "yes, that is correct."

With Gorbachev's shrug and almost offhand response, New Atlanticism gained a critical boost: Bush knew that Kohl's Germany would choose NATO, not neutrality or some other option. So did some of Gorbachev's advisors—including his security advisor Sergey Akhromeyev and German expert Valentin Falin—who "squirmed in their seats" and interrupted their boss to gain speaking time, before being finally shut down by Gorbachev. It was an extraordinary display of internal dissent during a presidential encounter. "An amazing performance," Bush recalled.[52]

New Atlanticism next depended on President Bush persuading his NATO colleagues to revamp the alliance for the "Age of Freedom." He decided the task was too important to leave to professional diplomats (provoking the fury of foreign ministries).[53] He pulled negotiations to the top level—heads of state and government, though also foreign ministers—and established special channels to the most important of them: German Chancellor Kohl, British Prime Minister Thatcher, Italian Prime Minister Andreotti, French President Mitterrand, and then also NATO Secretary General Wörner. Wörner, Kohl, and Andreotti were enthusiastic about Bush's draft proposals for NATO's transformation; Thatcher and Mitterrand were reluctant on certain issues, but were within reach of compromise.

NATO's transformation

NATO's most crucial summit meeting since the founding of the alliance took place in the stately mansion Lancaster House, in the heart of London, on July 5–6. President Bush was in no rush to get there, as he wanted to squeeze in one more round of golf at his Maine retreat before departing. He arrived looking tired, and sneezed his way through Prime Minister Thatcher's opening statement.[54]

Thatcher had prepared differently, reading books, including Alan Clark's *Barbarossa*—the story of the German invasion of Russia in 1941. This time around, though, Thatcher did not single out Germany. Instead, in her opening remarks to the North Atlantic Council, she spoke of the book's message, that "bravery be turned to the purposes of peace and not to the battles of war."[55] In the ensuing debate among NATO's heads of state and government, the meaning of Thatcher's opening remarks became fully apparent. Bravery in the purpose of peace, she reminded her colleagues, meant a dedication to strong defense. We are entering a new era, Thatcher stressed, but we should not give the impression that there is no longer any danger.[56]

Thatcher had been the least enthusiastic leader consulted on Scowcroft's draft communiqué in June. At one point, she had asked in vain for an entirely new draft that kept NATO's flexible response strategy in place and that downplayed the idea of establishing liaisons with the former adversaries. Her reservations on nuclear issues were of greater import. US officials sought to establish a "last resort" role for nuclear weapons, which went against NATO's flexible response strategy. Thatcher was weary that decreased confidence in nuclear deterrence might embolden the proponents of disarmament and of "no first use" doctrine. She found it a deceptive doctrine "on which Soviet propaganda had always insisted,"[57] and it might easily play into the hands of those who advocated new collective security measures (option 1). In the end, NATO embraced "last resort," but not "no first use."

French President Mitterrand also had nuclear reservations. The idea that nuclear weapons should be a "last resort" was foreign to the French tradition of deterrence by massive retaliation. He reminded his NATO colleagues of this in London, but also admitted that this was a French issue (given France's non-participation in the integrated command). Mitterrand's main objective was instead to soften the contours of option 2: he supported NATO's New Atlanticism, but sought enhanced political space for both the CSCE and the emerging European Union. It would be wise and useful, Mitterrand cautioned, to bear in mind that "the Europeans" must prepare within the alliance for an enhanced role in their own defense.[58] Mitterrand was thus behind the London Declaration, but also signaled a political debate inside option 2: NATO could be a cornerstone, but the role for "Europe" would have to grow.

President Bush urged his colleagues to keep the geopolitical context front and center. NATO's summit had been timed to coincide with the opening of the Soviet Communist Party Congress, in the hope that NATO's professed transformation would bolster Gorbachev's domestic standing.[59] Soon, Bush continued, the Soviets and Eastern Europeans would make their decisions on German unity, the CFE treaty, and the planned CSCE summit. The NATO summit, therefore, "may be our last chance" to shape their thinking.[60] By now unsurprisingly, Chancellor Kohl aligned with President Bush. "We have a responsibility to continue to build on proven foundations," Kohl stated, effectively endorsing option 2, "and at the same time to promote the historic transformation with far-sightedness and creativity," meaning adding a layer of collective security dialogue and partnership with former adversaries.[61]

And so it was, the NATO leaders agreed to the "transformation" of their alliance. They asked their foreign ministers to iron out tricky issues in the evening, as they themselves dined at Buckingham Palace with Queen Elizabeth. The next day, on the final day of the summit, the leaders addressed only minor issues of language and emphasis.[62] The ensuing London Declaration states: "NATO must become an institution where Europeans, Canadians and Americans work together not only for the common defence, but to build new partnerships with all the nations of Europe."[63] Reforms then fell into the four categories identified by President Bush back in May:

- *Partnership with former adversaries*: leaders of the Soviet Union and Central and Eastern European countries were invited to address the North Atlantic Council, establish regular diplomatic liaisons with NATO, and intensify military contacts.

– *Conventional force posture:* NATO offered to turn from large-scale forward defense to scaled-back readiness. NATO forces would be fewer, more multinational, and mobile. All on the presumption that Soviet withdrawals from Eastern Europe would continue.

– *Nuclear force posture:* NATO offered to reduce the number of American weapons stationed in Europe and its reliance on nuclear weapons in its strategy. The flexible response strategy, which had endured since the 1960s, was thus singled out for significant modification.

– *Continental reconciliation:* NATO welcomed an enhanced role for the CSCE in promoting free societies, in addition to the CSCE role in securing conventional arms control agreements, notably on conventional forces in Europe. The CSCE should be institutionally developed, the allies agreed.

German unity

There could be no rest for the weary. Some of the leaders jetted straight from London to Houston, Texas, for a G7 meeting to discuss, among other things, aid to the Soviet Union. Chancellor Kohl in addition prepared for a final round of meetings with Gorbachev in Moscow and Stavropol. NATO's transformation commitment had indeed strengthened Gorbachev's hand at the Party Congress. The question now was how it would impact the final Kohl–Gorbachev talks on German unity.

The Moscow and Stavropol meetings led to agreements going beyond the "wildest expectations" of the German team.[64] Gorbachev agreed to full NATO membership of a unified Germany, raising only minor issues that were easily resolved: Germany should renounce weapons of mass destruction (thus, also nuclear weapons); Soviet troops would gain a transition period of four years to leave the former GDR; NATO's scope could only be extended to the former GDR once those troops were out; and non-German NATO troops would not be permanently stationed in the former GDR. They also agreed on a force ceiling of 370,000 troops for the new Germany, a measure to limit its military size and thus its potentially destabilizing impact on Europe's geopolitics.

Gorbachev's prominent advisor, Valentin Falin, who had been so upset in the Oval Office in May, had urged Gorbachev to extract concessions of a different magnitude during these final meetings with Kohl, and to refuse to accept unification within the state structure of the Federal Republic of Germany. Falin wanted East as well as West Germany diluted into a wholly new German state construct. He preferred to see this new state become neutral—ideally outside NATO, though the next best thing would be to severely delay full NATO membership for Germany.[65] However, time had run out on Falin and other hardliners. Gorbachev was betting on a special relationship with the new Germany, not its obstruction. Chancellor Kohl was perfectly open to this special relationship, but only within the parameters of agreed Western policy, the robustness of which Gorbachev probably underestimated.

The path to German unity from here was, by and large, unproblematic. For a moment, in August and early September, the allies worried that a deal with the Soviet Union would permanently exclude non-German troops from the territory of the former GDR.[66] But the concern flared and faded. NATO gained full rights to defend its members, and the 2+4 treaty was signed on September 12. With this treaty, the allied powers terminated their rights and responsibilities that dated back to the settlement following the Second World War, dissolving all quadripartite institutions and practices. The united Germany, which came into being on October 3, 1990, gained "full sovereignty over its internal and external affairs."[67]

NATO strategy and Europe's security architecture

As Germany united, the Soviet Union fell apart. The central political institutions of the country had seen a "rapid decline" in their prestige and authority, the group of experts advising the NAC concluded in November 1990.[68] This included the presidency and role of Mikhail

Gorbachev. The Soviet republics were increasingly unwilling to bow to Moscow's instructions, and some of them (including the Baltic republics) were clamoring for outright independence. The republic of Russia was fast becoming the major usurper of central authority. Its leader, Boris Yeltsin, a Gorbachev rival, had in fact become president of the Russian parliament while Gorbachev was in the air, on his way to the May 30 summit with President Bush. It grievously undermined Gorbachev's momentum at a critical moment—this was the summit where Gorbachev, to the chagrin of his advisors, conceded Germany's right to choose its alliance membership—and Yeltsin was not relenting.

NATO's chosen path was to deliver on the London promise of its own "transformation," for the benefit of continental stability. Trouble was brewing in the Middle East, where Iraq had invaded Kuwait. And tensions were running high in the Soviet Union. But there were encouraging developments as well, and NATO highlighted them at its December 1990 meeting. Two CSCE documents had been agreed the preceding month, and they stood out. The Charter of Paris advanced a broad agenda of human liberty and security, and bolstered the CSCE organizationally.[69] Meanwhile, the Treaty on Conventional Armed Forces in Europe brought about the "equal ceilings" that NATO had sought in early 1989, but now in a wholly new context. NATO welcomed all of this, but also highlighted how its continued capacity to "spread the values of freedom and democracy" depended on its ability to sustain "the enduring principles and benefits of our transatlantic partnership, including those that flow from our collective defence."[70] This was option 2 in operation: NATO as the foundation; the CSCE in complementary development.

NATO's December 1990 stocktaking also clarified a couple of other issues internal to NATO. One was NATO's growing focus on a broad and varied set of risks. These risks—or "unforeseeable strategic consequences of instabilities that might emerge"—marked a new NATO, an alliance no longer focused primarily on East–West confrontation, but one in tune with contemporary security challenges. Still, NATO cautioned, "prudence requires NATO to counterbalance the Soviet Union's substantial residual military capabilities." New NATO was in the making, but old NATO in effect remained as a residual security guarantee. The other issue concerned Europe's scope for influence. In London, President Mitterrand had announced a debate over diversity *within* option 2, and here it was. NATO highlighted that the European allies would have to do more (enabling an equitable sharing of defense burdens), but in return would gain opportunities in the shape of "the construction of a European pillar in the alliance."

Through most of 1991, as a US coalition fought a war against Saddam Hussein's Iraq, and then as Soviet conservative hardliners botched an attempt to unseat Mikhail Gorbachev, the allies continued to direct work on military strategy and political transformation in NATO headquarters. On November 7–8, 1991, the job was done. NATO was able to issue both its first ever public Strategic Concept,[71] and then also its Rome Declaration on a new security architecture.[72] Symbolically, NATO's strategy came first, and the security architecture second. The former enabled the latter.

NATO's Strategic Concept adopted a broad approach to security, retooled the alliance's collective defense posture, and remained concerned with Europe's "strategic balance." The latter was a reference to the Soviet Union and the need for prudence. The rejigged collective defense posture involved notably a downscaled role for nuclear weapons (now "last resort"), the elimination of in-place linear forward defense lines, and instead the organization of mobile forces of layered readiness. In its ensuing Rome Declaration, NATO stressed how Europe's challenges "cannot be comprehensively addressed by one institution alone." NATO was thus readying politically and militarily to sustain an architecture of "interlocking" institutions. This included notably NATO's own evolving European Security and Defence Identity, its partnerships with former adversaries, and its support for the CSCE. A few weeks after it issued the Rome Declaration, on December 20, 1991, NATO opened a new forum for dialogue with its former adversaries—the North Atlantic Cooperation Council.

As NATO completed its security architecture policy and as it fleshed out the New Atlanticism of option 2, the Soviet Union fell apart. Boris Yeltsin and the republics were taking their revenge on the political center. In mid-December, Russia, Ukraine, and Belarus set up a Commonwealth of Independent States to take the place of the Soviet Union. On December 25, 1991, Mikhail Gorbachev resigned as Soviet president. The Soviet Union had vanished, and NATO had expanded in geography and political functionality within a security architecture largely of its own making.

NATO emerged from the geopolitical upheaval of 1989–91 as the cornerstone of transatlantic relations and Europe's security architecture. New Atlanticism represented a conscious choice to anticipate change by building on NATO as a tried and trusted institution.

NATO was not an altruistic foundation, of course. "In truth," Robert Gates, Brent Scowcroft's deputy, later wrote, we were trying "to bribe the Soviets out of Germany."[73] The bribe, if such it was, consisted of West German financial donations and US assurances that NATO would transform. Gates' statement has a stark ring to it. Some might even be tempted to conclude that NATO bribed the Soviet Union (and then Russia) into a political order against which it would sooner or later revolt. The result, one could then venture, is the war that Russia began in 2022 in Ukraine. However, to embark on that train of thought is to step on a slippery slope.

Countries do not offer gifts that go against their own interest, and the NATO allies' overwhelming interest in 1989–90 was to support and shape Germany's unification in such a way that Europe's balance-of-power past would not re-emerge. If the Soviet Union resisted or slow-walked this issue, a bribe was an option. It is critical to understand the extent to which Germany, not the Soviet Union, became the central and urgent challenge. Naturally, the Soviet Union's frail political condition was important, and President Bush and other leaders were greatly preoccupied by it. But the recipe found in 1949 for moving Europe beyond balance-of-power politics—transatlantic defense cooperation via NATO—could not be threatened by the Soviet Union. NATO had endured the Soviet Union. If anything could undo NATO, it would be Germany's unification on neutral terms. With an enhanced Germany unfettered by alliance ties, the transatlantic commitment to mutual defense guarantees would surely diminish, and possibly wither.

The Soviet Union essentially had no consistent policy on Germany through these critical years. "If one goes back and reviews all the evidence," writes Angela Stent, "one must conclude that prior to 1989 there was little innovative thinking in the Soviet Union on the future of Germany."[74] When the big changes of 1989–90 began to unfold, there was then a complete "lack of concepts" toward Germany, save for the conservative Soviet troop of German experts who sought to resist the country's unification and NATO membership. Gorbachev mainly saw Germany as a link to a new European order; but that order remained vaguely defined, and Gorbachev lacked the strength to think through the link and maintain it in the face of Western policy.[75]

Finally, there was a lot of wiggle room in the New Atlanticism framework. It was underdeveloped or "misty," to borrow from Thatcher. It had an undeniable core: a united Germany in NATO. But the wider architecture was a work in progress. It had been traced in London in July 1990 and in Rome in November 1991, but it had yet to spring to life. Subsequent statesmanship cannot, to evoke some drama, escape the judgement of history with simple references to decisions made in 1990–91. This goes for Western, as well as Russian leaders.

Europe's changes "did not come about by chance. They have been achieved by strength and resolution in defence, and by a refusal to ever be intimidated."[76] Thus spoke Margaret Thatcher in the House of Commons on November 22, 1990. She would no doubt have reveled in the opportunity to shape Europe further; but this was her resignation speech. Geoffrey Howe, whom Thatcher had fired on account of his alleged dimmed clarity of purpose, was among those in the Conservative Party who had revolted against her, not least over the issue of Britain's relationship to Europe. It was now up to John Major, Mrs Thatcher's successor, and colleagues in NATO (and wider in Europe) to act with Thatcherian strength and resolution to shape New Atlanticism.

NATO Grows Bigger and Softer

Some 14,000 km, or 8,600 miles, from NATO headquarters in Brussels, just east of the Kuzman Knoll in Antarctica, lies the Wörner Gap, a flat saddle of glacial landscape connecting two ridges. It is remarkable only for being named after NATO's late secretary general, Manfred Wörner, who succumbed to intestinal cancer in August 1994. The Bulgarian authorities felt so indebted to Wörner for his contribution to European unity that they decided to bestow this unusual honor on him. And they were not done. In 2019, by then a NATO member, Bulgaria donated a Soviet-era car, the unassuming and oft-ridiculed Trabant, for display outside NATO's new headquarters in Brussels. It was another unusual tribute to Wörner and an appreciation of his visit to Sofia—the first time a NATO secretary general had visited Bulgaria—in June 1991, when he agreed to be chauffeured in a Trabant by a private citizen, Solomon Passy, who, as things turned out, later became the Bulgarian foreign minister who negotiated his country's membership of NATO.

Wörner's finest hour as NATO secretary general (1988–94) came in April 1994, as he pushed the allies to do something about the war in Bosnia. Serb forces were strangling the Bosnian city of Goražde, NATO was deadlocked, and Wörner was hospitalized in Aachen, Germany. NATO's supreme commander, General Joulwan, recalls how he flew to the hospital, because he wanted to brief Wörner on the precarious situation in Goražde. Wörner assured Joulwan that, despite his poor condition, he would come back to NATO headquarters to hold a meeting with the other Council members. Visibly weak, Wörner accompanied Joulwan to the elevator: "I was nearly in tears," Joulwan confessed.[1] Wörner did make it to Brussels to chair an NAC meeting on April 22, 1994. His intravenous feeding tubes were visible near his shirt collar, his physician was seated right behind him, and yet he guided the alliance through a lengthy session and to the conclusion that NATO must do more.[2] It did not put an end to the war (that would come more than a year later), but Wörner had visibly become the conscience of the alliance.

At one point he joked that he was "leaner and meaner, like the alliance."[3] But Wörner was ill, and the alliance was not growing lean and mean. First and foremost, it was enlarging its functionality in Europe to become a hub for partnerships and dialogues. Determined adversaries in the Balkans were there to challenge it, though. NATO had to do something to "shape events," as Wörner wrote, "and not become their victim."[4] A phase of activism thus set in. But activism was hard. The United States took the lead, insisting on NATO's primacy; France and Russia grew frustrated; Germany made no claims; and Britain was looking for a role. Energized and active, NATO thus grew overwhelmingly dependent on US leadership. While the alliance succeeded in embracing general security tasks, it failed to define new ways and means of sharing the burden of leadership. Instead of leaner and meaner, NATO grew bigger, softer, and less military. The United States still offered a military backbone of sorts; but without that, NATO would be just big and soft.

More dialogue, limited action

NATO's expanded functionality followed from the July 1990 London summit's offer of political transformation and continental dialogue. In late 1991, as we have seen, the NATO allies set up the North Atlantic Cooperation Council (NACC) to embody and promote cooperation—at first with some former Soviet republics, and later with all of them plus the former Soviet client states in Central and Eastern Europe.

The NACC got off to an unexpectedly dramatic beginning in December 1991. The initial meeting's final communiqué had been agreed and sent to the press, when the Soviet ambassador, Afanassievsky was summoned and left the room for about half an hour. He returned "white-faced," recalled Chris Donnelly, a Wörner special advisor.[5] Afanassievsky had just been informed of the legal dissolution of the Soviet Union, and he conveyed this news to his NACC colleagues. Moments later, Secretary General Wörner announced that he had just received a telegram from Russian President Boris Yeltsin, stating that Russia wished to join not only the NACC, but ultimately NATO itself.[6] It was too late to remove any mention of the Soviet Union in the NACC communiqué, but a footnote was added to later editions. Thus, and whether befitting or not, the Soviet Union ended up as a NATO–NACC footnote.

Moving into 1992, NATO developed plans for continued dialogue and cooperation, as war-like situations raged on Europe's periphery and beyond. Major NATO allies were consumed by them in different ways, but NATO watched from the sidelines. The Gulf War of early 1991 had been fought by a US-led coalition, and by March it was over. Except that it was not, because the plight of the Kurdish minority in northern Iraq led the United States, along with France and Britain, back into a mission to shield Kurdish minorities from government repression. This mission, mandated by the UN Security Council in early April 1992, raised the tricky question of how to protect civilians from predatory governments hiding behind principles of sovereignty. The principle could not be absolute, the UN Security Council was saying.

But what to do if several republics engaged in a contest for sovereignty, and in the process harmed civilians? The emerging headache of Yugoslavia fell to European governments: "we don't have a dog in that fight," US Secretary of State James Baker famously said, adding, "we don't want to put a dog in that fight."[7] European governments at first seemed content to demonstrate their prowess at conflict resolution, but they were soon out of their depth in crisis management. On June 25, 1991, Slovenia and Croatia, two of the Yugoslav republics, declared their independence. Serbia, Yugoslavia's powerhouse, was spoiling for a fight. The European countries were divided: some—Italy, Belgium, and Denmark—favored independence for Slovenia and Croatia; France and Britain hesitated. Germany, the new heavyweight, tipped the balance. On December 16, it unilaterally came down on the side of the two breakaway republics being granted independence. This German assertiveness stunned some observers, including Richard Holbrooke, who later brokered the 1995 Dayton agreement that made NATO the keeper of Bosnia's peace.[8] But German Foreign Minister Genscher had a point when he claimed to be merely abiding by Europe's legal strategy to coerce Serbia into conflict resolution.[9] The real problem was not Germany, but Europe's complicated scheme—and insufficient political will.

Europe's descent into the cauldron continued in early 1992. Responding to what was, in retrospect, the wildly optimistic assessment of UN Secretary-General Boutros Boutros-Ghali that the UN could engender and maintain peace in Yugoslavia, European governments offered military forces for a UN Protection Force (UNPROFOR). The idea was that, as UN diplomacy probed for peace, UNPROFOR would safeguard key urban areas. The size and the mandate of UNPROFOR would grow, but never by enough to catch up with the political cunning and operational agility of the Serb forces. UNPROFOR areas of operations thus became small, isolated, and exposed pockets, supposedly protected by ill-equipped and politically constrained European forces.

NATO had not foreseen this challenge of operational crisis management in its December 1991 Strategic Concept. The alliance was not ready to act. Instead, the allies acted individually, in all too many directions. They did seek to muster the will to do something, though: through 1992, they offered case-by-case NATO military support to first CSCE and then UN peacekeeping missions. But these offers made no difference: the CSCE and the UN were not ready to authorize the use of force, and NATO was de facto not ready to offer it. It was this paralysis that tore at committed Atlanticists, such as Manfred Wörner.

The situation sparked a debate across NATO countries on whether the allies had to go "out-of-area" (beyond NATO territory), or else risk going "out-of-business."[10] It was a fraught and difficult debate. Allied governments saw the threat to their London promise of transformation and continental stability, but could not offer unity in action. Russia also served up an unexpected reminder of its role in Europe. This came on December 14, 1992, at a CSCE meeting, when Andrei Kozyrev, Russia's foreign minister, lashed out at NATO's alleged breach of Yugoslav sovereignty—this at a time of hardly any NATO involvement in Yugoslavia—and promised Serbia the support of "Great Russia." It was a threatening great-power play. However, it was also just a ploy, Kozyrev said afterwards: he merely wanted Western diplomats to be aware of the stakes involved in not catering to Russia's interests.[11]

President Clinton took office soon thereafter. He brought with him a philosophy of assertive liberalism—of fighting for principles and freedom. It was a rebuke to the carefully measured policy style of President Bush, who, Clinton argued during his election campaign, "simply does not seem at home in the mainstream prodemocratic tradition in American policy."[12] It was also a reflection of the buoyant mood of American liberals after the Cold War: Clinton made the defense of democracy the centerpiece of his foreign policy agenda. But his fellow democracies in NATO, the US allies, were less than buoyant about their situation in Bosnia and what the United States might do about it. Clinton's idea was to lift the arms embargo, in order to empower the non-Serb Bosnians, and simultaneously conduct air strikes against Serb forces. As British Foreign Secretary Douglas Hurd said rather indiscreetly, Clinton would be creating a "level killing field."[13] Team Clinton did indeed want a level playing field; but what Hurd meant—and what the exposed European UNPROFOR contributors meant—was that the killing had to stop.

European governments had put themselves in a position where they bowed to force. Hurd (and probably numerous other European diplomats) quite clearly felt that whatever the justice of the case, the Serbs were bound to prevail.[14] Such European realism was anathema to both President Clinton and Congressional leaders. It smacked of the Realpolitik that they had fought to overturn ever since the Second World War. They had not created and supported NATO through the

Cold War just to turn it now into an instrument of balanced Balkan power. But nor could Clinton expose European troops to risk. He thus hesitated. His secretary of state, Warren Christopher, visited Europe in February 1993, but he brought only questions about what should be done about Bosnia. "There was," recalled Robert Hunter, designated US NATO ambassador, "no sense of American leadership."[15]

A disputed architecture

In the quaint city of Travemünde, on the German Baltic Sea coast, NATO sought to stage its comeback. The allied defense ministers met there in October 1993, and it offered an opportunity for US Secretary of Defense Les Aspin to outline how the Clinton administration intended to take charge. There were three pillars to the US thinking:

- *Partnership for Peace (PfP)*: Further outreach to former Warsaw Pact countries, including Russia. Not in grand format, like the NACC, but in tailored formats suited to enhancing individual partners' abilities to operate alongside NATO forces in crisis management operations.
- *Combined Joint Task Forces (CJTF)*: A measure to reform NATO's static command structure and make it deployable for out-of-area missions. NATO required fewer military headquarters, but they needed to be more agile.
- *European Security and Defence Identity (ESDI)*: A new approach to the perpetual challenge of building a European community compatible with NATO. Instead of taking it outside NATO, which could happen with the new European Union, ESDI offered a path inside NATO, including the use of CJTF by the European allies only.

More outreach, greater flexibility, and more Europe inside NATO— that was the US recipe for NATO renewal. Allied defense ministers approved it with a "broad degree of consensus." The path was thus cleared for NATO heads of state and government, who, at a summit in January 1994, gave their blessings to the reforms.[16] Robert Hunter, now US NATO ambassador, considered NATO's Travemünde meeting to be a remarkable moment of architectural clarification.[17] But clear thinking did not, in fact, equate to political agreement. The French daily *Le Monde* found after the January 1994 summit that the Clinton administration had no idea of what to do with Europe.[18] And France was not the only point of concern.

Russian President Boris Yeltsin liked the Partnership for Peace, in that he saw it as an alternative to NATO enlargement, though he did also worry that it might actually be a precursor to enlargement. "I tell you plainly that we favor a different approach," Yeltsin wrote to Clinton on September 15, 1993. Copies of the letter were also sent to French President Mitterrand, German Chancellor Kohl, and British Prime Minister Major. Instead of NATO, Yeltsin wanted Europe's foundation to be a pan-European structure. If NATO did remain, then in the long run Russia should be able to join it. The bottom line, Yeltsin emphasized, was that Russia should have a special status: "In general, we advocate that relations between our country and NATO be a few degrees warmer than those between the alliance and Eastern Europe."[19]

Central and Eastern European countries predictably objected to Russia's desire for continued supremacy, and they reacted vigorously to any sign of NATO or US hesitancy in delivering on their hopes of inclusion in Western institutions. In April 1993, at the opening of Washington's Holocaust Museum, Clinton had assured Polish President Wałęsa and Czech President Václav Havel of his sympathy for their desire for NATO enlargement.[20] Moreover, in August 1993, in a move reminiscent of Gorbachev's May 1990 concession that Germany could choose for itself, Yeltsin had told Poland's Lech Wałęsa that Poland could choose for itself. Yeltsin's subsequent letter to Clinton and the other NATO leaders was an effort to backtrack—to claim special privileges for Russia. Central and Eastern European leaders were not about to allow that.

Uncertainty extended into the depths of the Clinton administration. As agencies were considering draft versions of NATO's January 1994 summit communiqué, Department of Defense representatives invoked the authority of Secretary Aspin and the incoming chairman of the joint chiefs of staff, General John Shalikashvili, to argue that while enlargement may be in the interests of Central and Eastern European countries, it was not in US interests.[21] The argument, which prevailed, was that enlargement would diminish NATO's defense effectiveness, and that military effectiveness would be best served by "Peacekeeping Partnerships." France's Mitterrand and Britain's Major happened to agree; but what clinched it for President Clinton was the plight of Boris Yeltsin in Russia.[22] His domestic reforms, which most certainly were in US interests, had provoked a backlash of nationalist-communist political resistance that, in early October 1993, led to a spectacular and violent standoff in Moscow. President Clinton decided to kick the can of NATO enlargement down the road. For now, NATO would have Partnerships for Peace.

But how far down the road did Clinton really kick the can? On his way to the Brussels summit in January 1994, he stopped off in Prague to meet with the leaders of the Czech Republic, Slovakia, Poland, and Hungary. The Partnership for Peace is not "a permanent holding room," Clinton assured them. "It changes the entire NATO dialogue so that now the question is no longer whether NATO will take on new members but when and how."[23] "Not whether, but when" was the message; but President Yeltsin was mostly hearing that NATO enlargement was not on the agenda. Secretary of State Warren Christopher and his deputy, Strobe Talbott, had been in Moscow to clarify US policy, but perhaps they had not spoken clearly enough; perhaps Yeltsin had had too much to drink (which Christopher later insinuated); or perhaps he had simply heard only what he wanted to hear.[24]

The ambiguity extended also to US allies. German opinion was divided. Defense Minister Volker Rühe—who brought his NATO colleagues to his hometown of Travemünde in October 1993—was outspoken in his support for NATO enlargement. He knew that his boss, Chancellor Kohl, agreed, but that he had to contend with coalition partners from Hans-Dietrich Genscher's liberal party who continued to long for an all-European security structure (as did the Social Democrat opposition). As Rühe later learned, Kohl also had to contend with Yeltsin's displeasure at Rühe himself. In fact, Yeltsin had attempted to use one of his and Chancellor Kohl's multiple sauna meetings to verbally skin the German defense minister, though Kohl had skillfully deflected the challenge.[25]

Britain and France were skeptical about NATO enlargement, but for distinct reasons. President Mitterrand's position was delicate, or perhaps simply complex. He prioritized the deepening of the European Union, but Germany, his indispensable partner, needed the EU to be widened, in order to cover its eastern flank. In terms of widening (or enlargement), Mitterrand was thus content to let NATO move first: it offered cover for EU deepening.[26] However, for the EU to succeed, NATO needed to be made compatible with the EU, and not the other way around. The problem was then France's limited clout in NATO. It upheld its position of non-military integration, and its defense minister, François Léotard, did not attend the decisive Travemünde meeting. Secretary of Defense Aspin courteously went to Paris in October 1993 to meet with Léotard, who assured Aspin that things were about to change:[27] France was intending to rejoin NATO at the level of defense ministers and military chiefs of staff. This was a first and critical signal that France intended to move back into NATO, in order to shape it for European purposes.

Britain had other ideas. NATO needed first and foremost to remain militarily effective and politically cohesive. British leaders maintained that crisis management in the Balkans (or elsewhere) should belong not to any one institution, but to flexible coalitions driven by national interests, on a case-by-case basis. And coalitions needed to run on military interoperability and shared command options, for which NATO efficacy was simply indispensable. The core British concern thus did not center on Moscow—Russia had lost an empire, but so had Britain, and Russia now needed to learn to live as a medium-rank power, rather than dreaming of empire.[28] Rather, Britain's concerns centered on especially France's alleged penchant for trading military muscle for institution-building, against which British policymakers never tired of warning.[29]

Thus, at NATO's January 1994 summit, President Clinton had policy ideas—PfP, CJTF, and ESDI—but no solid political ground. Solidity, in fact, took on an entirely different meaning at the opening of the summit, when President Clinton entered the room and went up to

Chancellor Helmut Kohl, a tall man who carried more weight than any other NATO leader. "I was thinking of you last night, Helmut, because I watched the sumo wrestling on television," Clinton told a puzzled Kohl. He went on to finesse the point: "You and I are the biggest people here and we are still a whole one hundred pounds too light."[30]

Bosnia blues

Anthony Lake, Clinton's national security advisor, felt that solid ground in the form of NATO consensus would follow from US leadership. It was no simple task to define US leadership, though. There was a slippery, stubborn, and painful war in the former Yugoslavia, and there was dissent in Washington over NATO enlargement. But Lake felt aligned with the president and was ready to do whatever, in his view, was necessary. And he was a formidable player. In Lake's four years as national security advisor, an aide confided, "I have never seen him lose a fight."[31]

Lake's first move after the January 1994 summit was to initiate an in-house US study of NATO enlargement to gain "momentum." Some European allies felt "misled" because they did not think this followed agreed policy.[32] Strobe Talbott, deputy secretary of state, was concerned about Russia, and was a skeptic, too.[33] But Lake had been clear that "partnership" (the PfP) did not cut it. When he first encountered the PfP concept, he had asked, "Where's the vision?" Later, he would complain, "What does the PfP do?"[34] With his encouragement, a troika of his senior aides, Alexander Vershbow, Daniel Fried, and Nick Burns, had, by the fall of 1994, developed a roadmap entitled "Moving Toward NATO Expansion." It foresaw NATO enlargement in the first half of Clinton's second term (thus, presuming he would win another term), in 1997 or 1998, allowing for time to build NATO consensus and to partner with Russia. "Over the next three years," Vershbow would write, "the United States followed this roadmap almost to the letter."[35]

Ending the Bosnian War was a critical first step: 1995 was teed up to be the decisive year. Western countries had hesitated throughout 1994—on Bosnia and the Rwanda genocide—and the Bosnian Serbs were looking to close the affair while they had the upper hand. Their plan for 1995 was to win by overrunning the UNPROFOR safe areas.[36] US President Clinton and Russian President Yeltsin were both facing elections in 1996, meaning that their political flexibility would run out in 1995. In addition, France's new president, Jacques Chirac, elected in May 1995, was a force for change. He was exasperated by UNPROFOR and the inability of the UN system to deliver decisive action. NATO's supreme commander, General Joulwan, was equally exasperated. "You don't understand the mission," he at one point vented against the British UNPROFOR commander, General Rose, who was reluctant to act more forcefully. "I was so angry I banged my fist down on the table," Joulwan recalled. "I couldn't believe what I was hearing. It was just shocking."

President Chirac sought change and was appropriately nicknamed "the bulldozer."[37] Perhaps more telling was his affection for sumo. Chirac was never overheard making jokes about the stature of German Chancellor Kohl, but he would sometimes muse about having the height but not the weight for sumo wrestling. (Nor did his dog, a Maltese, though he did name it Sumo.) Still, for Chirac, the time had come to throw France's weight around. Along with Britain, it was the major contributor to UNPROFOR, and Chirac's view was that the force was neutered and at the end of its useful existence. But Chirac did not want to pull it. Instead, he wanted to beef it up with a rapid reaction force (RRF), sideline the UN chain of command, and make it a force that the Serbs would have to reckon with.

President Chirac's indispensable partner was Britain's John Major, the two countries making up the backbone of UNPROFOR. However, Major was in a fragile position and was not amenable to bulldozer tactics over Bosnia. In early June, the two leaders agreed that the Serb forces had humiliated the French and British forces by taking them hostage, and they agreed to stand up the RRF.[38] Britain also put a forceful new commanding general, Rupert Smith, into Bosnia. He had none of the timidity of General Rose. But Britain's essential difficulty resided in London, where John Major was in a weak position and therefore hesitated. Major did not think particularly highly of France's ability to change things in Bosnia, and his RRF commitment mostly had to do with a desire to be able to pull the British troops out.[39] He probably also sensed that Chirac and Clinton were about to move things along, so that Britain risked being left out of a Franco-American rapprochement. With the RRF, Britain engaged—but, an observer noted, "for all the wrong reasons."[40] To some in the Clinton administration, Major's government could not move beyond a "profound cynicism" that made it an unreliable partner.[41]

Whatever his motive for backing the RRF, Prime Minister Major was soon forced into a battle for his domestic political survival. "We had to stop the rot," Major later wrote, and the rot included his predecessor, Margaret Thatcher, and the anti-European skeptics within the Conservative Party who were seeking to undo Major's more moderate leadership.[42] Thatcher had re-emerged on the political stage with her memoirs, and she spoke highly of "the most formidable leader" for more than thirty years—poisonously referring thus not to her political heir, John Major, but to his opponent, Labour leader Tony Blair.[43] To stop this rot, Major resigned as party leader on June 22, 1995, and initiated a leadership election campaign. He prevailed, but that did not restore his foreign policy credentials. Major's problems in foreign policy fueled the later Tony Blair premiership, from 1997 on, and especially its holier-than-thou attitude in foreign policy. In wanting to be everything but John Major, Blair set a new course that would impel Britain headlong into the war on terror. That came later, but it was all connected.

In 1995, Clinton and Chirac wanted change, but they were coming at it from opposite directions. Chirac sought to transform UNPROFOR into a lean and mean ground force. Clinton wanted the boots off the ground, so that he could mount an intensive bombing campaign against Serb forces.[44] As President Chirac pressed his case, though, President Clinton agreed to align with France, co-sponsor a new UN Security Council Resolution, and co-finance the RRF. However, Congress sought to tie Clinton's hands. The Congressional leadership wanted to punish Serb forces from the air, and they had no intention of funding ground operations—either via partnership with France or via UN funding for UNPROFOR.

President Clinton realized belatedly that his hands were also tied inside NATO. Since mid-1994, the United States had in fact been part of NATO's Operations Plan (Op-Plan) 40104 for evacuating allied troops. It was a hallmark of allied solidarity; but it also meant that, to get European and Canadian forces out, US troop deployments "would be *automatic*."[45] Richard Holbrooke, assistant secretary of state, felt that the Pentagon had not been totally forthcoming about the implications of Op-Plan 40104, and he took it upon himself to drive the point home to President Clinton. The occasion was a gathering in the North Portico of the White House, following a dinner with Chirac. Clinton reacted with "surprise" to the news that his hands were tied. "Is this true?" he asked Secretary of State Christopher, who was standing next to him. To this Christopher replied, "We have a problem."[46] The president then walked off, holding his wife's hand, but there it was: to renege on the NATO pledge would be to undermine not only the administration's Bosnia policy, but also its wider credibility in Europe.

Still, it took a continuing Serb offensive, including the fall of the safe area of Srebrenica and (it dawned on the international community later) the genocide of almost 8,000 Bosnian Muslims, to provoke allied agreement. The French position hardened. "We have to declare war on [Serb commander] Mladic, or get out," said a prominent member of the French general staff, General Philippe Morillon.[47] But France had limited means, and the allies were still not ready to support its proposed ground offensive. Finally, John Major called a London conference of the principal players—Russia included—that settled on a compromise: NATO air power was to be leveraged for a broad and punishing response; the RRF could move in to protect the capital, Sarajevo; and UNPROFOR would remain.[48] In a last hiccup, the United States, France, Britain, and UN Secretary-General Boutros-Ghali struggled to sort out the chain of command, and it was only following further Serb offenses in late August that matters were fully clarified.[49] On August 30, 1995, NATO Secretary General Javier Solana announced the onset of Operation Deliberate Force—an intensive air campaign of almost one month's duration—that finally brought the Serbs to the negotiating table.[50]

The Bosnian endgame had several important ramifications for NATO. Above all, a number of countries felt that it had validated their role and importance, and they would be looking to cash in on it. Russia was one of them. It had railed at points against NATO's plans, but it had joined NATO's Partnership for Peace in June 1994 and had stuck with the international diplomacy that in the end forced the Serbs to enter into negotiations. It expected to be fully part of the peace process, too. France, the bulldozer of UNPROFOR, felt it deserved a greater say in the alliance's strategic affairs, including on the issue of enabling European command. In addition, a full thirteen PfP countries (besides Russia) ended up participating in NATO's peace implementation force (IFOR), several of them with the intention of proving their worth as potential new allies. And finally, the EU was there, too, personified at the peace talks by EU Special Representative Carl Bildt. Richard Holbrooke and his boss, Warren Christopher, would win most of the acclaim for the "Dayton Peace" concluded at the Wright-Patterson Air Force Base, outside Dayton, Ohio, but Bildt co-chaired the peace conference, as did Russia's foreign minister, Igor Ivanov. Operation Deliberate Force and the Dayton Peace offered success; but, as noted by the *New York Times*, success has many fathers.[51]

American terms of enlargement

Could NATO manage all these expectations and still enlarge? The NATO allies could, at this point in late 1995, have shifted. They could have deepened the PfP and, by extension, the role of the Organization for Security and Co-operation in Europe (OSCE, the former CSCE) in the conduct of continental dialogue. That would have catered to Russia's declared interests. It could also have deepened its commitment to a European "identity" (ESDI) and an associated command option (CJTF), which would have catered to France's declared interests. But the allies did not shift. Instead, they followed through with enlargement and confirmed NATO's essential and enlarged role as Europe's security foundation.

The fact of the matter is that neither Russia nor France had the weight to undo what Lake and his enlargement team had put on track in late 1994 with the "Moving Toward NATO Expansion" roadmap.

"Not whether, but when and how" remained the dogma. Moreover, in multiple ways Bosnia bolstered the case for enlargement. The war had demonstrated the lack of capacity of UN command and the prowess of NATO command and action. "Those who still wonder why the east Europeans became so obsessed with NATO membership should search through the annals of the Yugoslav saga," wrote an astute observer, Jonathan Eyal.[52] This applied also to Washington, where decision-makers did not want to get drawn into more unchecked wars of rekindled nationalism. To pre-empt them was also to pre-empt Russia from taking advantage of them for balance-of-power gains. When Washington's lead architect of its Russia policy, Deputy Secretary of State Strobe Talbott, made all these arguments in August 1995, it was clear that the administration had made up its mind.[53]

In response to the US roadmap, which the allies received in late 1994, NATO initiated its own "Study on NATO Enlargement."[54] It appeared in early September 1995, a timing that mattered enormously. This was during Operation Deliberate Force, when NATO was bombing to win in Bosnia and had to keep the allies (as well as Russia and other partners) on side. The "Study on NATO Enlargement" thus had one overriding purpose: to buy NATO time.[55] It balanced all the big issues, emphasizing a more political and yet militarily effective NATO, an enlarged NATO, and yet more scope for partners such as Russia and the European Union. Nor did it rule out the option of Russian membership of NATO. In short, it anticipated change, but did not define it. The politics of inclusion could thus begin.

Russia's inclusion in the architecture began in October 1995. A ceasefire took effect in Bosnia on October 5; on October 7 NATO agreed to deploy a force in support of a peace deal. Russia's President Yeltsin would be in New York later in the month for the fiftieth anniversary of the UN, and President Clinton intended to persuade him there of NATO–Russia cooperation and partnership. To help matters along, Clinton had arranged for a meeting to take place with Yeltsin in the former home of Franklin Roosevelt, overlooking the Hudson River—thus playing on the wartime alliance of their two countries.

Persuasion was not going to be straightforward, and Clinton had been put on alert. Yeltsin had made a stopover in Paris, where he and

President Chirac had agreed on the importance of grand partnership between NATO and Russia.[56] In his UN speech, Yeltsin wasted no energy. "We are against the eastward expansion" of NATO, the Russian president declared. It is an "extremely acute" question that could herald "new confrontation tomorrow."[57] What followed in the Roosevelt apartment were "hours of intense and often highly personal discussion."[58] The meeting ended on a high note, though. Meeting the press afterwards, President Yeltsin said that going into the meeting he had feared a disaster, but "now for the first time I can tell you that you [journalists] are a disaster." President Clinton's body reportedly shook with laughter as he reminded journalists of the need to attribute the statement correctly.[59]

The meeting, in fact, focused not on NATO enlargement, but on the thorny issue of Russia's refusal to serve under NATO command. For NATO, unified command was sacrosanct. In the end, the two presidents agreed that Russia should contribute around 2,000 troops to IFOR, and that their defense ministers, William Perry and Pavel Grachev, should come up with a command solution. And this they did, not least thanks to an idea put forward by General Joulwan, supreme allied commander Europe (SACEUR), to appoint a Russian officer as deputy to SACEUR and let the Russian issue certain operational orders outside NATO's chain of command.[60] The agreement carried great significance: NATO and Russian troops now began serving side by side as full Partners for Peace. To President Clinton's advisors, it did not mean that NATO enlargement was off the agenda, but rather that practical cooperation was "lubricating" the process.[61] Through 1996, when both presidents were up for election, enlargement would involve simply consultations with prospective new members.[62] The big decisions were postponed until 1997.

France's inclusion in the architecture began in December 1995. It was a NATO member, of course, but it was not militarily integrated: and that was the issue. President Chirac offered France's reintegration in return for a European identity that could "assert itself fully," as he told the US Congress on February 1, 1996.[63] Prior to his visit to the US, in December 1995, Chirac had announced that France's chief of defense would henceforth take his seat on NATO's Military

Committee. And that was just a first step. If NATO would change, France would continue, step by step, to re-engage.[64]

Perhaps ominously, few senators or representatives attended the speech of the French president.[65] Missing the French president "had become no big deal," an observer remarked drily.[66] That did not mean that the French effort was in vain; merely that it stood a better chance of succeeding if it worked properly through the allied machinery. French and British officials did so through the spring of 1996—partly invoking the ire of the supreme commander, as they carved out a European command option centered on SACEUR's deputy (DSACEUR)—and they garnered political consensus. By June 1996, at a Berlin NAC ministerial meeting, NATO thus welcomed the "completion" of the CJTF concept.[67] A European option had been born. France henceforth rejoined NATO at the level of defense ministers, and Spain decided to fully integrate into NATO militarily.

Things then fell apart—essentially because France upped the ante. Its leadership aimed high for big concessions, pushing issues upward to the highest political levels. It thus violated what had worked through the spring—engaging NATO's machinery—in a sign that the decades of limited engagement in NATO's work culture carried a political cost. President Chirac at first eyed the position of SACEUR, but settled for the slightly more modest (but still audacious) demand that command of NATO's southern flank—AFSOUTH—be transferred to a European. He wrote to President Clinton personally to make the case, adding a handwritten note, "Bill, this is important to me."[68] But it was also important to President Clinton, who worried about the cohesion of AFSOUTH—to which the American Sixth Fleet was assigned—and NATO's wider political cohesion. Through tortuous negotiations that stretched into the spring of 1997, the United States offered to set up a distinct CJTF option in AFSOUTH, rather than hand over command entirely. It was a limited offer. When President Chirac called snap parliamentary elections in May 1997 and unexpectedly lost control of government to the socialist opposition—which was committed to French security policy dogmas—he gave up on the affair: France would not reintegrate with NATO militarily.

Attention meanwhile turned to NATO–Russia relations. The two sides struck a deal, a NATO–Russia Founding Act. On the NATO side, it was largely "made in Washington" and had very little NATO input, recalled the US ambassador to NATO at the time, Robert Hunter.[69] Alexander Vershbow, who penned the Founding Act, recalls how one sentence in particular involved such a political minefield that he labeled it "the sentence from hell."[70] He did write key elements of it at NATO headquarters, but on the back of a napkin at a US officials-only lunch.[71]

A lot of this was by design: the allies had agreed to the US lead. There was an exception, though, and it again related to France. In January 1997, in preparation for the endgame, Strobe Talbott visited London, Paris, and Berlin, and gained the support of Britain's John Major and Germany's Helmut Kohl. The United States could run things primarily in a US–Russia channel and involve NATO via its secretary general, Javier Solana. President Chirac saw things differently, though, suggesting to Talbott that the great powers—the United States, France, Germany, Britain, and Russia—hold a five-power summit to hammer out an agreement.[72] To Talbott, this spelt trouble. The United States wanted to create a sense of inevitability around NATO enlargement, in order to nudge Russia from protest to constructive engagement. A five-power summit would instead encourage Russia to protest further. France did not find support for its design, and so Talbott could proceed. But the allies did agree to come to Paris to sign the NATO–Russia Founding Act—on May 27, 1997.

The Founding Act is a cornerstone of post-Cold War NATO. It defines contractual obligations in support of "a lasting and inclusive peace."[73] NATO offered to continue its transformation into a broader and more political, open, and partnered organization. In return, Russia agreed to continue its democratization and economic transformation. That was the contract.

NATO's offer involved three aspects worth highlighting:

- In political terms, NATO spoke not of its coming geographical enlargement, but of "expansion," including notably the expansion of its "political function." NATO was thus about not geopolitics, but democratic values.

- In terms of nuclear weapons, NATO pledged to have "no intention, no plan and no reason" to deploy them on the territory of new members. Nor would it change its "last resort" doctrine, which obviously downplayed the role of nuclear weapons.
- In terms of conventional weapons, NATO pledged (in Vershbow's "sentence from hell") to carry out its collective defense and other missions by ensuring interoperability with new members, rather than "by additional permanent stationing of substantial combat forces" on their territory.

In essence, the alliance offered to enlarge politically, but not militarily. It would grow bigger, but also softer. The caveat was Russia's side of the bargain. NATO's hedge lay in the statements that it did "not foresee any future need" to alter its nuclear plans, just as its conventional force plans were intended for the "current and foreseeable future." If Russia changed, so NATO could alter its plans.

NATO at the turn of the century

With the Founding Act in place, NATO was ready to grow bigger and softer. Its Madrid summit in July 1997 showed the way. In the Spanish capital, NATO slimmed down its military command structure considerably. It instead upgraded the PfP and built a new home for partners, a Euro-Atlantic Partnership Council. And then, notably, it agreed to invite three countries—Poland, the Czech Republic, and Hungary—to begin accession talks. In less than two years, on March 12, 1999, those three countries would be able to sign the NATO treaty, symbolically at the Truman Presidential Library in Missouri, honoring the president who founded the alliance. And this was the beginning, not the end: "We reaffirm," the allies stated, "that NATO remains open to new members."[74]

The US team had, with overweening self-confidence, allowed the decision on how many countries would be invited to fester ahead of the summit, even if it wanted just three countries in. Coalitions had thus formed, some backing Romania, others in favor of Slovenia. President Chirac made the most of it, refusing a foreign ministers meeting on the eve of the summit to settle matters, and refusing to go straight into restricted session when the summit opened. He wanted a public *tour de table* to maximize pressure on the United States. In the end, though, Chancellor Kohl aligned with President Clinton, and once the dust settled, three countries made the cut.[75] The others would have to work their way differently through NATO's open door.

The summit rivalry between Presidents Clinton and Chirac was revelatory, though. These two activist leaders had not yet aligned their activism in support of NATO. For as long as that was the case, NATO would be entirely dependent on US policy and support. Contrary to the ideas of the Marshall Plan of 1947 and the subsequent push by Secretary Dulles and others to have Europe organize its own defense with US support, NATO would have political diversity, but just one military leg—its American one. It created a regrettable asymmetry that Russia could exploit in its diplomacy—as a nuclear superpower speaking bilaterally only with the United States, but also as a European country that appealed to (some) Europeans' desire for an order beyond America's hegemony. A more balanced Euro-Atlantic alliance was thus not only a question of dealing with the next Balkan crisis: it was a matter of not tempting Russian nationalists to divide and rule within big, soft NATO.

Into this Franco-American stalemate stepped British leader Tony Blair. He was an activist who was determined never to fall into the perceived foreign policy cynicism of his predecessor, and who made a point of elevating principles of human justice over strict interpretations of state sovereignty. Early on in his premiership, Blair's desire to be a force for good was energized by his ability, working in tandem with President Clinton, to secure the April 1998 Good Friday peace agreement in Northern Ireland. To do good, Blair would subsequently lead Britain into Iraq for Operation Desert Fox in 1998; into Kosovo in 1999; into Sierra Leone in 2000; and then later into Afghanistan and (again) Iraq. He would team up with President Chirac to advance European military capacity building, and he agreed to channel part of the effort into the EU, which had been institutionally upgraded, with the Amsterdam Treaty of 1997 enabling an EU security and defense policy. In their St. Malo Declaration of December 4, 1998, Blair and Chirac committed themselves to bringing this EU dimension to life. The enhanced EU should respect NATO's unique role in collective defense, but simultaneously give the Union the capacity for "autonomous action," backed by credible military forces in the management of crises.[76]

The Kosovo crisis of 1998 (and then war in 1999) would demonstrate the need for a balanced Atlantic partnership (which is what Blair and Chirac had in mind), but also the dangers of precipitate action. It also demonstrated that Europe's leading powers could not intimidate Serbia, that Russia remained potentially revanchist, and that NATO depended almost entirely on US military power for effective crisis management. It further showed that if the United States exercised this power via NATO, the allies could slow it down. Beginning on March 24, 1999, it took Operation Allied Force a full eleven weeks of bombing—with the involvement of more than 900 aircraft and 35 ships—to coerce Serbia into a political solution for Kosovo (at the time an autonomous region of Serbia). The war thus demonstrated both NATO's centrality and its strategic limitations, indirectly encouraging the idea of coalition warfare unconstrained by institutional rules and procedures.[77]

To an extent, Blair was simply unlucky. The timing of his Kosovo activism was bad: after a couple of years of elevated activity, President Chirac had simply run out of steam. He signed up to the St. Malo Declaration, but not action in Kosovo. President Clinton was faced with impeachment hearings in Congress, and his secretary of state, Madeleine Albright, was not impressed with the St. Malo Declaration. And Germany's new chancellor, Gerhard Schröder, was prepared for partnership with Russia, but not military activism. Following a particularly intense argument with Schröder, Blair sighed, "I thought he was going to hit me."[78] Blair would later strike back, once NATO's Operation Allied Force had begun, with a speech so bold on intervention that it became known as the Blair Doctrine.[79] Lawrence Freedman, who contributed portions of the speech to Blair's advisors, later wrote that the key challenge of the doctrine was not to follow its righteous impulse, but to control it for political purposes.[80]

NATO's declared purpose was increasingly the security and stability of the Euro-Atlantic area. The alliance maintained its purpose of collective defense, but crisis management and crisis response operations, as well as wide-ranging partnerships, were the main novelties of its updated Strategic Concept.[81] The Kosovo War raged as NATO leaders met in Washington to adopt this Strategic Concept and to mark the alliance's fiftieth anniversary. Bosnia, and now Kosovo, had forced NATO to search for a new role, beyond that of a mutual defense pact, noted the *New York Times*; and the alliance essentially chose the role of regional policeman.[82] This was collective-security NATO, acting outside of its territory, in the Euro-Atlantic region, as a force for good.

It raised the obvious question of who would control this force for good. France and Russia—the two big, frustrated reformers of the 1990s—agreed that only the UN Security Council could do this. Both countries were permanent members of the UNSC, and they, as well as China, felt that the UN Charter was clear on the Council's prerogatives in authorizing action to restore peace and security. But other NATO leaders were reluctant to grant the UNSC a veto over NATO. The alliance thus divided: a "Catholic" camp, led by Chirac and his Italian colleague Massimo D'Alema, insisted on UN mandates; a "Lutheran" camp, led by Blair and Schröder, devised a new doctrine, whereby human plight could sometimes trump sovereign rights; and an "agnostic" camp, led by Clinton, argued that UN mandates were desirable, but not imperative.[83] In Kosovo, the allies agreed that existing UNSC resolutions—along with human plight—justified action. Moving forward, they fudged the issue in their Strategic Concept, by pledging to pursue crisis management action "consistent with international law."

That a force for good could be politically divisive was thus clear. Legal doctrine did, on balance, offer NATO a basis for action in Kosovo; but legal doctrine could not be separated from questions of political credibility and selectivity.[84] Russian Prime Minister Primakov, who had been en route to Washington when NATO's Kosovo air campaign began, ordered, in a display of political fury, his plane to turn around over the Atlantic and return to Russia. Russia later joined in the diplomacy to get Serbia to enter a peace deal, and it enlisted in the NATO-led international peacekeeping force (KFOR). But its declared intention was to anchor the deal in the UN and make NATO an appendix.[85] In mid-June, Russia abruptly moved its forces in Bosnia into the airport at Pristina, Kosovo's capital, leading to a brief, but intense, standoff with the UK's NATO forces. British Lieutenant-General Michael Jackson, in charge on the ground, refused to follow the orders of SACEUR, General Wesley Clark, to interfere with the Russian move. "I'm not going to start Third World War for you," Jackson told Clark.[86] The crisis was defused, but it drove home Russia's refusal to substitute legal and humanitarian doctrine for political control.

The year 1997 was a pivotal one for NATO. It was when the NATO allies struck a deal with Russia, decided to enlarge NATO with three countries, and took further steps to enhance NATO's general security role. In Paris to discuss preparations with President Chirac, US national security advisor Anthony Lake foresaw how all this could come together in a 1997 "super summit." "This would be of huge, historic significance, on the order of 1815," Lake told the French president, alluding to the historic Congress of Vienna and its outcome, a stabilizing Concert of Europe. "That should be our objective."[87]

That NATO allies had come to the point where they could credibly entertain such a historical analogy was telling. They had overcome the crisis of inaction that had dragged the late secretary general, Manfred Wörner, from his sickbed to run NAC meetings into the night. The fact that a NATO transformed for post-Cold War Europe would have to spring into action to solve other people's crises had been hard to digest; but the decision to engage Operation Deliberate Force and coerce the Serbs into peacemaking was truly transformative. It was a fitting conclusion to Wörner's efforts.

It was transformative in that NATO gained a sharp edge in Europe's new political order. For the European allies, it implied limits to the European Union and its defense arm, the Western European Union. For Russia, it implied limits to its continental role, in that it had no legal or formal right to shape NATO's decision-making. The endgame to Bosnia's war thus established the fact that at the core of Europe's set of interlocking institutions was NATO.

This did not speak against Lake's desire for an 1815 moment in 1997. But it did mean that the NATO allies had to be especially cognizant of the potential contradiction between their general security aspiration and Russia's sense of being boxed in. And in 1997 the allies were explicit: they offered Russia big and soft NATO as a path to mutual political renewal. To do otherwise, to make NATO enlargement contingent on Russian consent, the allies decided, would be to stoke nationalist and great-power aspirations in Russia. By this logic, NATO could not simply stay with the Partnership for Peace—which is what the Pentagon preferred—it had to open up to enlargement. But it had to go easy on the first round of enlargement, staying well clear of the three Baltic states—former Soviet republics—that bordered on Russia. That was the deal Presidents Clinton and Yeltsin struck in Helsinki, in March 1997.

NATO's main challenge moving forward from 1997 was not Russia. Rather, it was its own political sense of what it would take to get the balance between Russia and enlargement right, while running crisis response operations, such as that in Kosovo. What it would take was an inherently political question. But the NATO allies were attracted to new aspirations of human justice baked into its general security role. Along with the war on terror, these would cause NATO to lose its balance in the twenty-first century.

9

Runaway Aspiration

"I choked back tears," recalls Condoleezza Rice, national security advisor to President George W. Bush. The occasion was the message of Nicholas Burns, US NATO ambassador, that NATO was preparing to invoke Article 5 for the first time. The initiative came from Secretary General George Robertson and a handful of NATO ambassadors and advisors gathered in the headquarters, and it was in response to the terrorist attacks of September 11, 2001. Rice assured Burns of approval for the initiative. NATO's Article 5 is in fact triggered by an armed attack, meaning that, technically speaking, an Article 5 declaration by the NAC is superfluous. But because NATO had never before been in such a situation, and to sweep aside any political ambiguity, the headquarters leadership decided to go for a formal declaration. Robertson, who would have to break new ground, recalled the sage advice of his predecessor, Javier Solana: never put anything before the North Atlantic Council unless you know the answer is "yes." "It was good advice," Robertson thought, but "I ignored it."[1]

Robertson would next have "fraught, nerve-racking telephone conversations with Prime Ministers, Foreign Ministers and in one case, through the Foreign Minister's mobile phone, with a whole Cabinet meeting."[2] The NAC had met on the morning of September 12, when the permanent representatives—ambassadors—asked for five hours to run consultations with their capitals. There was a legal concern—whether the attack was "directed from abroad," as stipulated

213

in Article 5—and then there were political anxieties and questions to massage. When the NAC reconvened some hours later, all the allies agreed that the attack had triggered NATO's Article 5. The NAC thus issued its first ever Article 5 declaration.[3] It came with the caveat that the United States must present persuasive evidence of the attack originating from abroad, which it later did. Through all this, Robertson maintained a focus on getting the job done. It was only when he read the declaration to a packed press conference that he allowed himself the thought, "My God, this is pretty dramatic stuff." The decision to seek a NAC declaration could have gone into reverse, damaging NATO. Making the decision was "high risk," Robertson noted. When it bore fruit, he commented wryly, the Article 5 declaration became "everybody's idea."[4]

NATO's entry into the war on terror would transform the alliance yet again. To be ready and relevant, it needed a global outlook, and agile and ready military forces. But the war on terror—and especially the 2003 war in Iraq—threw the allies into a "near-death" experience.[5] To overcome their crisis, the allies needed a mission of great aspiration. This led to NATO's vast commitment to Afghan stabilization. Afghanistan offered NATO a role in the war on terror, and a seemingly manageable general security task that built on the alliance's Balkan experience. But war was thrust upon NATO by a skillful Taliban insurgency. And the mighty alliance discovered the brutal reality that in war, the ability to relate military means to political ends is paramount. But NATO's mindset was elsewhere, and the alliance made mistakes—in Afghanistan, in Europe, and then in Libya. By the end of it all, it was exhausted.

Marginalized NATO

The NATO allies were not ready for a military engagement in Afghanistan, even if they supported the Article 5 declaration. They had spent the better part of a decade adjusting to big, soft, security NATO. They had reduced their military forces, put some of them in storage, and readied a portion of them for crisis management operations in the Euro-Atlantic area. Anything beyond that would have to be pulled from dormant structures and greatly improvised. The September 2001 terrorist attacks did not leave the allies the luxury of time. In a matter of weeks, on October 7, 2001, the United States began its war, Operation Enduring Freedom, on Al Qaeda and its Afghan hosts, the Taliban regime. Only one ally, Britain, was ready to take part in the opening phase of this operation. British leader Tony Blair, President Bush later recalled, never wavered. It cemented, Bush wrote, "the closest friendship I would form with any foreign leader."[6]

Thus opened the coalition phase of the war on terror. It was a US effort with flexible, ad hoc, improvised contributions from allies and partners. It was certainly not a war decided by the North Atlantic Council, nor a mission run through NATO's chain of command. Nor would it be anytime soon, Deputy Secretary of Defense Paul Wolfowitz told NATO defense ministers on September 26. Wolfowitz had come to NATO headquarters to seek coalition contributions, not to ask the alliance to take collective action. "If we need collective action, we'll ask for it," he assured those attending, effectively downplaying the idea. Wolfowitz thus mostly ran bilateral meetings with allies and partners, including Russia, to request specific contributions to the US-led coalition.[7] He was dovetailing with his boss, Donald Rumsfeld, who argued both inside the administration and to the public that the war on terror could only be fought by flexible coalitions, not institutionalized alliances.[8] Tellingly, Rumsfeld's 2002 presentation of a grand "military transformation" agenda at no point referred to NATO.[9]

NATO did contribute to the fight against Al Qaeda. But the measures were indirect, including intelligence sharing, port and airfield access, and overflight clearances. They also included a naval operation (Active Endeavour) in the Eastern Mediterranean and, perhaps most notably, the deployment of NATO airborne warning and control planes (AWACS) to the United States, allowing US assets to deploy abroad. But all this happened within a coalition framework, and NATO's contributions came only after the US government had decided that it could not leave NATO hanging entirely. Ambassador Burns was thus instructed to seek the aforementioned NATO contributions. And this was the rub. Edgar Buckley, a deputy to George

Robertson who had helped draft the Article 5 declaration, saw in the US decisions "a fundamental misjudgment about the nature of the Alliance."[10] If NATO was merely a coalition toolbox, the alliance's solidarity would go out the window. Condoleezza Rice retrospectively agreed. "We left the alliance dressed up with nowhere to go. I wish we'd done better."[11]

To be relevant, NATO needed yet again to "transform." On this there was agreement. But could the allies remain politically cohesive in the day and age of global terror? President Bush had in his January 2002 State of the Union address, invoked an "axis of evil" that had allies worried. If they transformed their alliance for expeditionary operations in faraway countries, would they become simply a toolkit for America's war on terror? Karl Franz Lamers of the German conservative CDU spoke for many Europeans when he drew a distinction between NATO and coalitions.[12] Decisions on war and peace would have to be collective, not issued from any one capital. However, decisions would only be collective if the alliance was ready. And for NATO, this meant not only building expeditionary muscle for global tasks, but also completing its security mission in Europe.

On to transformation

NATO notably needed to move its relationship with Russia beyond the freeze provoked by the Kosovo intervention. Relations chilled to the point where Russian officials would only talk to NATO officials about the Balkans, nothing else. Vladimir Putin's rise to power in December 1999 changed things, because Putin wanted "to improve relations with the West as a means to strengthen the Russian state."[13] In February 2000, he and NATO Secretary General Robertson met in Moscow to reset relations. As secretary general, Robertson did not have a plane, but the German government put one at his disposal for the occasion. He recalls with good humor the historical irony of the moment he stepped onto the tarmac, with plenty of media to report it: how he, a Brit, in Moscow, was stepping out of a Luftwaffe aircraft.[14]

The puzzle for NATO was how to enhance the partnership with Russia, while continuing its enlargement in Central and Eastern

Europe and building its military muscle. To solve the conundrum, NATO turned its military eyes to forging lean and agile national forces that could deploy across great geographical distance—too lean to threaten Russia, but capable of chasing terrorists in Afghanistan's Hindu Kush mountains. New allies would be asked to do the same thing, which, again, would rob them of the military mass that Russian leaders might see as potentially threatening. And there was more. NATO's integrated command structure would transform. The old structure, organized around an East–West geography, including strategic commands for the Atlantic and for Europe, and then sub-commands for Europe's distinct theaters, would disappear. A new structure would go beyond geography, with one major strategic command focused on current "operations," wherever they may be taking place, and another major strategic command focused on the future (or, in the jargon of the time, military "transformation"). In short, NATO's political-military preoccupation was no longer primarily Europe, where NATO remained big and soft, but hotspots around the globe, for which NATO needed new tools.

President Putin was touchy about NATO enlargement, but open to it, so long as the first priority was a new and upgraded NATO–Russia partnership deal. It had been in the making since the reset of Putin and Robertson. In the end it would essentially consist of an upgrade to their NATO–Russia Permanent Joint Council (PJC), which dated back to 1997. The PJC had operated in "format 19+1" (nineteen NATO countries plus Russia). With the upgrade, a new NATO–Russia Council (NRC) would meet in "format 20" (all countries on an equal footing). Attached to the NRC would be a number of working groups, staffed by national experts, to address issues such as terrorism, ballistic missile defense, and airspace management, and ultimately to tee up political decision-making. But it took a long time to reach the deal, and by early 2002 it seemed to have got bogged down. Italy's Prime Minister Berlusconi then seized the moment. He had excellent relations to both Putin and Bush, and at his urging, in early April Putin called Bush and asked to accelerate the negotiations. Time was of the essence, Berlusconi also felt, and he offered to provide "an appropriate historic setting" in Italy for a signing event in late May.[15]

NATO and Russia delivered. In mid-May 2002, NATO foreign ministers met in Reykjavik to finalize an overall roadmap for alliance transformation: new and slim military tools, continued enlargement, and a new security relationship with Russia.[16] On the sidelines, NATO and Russian officials agreed to the NRC upgrade and what promised to be a new beginning in NATO–Russia relations. Attention then turned to Italy and the "historic setting" promised by Berlusconi for the NATO–Russia deal.

The parties convened at Pratica di Mare on May 28 and signed the deal.[17] They invoked a Pratica di Mare spirit of cooperation, which sounded splendid. But the name referred not to a sumptuous palace in the capital of Rome, but to an air base next to modest Pomezia, outside of Rome. In the new age of terrorist threats, Prime Minister Silvio Berlusconi considered it better to gather the leaders at an air base and surround it with some 15,000 security forces. Instead of bringing the leaders to Rome's marbled splendors, Berlusconi brought faux marble to the leaders: he had the air base scaffolded into an ancient Roman setting, replete with arches and statues. It was all a magnificent show.[18] Russian Foreign Minister Igor Ivanov played his part, perceiving in the NRC the germ of "a future European security architecture."[19] The *New York Times* seemed persuaded, seeing two sides "well on their way to ending Russia's longstanding estrangement from the West."[20] Berlusconi would later reminisce that "I guess of all the things I did in my life, this may be the one I am most proud of ... This really was the moment that marked the end of the Cold War."[21] But the scaffolding also indicated how fragile it all was. The NRC would only be as strong as the trust that the NATO allies and Russia could build.

The "war on terror" would corrode relations, and it was inside the alliance that the rot began: most allies disagreed with the label "war on terror." They regarded terrorism as a criminal matter, to be dealt with by various means, ranging from police forces, courts of law, intelligence, special operations forces, and development aid. War was too biased toward massive military engagement, they felt.[22] And as President Bush and his principal deputies increasingly singled out Iraq as a threat to be disarmed, some allied leaders worried. Fighting

Iraq could "shatter" allied unity, German Chancellor Schröder warned in September 2002. "It would be a big mistake."[23]

The most urgent issue on NATO's agenda was not Iraq, but Afghanistan. Following the fall of the Taliban regime, which had supported Al Qaeda, a UN mission had been set up, and with it an International Security Assistance Force (ISAF). ISAF was not part of the war of terror: it was a small force policing the streets of Kabul to protect and enable the government. Through 2002, NATO was deeply divided on whether the alliance should take a greater role in supporting and running ISAF. Britain and Turkey had run ISAF in its early rotations largely by national means. Now Germany and the Netherlands were slated to take over, and they found it heavy going. They wanted NATO to help. Canada and Italy, next in line, had similar thoughts. But France and Belgium were opposed: they simply did not want NATO to buy a share, however indirect, in the war with terrorists. In short, NATO was stuck.

US Secretary of Defense Donald Rumsfeld charged into this delicate situation with hobnailed boots. As he met with his NATO colleagues to prepare for a November summit in Prague, and as a possible war in Iraq was on everybody's mind, Rumsfeld simply ignored how such a war related to NATO: "It hasn't crossed my mind."[24] Remarkably, the snub came as NATO defense ministers approved a new concept for force readiness—a NATO Response Force (NRF)—that would sideline and eventually finish off the CJTF concept. Technically, it was clear that the CJTF had become heavy, bloated, and unfit for expeditionary operations.[25] But politically, CJTF harbored aspirations for greater European influence and a degree of operational autonomy. In ignoring these aspirations, Secretary Rumsfeld provoked the ire of several European allies.

President Bush thus went to the Prague summit with one important mission in mind: to dispel allied unease and bolster confidence in US policy. And that mission was accomplished, at least for the time being. The allies sidestepped Afghanistan and Iraq and delivered on the three big themes of their earlier Reykjavik meeting. The single biggest decision was to invite seven new countries to begin accession talks with the alliance: Estonia, Latvia, Lithuania, Slovakia, Slovenia, Romania, and Bulgaria. This was NATO's big-bang enlargement eastwards, overshadowing the 1997 decision to invite just three countries. The Prague summit also celebrated the upgraded partnership with Russia, just as it readied other NATO partnerships for joint efforts against terrorism. And then finally it offered a package of military reforms to prepare NATO for expeditionary operations.[26] President Bush had done well. "Hmmm, not bad," a European diplomat noted; President Bush seems "a decent guy who's up to the job."[27]

Near-death experience

The beautiful, but potentially brutal, volcanic Azores in mid-Atlantic symbolically captured the drama of how NATO next descended into a spiral of diplomatic conflict that threatened to undo the alliance. It was on the Azores that President Bush, Prime Minister Blair, Prime Minister Aznar of Spain, and Prime Minister Barroso of Portugal gathered on March 16, 2003, for a final diplomatic act before they unleashed war on Saddam Hussein's Iraq on March 20. NATO was divided and left behind.

Observers wrote of a transatlantic division of outlooks—of American Mars and European Venus.[28] And it is true that the United States and Britain were pitted against the leading continental countries of France, Germany, and Russia. But it is also true that the conflict ran deep in most allied countries. The Azores summit was widely seen as offering a helping hand to Blair, Aznar, and Barroso, all of whom struggled to carry parliamentary majorities for the war. Viewed more broadly, the Iraq War was a political trauma of such magnitude for NATO that only an extraordinary new mission could offer relief; and that became the alliance's Afghanistan mission.

President Bush, Prime Minister Blair, and President Chirac in a sense transplanted to NATO their conflict in the UN Security Council. They had agreed in the UNSC to let UN inspections disarm Saddam Hussein's Iraq, but they disagreed on the consequences of Iraqi non-compliance. As 2002 made way for 2003, diplomatic trench-digging went into overdrive. President Chirac and Chancellor Schröder aligned with President Putin to arrest further decision-making in the UNSC. It created a particular headache for Prime Minister Blair, who needed UN cover to avoid regime change in London, as an advisor put it to him. With the help of President Bush, Blair sought both a last-minute UNSC resolution and a roadmap for a Middle Eastern peace process.[29] But all to no avail: on March 20, Blair decided to go to war with the United States without added UNSC cover and in opposition to multiple NATO allies. It was an ignoble fate for the interventionist doctrine that Blair had prescribed as an antidote to the allied fragmentation and paralysis over Bosnia. It was likewise a troubled outcome for Chirac and Schröder, whose European project had come to rely not on the United States, but on Russia.

Shortly before the war, Turkey brought allied tensions to a new pitch. Prime Minister Recep Erdoğan, newly elected in 2003, did not support his country's role as a northern conduit for American forces attacking Iraq. He no doubt worried that a weakening of Iraq's central government would empower Kurdish forces in the borderland, with whom Turkey had a longstanding conflict. Officially, Erdoğan worried about the risk of Iraqi retaliatory missile strikes and possible use of chemical weapons. He thus sought NATO Article 4 consultations—which any ally can do if threatened—and the pre-emptive NATO deployment of missile defense systems and decontamination units to Turkey. But four allies—France, Germany, Belgium, and Luxembourg—did not want to grant these consultations, on the grounds that they were a barely veiled attempt to drag NATO into a war effort they did not support. Denying their ally, Turkey, consultation rights meant that NATO was not only stuck: it was at breaking point.

NATO Secretary General George Robertson and US NATO Ambassador Nicholas Burns teamed up to solve the problem. Luxembourg and Germany relented, and Robertson removed France from the equation by handing the affair to NATO's Defence Planning Committee—the decision-making forum where France, on account of its military opt-out, was not represented. Robertson then found a loophole that would allow NATO's supreme military commander to deploy assets in support of Turkey. Belgium was now politically isolated, and by mid-February it, too, relented.[30] NATO assistance to Turkey, Operation Display Deterrence, went ahead. NATO did not break, but it had been a close call.

The Bush team knew this, and four days later, when George Robertson visited the White House, he received a standing ovation in the Oval Office, led by President Bush. All the principals were there, including security advisor Condoleezza Rice, Secretary of State Colin Powell, and Secretary of Defense Donald Rumsfeld. To his credit, at the end of the meeting George Robertson decided to address the alliance malaise. Having asked President Bush whether he could be frank with him, Robertson warned that the president's language and his appearance—often in a military flight jacket—was turning European opinion against him. Language that works here doesn't work in Europe, Robertson told the president.[31] It was unusual for Oval Office guests to criticize the president, and all the principals looked on sternly. Robertson remembers how "the temperature in the room fell below zero." Bush broke the ice with a playful question about who would score higher on a scale of warmongering, himself or—and he then pointed at him—Secretary of Defense Rumsfeld. "It is not easy to step into the Oval Office and say critical things," Robertson would recollect, but "I needed to say it for the sake of alliance cohesion."[32]

Overreach

The best way to shelter NATO from the disputed war in Iraq was then to wed it to the Afghanistan mission. In mid-April 2003, NATO allies took charge of ISAF. In early December 2003 they upped the ante, deciding to expand ISAF progressively from the city of Kabul to all major provinces of the country. US NATO Ambassador Burns recalls how "We were not arguing about Afghanistan in the North Atlantic Council. The fact that we were divided on Iraq encouraged countries to be more engaged in Afghanistan."[33] George Robertson's mandate as NATO secretary general expired at the end of 2003, and his replacement, Dutch Foreign Minister Jaap de Hoop Scheffer, knew what he was stepping into: a bruised alliance that needed to get Afghanistan right.[34] Behind the scenes, the United States, France, and Germany had come together around his candidacy. Apart from his personal qualities, Scheffer's appeal also had to do with the fact that the

Netherlands had a foot in both camps: it supported the Iraq War, but did not send any troops. "My mandate from the key allies was clear," de Scheffer recalls, and it was to "heal the rift."[35]

"All hell broke loose," a British Chinook pilot, Mark Hammond, recalled, as he flew into Musa Qala in northern Helmand province in mid-2006, completing his medical evacuation mission as four Apache helicopters and an A-10 Warthog "ripped the place to pieces."[36] For British forces, for whom Helmand province was supposed to be a relief after bruising years in Iraq, it was a rude awakening to Afghanistan's reality. It was the same for NATO, which by early 2007 had fully rolled out its footprint of provincial reconstruction teams (PRTs). These combined security assistance, development aid, and governance advice, and there was a PRT in most of Afghanistan's provinces, protected by some 35,000 ISAF troops under NATO command.[37] But the troops were spread thin and were not ready for the Taliban's skillful insurgency. All hell thus broke loose not only for Mark Hammond, but for the entire ISAF mission.

Healing the rift now meant finding a recipe to gain control of events in Afghanistan. When British General David Richards moved into Kabul, he saw political and organizational "anarchy"—a "startling lack of coordination" among essentially all actors.[38] Something needed to be done. The lessons learned from the Balkans and an integrated approach in the UN system became the building blocks of the new thinking. The Bush administration pulled these elements into its December 2005 National Security Presidential Directive for inter-agency coordination and action.[39] It spilled over into an Afghanistan Compact adopted in London in January 2006, which promised coordinated action to bring national development to the country.[40] Hopes for a coordinated effect ran high.[41] But de facto the compact committed the international community to build a nation for the state, rather than the other way around. It offered the Taliban, better aligned with rural Afghan society than the government, a durable advantage.[42]

The NATO allies embraced the Afghanistan Compact, but also sought their own "Comprehensive Approach." These were conclusions of NATO's Riga summit in November 2006. It immediately caused a political headache for allies, though. NATO leaders warned that the alliance "cannot assume the entire burden,"[43] but who would help NATO carry the burden? And what should NATO do if no one showed up? Should it develop its own global partnerships with, say, Australia and Japan, and begin to coordinate civilian and military assistance? The questions inflamed the political wounds from the Iraq War: the United States supported NATO going big; France resisted. For a while, the Comprehensive Approach offered relief, because it was so broad that compromise seemed possible. But it failed to pinpoint the essential challenge of the Afghan mission: namely, to think through the relationship between campaign ends and means. For as long as the end was the Afghanistan Compact, NATO would always be short on means. The Comprehensive Approach was ultimately not fit for political purpose, and NATO was about to find that out.

Three strong political actors would undo NATO's theory of Comprehensive Approach before it was fully formulated. They acted out of self-interest and did not coordinate, but the sum total was the same: renewed deadlock in the alliance, and the realization that, even if it did not want to, NATO was increasingly holding the baby in Afghanistan.

Afghanistan's President Hamid Karzai was becoming a difficult partner. Impatient, in late 2007 the United States and Britain sought to accelerate the coordination of security, aid, and governance in Afghanistan through the appointment of a "civilian czar"—a high commissioner—to run things. And they had a candidate in mind: Paddy Ashdown, a centrist British politician with experience from Bosnia-Herzegovina, where he had served as a plenipotentiary representative of the international community between 2002 and 2006. Ashdown accepted the Afghan job, and Karzai also indicated that he would approve the appointment; but then the mood in the presidential palace shifted. Fearful that Ashdown would become too strong, and that he would inhibit the distribution of political favors "Afghan style," in early 2008 Karzai simply vetoed the whole idea.[44]

Western leaders could, of course, have set up their own in-house coordination; but that is where Turkey's Prime Minister Recep Erdoğan put his foot down. Turkey, more activist and mindful of its own interests following the Iraq War,[45] nurtured distinct grievances against the EU's security and defense dimension. The country had had a partnership deal with the old vessel of European cooperation, the Western European Union. But the EU had begun shutting down the WEU, taking over its functions with greater vigor, but also with a poorer offer of access to Turkey. That country lost no time in retaliating, vetoing NATO's cooperation with the EU. In 2006–7, Turkey was not about to let the allies' search for an Afghan-centric Comprehensive Approach overrule these reservations. Time and time again within NATO, Turkish diplomats refused to open the door to the improved NATO–EU relations presumed by the Comprehensive Approach. As NATO approached its Bucharest summit in April 2008, therefore, it was increasingly clear that at best it could develop a plan for its own actions. As for comprehensive international collaboration, it would have to dial down its ambitions.

Putin would likewise do his best to derail NATO's planning. He had signaled his intent in February 2007, when, at the Munich Security Conference—an annual gathering at the highest political levels—he spoke out bluntly against American leadership and a "unipolar" world, in which Washington was insinuating itself in place of the UNSC. NATO expansion, President Putin continued, was a plain "provocation" for Russia.[46] Though Putin's grievances focused on Europe—on NATO's geographical enlargement, the use of force in Kosovo, US plans for building up missile defenses, and Western meddling in Ukraine—they were fueled by his sense that NATO was in over its head in Afghanistan. Putin's Munich speech "reflected Russia's rediscovered swagger on the world stage."[47]

In January 2008, Putin brought that swagger to NATO headquarters, as he replaced the rather unassuming General Konstantin Totsky as Russia's representative to NATO and the NRC with the colorful Dmitry Rogozin. Famously, Rogozin would put up a portrait of former Soviet leader Joseph Stalin in his office next to NATO headquarters. Jaap de Hoop Scheffer recalls the sense of astonishment and political ambiguity that Rogozin's first visit to his office provoked. As per protocol, Rogozin visited Scheffer before taking up his position at the headquarters. Unexpectedly, he brought a present to the secretary general's office in a huge, gift-wrapped box. This Scheffer unwrapped, only to find a large parcel inside. On opening the package, to his astonishment he discovered that it contained a big ax in carved wood. Rogozin broke into a smile: "I have come to bury the hatchet."[48] Rogozin in fact turned out to have a liking for handing out replica weaponry at the headquarters: when the Italian NATO ambassador, Stefano Stefanini, ended his term, Rogozin offered him as a parting gift a (deactivated) Kalashnikov automatic rifle.[49]

Rogozin and his boss, Vladimir Putin, could not have failed to notice how deeply the issue of membership for Ukraine and Georgia divided the allies in the run-up to the Bucharest summit. Most allies—and certainly all the major ones, except for Spain—had come together in February 2008 to recognize Kosovo's independence, which upset Putin. But now they were in open disagreement—pitting the United States and its eastern allies, such as Poland and the Baltic states, against Germany and France—and this provided Russia with a golden opportunity. Ukraine and Georgia were not easy enlargement cases: their governments suffered from corruption, and in Ukraine public opinion was deeply divided. But Russia was the real issue. Should the allies engage Ukraine and Georgia at the risk of Russian aggression?

Shortly after Rogozin's entry to the headquarters, President Putin accepted NATO's invitation to join the summit in Bucharest.[50] It was standard protocol to issue such an invitation, but Putin had never before acted on it.

Bucharest disunity

Putin was invited to the second day of the summit, which was normally set aside for partnership events. But he unexpectedly showed up for dinner on the summit's first day. Luckily, Afghan President Karzai had been unable to attend, and so there was a vacant seat. Putin took his place next to Jeannine de Hoop Scheffer, wife of the NATO secretary general, and put up a civil performance.

The next day, at the opening of a bilateral meeting, Putin told Scheffer, "I'd rather talk to your wife than you." It seemed like a joke, but in fact was not. The bilateral meeting turned unfriendly, as Putin lashed out at NATO's enlargement policy. The preceding day, the allies had agreed to invite two new countries to begin accession talks: Albania and Croatia. Macedonia was likewise issued with an invitation, pending resolution of the dispute between it and Greece over the its name. But this was not the rub. The real cause of Putin's disgruntlement was NATO's statement that Ukraine and Georgia "will become members of NATO."[51] The allies set no date for this, and nor did they allow the two countries to enter NATO's Membership Action Plan (MAP), normally the track to membership. They were categorical about the end state (membership), but slow-walked the process—an ambiguity that Putin tore into.

Remarkably, instead of buying time, NATO leaders went head to head with Putin. They could have asked staff to establish a process for evaluating the performance of Ukraine and Georgia in this or that direction (something staff excels at doing). But the leaders had convinced themselves that they could settle disagreements at the summit, even if those disagreements had proven intractable during the summit preparations. This is very rarely done, and hindsight shows why. The text they came up with was a bad compromise. President Bush added the phrase—often cited—that Ukraine and Georgia "will become members." German Chancellor Angela Merkel and French President Nicolas Sarkozy ensured that Ukraine and Georgia were not put on track to membership (MAP). Thus, NATO said both "yes" and "no." NATO offered a vision of Ukrainian and Georgian membership, but in fact had no consensus. NATO's ambiguity was an open invitation to Russian resistance: an invitation to turn NATO's eastern flank into a competitive space.

Jaap de Hoop Scheffer recalls how on the first day he restricted access to the NAC: out went everyone but the leaders themselves, and one advisor each. But it was all to no avail: the rifts ran too deep. It took corridor diplomacy in the evening, an emergency breakfast at 5 a.m. the next day, and then some further corridor diplomacy to get to an agreed text.[52] President Bush downplayed all this in his memoirs, stating that he thought the threat from Russia strengthened the case for Ukraine and Georgia's fast-track (MAP) status, and that the allies found a compromise.[53] In fact, Bush's determined position fully crystallized just five weeks ahead of the summit, and only during a direct meeting in late February at the White House between himself and the NATO secretary general.[54] Bush knew of the opposition from key allies. His own ambassador to Russia, William Burns, warned him that President Putin would see fast-track membership status for Ukraine and Georgia as a "direct strategic challenge."[55] President Bush had long pursued a freedom agenda that involved not only a war on terror, but also a global campaign for local choice, empowerment, and accountability.[56] On Ukraine and Georgia, at the Bucharest NATO summit, Bush conspicuously failed to empower allied viewpoints, and ultimately did NATO damage.

Other allied leaders, especially Germany's Chancellor Merkel and France's President Sarkozy, must share the blame, though. They coordinated their summit opposition to President Bush, and each, in his or her own way, pursued national agendas.[57] Sarkozy, in line with French diplomatic tradition, sought a privileged high-level dialogue with Putin, which of course relegated Ukraine and Georgia to the second row. Merkel, in line with Germany's Ostpolitik tradition, sought trade and interdependence, meaning that she refused to let energy security become a NATO topic.[58] These two leaders drew back out of fear of upsetting Russia and in the belief that they could reason with it—through privileged dialogue or trade. They downplayed President Putin's warnings to the West, and then agreed to a NATO text they did not support ("will become members"). It was a weak position that could all too easily embolden a counterpart who was determined to alter the course of European security, and especially block NATO enlargement.

All this rather dampens the summit's achievements surrounding Afghanistan. President Sarkozy boosted the ISAF mission by offering a French force contribution—a gesture that went hand in hand with his decision to have France rejoin NATO's integrated command. The split of 1966 was thus ended. The allies also adopted a Comprehensive Approach policy. However, as one involved staffer noted, the outcome was so broad and loose that you could drive a truck through it and not notice.[59] The policy also divided between a vision for broad international cooperation—issued by all ISAF partners (also gathered in Bucharest)—and an action plan (a Comprehensive Strategic Political-Military Plan) that belonged to just NATO.[60] This division of labor—between global vision and NATO action—underscored a fear inside NATO: namely, that if the vision failed to translate into global action, then the alliance would be on its own and would in the end be held responsible for Afghanistan. As with Ukraine and Georgia, in Afghanistan NATO was about to bite off more than it wanted to chew.

Russia's new president, Dmitry Medvedev, an ally of Putin's, did not hesitate to exploit the situation. On August 7, Russia provoked Georgian President Mikheil Saakashvili into picking a fight, and Russian forces rolled into Georgia, strengthening their control over two of Georgia's republics—Abkhazia and South Ossetia, today nominally integrated into the Russian Federation. France, the United States, and others helped negotiate a quick end to the war, which perhaps obscured what, with hindsight, was a clear sign that Russia would no longer accept the security framework established by NATO in the 1990s.[61] Adding insult to injury, Russia blocked approval of a Comprehensive Approach agreement between the United Nations— where it has a veto—and NATO. As for NATO–UN relations, all that could be done was to have the two secretaries general of their respective organizations sign an agreement on "secretariat cooperation." And even then, the agreement was kept secret to minimize political controversy with, again, Russia.[62]

Limits to aspiration

By late 2008, it was clear that NATO was short on political oxygen. It lacked coherent leadership in Afghanistan and on Russia in Europe. The United States had doubled down in Iraq, boosting its 2006–7 effort under the leadership of General David Petraeus. And this took its toll: it was to be the last and defining effort by the Bush presidency. NATO's foreign ministerial communiqué of December 2008 was consequently all about continuity on Afghanistan, Ukraine, and other main issues.[63] It was an alliance that stood the course while awaiting leadership.

President Barack Obama offered leadership, but on terms that Americanized the Afghan mission and strategy. It took Team Obama almost a full year to chart its course—a lengthy span of time. It first tasked Bruce Riedel, a former CIA analyst and diplomat, with running a strategic assessment, which called for more attention to be paid to Afghanistan–Pakistan relations. This was no surprise: analysts knew that the border area represented not a division, but an integrated area controlled by the Pashtun, from which the Taliban had sprung. The previous Bush administration's recommendation to the Obama team was to "induce a strategic shift in Afghan-Pakistani relations."[64] The allies signed up to this shift at their sixtieth anniversary summit in April 2009. The real surprise came when Team Obama decided to put General Stanley McChrystal, a wingman of General Petraeus, in command of the ISAF operation: in August 2009, McChrystal recommended a fully resourced counterinsurgency strategy that would increase US and allied commitments in every way. This unsettled Team Obama and triggered another strategy review in Washington.[65] The NATO allies were consulted, but mostly awaited President Obama's lead. On December 1, he finally came out in support of stepping up the counterinsurgency effort. Three days later, the NATO allies followed suit.[66]

President Obama had become NATO's best hope for turning around the Afghanistan mission. The NATO allies were ready to break past taboos—endorsing counterinsurgency as a strategy and committing to a large NATO training mission for Afghan security forces. But the alliance was not necessarily reinforced. It had not mobilized comprehensive international cooperation: rather, it had rallied around US strategy. The mission, now surging, was taxing for the individual allies, who struggled to deliver both forces and domestic support. Many of them hedged their contributions with caveats, hampering overall command of the mission.[67]

Dissent within Obama's team also tested alliance coherence. The president struggled to define the right level of ambition. He started out seeking the "defeat" of Al Qaeda, but settled on "degrading" it, which seemed more modest. But he then also decided that this would require a fully resourced counterinsurgency operation, a vast undertaking. Its timeline then set off a struggle inside the administration, with military commanders recommending a lengthy campaign, and civilian advisors seeking a faster transition to diplomacy. In June 2011, six months into the main surge, Obama settled the issue: the full surge would be over by mid-2012.[68]

One of the primary tasks of NATO's new secretary general, Anders Fogh Rasmussen, appointed in 2009, was to ensure NATO cohesion as the Obama administration worked out its strategy. As Team Obama settled on going big not to stay engaged, but to go home—that is, surging to put the Afghan government on its feet and then draw down—NATO developed a plan for the "phased transfer" of security responsibility to the Afghan authorities, to be followed by a partnership and downscaled training mission. To enable all this (which obviously relied heavily on political decision-making in the main capitals), Rasmussen had to take the sting out of war-on-terror controversies. In particular, it was his task to craft a new Strategic Concept for the alliance, which laid to rest tensions related to NATO's regional versus global role and its defense versus crisis management role. The allies had said as much when they appointed Rasmussen in April 2009, beginning and ending their summit communiqué with reference to a "new Strategic Concept" that "will define NATO's longer-term role in the new security environment of the 21st century."[69]

NATO's new Strategic Concept, adopted in November 2010 at the alliance's Lisbon summit, was notable in two ways. Unlike its 1999 predecessor, it was short and readable: it was good public diplomacy. This owed much to Fogh Rasmussen, the first former prime minister to have been secretary general since Paul-Henri Spaak: he carried political weight, and he leveraged it to take control of the writing of the document, once a phase of consultation had concluded.[70] And the Strategic Concept was also remarkable in that it did not prioritize among missions or fundamental tasks; it did not indicate which of collective defense or general security was the more important. Instead, it defined three fundamental tasks—collective defense, crisis management, and cooperative security—and put them all on a par with one another.[71] This was a NATO for everyone, a 360-degree alliance that appealed to allies looking east, south, globally, or simply for human betterment. It was a Strategic Concept crafted to build consensus, soothe allied nerves, and strengthen NATO's public communication. It was a Strategic Concept to keep the ducks in a row while Obama's Afghan lead played out.

A Russia opening?

Russia remained a dynamic concern for NATO. The allies confronted a big question: was NATO's big and soft formula for European security working, or did the alliance need to anticipate Russian revisionism? President Putin's performance in 2007–8 indicated revisionism; but (in accordance with the term limits placed on him by the constitution) Putin had stepped down as president in March 2008 and had allowed a successor, Dmitry Medvedev, to ascend to the presidency. Medvedev at first imitated Putin, leading the war in Georgia. But he gained his own voice, speaking of the need to reform Russia and to gain access to the World Trade Organization.[72]

The hope for convergence, as envisaged in the NATO–Russia Founding Act, grew as Medvedev settled in as president. In early 2009, US Secretary of State Hillary Clinton offered Russian Foreign Minister Sergey Lavrov a "reset" of relations, which in time would lead to enhanced US–Russian cooperation on non-proliferation (which is to say, sanctions on Iran and North Korea). They also agreed, as part of the New START treaty of April 2010, to limit their nuclear arsenals. A "hamburger summit" between Presidents Medvedev and Obama became a high point of sorts. It took place in June 2010, when the two leaders made a burger run to Ray's Hell Burger in Arlington, Virginia, where they had cheeseburgers and symbolically decided to split the fries.[73]

The spillover effect on NATO was obvious. If the United States and Russia could agree to limit their own nuclear arsenals and to cooperate on non-proliferation, might NATO not become home to a new and continental-wide agreement on missile defense? Russia had long protested US missile defense plans, claiming they were directed at Russia, whereas the United States and its allies professed to be concerned with southern threats, including from Iran. The Obama administration was ready to change course, and NATO Secretary General Rasmussen spoke of an architecture of "one security roof that protects us all."[74] In November, President Medvedev attended NATO's Lisbon summit, at which the NATO allies and Russia agreed to a cooperative policy on missile defense.[75] French President Sarkozy felt so confident in Russia's course that in December 2010 he approved the sale of two Mistral-class helicopter carriers to Russia, granting the country access to significant Western military technology and force projection capacity. And this was possibly just the beginning.

Ideas of a wider NATO–Russia rapprochement were stirring just beneath the official political level, in what experts call Track-II diplomacy, where former officials and current advisors test ideas and fertilize the ground for political initiative. Among them were the former German minister of defense, Volker Rühe, and the former chairman of NATO's Military Committee, General Klaus Naumann, who argued that "the door to NATO membership should be opened for Russia."[76] "The idea isn't as crazy as it sounds," replied James Joyner of the Atlantic Council.[77] On the Russian side, President Medvedev offered discreet support to policy ideas launched by the Institute of Contemporary Development (INSOR), headed by long-time Medvedev ally Igor Yurgens, and a new think tank, the Russia International Affairs Council (RIAC), which Medvedev had set up and asked a former foreign minister, Igor Ivanov, to run. In the run-up to the Lisbon summit, Yurgens' INSOR cooperated with the UK's International Institute for Strategic Studies to suggest how "pragmatic cooperation" could render the prospect of Russian NATO membership "more plausible."[78] A debate on this thought-provoking question simultaneously unfolded in the pages of the *Moscow Times* and in Western publications.[79] The so-called Albright Group—chaired by former Secretary of State Madeleine Albright—had run consultations leading up to the new Strategic Concept, and the group had visited Moscow. However, the Albright Group had to walk a fine line between partnership with Russia and reassuring NATO allies in Central and Eastern Europe that their interests would be considered.[80] The same balancing act could be found in NATO's Strategic Concept, where the allies confessed to wanting "a true strategic partnership between NATO and Russia," but "with the expectation of reciprocity from Russia."[81] But the Strategic Concept was Track-I, government level. The wider debate on NATO–Russia relations continued at Track-II levels.

The horizon of a Russian membership of NATO was not impossible to draw for all the experienced hands involved in Track-II conversations. They could look to the NRC and imagine it upgraded around issues of common interest. They could also look to France's withdrawal from the integrated command, suggesting that a large country could be in, but not fully in. The French experience also suggested that other allies could maintain an integrated military command, common defense planning, and separate decision-making (in the Defence Planning Committee). However, in the end it all came to naught. Perhaps it was written in the stars. Perhaps the high-minded atmosphere of the November 2010 summit was fueled by ambiguity on the important issues that would block deeper rapprochement. Diplomatic stumbles in 2011 contributed, though.

NATO allies stepped into the Arab Spring in an unfortunate way, seeking to protect civilians in Libya, but in the end becoming embroiled in a mission to unsettle the Qaddafi regime.[82] NATO's Operation Unified Protector began in March and ran until the end of October 2011. It took place with Russia's blessing—or at least not its opposition, as President Medvedev instructed his diplomats to abstain on the UNSC Resolution 1973 of March 17, 2011. This led first to a US, British, and French-led coalition operation, and then, ten days later, to NATO command of the operation. President Medvedev continued to warn of Russia's interests in the region, but he played along and famously rebuked his prime minister, Vladimir Putin, for comparing the intervention to a Western "crusade."[83] How the rebuke affected Putin's calculus is uncertain, but it seems safe to conclude that it did not diminish his desire to return to the presidency.

In the meantime, NATO allied relations frayed. France and Britain were driving the alliance's diplomacy harder than it could handle. Only fourteen of the twenty-eight allies contributed military assets to the Libya mission; and of those fourteen, only seven (the United

States, Britain, France, Canada, Belgium, Denmark, and Norway) carried out strike missions. There was bad blood between Sarkozy of France and Berlusconi of Italy.[84] Germany's foreign minister, Guido Westerwelle, who modeled himself on his predecessor, Hans-Dietrich Genscher, opted for restraint, rather than alliance solidarity; this meant that Germany not only abstained on UNSC Resolution 1973, but actually withdrew its personnel from NATO AWACS airplanes. President Obama's frustration with his allies' inability to step out in front (the so-called leading from behind doctrine) caused Secretary of Defense Robert Gates to warn them of their "collective military irrelevance" and of a "dim, if not dismal future" for NATO.[85] The glaring problem for the allies was that they had de facto handed the Libya operation to a small coalition of the most active nations— the strike nations—inside NATO, and disagreed about what to do next.

Prime Minister Putin had no such qualms about his political future. Russia had scheduled presidential elections for March 2012, and the big question was whether Medvedev would run and thereby maintain the hope for a new NATO–Russia relationship. Medvedev ended all speculation in September 2011, when he announced that Putin would be the candidate for the political party to which they both belonged. There would be no political contest in Russia. NATO–Russia relations would soon again in part depend on Vladimir Putin's thoughts and ambitions.

The war-on-terror years were bruising for the transatlantic alliance, and the aftershocks were felt long after the terrorist attacks of September 2001. The NATO allies had responded to the attacks with a powerful statement of solidarity—the Article 5 declaration—and offered to transform their alliance yet again. However, the Bush administration marginalized the alliance, and the Iraq War deeply divided it. NATO was a victim even before the intervention in Iraq started. What good was NATO's investment in expeditionary capabilities, if its governments were so fundamentally at odds with one another? For people like Secretary General Robertson, who invested heavily in NATO's relevance and steered the alliance to its first-ever Article 5 declaration, the marginalization of NATO and the predominance of coalitions in the operations in Afghanistan and Libya—and therefore the predominance of coalitions in NATO decision-making—were great disappointments.

"Justice has been done," remarked President Obama on May 2, 2011, as he announced the killing of Al Qaeda leader Osama bin Laden.[86] Bringing justice to bin Laden was a political relief, but it did not guarantee that political order would follow in either Afghanistan or NATO. Would the allies welcome the pursuit of justice at the expense of political order? The question is age-old in international affairs; and like many before them, the allies sought to have it both ways. They pursued terrorists and sought to build order. But they were also growing tired. After the killing of bin Laden, they began to offer Afghanistan a dialed-down partnership. They fought from the air over Libya, but let the ground be dominated by proxy forces and armed factions that took Libya into a civil war. They had high hopes for NATO–Russia relations, but lacked policy on what to do now that President Medvedev's term was coming to an end. Their 2010 Strategic Concept was designed to heal past wounds and offered little guidance for prioritized action or policy.

The NATO allies committed the sin of hitching their alliance to aspirations they could not fulfill. They invested in Afghanistan because it was the good fight, whereas Iraq was the bad fight. They subscribed to the lofty Afghanistan Compact, which was impossibly broad and infinite. Instead of lowering the bar, the allies repeatedly searched for more means. In 2008, at their Bucharest summit, they promised Ukraine and Georgia a future—but one on which they, the allies, disagreed. The leaders had been warned, but they insisted. In a circumscribed way, the leaders recognized their mistake, and henceforth chose a NATO secretary general from within their own ranks—a former head of state or government. They needed someone who could comfortably speak truth to power. But at the end of the day, the leaders were in charge. By 2012, they had left their political-military alliance weak at its very core, where political ends connect to military means. It did not augur well for what was to come next.

PART IV

Retreat and Resurrection? Nato from Afghanistan to Ukraine, 2012–24

10

NATO's Nationalization

"Having NATO in town is kind of exciting," Esther Westlake, a Chicago university graduate, told the visiting journalists.[1] Westlake had been involved in marches before, but never one as big as the May 2012 Chicago march to protest against NATO. She did find the excitement and the march a bit "crazy," because it attracted such a wealth of disparate activists—anti-capitalists, union laborers, war protesters, and proponents of many shades of peace and justice. They all descended on McCormick Place, the convention center on Chicago's lakefront, where NATO heads of state and government assembled for their summit. But the protesters and NATO leaders did not interact directly. The protesters wanted to hold NATO leaders to account for the world's ills, but the leaders were preoccupied with their own shortcomings and not least their dwindling resource base—"security in an age of austerity," they would call it—as well as their beleaguered campaign in Afghanistan.[2]

Perhaps the NATO leaders should have been flattered by the protesters' idea of an all-powerful NATO alliance. There was a whiff of purpose and power in the air, in the sense that President Obama had begun to eye an enhanced role for the United States in Asian geopolitics. He had thus been unusually involved in the making of a Defense Strategic Guidance, issued in January 2012, that foresaw how the United States "of necessity" would "rebalance toward the Asia-Pacific region."[3] But NATO was not on this page. Its Chicago summit

239

communiqué did invoke a "Heart of Asia" policy, but this was related to the desire to get out of Afghanistan on good terms, not to a vision of greater engagement. NATO's in-house negotiations on a down-scaled future mission in Afghanistan involved an all-too-familiar debate between, on the one hand, the United States and Britain, and on the other France, over the necessity of a "combat" role. In the end, and as a sign of the times of austerity, they agreed that the new mission would "not be a combat mission."[4]

Political fatigue was thus NATO's bigger story. The allies were not ready to ponder their role in Asia's geopolitics, but were ready to go home and rebuild their nations. President Trump was famously elected on this agenda; but a lengthy war and fiscal crisis had made it a common international concern before his election. In 2014, when Russia mounted aggression against Ukraine, the allies could muster only a weak response. They saw—or perhaps wished for—a mere regional dispute that did not seriously impinge on NATO. They thus let Germany and France take the lead in bringing Russia and Ukraine to a diplomatic agreement. A similar type of sidelining of NATO took place in Iraq, where Islamic State grew into a force to be reckoned with. The United States formed a "Global Coalition" to intervene and left NATO behind. NATO instead moved through a string of three summits—in Wales (2014), Warsaw (2016), and Brussels (2018)—where the allies tinkered with their posture, but lacked the energy to renew the alliance's collective aspiration. In Chicago, behind closed doors, NATO was everything but the all-powerful alliance that Esther Westlake and her fellow marchers from Chicago imagined. Rather, its indecisiveness contributed to a train of deteriorating events that would culminate in Russia's February 2022 all-out assault on Ukraine.

A gathering storm

Vladimir Putin and Bashar al-Assad have a lot in common. Their countries, Russia and Syria, are traditionally aligned, and they both became president in 2000. They oppose efforts to unseat autocratic leaders, including NATO's 2011 Libya operation, and they have both been challenged by domestic resistance. Putin weathered widespread anti-government protests after his March 2012 presidential election, while at the same time al-Assad's rule descended into civil war. Their coordinated campaign against Western interests would come later, in 2015; but by 2012–13 they were unmistakably testing NATO. They were autocratic rulers generating instability: would NATO allies know how to handle them?

Putin's return to power in 2012 did not cause NATO to give up its main line of cooperation with Russia, namely on missile defense. President Obama had deliberately retooled US missile defense policy—to a so-called European Phased Adaptive Approach, where missile defense deployments would happen more slowly and further away from Russian territory—to facilitate dialogue, and NATO agreement on it had led to the NATO–Russia missile defense deal in Lisbon in November 2010. The allies did remain prudent, because they did not want to give President Medvedev all that he wanted, not least NATO legal guarantees and a missile defense architecture that de facto would offer Russia control over core components in NATO's territorial defense.[5] But missile defense cooperation seemed promising. Moreover, the allies assumed that whatever President Medvedev agreed to must have been approved by Prime Minister Putin.[6] Perhaps, therefore, the allies and Russia had found a way to let the good times roll, and once and for all put the tension of the Bucharest summit behind them.

The allies had another reason to hope for better times: nuclear weapons were once again dividing governments and energizing public opinion against NATO strategy. The source of anxiety was in some ways President Obama. With his April 2009 vision of a world without nuclear weapons, the president had encouraged a "global zero" campaign that wanted NATO and others to let go of nuclear deterrence. As during the Cold War, Germany moved to the front line of this debate, causing the alliance a headache. German Chancellor Angela Merkel demanded reduced reliance on nuclear weapons and nuclear energy, which made for good politics at home in Berlin. But it was certainly not agreed NATO policy. Eastern European allies felt that Germany had disregarded their need for extended deterrence. France wanted both nuclear deterrence and nuclear energy—two issues intrinsically linked in its national capability. And other allies hosting US nuclear weapons—Belgium, Italy, the Netherlands, and Turkey, in addition to Germany—simply did not want to handle the passionate public nuclear debate that Chancellor Merkel was stoking.[7]

Thus, while Prime Minister Putin was contemplating his presidential comeback, NATO got caught in an introverted debate on weapons. In the end, the allies punted the football into the long grass. They stuck to their catchphrase from the Strategic Concept that "as long as nuclear weapons exist, NATO will remain a nuclear alliance," and they then handed deterrence and disarmament issues to an in-house review team tasked with developing a Posture Review for NATO's Chicago summit in May 2012. The review touched on the full array of thorny issues: nuclear weapons, conventional weapons, missile defense, and disarmament. But the purpose was to bundle things together and make sure nothing major happened. The review's underwhelming conclusion was that NATO's "existing mix of capabilities" was sound, and that in responding to a complex and evolving security environment, NATO should continue to maintain "an appropriate mix."[8] In other words, the NATO allies were betting that time would be on their side—that they did not need to rock the boat.

Bashar al-Assad was not similarly blessed with the luxury of time. A civil war threatened his regime, and in response he threatened his adversaries. This included the menace that he might use chemical weapons against them. But chemical weapons use is a "red line" that "would change my calculus," Obama stated in August 2012.[9] A year later, al-Assad crossed that red line, using chemical weapons—sarin gas—in a rebel-held Damascus suburb. It was a defining moment not only for President Obama, but also for the allies and partners who backed him. The president dithered, but the failure of leadership was collective. Chancellor Merkel cautioned restraint; British Prime Minister David Cameron was voted down in parliament and called Obama to apologize; and the US Congress, where the Republicans held the House of Representatives, wanted to turn the affair into a test of President Obama, rather than the national interest. Obama played into this, hitching his decision to Congressional authorization for military action. In the end, he struck a deal with President Putin to have their countries remove tons of chemical weapons from Syria.

"Don't do stupid shit," was how Obama later characterized his guiding foreign policy principle.[10] It was hard to disagree in the abstract, of course, but did it mean that Obama was right to step back in Syria, effectively allowing Putin to secure the political life of his ally, al-Assad? Or was Obama, as an influential critic, Charles Krauthammer, maintained, choosing national decline—for the purpose of having the United States live as a nation among many?[11] And did this restraint cause the threats against the United States and NATO to grow? Undeniably, Obama's red line in Syria affected NATO's reputation for resolve.[12] It revived memories of NATO's 2008 Bucharest summit, at which the NATO allies made a promise to Ukraine and Georgia that they did not really mean. The crisis of reputation seemed to have passed—until now, in 2012, when the American leader issued a threat that he did not really follow up on.

In 2008, Russia had chosen war on Georgia. In 2012–13, it was not clear how Russia would respond. It had cooperated on Syrian chemical weapons, but what would come next? NATO's oft-repeated formulation during these years was that it was "prepared," though it did not specify for what. And judging by the political fatigue and the homecoming of its forces, it was not prepared for much. "Bonsai armies"— that would be the nickname attached to Europe's armies: small, artful, and ineffective.[13] NATO Secretary General Rasmussen knew this and pushed a variety of policy concepts—Smart Defense, Connected Forces Initiative, and NATO Forces 2020—to change things.[14] But they barely masked the reality that the allies were not investing.

A limited defense architecture

At an unassuming Italian restaurant in Brussels' Zaventem airport, not far from NATO headquarters, Russia's ambassador to NATO, Alexander Grushko, had a message for NATO Deputy Secretary General Alexander Vershbow. Vershbow had in fact invited Grushko for lunch some days earlier, not knowing that it would coincide with Russia's formal annexation of Crimea on March 21, 2014. In the preceding weeks, Russia had sent unmarked troops into Ukraine's Black Sea peninsula, staged a manipulated referendum for independence, and then prepared legislation for the inclusion of Crimea in Russia. It all happened within a month. "From this day forward," Grushko told Vershbow over lunch, "the West will no longer be able to impose its will on Russia."[15]

The Russian aggression brought NATO back to basics. It could no longer talk vaguely of being "prepared"; rather, it needed to revisit and bolster its collective defense function. Of this there could be no question. But NATO's need for adaptation depended on the depth of Russia's desire for continental revision. Did it run so deep and was it so dangerous that NATO should give up on its big, soft, security design? Or could and should NATO limit its adaptation in the interest of continental stability? These questions roiled through NATO in the months following the Crimea seizure and annexation. In the end, the organization adapted in limited ways, as it prescribed a dose of collective defense medicine for itself. But only for the alliance: for the continent—and thus for Ukraine, or the Balkans, or other troubled "peripheries" beyond its perimeter—NATO did not ramp up on defense measures. The cooperative continental order was alive, though on a degree of life support.

French President François Hollande presumably knew better than most how hard it was to recalibrate both Russia policy and national security priorities. His predecessor, President Nicolas Sarkozy, had with optimism struck a deal with Russia in 2011 to sell it two high-class Mistral helicopter carriers. This had occurred in the teeth of warnings from some NATO allies; but political optimism and national interests—the deal was worth $1.66 billion—carried the day. After the Crimea seizure, President Hollande at first refused to reconsider the affair: the ships—already named *Vladivostok* and *Sevastopol*—were due to be delivered later in 2014 and in 2016, and Russian sailors had begun training on them. However, one day ahead of NATO's September 5, 2014, summit, Hollande relented and postponed the deal.[16] It would take almost a further year before it was finally canceled.

Adaptation was thus on NATO's agenda for the September 2014 alliance summit at the Celtic Manor Resort in Newport, South Wales.

In 2010, the resort had hosted the prestigious US–European Ryder Cup golf competition—a tournament where a team from either Europe or America triumphs. Now, in 2014, the idea was to have both sides win. The summit communiqué details how the allies balanced the issues to reach agreement. Three measures stand out in terms of both their novelty and the political caveats built into them.

First, the allies adopted a *Readiness Action Plan* (RAP) to respond militarily to Russia. This consisted of an enhanced air, land, and maritime presence in the eastern part of the alliance, to reassure exposed allies. And it consisted of a reinforcement of the NATO Response Force (NRF), including the creation of a spearhead force, the Very High Readiness Joint Task Force (VJTF). However, not wanting to focus exclusively on the east, NATO also said that the RAP package would respond to "risks and threats emanating from our southern neighborhood."[17]

In addition, the allies agreed to put more defense money on the table. NATO's guidelines already stipulated that countries should spend a minimum of 2 percent of GDP on defense, but that had not been taken seriously. Now, in Wales, the heads of state and government entered a *Defense Investment Pledge* (DIP) to this effect: 2 percent of GDP for defense, of which 20 percent would go on research, development, and equipment. They promised to strive to meet these targets within a decade. But the language was vague, as they committed "to move towards the 2% guideline." In practice, with some budgetary increase, they could slip off the hook.[18]

Finally, on *Russia*, the allies got tough—but only to an extent. They condemned "in the strongest terms Russia's escalating and illegal military intervention in Ukraine" and worried more broadly about "Russia's pattern of disregard for international law." However, the allies also continued to believe that "a partnership between NATO and Russia based on respect for international law would be of strategic value." They made partnership contingent on Russia's good behavior, but kept the aspiration alive.[19]

In sum, and with hindsight, NATO's Wales summit was a scene-setter, but not much more than that. It defined new priorities, but left considerable wiggle room. The hard work of hammering out the details of NATO's enhanced defense and deterrence profile remained to be done. A new helmsman would lead the charge: Anders Fogh Rasmussen was leaving the building after five years as secretary general, and another Nordic former prime minister, Jens Stoltenberg, took over. Stoltenberg and the headquarters team would be pivotal in driving the alliance to more substantial agreement at upcoming summits—in Warsaw in 2016 and Brussels in 2018.

This adaptive defense work was facilitated by a narrowing of NATO's political remit. It followed first an incident, and then the allies' decision to limit NATO in two key respects. The incident was the downing by Russian-backed rebels on July 17, 2014, of a civilian aircraft—Malaysia Airlines Flight 17 (MH17)—in Ukrainian airspace. On board were 283 passengers, 196 of whom were Dutch. The incident galvanized Western sanctions and led the Dutch authorities to investigate the crime. But none of this involved NATO, which does not manage sanctions: these are adopted either nationally or at the EU level.

An explicit decision to limit NATO came from the Obama administration's approach to the burgeoning civil war in Syria. President Obama had declined to intervene in 2013; but in 2014 the time had come to act, and Obama and Secretary of State John Kerry used the NATO Wales summit for the occasion. They pulled together a "core coalition" to fight Sunni militants and Islamic State (ISIL) terrorists. Days later, Obama pledged to degrade and "ultimately destroy" ISIL.[20] As in Libya in 2011, a strike (or core) coalition took action. In 2014, it consisted of eight NATO allies (Britain, France, Canada, Germany, Turkey, Italy, Poland, and Denmark) and one non-NATO ally (Australia). Unlike in Libya in 2011, though, NATO would have no role in or command of the mission. Lending NATO to a coalition had been a headache, and the allies were not about to repeat the experience.

NATO was equally limited by a decision by French President Hollande and German Chancellor Merkel to take the lead in the diplomacy to settle affairs in Ukraine. They assumed this leadership, it should be noted, with the backing of President Obama and other allied leaders. Merkel and Hollande met up with the leaders of Russia and Ukraine in what became known as the Normandy Format—following their initial meeting in Normandy, France, in early June 2014, where they were gathered to mark the seventieth anniversary of the allied invasion, D-Day. The Normandy Format got off to a brisk start: it facilitated a ceasefire in early September 2014, and then in February 2015, it defined a framework to resolve the war. Both agreements were worked out in the Belarus capital, Minsk, and so the diplomatic effort was baptized the "Minsk process." But the framework was only that—a framework. Lengthy and (we now know) ultimately futile, negotiations followed on Ukraine's constitutional order and Russia's influence.[21] Russia wanted to shape Ukraine's constitution; Ukraine wanted Russia out; Merkel and Hollande tried in vain to foster a compromise; and NATO was out of the equation.

The sum of all this was a limited defense architecture, coupled with a hope for change. The limited defense architecture was NATO's: more exercises in the eastern part of the alliance, more reaction forces, and a stern warning to Russia. The security of a big, inclusive, and, to an extent, demilitarized Europe was not so much in NATO hands as in the hands of many others: a US-led coalition in Syria to keep trouble at bay, national sanctions to incentivize diplomacy, and Franco-German leadership in search of a continental deal.

NATO stalls

The energy had left the room in 2014 before the real work of NATO reform began. NATO chiefs—the heads of state and government—were not looking to NATO to settle the big political questions of continental order. It was very unlike 1990, when NATO defined the contours of order. Back then, President George H.W. Bush and Chancellor Kohl had been in the lead and wanted NATO decisions to guide continental diplomacy. There was no such search for a NATO mobilization in 2014–18. The fatigue of the war on terror had taken deep root and now caused NATO defense and continental diplomacy to disconnect from each other.

NATO ministers and staff did get on with defense reforms, confronting all the hard nuts of military change. The wall they ran into was the Readiness Action Plan, which raised more questions than it answered. Should NATO station Western forces on the territory of the eastern allies, or should it merely rotate forces in and out? How much kit and gear should it store—"pre-position," in NATO-speak—on these territories to enable deployment? Would NATO allies have the air- and sealift muscle to do the job? How could NATO ensure command and control? And how could the allies re-learn what they had not used since the Cold War—i.e., the skills of joint maneuver combat against a peer competitor?

Three positions emerged in the alliance.[22] Poland, the Baltic countries, Romania, Slovakia, and Slovenia sought a maximalist solution, a RAP 2.0, meaning permanently forward-deployed Western troops. The southern allies of Italy and Spain, but also Denmark and Belgium, had different interests (and small pocketbooks) and were instead happy to stick with RAP 1.0, the Wales design of enhanced reaction forces stationed in the West that, if needed, could come to the rescue in the East. The United States and Britain were in between: they supported not permanent deployments, but rather long-term rotations, enabled by the pre-positioning of significant amounts of kit and gear. The NATO allies and staff had to consider these positions with an eye to the upcoming July 2016 Warsaw summit; they knew that time was short and the challenge of consensus considerable.

Perhaps all this weighed on the foreign ministers of Turkey and Greece, Mevlüt Çavuşoğlu and Nikos Kotzias. In mid-May 2015, Çavuşoğlu hosted a meeting of NATO foreign ministers in Antalya, Turkey. In the evening, he thanked the band that had entertained the guests after a first day of discussions. When the group next proceeded to play the hopeful 1980s hit "We Are the World," written by Michael Jackson and Lionel Richie, Kotzias climbed onto the stage next to Çavuşoğlu and enticed Secretary General Stoltenberg, the EU's foreign policy chief Federica Mogherini, and others to join him. Then, hand in hand, they sang along, Stoltenberg with a microphone for special effect.[23] It was an odd scene. The encouraging news, as one journalist drily noted, was that "At last check, they were all keeping their day jobs."[24]

As officials let their hair down in Antalya, the leading allies were finding it hard to set priorities that brought all the allies together.

Germany was a case in point: Chancellor Merkel and her foreign minister, Frank-Walter Steinmeier, believed that they were being tough on Russia, while simultaneously furthering multilateral cooperation in Europe. In fact, their policy was in large parts based on old precepts of German policy on Russia, and it was notably at odds with the interests of eastern NATO allies.[25] It certainly did not help with the decision-making that Merkel and Steinmeier were political competitors, pushed together in a grand governing coalition. Their point of consensus was the virtue of diplomacy based on patience and trade. Steinmeier was in the Willy Brandt mold of SPD politicians, and thus heir to the Ostpolitik tradition. He was not oblivious to Russian manipulation, of course, but he struggled to connect diplomacy and defense: he warned that the latter could lead to a "spiral of escalation." He believed Germany had the "staying power" and "broad horizon" to take responsibility for Europe's security and produce the reverse outcome of de-escalation.[26]

But the Steinmeier–Merkel approach did not assuage the Eastern European allies. They protested about the construction of a new Russian–German pipeline, Nord Stream-2, which the Merkel government was supporting. This pipeline was not about trade, they warned (with Ukraine's President Poroshenko joining the chorus), but was a Russian geopolitical plot.[27] They looked with similar skepticism at the so-called Steinmeier formula for unlocking the Minsk negotiations between Russia and Ukraine. The German foreign minister believed he had found a path toward de-escalation, but revealingly, only Russia supported it: Ukraine saw mostly a path toward permanent Russian interference in its constitutional order, and the negotiations went nowhere. In a revealing foretaste of things to come, in October 2014 Russian President Putin snubbed Chancellor Merkel, making her wait a full five hours before a private meeting.[28]

Problems meanwhile burgeoned in Syria, spilling over into NATO politics. Most visibly, in November 2015, a Turkish F-16 shot down a Russian Sukhoi Su-24 after it violated Turkish airspace. It was the first shooting encounter between a NATO ally and Russia. The problem was that Russia had gotten into the Syrian game, bombing the opposition to al-Assad in a pattern that repeatedly, if very briefly, brought

Russian planes into Turkish airspace. The wider problem was that Turkey was on its own. It had a conflict with Russia. And it had one with the United States, whose Global Coalition had teamed up with Kurdish forces on the ground. The United States pretended to have organized the Kurds in such a way that did not impinge on the struggle between them and Turkey; but the fiction was hard to sustain. Turkey's President Erdoğan did not take kindly to the situation; in addition, he had boldly gambled his country's interests on the seeming rise of the Muslim Brotherhood in the region. For as long as this political force rode the crest of the Arab Spring—the regional desire for greater democracy—Erdoğan's wager seemed solid. However, the Brotherhood stumbled in Tunisia, in Egypt, and then in Syria. Erdoğan then found himself allied to an increasingly sectarian movement in opposition to virtually all regional governments. Turkey was isolated, and a power struggle developed inside Turkey between President Erdoğan and political Islamist Fethullah Gülen. Once friends, now suddenly they were uncompromising rivals.[29]

Russia's President Putin was adding to President Erdoğan's political pain, and thus also to the fragmentation of the NATO allies. Putin reacted with brutality to the downing of the Su-24: he adopted sweeping economic sanctions against Turkey and mobilized Iraq and Armenia to enhance Turkey's sense of Russian encirclement.[30] As NATO approached its mid-2016 Warsaw summit, therefore, President Erdoğan was in need of a Russia policy that covered much more ground than simply NATO's eastern flank. Britain's ambassador to NATO, Adam Thomson, perceived the situation clearly: he suggested that the Eastern European allies could only hope to get more on their flank—something like RAP 2.0—if they were prepared to give something on the southern front.[31]

A sense of impeding fragmentation thus took hold. The United States struggled to gain the upper hand against Islamic State and could not forsake the Kurds, meaning Turkey's ire would continue. The Eastern European allies meanwhile worried about Russia's future intentions. Nine of them—the Baltic states, Poland, Romania, Bulgaria, the Czech Republic, Slovakia, and Slovenia—worried so much that they decided to meet and coordinate ahead of the NATO foreign ministerial meeting in December 2015. They wanted as much RAP as possible; but they also managed to convey the image of alliance fragmentation—else why would they be meeting on their own? This was the clear perception in the headquarters, whose leadership felt that the eastern allies' drive for RAP 2.0 put the alliance's overall deterrence posture at risk.[32]

Fragmentation continued on June 23, 2016, when in a referendum, British voters decided to have Britain leave the European Union. The next day, Prime Minister David Cameron announced that he was stepping down. This might have been an EU matter, but the political uncertainty, Britain's long-drawn-out domestic transition to a more Euro-skeptic leadership, and the friction it generated with continental countries, Britain's allies, also mattered to NATO. The political mood soured, and NATO's leadership—the secretary general and his deputies—could do nothing, because the decisions belonged to the EU and Britain. NATO was again, relatively speaking, politically marginalized in continental matters.

NATO's Warsaw summit took place the following month. Leaders zoomed in on NATO defense efforts. And they sought an East–South compromise, offering a little bit to both sides. On counter-ISIL strategy, NATO leaders agreed to offer Iraq in-country training for its security and military forces, and also to give the US-led coalition access to NATO air surveillance data.[33] It was a NATO stake in the south, even if a very limited one. To the east, on Russia, the allies beefed up the language—"we cannot return to 'business as usual.'"[34] This greater sense of threat, as opposed to missed partnership opportunity, led them to agree to RAP 1.5, in the shape of "an enhanced forward presence" (eFP) of allied forces in Poland and the three Baltic states, along with a more varied enhanced "tailored" presence in Romania and Bulgaria.

The NATO allies had thus gotten to the point where they put up a "tripwire" along the eastern frontier. If Russia ran over these tripwire forces, NATO warned, the balloon would go up and NATO would mobilize its full military force in response.[35] All this was meant to be politically astute: because the eFP forces were small (battalion sized), and because they rotated in and out, they were not in violation of the 1997 NATO–Russia Founding Act. In other words, NATO did not have to forsake the aspirational partnership option. However, there were limits to the astuteness. The tripwire forces de facto shed light on the reaction forces that were supposed to show up, if called upon. These forces were heavy, slow, and generally unfit for purpose. To reform them, NATO needed a political drive. But the allies were fatigued. And they faced an emboldened Russia which, as Grushko had warned Vershbow in 2014, did not want to be pushed around.

Grushko and Vershbow would meet again, this time in late 2016, for a farewell dinner organized in Vershbow's honor by the Czech ambassador to NATO. Vershbow's stint as deputy secretary general was coming to an end. At the dinner, Grushko presented Vershbow with a gift that was shot through with politics—a 2014 Crimean champagne. Vershbow knew how to reply, though. The Czech ambassador, a guitarist, knew that Vershbow played the drums, and he had put together a band. On Vershbow's cue, they played and Vershbow sang the old Beatles number, "Back in the USSR"—which could be seen as a comment on the enduring communist mindset of Grushko and his government. The next day, at a private meeting with a handful of Russia experts from NATO headquarters, Vershbow ceremoniously poured the Crimean champagne down the toilet.[36]

NATO divided

The Donald J. Trump presidency drove a coach and horses through NATO's carefully stitched-together compromises. Of the three core items on NATO's Wales agenda—defense posture (RAP), defense investment (DIP), and Russia policy—President Trump had eyes for only one: DIP. He would time and time again berate the allies for not paying what he considered their fair share. Other US presidents had taken the allies to task, of course; but President Trump's focus and style became dysfunctional, and this paralyzed NATO politically. That was bad enough. Adding further to the pain were indications that continued work on the RAP inside NATO's "machinery" was causing a political-military divide within the alliance. It threatened NATO's own values of civilian leadership of military affairs, and the fault rested squarely with the political leadership.

Trump had a history of criticizing US allies and NATO. In 1987, he placed an ad in the *New York Times* berating allies for being cheap and for making a "laughingstock of the United States."[37] In mid-2016, while still a presidential candidate, Trump made NATO's Article 5 solidarity contingent on allied defense spending. As president-elect, he then declared NATO to be "obsolete."[38] He most certainly was not of a transatlantic mold, and did not venerate the alliance. If Trump did keep the United States in NATO, the allies could expect to be treated like his subcontractors in a New York real-estate deal—that is, with a degree of brutality. The allies braced themselves.

Trump's more recent history as a presidential candidate impinged on NATO's Russia policy, too. Opponents, critics, and analysts repeatedly questioned the extent and nature of the links between Trump himself, his campaign, and Russia. A widely cited dossier put together by a former British intelligence officer, Christopher Steele, suggested that Russia had a hold on Trump. In January 2017, FBI Director James Comey felt compelled to inform president-elect Trump of these allegations, which ultimately placed a question mark over the legitimacy of Trump's presidential victory. Policy on Russia was thus inherently problematic for the Trump presidency from the outset, and NATO got caught up in this. There would be no renewal or evolution of NATO's Russia policy during the Trump presidency.

The best that the allied leaders and Secretary General Jens Stoltenberg could do was to prepare carefully for their first meeting with President Trump and get NATO off to a promising start. The meeting was scheduled for May 25, 2017, and was intended as a short meet-and-greet summit to acquaint allied leaders with the new president. This was customary. What was not customary were the high stakes involved. NATO's cohesion was on the line, and the meeting simply could not go wrong. And yet it did.

The NATO headquarters team, led by Secretary General Stoltenberg, and Trump's national security team (national security advisor H.R. McMaster, Secretary of Defense James Mattis, and Secretary of State Rex Tillerson) had laid the groundwork to near perfection. Stoltenberg's preparatory visit to Washington had prompted President Trump to say that NATO is "no longer obsolete."[39] Trump knew that France and

Germany were preparing to allow NATO a role in the US-led Global Coalition. Even if that role was limited, it was a significant political gesture, and Trump could pocket it.[40] The president would also be able to inaugurate NATO's new headquarters building. Outside its entrance, a new memorial to commemorate September 11, 2001, would be dedicated—a large metal piece from the World Trade Center. It stood alongside another memorial, a section of the Berlin Wall that had come down in 1989. Both were manifestations of alliance solidarity, and Trump was given an opportunity to leverage them to his own political benefit.

The critical piece in all this was President Trump's affirmation of alliance solidarity. The national security team had succeeded in inserting it into Trump's prepared speech. Copies of the speech, which were distributed to NATO officials, included a twenty-seven-word statement declaring an "unwavering" US commitment to NATO and its Article 5.[41] As Trump walked on stage, Gary Cohn, an advisor, told him, "You have one thing to say, one thing only to say: Article 5."[42] Yet, and unbeknownst to his national security team, President Trump had decided to omit this part of the speech. Article 5 solidarity was thus not to be. Instead, the president berated the allies for not being "fair to the people and taxpayers of the United States."[43] It was a jolt and a shock. Mehmet Fatih Ceylan, the Turkish ambassador to NATO, would recall the scene with dismay, finding Trump's choice of language and message "uncompromising and repulsive."[44]

And the NATO allies had not seen the worst of it yet. Through 2018, President Trump repeatedly discussed with his advisors the option of leaving NATO.[45] The rumors grew so persistent that, as Trump was on his way to the 2018 summit, the US Senate passed a resolution by 97-2 in favor of NATO. At the summit, Trump used a breakfast meeting on the first day to complain so bitterly about NATO—including Germany's continuing dependence on Russian energy—that his national security advisor, John Bolton, afterwards wondered, "Could it get any worse?"[46] The answer was "Yes." Staff had had the foresight to fully draft and agree the communiqué beforehand, but still the summit was thrown off track by Trump's ire and his threat to withdraw from NATO within a year unless allies paid their dues. The allies managed to muddle through, but it was, Bolton found, a "wild ride." And at the end of it all, incredibly, President Trump told the press that he was a "stable genius" who had turned NATO into a "fine-tuned machine."[47]

NATO's crisis was not related to the substance of Trump's criticisms. The president had a point: the allies were not sharing the defense burden adequately, and Germany's and Europe's energy dependence on Russia was a great geopolitical vulnerability. The allies had been forewarned that these concerns preoccupied the president.[48] NATO went off the rails because he did not appreciate, did not perceive, that political solidarity was NATO's core asset. Instead, Trump put his own persona at the center of NATO politics. The lack of solidarity and the personalized politics made it almost inconceivable for allied leaders that they should return to their parliaments to ask for more defense spending in the name of Donald Trump. For this, they needed not only Trump's stick, but also the carrot of a politically meaningful alliance that they could weave into national security concerns. In short, they needed a solid and aspirational alliance that they could sell to the voters. With his punitive expedition against European cooperation and his soft touch with regard to Russian President Putin, Trump was not offering it.[49]

While NATO politics were at a standstill, NATO military planning forged ahead. The Brussels summit delivered on two counts. One was more available reaction forces. US Secretary of Defense James Mattis had been the prime mover of the "four thirties" initiative that was approved at the summit. Under it, the allies committed, by 2020, to having thirty battalions, thirty air squadrons, and thirty naval combat vessels ready to use within thirty days.[50] To move these forces, to get them from A to B, the allies simultaneously agreed to set up two new military commands—a naval command for the Atlantic, located in Norfolk, Virginia, next to NATO's Transformation Command, and a logistics command in Ulm, Germany. The 2018 summit thus promised to deliver the capability that the "tripwire" of 2016 presupposed.

Where political-military tensions began, though, was in respect of the overarching military view of what to do. Through 2014–16, NATO had a Military Strategy (MC400/3) so short and thin on detail that it was totally inadequate as a foil to Russia's assertiveness. For reasons of its superficiality, and remarkably for a NATO Military Strategy, it was not highly classified.[51] MC400/3 reflected the broad and open-ended Strategic Concept of 2010; but the strategic game had changed. From a military perspective, Russia's actions meant that NATO forces should not be prepared for the odd contingency in faraway countries, but rather, in a worst-case scenario, for war with Russia. Without this warfighting capability, NATO could not hope to deter Russia.

US General Curtis Scaparrotti became a real force for change in this context.[52] He arrived at the military helm of NATO, as supreme commander (SACEUR), in late spring of 2016, having completed a tour as supreme commander in South Korea. In that theater, Korean, US, and allied forces were united around a single plan, and Scaparrotti had tended to it. What he found in 2016 in NATO was, worryingly, a lack of any such unified plan; and then, in addition, an indecisive political debate on whether Russia was in fact a threat. He thus set about building political-military consensus on the nature of the threat and what NATO should do about it militarily. Scaparrotti wanted to shape a new NATO Military Strategy, and to this end he began drafting "SACEUR's Strategic Thoughts."

Scaparrotti worked the NATO system. He had a dialogue with governments, which at the 2018 summit formally tasked him with submitting his Strategic Thoughts for their review. He also had a dialogue with the national chiefs of staff seated at the top of NATO's military hierarchy, in the Military Committee. The chiefs of staff had already agreed that NATO needed new strategic thinking, and they had directed their NATO staff to draft a strategy. But Scaparrotti was also pushy. He wanted a real and unified plan that set out clear military objectives and that committed resources to them. In this, he rubbed up against the tendency of national representatives to compromise and to fudge objectives and requirements to suit national caveats.

Collective defense against Russia needed to focus on Russia's core capabilities—its "centers of gravity," in classical strategic parlance. It needed to plan for how to counter these; and for this, it needed to commit forces to achieve certain effects at certain geographical points. It all promised to be quite constraining on the NATO allies, and Scaparrotti was making this constraint clear. In the end, leading chiefs of staff, such as Czech General (later President) Petr Pavel and British Air Chief Marshal Stuart Peach, supported Scaparrotti's thinking, though it had a bumpy ride through the military staff. More importantly, allied political authorities were divided. When, in May 2019, they received the new Military Strategy (MC400/4) for approval, they declined to provide it. Instead, they merely "noted" the strategy, which was to say that the governments had political reservations.[53]

General Scaparrotti stepped down as SACEUR in mid-2019, handing the baton to General Tod Wolters. Wolters was enthusiastic about the new strategy: the first true military strategy by NATO in "50-plus years," he ventured.[54] And he would be able to develop follow-on strategy plans with greater detail and substance—a concept for the "Deterrence and Defence of the Euro-Atlantic Area" (so-called DDA) and a plan for managing multiple crises in SACEUR's area of responsibility (so-called SASP). National governments were happy to approve these follow-on documents, which was an improvement. But they did so also with the intention of controlling the planning that went into the documents. Exposed allies did not intend to let forces leave their geographical neighborhood, meaning they wanted to tie SACEUR's hands with geographical response plans. Allies that were supposed to deploy forces far from home, such as Britain, objected to requirements for armor and equipment that would weigh their forces down and make deployment exceedingly costly. And southern allies, stuck in out-of-area contingencies, objected to the more detailed eastern flank planning, fearing that it would swallow up attention and resources.

In short, the military level in NATO pushed for stringent and classical center-of-gravity planning, and the political level pushed back. SACEUR Scaparrotti succeeded in shaping a Military Strategy that promised quality for the follow-on documents, DDA and SASP, but political reservations then kicked in and halted development. This amounted to a political-military crisis. The culprit was political paralysis through 2016–19. The Trump presidency was politically debilitating, but the European allies' lack of will and investment was also problematic. Their political disunity had come to harm military planning and, therefore, NATO deterrence. As a NATO military staffer put it, it was high time for NATO to get "its political ducks in a row."[55]

NATO punts the football

"What we are currently experiencing," President Macron of France told *The Economist* in November 2019, "is the brain death of NATO."[56] It was a blunt statement just one month away from a NATO leaders' meeting in London. Macron's ire was directed at "Washington," meaning President Trump, whose erratic decisions on Syria—whether or not to stand with the Kurds, and whether or not to keep the Global Coalition together—seemed to have particularly upset Macron. James Mattis, Trump's first secretary of defense, had resigned over the issue of US fidelity to allies and partners, the Kurds included, in late 2018.[57] But Macron, of course, had no intention of resigning. What he wanted was a geopolitical awakening in Europe and a recasting of the transatlantic bargain.

Macron's was a blunt statement, but also an odd one, as if the French president and France were not somehow part of NATO's brain. And it was not the first sign of fragmentation at the highest levels of the alliance. NATO had turned seventy on April 4, 2019, but the chiefs, the heads of state and government, did not show up for the occasion. Instead, they dispatched their foreign ministers for a low-key celebration in Washington. Leading US politicians and former ambassadors pointed the finger at the White House incumbent.[58] But still President Macron managed to surprise his closest allies with his "brain dead" dissection and his call for European strategic autonomy.[59] Macron's remarks were more eloquent than Trump's prose, but his blunt message was Trumpian in character. At the London get-together, therefore—in any case planned as a short "leaders' meeting," rather than a real "summit"—the NATO leaders had one task: to give themselves a break.

"We will meet again in 2021," the leaders symbolically declared in London.[60] In other words, they would not meet in 2020, and there would be no more leaders' meetings or summits on President Trump's watch. What would come after the US presidential elections remained to be seen (though it seems safe to infer that many of the allies hoped for a US leader who was more amenable to Atlantic cooperation). To pass the time, they instructed Secretary General Jens Stoltenberg to lead a "reflection process," the main purpose of which was to "further strengthen NATO's political dimension including consultation." Here it was: the heads of state and government had acknowledged, albeit in diplomatic terms, that they had a political problem.

The secretary general and his team now looked into a two-step process.[61] Through 2020 and up until mid-2021, when the NATO chiefs would meet again, he, the secretary general, would tee up NATO for a decision to begin renewal of the alliance's Strategic Concept. As a next step, and following political approval of his own set of reflections, the secretary general would then steer the work on this renewed Strategic Concept. Ever the politician, Stoltenberg captured all this under the heading of "NATO 2030"—communicating the fact that NATO had both a future and a sense of direction.

In the first phase, Stoltenberg pursued the tried-and-tested method of appointing an experts' group to develop and test out ideas. This eight-person group began its work in April 2020, only to find itself hamstrung by the COVID pandemic. Still, they issued a report in December 2020 constructed around the new mantra of "strategic competition" and containing a wealth of ideas for how to enhance NATO politically.[62] In parallel, and of greater importance, the secretary general began developing his own "Food for Thought" paper, with key policy priorities and the Strategic Concept ambition. In February 2021, this paper (unclassified) began to circulate.[63] It was this paper, not the expert group report, that was up for political approval at NATO's Brussels summit in June 2021. And Stoltenberg had done his homework well. The summit invited him to begin phase two—the fashioning of a new Strategic Concept.[64]

Phase one had offered relief, but no panacea. Team Trump had succeeded in placing China on NATO's agenda, but only vaguely, as a combination of "opportunities and challenges that we need to address together as an Alliance."[65] It had taken the Trump team all of three years of persistent and sometimes controversial diplomacy to get NATO to this point. It wanted NATO to be more forward leaning, but China was a mouthful, and European leaders were not keen to bite off more than they could easily chew.[66] During phase one, therefore, NATO staff and diplomats mostly marked time, streamlining policy planning to consider China, without really confronting the challenge head on. The political consensus was that China represented both "opportunities and challenges." If the allies wanted less ambiguity, they would have to hammer it out politically.

Oddly, Joe Biden's election as US president would demonstrate the same point: namely, that NATO's political problems were not easily solved. The allies welcomed Biden's election, and early consultations were designed to soothe the political wounds of recent years. "We will consult with our friends, early and often," Secretary of State Antony Blinken assured them.[67] But things did not turn out that way. The Biden administration's early decision, in February 2021, to lift the threat of US sanctions on the German–Russian Nord Stream-2 pipeline was an obvious gesture to Germany, whose leadership had repeatedly been singled out by President Trump for political censure; but the Eastern European allies felt let down by Biden's decision. They did not trust Russia, and they did not trust Germany to look beyond trade and business opportunity.

President Biden and his national security team also managed to deeply upset France. On the sidelines of the G7 summit in Cornwall, Britain, in June 2021, Team Biden accepted British Prime Minister Boris Johnson's idea of an AUKUS (Australia, UK, and the US) alliance centered on the delivery of nuclear submarines to Australia. When news of AUKUS became public some months later, it not only wrecked France's billion-dollar deal with Australia to deliver non-nuclear submarines, but it also undermined France's self-identified role as an Indo-Pacific power. And finally, it energized Boris Johnson's "global Britain" vision that, because of Brexit, had come into direct competition with Macron's continental geopolitical awakening.[68] How Team Biden missed all this is something of a mystery. It left no doubt that on NATO's China policy, France could be trusted to return the favor and block any American initiative.

Most alarming was the sudden and chaotic US and allied retreat from Afghanistan in August 2021. The imagery of the Taliban re-entering the capital of Kabul and taking power once again, after twenty years of massive Western aid and engagement, was depressing enough. But the human plight and the uncoordinated and frantic departure of Western troops added insult to injury. The mission was collapsing, US forces were leaving, and the allies were mostly fending for themselves. President Biden would later blame his predecessor, President Trump, for creating an untenable position for the United States by striking a deal with the Taliban in 2020 and pulling US troops out, in the belief that a peace deal would follow.[69] For the alliance, it was one long dark moment. The mission failed, and the consultations on both the botched peace deal and the mission's exit strategy also collapsed. The allies subsequently spoke of a lack of "meaningful discussions" among themselves on US–Taliban negotiations and a broader lack of "more interactive discussions."[70] The language was convoluted, but the wider point was clear enough: NATO was not in a stellar condition.

❃

What a difference a few years can make, European and Canadian leaders must have thought in June 2021, during their meet-and-greet summit meeting with President Biden. The atmosphere was much better than four years earlier, when President Trump failed to support NATO's solidarity clause and berated his allies. In contrast, President Biden called Article 5 a "sacred obligation." "I just want all of Europe to know that the United States is there," he reassured his listeners.[71] Enthused, the allies agreed to brand Russia a "threat" and China a "challenge," and to direct their secretary general to draft a new Strategic Concept.

But NATO's timidity had, in a way, not changed since the 2012 Chicago summit. Then, the allies lacked resources and sought to reduce their mission commitment (in Afghanistan). In 2021, they still lacked resources and sought to diminish their collective defense commitment to what was strictly necessary. And importantly, that amounted to not very much. The allies had put up a "tripwire" in the

East and had begun work to energize their reaction forces; but the deterrence and defense posture was not strong. This was a political choice. France and Germany were still negotiating with Russia and Ukraine. The United States coalition had prevailed against Islamic State, but relations with Turkey were hard to patch up. And China was a headache, with any strategic commitment requiring potentially vast amounts of resource commitments across all sectors of society. Prudent as ever, Chancellor Merkel cautioned against overstating the China challenge: "We need to find the right balance."[72]

By around 2020, the allies had come to recognize the political crisis in which they found themselves. They ordered their secretary general to do something, and he envisioned NATO 2030. Several deep and underlying trends had produced this crisis: exhaustion in Afghanistan, a controversial war on terror, a fiscal crisis, a Europe seemingly at peace, and a sense that NATO could remain big, soft, and security focused, while the individual allies returned home to rebuild their nations. This undercurrent of "nationalization" was the condition NATO found itself in through the 2010s, and it manifested itself in NATO's feeble response to Russia's 2014 aggression. The culmination was the Trump presidency. The challenge for the future was to reinvigorate NATO's geopolitical role.

Comeback?
Classical NATO for a New Era

"I refuse to believe that you welcome the killing of innocent children and grandparents," said President Biden in March 2022, in Warsaw, in a statement directed to the Russian people, "or that you accept hospitals, schools, maternity wards that, for God's sake, are being pummeled with Russian missiles and bombs." The president thus drew a sharp contrast between the hopes of democracy and the brutality of dictatorship, between people and dictators. And as far as the Russian dictator, President Putin, was concerned, Biden was equally blunt: "For God's sake, this man cannot remain in power."[1] The United States, Biden was saying, is back in Europe and back to lead.[2]

But NATO was treading carefully. The allies did see Russia's war on Ukraine—its attempt to overturn the government, annex the four provinces of Donetsk, Kherson, Luhansk, and Zaporizhzhia, and asphyxiate the rest of Ukraine—as a new battle for freedom. They did offer increasing amounts of materiel and training to Ukrainian forces. And the aid was urgently needed, because the Russo-Ukraine war quickly became one of attrition: victory would go to the side with the greatest military and political endurance. However, while Russian politics descended into xenophobic radicalism, which portended a lengthy war, the allies did not ramp up their production of weapons, but drew down stocks.[3] The mantra to stand with Ukraine "for as long as it takes" was at risk of becoming "for as long as stocks last."

The allies were holding back because they did not want to escalate the war to a continental or nuclear scale. They did not commit their own troops to the fighting, and the increase in aid to Ukraine was carefully orchestrated, so as to let Russia absorb the fact that this mission was going to be costly. But they held back also because the political consequences of the war were difficult to foresee, though they promised to be of great impact. "Let me be clear," NATO Secretary General Stoltenberg said in Kyiv in April 2023, as he stood next to Ukrainian President Volodymyr Zelenskyy, "Ukraine's rightful place is in the Euro-Atlantic family. Ukraine's rightful place is in NATO."[4] Yet, and symbolically, the allies did not dispatch Stoltenberg until the war had dragged on for almost a year and a half, and they could not agree to fast-track Ukraine into NATO membership. The allies knew that they would have to build an architecture for continental order, as they had done in 1949 and again in 1990–91; but they were visibly unsure of how to go about it.

Critically, time is no longer on NATO's side. A stalemated frozen conflict in Ukraine would buy time not for NATO, but for Russia and China. And with China as the preeminent rising power, that would suggest that NATO's future needs to be not only linked to, but centered on, China. However, NATO's attempt to build a primarily global future for itself would be wrong-footed and would exacerbate the rifts within the alliance. NATO's best bet is to rediscover its classical Euro-Atlantic character and make it fit for purpose.

NATO confronts great-power revisionism

On February 24, 2022, Putin's Russia invaded Ukraine to change the regime in a pro-Russian direction, or, in Russia's words, to "denazify" Ukraine's leadership and political order.[5] Ukraine's right to live as a sovereign nation was thus at risk. Moreover, with the likelihood that Putin's appetite could grow, NATO suddenly appeared vulnerable.[6] If Putin's war went well, and if he pulled Belarus fully into its orbit, NATO's Baltic area would be severely exposed. Some analysts later claimed that Putin had moderate war aims in mind all along,[7] but treaty proposals put on the table by the Russian Ministry of Foreign

Affairs in December 2021 suggest otherwise.[8] As always in diplomacy, bold measures announced in public without prior consultation are not an invitation to serious negotiations, but rather an airing of political grievances. And Russia had significant grievances.

One treaty proposal was intended for NATO. Russia wanted the alliance to close its doors to potential new members and, for special emphasis, to explicitly rule out the possibility that Ukraine could join NATO. Significantly, Russia also wanted NATO to demilitarize its presence in Central and Eastern Europe, calling for the roll-back of whatever Western military presence had been introduced since May 27, 1997—that is, when NATO and Russia signed the Founding Act. In fact, Russia wanted the territory east of Germany—including NATO's post-Cold War members, prospective members, and other countries—to become a buffer zone between East and West. NATO's solidarity clause, Article 5, would then de facto not extend beyond the alliance that existed when the Cold War ended. It was tantamount to a cancellation of NATO's post-Cold War enlargement.

The other proposal was Russia's attempt to tie the United States to its vision. It committed the United States to prevent further expansion of NATO and to desist from any type of military relationship with countries of the former Soviet bloc that are not NATO members. And it upped the ante, seeking to pull the United States further off the European continent and committing both sides to deploying short- and intermediate-range missiles, as well as nuclear weapons, only on their national territories. In addition, the treaty would have obliged both sides to refrain from any military deployment that the other party deemed to be a threat to its national security; given Russia's expansive view of its national security interests, this would have meant that US extended deterrence would have ceased to function.

Though all of this was couched in language referring to the UN Charter, the Helsinki Final Act, and the Paris Charter for a new Europe, it was a blatant attempt to revise Europe's security order. At best, it was a more aggressive advancement of the ideas sketched out by Medvedev's Russia in 2009 in response to NATO's 2008 Bucharest promise to bring Ukraine and Georgia into the fold.[9] At worst, it was a commitment by Putin's Russia to the ideology of "Eurasianism" that premised Russia's nationalist revival on the Mongol legacy, Russian Orthodoxy, and a firm rejection of Western thought.[10] Most likely, President Putin was gathering different threads of Russian legacies to weave a more complex tapestry of state conservatism.[11]

The NATO allies did not buy into Putin's philosophy, and instead decided to probe the potential for negotiations on arms control and confidence-building measures. They had long been concerned that all East–West arms control agreements—save for the US–Russia strategic nuclear arms treaty, START—had fallen by the wayside. The airing of Russia's grievances provided an occasion to test its thinking and its readiness to engage in "meaningful dialogue," as the allies stated in December 2021.[12] And by "meaningful" they meant a dialogue based on reciprocity and other "core principles" of European security, including respect for sovereignty and freedom for all European states to choose their alliances. From December 2021 through February 2022, allied diplomats coordinated and probed. Intelligence told the alliance leaders that Putin was preparing for war, but diplomatically they were offering him a way out.

Secretary General Stoltenberg went to bed on the eve of February 24, 2022, knowing that it would be a short night: "I knew that at some stage, within hours, someone was going to wake me up" with news of war.[13] Kaja Kallas, prime minister of Estonia, had warned her Cabinet members to be ready, but still, "I went to bed hoping that I was not right." Ukrainian President Zelenskyy likewise had a short night and was busy on the phone on the morning of Russia's attack. French President Macron was among Zelenskyy's interlocutors and on his suggestion, Macron claimed, the French president called President Putin to try to persuade him to stop the invasion. But it was no good, Macron said. "The Russian President has chosen war."[14] By early morning, they all knew not only that Russia had chosen war, but also that NATO (or the NATO allies) had not been able to deter it. True, Ukraine was not a NATO ally, but a major war in Europe's midst was a geopolitical earthquake.

Most of what happened next did not directly involve NATO. Western countries adopted sanctions against Russia, but these were either national or EU based. Western countries likewise adopted a coordinated approach to aiding Ukraine with weaponry and training, but this effort was anchored not in NATO, but in an improvised Ukraine Defense Contact Group. This group would gain its unofficial name, the Ramstein Group, after its meeting venue of the US Ramstein Air Base in Germany. Like other coalitions assembled for out-of-area crises, this one included both allied and non-allied countries, including Israel, Morocco, and Qatar, as well as representatives from both the EU and NATO. It was also clearly US led and orchestrated.[15] But still, this was not NATO.

NATO's role, the allies thought, should be to stabilize the continent without being on the Ukrainian front line. It was perhaps a tough distinction to make as war raged. But it implied three priorities for NATO.[16]

The first was to bolster NATO's ability to defend its own territory. To the East, NATO had hitherto put up "tripwires" of smaller forces (battalions), the idea being that Russia would be deterred by the response they could trigger. Now, NATO shifted to forward defense planning. Ideally, it would want to be able to stop a Russian aggression at the border. But this strategy of defense by denial would be immensely costly to implement in full. So the allies compromised: they undertook to triple NATO's forward presence; but as that would still not be enough stop an aggression at the border, they further promised to bolster the defense line with a powerful rapid-reaction force of up to 300,000 troops.

The second priority was to maintain its open-door policy, in order to signal that it would not give in to Russia's demands for a continental divide. NATO's first task was to facilitate the entry of Finland and Sweden into the alliance: in May 2022, in a stunning political reversal, those Cold War neutrals had concluded that Russia left them with no choice but to seek security inside NATO. Turkish reservations over Sweden's counter-terrorist policy dragged out the accession process, but it was still rapid by historical standards: in April 2023, Finland acceded; and by mid-2024, Sweden was likely to join. NATO's membership would thus grow to thirty-two.

And finally, the third priority was to enhance NATO's aid to Ukraine. This was about building Ukrainian institutions and leadership: it was not about guns and ammunition. And this was also a point in and of itself: NATO was non-lethal. NATO was not on the front line. The allies thus gave the green light to Secretary General Stoltenberg's April 2023 visit to Kyiv only after so many other leadership visits there, including by EU representatives Ursula von der Leyen and Charles Michel.

The allies also looked more broadly into the future. In it they saw an urgent Russia threat and, in the longer run, a looming China challenge. That is the gist of the Strategic Concept adopted at the Madrid summit.[17] Russia, the allies said, is "the most significant and direct threat" to allied security and to peace and stability in the Euro-Atlantic area.[18] This was tough language, but Russia's war had made it simple for the alliance to agree to it.

The wording on China was much harder to negotiate. Allied views varied, with the United States pushing for firm language, and some European allies preferring a softer approach. NATO's point of consensus became the view that China is a "systemic threat." This label was not new—the alliance had already employed it in 2021— but it was now wrapped in a more direct and dire assessment of China's actions and intentions. Thus, in NATO's Strategic Concept, China is variously "coercive," "opaque," and "malicious."

Fortunes on the Ukrainian battlefield shifted. Amid high expectations, Ukraine launched a counter-offensive. As Russia's forces dug in, its political structures cracked, even if only slightly. In June 2023, Yevgeny Prigozhin's significant Wagner force turned on the high command and, for a moment, appeared to march on Moscow. President Putin talked tough, but looked weakened. At the outbreak of the war, it had seemed inconceivable that Russia would both lose the war and fragment politically. Deep into the war, it no longer does. The war has developed into a test of strategic leadership, skill, and patience in Russia, in Ukraine, and in the Western alliance, and is likely to yield outcomes that we cannot yet fully imagine.

Into the future

The evolution of the war and Russia's condition are useful reminders of the wise words of Winston Churchill, who once said about politics that it involves "the ability to foretell what is going to happen tomorrow, next week, next month and next year. And to have the ability afterwards to explain why it didn't happen." We do not have, as Henry Kissinger has stressed, rules for predicting history's path.[19] Of course, ideologies have easy and clear maxims: in Marxism, history moves toward socialism; in Liberalism, it moves toward democracy. But history is complicated. To probe the present and the future, the best we can do is to trace a pattern of what remains and what has changed. We trace this pattern here, and we begin with issues of continuity—issues that have remained with the alliance through all its twists and turns.

A permanent East–West axis

Continuity is first and foremost evident in NATO's self-defined challenge of building and protecting a free community. This is where NATO begins, and it is the alliance's enduring challenge. The challenge has a geographical, a transatlantic, and a budgetary dimension.

Geographically, NATO's ambition to be free has anchored the alliance along an East–West axis. Details vary, but the theme remains. Back when the alliance was born, it was all about keeping the Soviet bloc out; today, it is about defending against Russia. At the beginning, it was about getting West Germany on its feet inside a strong transatlantic institution of restraint; today, it is about building German and European leadership for a more balanced community. In the early days, it was about keeping the United States engaged as a European power; today, it still is.

The global war on terror might be considered an aberration in this respect: the NATO allies squandered twenty years and untold resources in Afghanistan, which naturally falls outside the Washington–Brussels–Moscow axis. But as NATO's collective mind wandered, Russia remained; and it grew estranged from the offer of partnership in a Euro-Atlantic community. When President Putin put Ukraine in his revisionist crosshairs, in 2014, NATO was unprepared. And even though it improved its defenses somewhat and began talking about strategic competition, it was again unprepared for Russia's choice of war in 2022. In short, whatever else happens, in Afghanistan or in other places, NATO ignores the East–West axis at its expense, if not its peril.

The transatlantic dimension here has to do with balanced leadership. The United States was always the strongest ally, and after the outbreak of the Korean War in 1950 and the realization that Western Europe simply had limited military muscle, America's military leadership became a hard fact. It got embedded in NATO's military command structure, whose leading voice is SACEUR—supreme allied commander Europe—always an American and always dual-hatted as the commander of US European Command. The United States brings a command structure, a command culture, and ready and able forces; and the alliance builds a military posture around it.

Politically, this means that the US president is a first among equals in the North Atlantic Council. It also means that NATO has had to be imaginative to give voice and influence to the European allies, as well as Canada. Some of this sharing of influence takes place at the military level, where NATO strategy is not only about an adversary's capabilities and intents, but also about the distribution of responsibilities among the allies. NATO could thus agree to the 1967 flexible response strategy because it was coupled to a mechanism of allied influence, the NPG. Shared responsibility also takes place at the political-organizational level. NATO's secretary general is always a European, even if on occasion Canada would like to see the post rotate in its direction. The secretary general must know Europe's complicated political and diplomatic scene and shape the agenda of the North Atlantic Council for consensus. The secretary general must lean in, but not be pushy. It is a delicate balancing act, and if the push were to become a shove, he or she could go the way of Paul-Henri Spaak—rejected by the big allies who wanted wiggle room. Finding the right person for the right balance is a recurring challenge.

The budgetary dimension is about resourcing the defense of the community equitably. It is a staple of NATO diplomacy that the United States does not want to cover the bulk of NATO's defense, and that the European allies do not like to be told what to do. Budgets become focal points in this debate because they are so easy to understand—who spends what, who is spending more, and who is not carrying their fair share of the burden. But it is a minefield. Most European allies devote most of what they spend on defense to the NATO area; the United States puts a lot of its defense effort into the Indo-Pacific and other theaters. Some European allies offer substantial infrastructure support for NATO contingencies, some of it significantly coming from civilian budgets. Other European allies have intelligence or other assets that support NATO, but which again may or may not be fully accounted for in defense budgets. Finding consensus in this minefield is a permanent challenge for NATO diplomats.

Russia's war and NATO's defense plans will not make it any easier. NATO's summits in 2022 and 2023 produced a lot of essential paperwork (strategy and plans); but the hard part of putting flesh on the bones—of building military muscle—comes next. Unlike in the Cold War, the allies downplay nuclear deterrence; the key piece in NATO's strategy in this new era will be major, rapid, and resilient conventional forces. As before, though, these forces will be expensive, and allied governments will not gladly pick up the bill.

A sprawling alliance

Change has come to NATO as well, particularly in the way in which it has become harder to separate Euro-Atlantic security issues from global security issues. During the Cold War, NATO could delimit its policies, distinguishing between core business in Europe and events outside the Euro-Atlantic area that called for consultations, but not collective action. War and conflict in Asia (Vietnam) and the Middle East are cases in point. Increasingly, though, other such conflicts started to pull NATO out of its regional confines. At first it was Balkan crisis management (which was close to home), but then came international terrorism and China. The sum total for NATO has been policy sprawl, enhanced political diversity, and a marked recourse to summitry to move the alliance forward.

Policy sprawl has been one consequence of NATO's attempt to deal with this situation. Part of it has to do with the nature of the threat or challenge. Counter-terrorist policies demand efforts to stabilize governments, to offer development opportunities for local communities, and to coordinate international relief and assistance— all in addition to a security mission to combat terrorist forces. NATO has been pulled into all of this; and in Afghanistan, it became more than it could handle. Similarly with China. China is a global power with command of every tool in the foreign policy toolbox; NATO has limited tools and is politically diverse. It is broadening its aperture to China, but it continues to grapple with the risk that even limited policy angles—such as resilience—could pull the alliance into a variety of civilian domains reserved for either national or, in the European case, EU policy (e.g., energy policy). NATO is aware of the need to prioritize, but its policy agenda sprawls nonetheless.

Policy sprawl results also from NATO's enhanced diversity. The numbers tell the story: at the time of its founding, NATO had twelve member states; seventy-five years later, it is on the path to have thirty-two. It is a political success story to have so many countries wanting to join the club; but enlargement has also brought a real mix of national histories, political sensibilities, and geopolitical vulnerabilities. NATO allies are democracies, but democracy comes in a variety of shades, and democracy amplifies local and national concerns. And again, the way in which the outside world impinges on this diversity is changing and complex.

The Arctic region contains Russia and is drawing in China, but NATO is in two minds about whether to engage. So far, NATO policy extends only to the "High North," a less ambitious term indicative of allied disagreement on whether to look beyond SACEUR's current area of responsibility in the North Atlantic.[20] The Indo-Pacific is testing NATO as well, such as when the United States, Britain, and France become engaged in either contests of influence (e.g., with AUKUS) or contests about which should be the privileged power seeking to shape Beijing's view of things.[21] Most notably, perhaps, is the way in which Russia's war on Ukraine will shift influence within the alliance eastwards: Finland, Poland, and Romania stand to become pillars of influence, because of their capacity to defend NATO's eastern frontier. The countries of NATO's "Club Med"—Turkey, Greece, Italy,

272

Spain, and Portugal—worry, and Turkey has taken the unusual step of being the only ally to adopt a policy of neutrality on Russia.

Germany is in the midst of all this. With Ukraine on fire and NATO's frontier threatened, it needs to shed its reluctance and assume alliance leadership. Chancellor Merkel failed to grasp the nettle, but her successor, Chancellor Scholz, is trying to, with his supposedly watershed (*Zeitenwende*) declaration of February 2022.[22] But it is important to note the limits of what we can expect. Germany's political imagination is shifting, at both the popular and the leadership level,[23] and adjustments in German defense leadership—from Christine Lambrecht to Boris Pistorius—have had a real effect. Still, Germany's political imagination does not—and in all likelihood will not—extend beyond the status quo ante of US leadership. Partly this has to do with history: Germany has not projected military power since 1945, and memories are long both in Germany and in the neighboring countries. And partly it has to do with nuclear deterrence: the United States can offer it, and the German political elites are simply not willing to consider an alternative—meaning either French leadership or a German nuclear deterrent. Thus, Germany's growing willingness to supply military power is new, but Germany alone cannot offer Europe defense leadership.

For about two decades, NATO has resorted to increased summitry to deal with such questions. That is, the alliance has come to depend more on the involvement of the chiefs—the heads of state and government. This trend goes back to the war on terror, which drove the alliance to the brink of fragmentation. Enhanced summitry became part of the answer. Conflicts of interests ran so deep that it took the chiefs to untie the knots: foreign ministers did not have sufficient pull. Back in the Cold War years, the chiefs stood back and let the alliance of foreign and defense ministers steer a course. But that was then. Today, enhanced summitry is a NATO staple.

NATO's machinery is correspondingly oriented toward summits, delivering on the last one and preparing for the next one. The secretary general, who is at the helm of the machinery, has since 2009 been recruited from the ranks of chiefs. This upgrade is, in no small part, due to the botched 2008 Bucharest summit, where the chiefs made a mess of their Ukraine decision and did not listen to their foreign ministerial secretary general. They need a peer to restrain them, at least to a degree. The upgraded secretary general has become a more visible political salesman for the alliance: frequently appearing in public, publishing an annual report (since 2011) detailing the merits and missions of the alliance, and messaging policy in order to set up the next summit for success. This salesmanship has, in many ways, become a driver of the underlying trend of policy sprawl.

Towards the twenty-second century?

NATO's pattern of continuity and change suggests that it can place its emphasis on one of two options: NATO classic, or NATO transformed. The former is the better option, though it should carefully address the role of China and global events.

NATO's transformation would follow from a political desire to assign equal weight to Russia and China; and perhaps even in due course to shift the weight to China. Inevitably, such a shift would build on NATO's democratic values and be justified by a global clash between democracy and dictatorship. And as we know, NATO has both democratic values and a political impulse to pursue high aspirations. It is thus not inconceivable that a majority of the allies, led by the United States, could push for NATO's conversion into a more globally oriented bastion of democracy, drawing Japan, South Korea, Taiwan, New Zealand, Australia, and other democracies across the globe closer into its orbit. Such a shift would have to overcome the difficulty the allies have in agreeing on trade and investment policy with respect to China, but it would be furthered by their propensity to agree on values vis-à-vis China.[24] It could likewise be furthered by Asian democracies' desire to multiply their external security relationships and by a collective desire to counter China's seemingly growing appetite for isolating and perhaps antagonizing Taiwan.[25]

However, history speaks against such a NATO transformation. China is a broad global power, but Western countries decided long ago that they would compartmentalize their global policies. Canada's original NATO vision was for coordination and even integration

274

across a range of policy areas, and Paul-Henri Spaak wanted the same thing. But the decision was to segment. NATO thus remained political-military, while economic and financial affairs passed to the European communities, the G6, and other organs of coordination. The United States, Britain, and France were also content to uphold the influence conferred on them by their permanent seats on the UN Security Council, an exclusive status affirmed by the Non-Proliferation Treaty of 1968, which denies other allies and countries access to nuclear weapons. In short, the decision to keep NATO both narrow and Euro-Atlantic has been repeatedly made throughout the decades. To think otherwise in a moment of aspirational enthusiasm is to invite the allies to bite off more than they can chew.

NATO classic remains the more credible scenario for a continued vibrant transatlantic alliance. Naturally, NATO classic cannot afford to ignore the Indo-Pacific, because this theater has become the primary geopolitical preoccupation of the United States. The Korean War of 1950–53 offers European allies a lesson here. Back then, the United States fought a war in Korea, but had its eyes on the European prize in geopolitical terms: it did not want to leave Europe, but because of the war it needed Europeans to do some of the heavy defense lifting. West Germany's rearmament, the debacle over the European Defense Community, and eventually NATO's nuclearization and Americanization followed. Today, with America's eyes turning to the Indo-Pacific, none of the allies can afford a rerun of this affair. Simply put, it could irrevocably split the alliance. Taiwan's independence—which China has threatened to end—is thus not a freak issue that the allies can choose to ignore. But this does not mean that they should extend NATO to the Indo-Pacific. It merely means that the allies should revitalize classical NATO— protecting the Euro-Atlantic community and offering equitable leadership mainly along the East–West axis—and consider how this revitalized NATO should relate to the wider world. Three principles thus suggest themselves:

1. NATO must primarily build on the management of the East–West axis and tailor policy on Russia and China from this perspective. In the words of an American colleague who spoke

informally, both Russia and China are front-page news for NATO, but Russia is above the fold. NATO must contain Russia militarily, but really needs to rethink its approach to continental political order. This will include a China policy, but it will primarily be about Ukraine's NATO membership and political relations with Russia.[26]

2. NATO must counter the risk in a diverse alliance of thirty-two countries of always falling back on American leadership. The Americanization of NATO strategy is tempting—both for American leaders who prefer not to have to deal with a European caucus in NATO, and for European leaders who prefer to sit back—but it is inherently problematic. It feeds both burden-sharing frustrations in Washington and frustrations of exclusion and marginalization in Europe.

3. NATO must offer the leadership capable of prioritizing and delivering real political-military strategies.

NATO classic has a future, provided NATO's leaders can manage these challenges. We consider the three principles in reverse order.

Leadership

Since about 2020, NATO leaders have been busy revitalizing NATO politically. This level of activity comes out of a shared conviction that NATO cannot afford to once again be subjected to the wrecking ball of nationalist fervor—epitomized by President Trump's challenge and President Macron's accusation of allied brain death.

President Macron has since, in May 2023, changed his diagnosis: NATO is back, and it is back because of the electric shock treatment administered by President Putin.[27] This, of course, is encouraging from a NATO perspective. But the need for an externally generated shock suggests that NATO's chiefs, the heads of state and government, did not by themselves come up with adequate answers to NATO's fatigued condition. Oddly, the chiefs are as centrally involved in charting NATO's course as ever. Since the Cold War waned, NATO has held an impressive thirty summits—that is, North Atlantic

Council meetings in the format of heads of state and government. By way of comparison, during the entire Cold War, the organization held only eight such summits. Moreover, the pace seems to be quickening: including two emergency sessions on Russia's war in Ukraine and the summits planned for 2024 and 2025, the count will be seven summits in the first five years of this decade; and by the close of the 2020s, the figure will likely have topped ten summits, a record.[28]

But fast-paced summitry is no relief, and NATO would be better off with less of it. One side-effect of constant summitry is policy sprawl. Chiefs think in broad terms, across all sectors of government, and their main concern is not to be hemmed in by sectoral policy—political-military policy—but rather to secure a broad range of interests and to stitch together compromises. The NATO "machinery" knows this. It also knows that summits cannot fail: they must be successful. Thus, the "machinery" becomes increasingly focused on short-term horizons—the next meeting. Political astuteness then crowds out what ought to be NATO's primary virtue—strategic foresight and defense planning. Optics and compromises come to define strategic planning. NATO's 2010 Strategic Concept offered no priorities, just policy options on equal priority; and NATO's 2022 Strategic Concept claims to have woven climate change, human security, and Women, Peace, and Security issues into all of NATO's core tasks, collective defense included. These may offer good optics; but they also certainly lead to sprawling policies that challenge the core discipline of defense planning.

The chiefs should consider a change of pace. During the Cold War, as mentioned, they mostly delegated NATO business to foreign and defense ministers and their staff at home and at headquarters. With the exception of Paul-Henri Spaak, the secretary general was drawn from the ranks of foreign and defense ministers. The advantage of this was cohesion among colleagues and a greater sense of policy community, or of security policy brotherhood, which at the end of the day made NATO better able to define strategy and long-term policy.

NATO chiefs are indisputably part of the solution to the complexity that faces NATO. Ultimately, they set the direction for NATO. They are also the masters of their domestic political coalitions, which have become more difficult on account of identity and nationalist politics. The truth is that some political chiefs may simply not trust their foreign and defense ministers enough to let them run NATO. Still, the chiefs should consider the distinction between ongoing involvement in NATO and NATO leadership. To lead, they should define geopolitical priorities, stay abreast of the fine print of NATO policy, and not meet too often. They should have NATO summits only every second or third year, and they should do more to build and facilitate a skillful alliance organization and network of national experts that can derive and formulate policy. Their mission should be to have NATO attract the brightest and best policy planners.

For the "machinery," this means a shift of pace away from summitry preparations and back to conceptual policy work. This is incredibly important, because policy runs on conceptual tracks. NATO leaders and staff must get to the nub of what policy is supposed to do. Is it supposed to "deter" Russia and "contain" China? Is it supposed to "promote democracy" or "counter imperialism"? Is it supposed to "enable" leading allies' policies in Asia or to build a "NATO network" across the globe? This conceptual ground has been slipping from under NATO for some years, on account of fatigue, diversity, and summit priority. It is time to reverse the trend.

A greater role for Europe

For about a decade now, NATO's leaders have sought a more equitable alliance, by focusing on defense spending. It has been a limited success. To really change things, the allies need to reconsider how the European component—so central in the early years of the alliance—can finally mature in partnership with the United States and Canada.

European defense spending is too limited—on that score there can be no question. It encourages both the Americanization of the alliance and US recriminations about lax allies. The annual rate of defense expenditure for NATO Europe and Canada has, in fact, increased every year since 2015 (though so has US spending on defense). Whereas in 2015 the United States shouldered 71.5 percent of combined allied defense expenditure, in 2022 that figure was

68.7 percent.[29] Recurring debate in Washington over the size of the federal deficit and ways of offsetting it will certainly ensure that the numbers remain politically charged.

Inevitably, the allies must confront the fact that defense money is also about jobs and, increasingly, cutting-edge technology. If Europe is to spend more, it needs assurance that this will help European economies. Complicating matters is the fact that Europe's defense industrial base, once strictly a national policy domain protected by national security interests, is increasingly becoming a European Union domain and interest. The European allies continue to have national interests and will continue to be willing to buy weapons off the American shelf; but what is new is their increased desire to build up and protect the high-tech defense industrial interests woven into their common market.

If the allies do not unite to grapple with this issue, it could escape NATO. Defense industry and technology is already anchored in a separate US–EU dialogue and a US–EU Trade and Technology Council. However, all this encourages the idea that Europe's big political-economic issues are defined *outside* NATO. At worst, it encourages the idea that NATO is a military shield that can be taken for granted, and that it is fair for Europeans to think in terms of strategic autonomy in the EU. Things could spiral out of political control. Europe could lose American support, perhaps especially in Congress, and Americans could likewise find that NATO becomes a political dead end in Europe.

Aware of this, the allies have upgraded NATO's technology profile, stepping up their common efforts to both accelerate the development of and protect key technological innovations, such as hypersonic or quantum-enabled technologies. This is a start, but the political level needs reinforcement. Smart staffers can develop policy ideas, of course, but they might consider how in the past NATO set up the NPG, based on the technology of the day (nuclear) and organized around US leadership. They could match this, but reverse the roles, to create a NATO *Technology Planning Group* with European leadership, but a US and Canadian presence. This group could interact closely with NATO's defense planning organization, which remains a core asset of the alliance.

The allies could think of other ways to enhance Europe's role and voice inside the alliance. NATO's European-led strategic-level Transformation Command is, for reasons of legacy, located in Norfolk, Virginia. In a bold move, the allies could transfer this command to Belgium, where it could interact more easily with the political headquarters and the US-led strategic-level Operations Command. What matters is that NATO should not let the growing connection between technological, industrial, and defense interests slip out of its politics. It is the key to equitable leadership and will act as a leveler, raising Europe's investment and profile in NATO.

Collective defense

NATO's aspiration is to make war impossible and unthinkable. It is a demanding ambition that requires power—and not least, power restrained by free counsel. And yet things can go wrong. In Afghanistan, they did; in Ukraine, they have. The NATO allies failed to see the challenge clearly in 2014, and subsequently adjusted only in minor ways. Some leaders and analysts were alarmed at Russia's actions, but collectively NATO was not so perturbed: Ukraine's house was on fire, but it seemed only a small fire and quite manageable. Russia's war of 2022 has changed those perceptions: the house that is ablaze is Europe's. For NATO, that has meant a rediscovery of its Harmel doctrine and new thinking about Ukraine's place in the security order.

The Harmel doctrine was about defense and dialogue: and critically, in that specific order. There is no short-cut to a continent at peace: defense must come first. And NATO's rebuilding of "forward defense" on its eastern frontier will be expensive and long in the making. With enlargement, this frontier has moved eastwards, farther away from the older and more capable allies. And allied militaries are mostly small and inadequate, especially when it comes to enablers—that is, logistics, fire support, air defense, intelligence gathering, communication systems, and so forth. NATO allies must confront this reality, just as they must confront the reality that nuclear weapons remain the backbone of US extended deterrence. Some allies do not like to talk about nuclear weapons, which are anathema to many of their publics; but for the alliance, there is no alternative. A balanced approach to conventional defense and nuclear deterrence must thus be a NATO priority.

The next step in rediscovering Harmel is to reconsider the Bucharest vision of Ukrainian NATO membership. The stakes are simple: either NATO will be able to continue to uphold an inclusive order, or Russia will have succeeded in dividing it. The NATO allies had no compunction about accepting Finland and Sweden into NATO outside the so-called Membership Action Plan, a clearing-house for prospective applicants. At NATO's 2023 Vilnius summit, allies agreed that Ukraine could get on the same fast track to member-ship; though for now, they also said, it would have to settle for a rein-forced partnership and a commitment to arms deliveries. In effect, NATO kicked the can of Ukrainian membership further down the road. In 2024, at their July Washington summit, if they are to avoid looking like the alliance of the 2008 Bucharest summit, the allies will have to be quite clear about how Ukraine can cross the finishing line of NATO membership.

The third and final step in the direction of the Harmel doctrine is to develop ideas for continental dialogue. This cannot be a grand vision of peace with Russia: Russia has chosen war, and the trust is simply not there. If the Putin regime in Russia changes, then the vision of the 1990s—of political convergence and partnership—could re-emerge; but at the time of writing, this remains only a remote possi-bility. More important is therefore carefully calibrated dialogue with Putin's Russia on limited issues. The United States could talk strategic nuclear arms control with Russia. The United States, Britain, and France could dialogue with Russia on certain issues in the UN Security Council. And NATO could, in a small but significant way, indicate how arms control could return to Euro-Atlantic diplomacy. The OSCE, the child of the 1975 Helsinki agreement, would be the natural home for arms control agreements, but the OSCE has been emptied of agree-ment and dialogue. NATO should think how to reactivate it.

This third step of limited but real dialogue may seem difficult as war rages. But it has an important global dimension: the NATO allies should be concerned that most Global South countries have not chosen sides in the Ukraine war. They are sitting on the fence. NATO needs to engage them. It should see arms control as a gateway to a wider discussion on global order with those countries. NATO should come to them and should listen to them. It should tailor its vision of European stability to the concerns and priorities not only of itself, but also of this wider international community. This will also be the key to the success of NATO's China policy and, in fact, the means by which NATO can begin to prioritize among the welter of issues inherent in its China policy dossier. The goal of East–West dialogue is not new, but the means will have to be. In short, to go east, NATO must look south.

NATO has a future: to secure the Euro-Atlantic area and enable the free exercise of open government within it and among its partners. Poor political management could wreck that future, just as good leadership could secure it. Leadership must involve less summitry, less policy sprawl, and less reliance on political optics; it must build long-term policy that is centered on the East–West axis, the geopolitical bedrock of NATO's big idea of a transatlantic community at peace.

"People tire of armies," wrote André de Staercke, Belgium's ambassador to NATO for twenty-six years, "however much they need them."[30] To counter this fatigue, the alliance needed a big idea; and de Staercke captured it in the maxim that he offered Secretary General Spaak and that became NATO's motto: *Animus in consulendo liber*. It represented, said de Staercke in his parting speech as NATO ambassador, "the ultimate resource and the goal of this free-ranging Alliance which we formed to safeguard our future."[31]

The future is as ephemeral as leadership, as André de Staercke knew. In his memoirs, he wrote intimately of Winston Churchill, a long-time friend, and of how the political curtain fell on him during his final years in government. Churchill overstayed his welcome. History wanted to stage a familiar political play, but with new actors suited to new publics.[32] But de Staercke did not believe that NATO was bound to suffer a fate similar to that of Churchill. So convinced was he of the enduring power of NATO's idea of wanting to live and to survive in peace that he saw the alliance as an enduring political play that successive leaders would keep going. In the conclusion to his assessment of the alliance, André de Staercke thus invoked the words of the Angel of the Apocalypse: "I have opened before you a door which no one can close."[33]

The North Atlantic Treaty
Washington, DC, April 4, 1949

The Parties to this Treaty reaffirm their faith in the purposes and principles of the Charter of the United Nations and their desire to live in peace with all peoples and all governments.

They are determined to safeguard the freedom, common heritage and civilisation of their peoples, founded on the principles of democracy, individual liberty and the rule of law. They seek to promote stability and well-being in the North Atlantic area.

They are resolved to unite their efforts for collective defence and for the preservation of peace and security. They therefore agree to this North Atlantic Treaty:

Article 1
The Parties undertake, as set forth in the Charter of the United Nations, to settle any international dispute in which they may be involved by peaceful means in such a manner that international peace and security and justice are not endangered, and to refrain in their international relations from the threat or use of force in any manner inconsistent with the purposes of the United Nations.

Article 2

The Parties will contribute toward the further development of peaceful and friendly international relations by strengthening their free institutions, by bringing about a better understanding of the principles upon which these institutions are founded, and by promoting conditions of stability and well-being. They will seek to eliminate conflict in their international economic policies and will encourage economic collaboration between any or all of them.

Article 3

In order more effectively to achieve the objectives of this Treaty, the Parties, separately and jointly, by means of continuous and effective self-help and mutual aid, will maintain and develop their individual and collective capacity to resist armed attack.

Article 4

The Parties will consult together whenever, in the opinion of any of them, the territorial integrity, political independence or security of any of the Parties is threatened.

Article 5

The Parties agree that an armed attack against one or more of them in Europe or North America shall be considered an attack against them all and consequently they agree that, if such an armed attack occurs, each of them, in exercise of the right of individual or collective self-defence recognised by Article 51 of the Charter of the United Nations, will assist the Party or Parties so attacked by taking forthwith, individually and in concert with the other Parties, such action as it deems necessary, including the use of armed force, to restore and maintain the security of the North Atlantic area.

Any such armed attack and all measures taken as a result thereof shall immediately be reported to the Security Council. Such measures shall be terminated when the Security Council has taken the measures necessary to restore and maintain international peace and security.

Article 6[1]

For the purpose of Article 5, an armed attack on one or more of the Parties is deemed to include an armed attack:

- on the territory of any of the Parties in Europe or North America, on the Algerian Departments of France,[2] on the territory of Turkey or on the Islands under the jurisdiction of any of the Parties in the North Atlantic area north of the Tropic of Cancer;
- on the forces, vessels, or aircraft of any of the Parties, when in or over these territories or any other area in Europe in which occupation forces of any of the Parties were stationed on the date when the Treaty entered into force or the Mediterranean Sea or the North Atlantic area north of the Tropic of Cancer.

Article 7

This Treaty does not affect, and shall not be interpreted as affecting in any way the rights and obligations under the Charter of the Parties which are members of the United Nations, or the primary responsibility of the Security Council for the maintenance of international peace and security.

Article 8

Each Party declares that none of the international engagements now in force between it and any other of the Parties or any third State is in conflict with the provisions of this Treaty, and undertakes not to enter into any international engagement in conflict with this Treaty.

Article 9

The Parties hereby establish a Council, on which each of them shall be represented, to consider matters concerning the implementation of this Treaty. The Council shall be so organised as to be able to meet promptly at any time. The Council shall set up such subsidiary bodies as may be necessary; in particular it shall establish immediately a defence committee which shall recommend measures for the implementation of Articles 3 and 5.

Article 10

The Parties may, by unanimous agreement, invite any other European State in a position to further the principles of this Treaty and to contribute to the security of the North Atlantic area to accede to this Treaty. Any State so invited may become a Party to the Treaty by depositing its instrument of accession with the Government of the United States of America. The Government of the United States of America will inform each of the Parties of the deposit of each such instrument of accession.

Article 11

This Treaty shall be ratified and its provisions carried out by the Parties in accordance with their respective constitutional processes. The instruments of ratification shall be deposited as soon as possible with the Government of the United States of America, which will notify all the other signatories of each deposit. The Treaty shall enter into force between the States which have ratified it as soon as the ratifications of the majority of the signatories, including the ratifications of Belgium, Canada, France, Luxembourg, the Netherlands, the United Kingdom and the United States, have been deposited and shall come into effect with respect to other States on the date of the deposit of their ratifications.[3]

Article 12

After the Treaty has been in force for ten years, or at any time thereafter, the Parties shall, if any of them so requests, consult together for the purpose of reviewing the Treaty, having regard for the factors then affecting peace and security in the North Atlantic area, including the development of universal as well as regional arrangements under the Charter of the United Nations for the maintenance of international peace and security.

Article 13

After the Treaty has been in force for twenty years, any Party may cease to be a Party one year after its notice of denunciation has been given to the Government of the United States of America, which will inform the Governments of the other Parties of the deposit of each notice of denunciation.

Article 14

This Treaty, of which the English and French texts are equally authentic, shall be deposited in the archives of the Government of the United States of America. Duly certified copies will be transmitted by that Government to the Governments of other signatories.

Notes

Introduction

1. Christoph Heusgen, "Foreword – Munich Security Conference," February 2023, https://securityconference.org/en/publications/munich-security-report-2023/foreword/; Melinda Rankin, "Russia in Ukraine: Accountability and global order on the precipice," Lowy Institute, February 22, 2023, https://www.lowyinstitute.org/the-interpreter/russia-ukraine-accountability-global-order-precipice.
2. André de Staercke would recall Spaak's request for "a maxim reflecting in a few words the collective aim of the Atlantic alliance and the independence of its members." NATO, "Summary record of a meeting of the Council held at the NATO headquarters, Brussels (C-R(76)4)," NATO, January 29, 1976, https://www.nato.int/nato_static_fl2014/assets/pdf/pdf_history/20161027_E1-Symbols-NATOMotto-c-r764.pdf. De Staercke was the right person for Spaak's unusual request. The young de Staercke had studied classical literature in the Jesuit order, and had at one point traveled through the small but imposing Italian village of San Gimignano. There he had noticed how, in the village's central Palazzo del Podestà was inscribed a tribute to free intellects and free counsel in the exercise of power. The tribute *Animus in consulendo liber* originated with the Roman politician and philosopher Marcus Porcius Cato, and it had become widely used in medieval Italy. De Staercke committed it to memory and, decades later, handed it to Spaak and NATO. De Staercke served as Belgium's deputy ambassador to NATO for almost two years, June 1950–April 1952, before taking up the ambassadorship, which he held until January 1976. NATO's translations of the Latin motto into English are the slightly contorted "Man's mind ranges unrestrained in counsel" or, slightly more simply, "In discussion a free mind." NATO, "NATO : The official motto of NATO," accessed June 6, 2023, https://www.nato.int/multi/animus.htm.
3. Alvin Shusters, "Leaders of NATO sign declaration," *New York Times*, June 27, 1974.
4. Antony J. Blinken and Lloyd J. Austin III, "America's partnerships are 'force multipliers' in the world," *Washington Post*, March 14, 2021, https://www.washingtonpost.com/opinions/2021/03/14/americas-partnerships-are-force-multipliers-world/.

5. Alexander Gabuev, "What's really going on between Russia and China," *Foreign Affairs*, April 12, 2023, https://www.foreignaffairs.com/united-states/whats-really-going-between-russia-and-china.
6. Ministry of Foreign Affairs of the People's Republic of China, "Wang Yi expounds China's five-point position on the current Ukraine issue," February 26, 2022, https://www.fmprc.gov.cn/eng/zxxx_662805/202202/t20220226_10645855.html.
7. David P. Calleo, *The Atlantic Fantasy: The US, NATO, and Europe*, Baltimore, MD, Johns Hopkins University Press, 1970; David P. Calleo, *Follies of Power: America's unipolar fantasy*, Cambridge, Cambridge University Press, 2009.
8. Giulio Andreotti, *The U.S.A. Up Close*, New York, New York University Press, 1992, 336.
9. NATO, "NATO 2022 Strategic Concept," June 29, 2022, https://www.nato.int/nato_static_fl2014/assets/pdf/2022/6/pdf/290622-strategic-concept.pdf; Joe Biden, "Remarks by President Biden on the united efforts of the free world to support the people of Ukraine," White House, March 26, 2022, https://www.whitehouse.gov/briefing-room/speeches-remarks/2022/03/26/remarks-by-president-biden-on-the-united-efforts-of-the-free-world-to-support-the-people-of-ukraine/.
10. Stanley R. Sloan and Lawrence Freedman, *Defense of the West: Transatlantic security from Truman to Trump*, Manchester, Manchester University Press, 2020; Wallace J. Thies, *Why NATO Endures*, Cambridge, Cambridge University Press, 2009; Wallace J. Thies, *Friendly Rivals: Bargaining and burden-shifting in NATO*, London, Routledge, 2015; Thomas Risse-Kappen, *Cooperation among Democracies: The European influence on US foreign policy*, Princeton, NJ, Princeton University Press, 1995; Jeffrey J. Anderson, G. John Ikenberry, and Thomas Risse-Kappen, *The End of the West?: Crisis and change in the Atlantic Order*, Ithaca, NY, Cornell University Press, 2008; Seth A. Johnston, *How NATO Adapts: Strategy and organization in the Atlantic alliance since 1950*, Baltimore, MD, Johns Hopkins University Press, 2017. On the broader dynamics of security community building, see Karl Wolfgang Deutsch, *Political Community and the North American Area: International organization in the light of historical experience*, Princeton, NJ, Princeton University Press, 1957, and Emanuel Adler and Michael Barnett, *Security Communities*, Cambridge, Cambridge University Press, 1998.
11. Ivo Daalder and James Goldgeier, "Global NATO," *Foreign Affairs*, 85:5 (2006), 105–113; Zbigniew Brzezinski, "An agenda for NATO," *Foreign Affairs*, 88:5 (2009), 2–20; Ellen Hallams, "NATO at 60: Going global?," *International Journal*, 64:2 (2009), 423–450; Yonah Alexander and Richard Prosen, *NATO: From regional to global security provider*, Lanham, MD, Lexington Books, 2015; Michael O. Slobodchikoff, G. Doug Davis, and Brandon Stewart, *The Challenge to NATO: Global security and the Atlantic alliance*, Lincoln, NE, Potomac Books, 2021.
12. Michael J. Williams, *The Good War: NATO and the liberal conscience in Afghanistan*, London, Palgrave, 2011; Sten Rynning, *NATO in Afghanistan: The liberal disconnect*, Stanford, CA, Stanford University Press, 2012.
13. Serhii Plokhy, *The Russo-Ukrainian War: The return of history*, New York, Norton, 2023.
14. Sheryn Lee and Benjamin Schreer, "Will Europe defend Taiwan?," *Washington Quarterly*, 45:3 (2022), 163–182.
15. John J. Mearsheimer, *The Great Delusion: Liberal dreams and international realities*, The Henry L. Stimson Lectures Series, New Haven, CT, Yale University Press, 2018.

16. Joshua R. Itzkowitz Shifrinson, "Deal or no deal? The end of the Cold War and the US offer to limit NATO expansion," *International Security*, 40:4 (2016), 7–44; Joshua R. Itzkowitz Shifrinson, "Eastbound and down: The United States, NATO enlargement, and suppressing the Soviet and Western European alternatives, 1990–1992," *Journal of Strategic Studies*, 43:6–7 (2020), 816–846; Mary Elise Sarotte, *Not One Inch: America, Russia, and the making of Post-Cold War stalemate*, New Haven, CT, Yale University Press, 2021; Mary Elise Sarotte, "Not one inch eastward? Bush, Baker, Kohl, Genscher, Gorbachev, and the origin of Russian resentment toward NATO enlargement in February 1990," *Diplomatic History*, 34:1 (2010), 119–140.

17. John J. Mearsheimer, "Why the Ukraine crisis is the west's fault: The liberal delusions that provoked Putin," *Foreign Affairs*, 93:5 (2014), 1–12; John J. Mearsheimer, "John Mearsheimer on why the West is principally responsible for the Ukrainian crisis; Russia and Ukraine," *The Economist*, March 19, 2022; Ted Galen Carpenter, "Many predicted NATO expansion would lead to war. Those warnings were ignored," *Guardian*, February 28, 2022.

18. John Lewis Gaddis, "History, grand strategy and NATO enlargement," *Survival*, 40:1 (1998), 145–151; George F. Kennan, "Opinion: A fateful error," *New York Times*, February 5, 1997, https://www.nytimes.com/1997/02/05/opinion/a-fateful-error.html.

19. Charles A. Kupchan, "The origins and future of NATO enlargement," *Contemporary Security Policy*, 21:2 (2000), 127–148.

20. Patrick Porter, "Why America's grand strategy has not changed: Power, habit, and the US foreign policy establishment," *International Security*, 42:4 (2018), 9–46; Paul van Hooft, "Land rush: American grand strategy, NATO enlargement, and European fragmentation," *International Politics*, 57:3 (2020), 530–553; Christopher Layne, "The US foreign policy establishment and grand strategy: How American elites obstruct strategic adjustment," *International Politics*, 54:3 (2017), 260–275.

21. Timothy Andrews Sayle, *Enduring Alliance: The history of NATO and the postwar global order*, Ithaca, NY, Cornell University Press, 2019.

22. Charles Kupchan, *No One's World: The West, the rising rest, and the coming global turn*, New York, Oxford University Press, 2012.

23. Barry R. Posen, "Europe can defend itself," *Survival*, 62:6 (2020), 7–34; Barry R. Posen, "A new transatlantic division of labor could save billions every year," *Bulletin of the Atomic Scientists*, 77:5 (2021), 239–243; Barry Posen, *Restraint: A new foundation for US grand strategy*, Ithaca, NY, Cornell University Press, 2015; Christopher Layne, "America's Middle East grand strategy after Iraq: The moment for offshore balancing has arrived," *Review of International Studies*, 35:1 (2009), 5–25; Christopher Layne, "Hyping the China threat," *National Interest*, 169 (2020), 21–31.

24. Sten Rynning, "Critical, restless, and relevant: Realism as normative thought," in Bertel Heurlin et al. (eds), *Polarity in International Relations: Past, present, future*, Cham, Palgrave Macmillan, 2022, 149–168.

25. See references in note 17.

26. Kimberly Marten, "Reconsidering NATO expansion: A counterfactual analysis of Russia and the West in the 1990s," *European Journal of International Security*, 3:2 (2018), 135–161; Kimberly Marten, "NATO enlargement: Evaluating its consequences in Russia," *International Politics*, 57:3 (2020), 401–426; Keir Giles, *Russia's War on Everybody – And what it means for you*, London, Bloomsbury, 2023.

27. Henry A. Kissinger, *A World Restored: Metternich, Castlereagh and the problems of peace, 1812–22*, London, Weidenfeld and Nicolson, 1957; Hans Morgenthau, *Politics among Nations: The struggle for power and peace*, Boston, MA, McGraw-Hill, 1993; Arnold Wolfers, "'National security' as an ambiguous symbol," *Political Science Quarterly*, 67:4 (1952), 481–502; Stanley Hoffmann, "Obstinate or obsolete? The fate of the nation-state and the case of Western Europe," *Daedalus*, 95:3 (1966), 862–915; David P. Calleo, *Rethinking Europe's Future*, Princeton, NJ, Princeton University Press, 2001; Henry R. Nau, *At Home Abroad: Identity and power in American foreign policy*, Cornell Studies in Political Economy, Ithaca, NY, Cornell University Press, 2002; Henry R. Nau, *Conservative Internationalism: Armed diplomacy under Jefferson, Polk, Truman, and Reagan*, Princeton, NJ, Princeton University Press, 2013; Max Weber, Hans Heinrich Gerth, and C. Wright Mills, *From Max Weber: Essays in sociology*, Routledge Classics in Sociology, New York, Routledge, 2009; Stephen Turner and George Mazur, "Morgenthau as a Weberian methodologist," *European Journal of International Relations*, 15:3 (2009), 477–504.

28. William H. McNeill, *The Rise of the West: A history of the human community*, Chicago, IL, University of Chicago Press, 1963; James Burnham, *Suicide of the West: An essay on the meaning and destiny of liberalism*, New York, John Day, 1964; Doyne Dawson, *The Origins of Western Warfare: Militarism and morality in the ancient world*, Boulder, CO, Westview Press, 1996; David Gress, *From Plato to NATO: The idea of the West and its opponents*, New York, Free Press, 1998; Patrick Thaddeus Jackson, *Civilizing the Enemy: German reconstruction and the invention of the west*, Ann Arbor, MI, University of Michigan Press, 2009; Michael Kimmage, *The Abandonment of the West: The history of an idea in American foreign policy*, New York, Basic Books, 2020; Sten Rynning, Olivier Schmitt, and Amelie Theussen (eds), *War Time: Temporality and the decline of western military power*, Washington, DC, Brookings Institution Press, 2021.

29. Lawrence Freedman, *A Choice of Enemies: America confronts the Middle East*, London, Phoenix, 2009, xxvi.

30. Henry A. Kissinger, *World Order: Reflections on the character of nations and the course of history*, London, Allen Lane, 2014; Sten Rynning, "The geography of the Atlantic peace: NATO 25 years after the fall of the Berlin Wall," *International Affairs*, 90:6 (2014), 1383–1401.

31. Kissinger, *World Order*, 90.

32. Alexander L. George, *Bridging the Gap: Theory and practice in foreign policy*, Washington, DC: United States Institute of Peace Press, 1993; Raymond Aron, *The Committed Observer: Interviews with Jean-Louis Missika and Dominique Wolton*, Chicago, IL, Regnery Gateway, 1983; Michael C. Desch (ed.), *Public Intellectuals in the Global Arena: Professors or pundits?* Notre Dame, IN, University of Notre Dame Press, 2016; Michael C. Desch, *Cult of the Irrelevant: The waning influence of social science on national security*, Princeton Studies in International History and Politics, Princeton, NJ, Princeton University Press, 2018.

33. According to André de Staercke, Spaak wanted a motto in Latin because it was a language of "wisdom." NATO, "Summary record of a meeting of the Council held at the NATO headquarters, Brussels (C-R(76)4)."

34. J.H. Huizinga, *Mr. Europe: A political biography of Paul Henri Spaak*, London, Weidenfeld and Nicolson, 1961, 75.

Chapter 1 America's Search for United Nations

1. Franklin D. Roosevelt, "Address," *New York Times*, December 10, 1941.
2. John Lewis Gaddis, *The United States and the Origins of the Cold War, 1941–1947*, New York, Columbia University Press, 2000; Stephen Wertheim, *Tomorrow, the World: The birth of US global supremacy*, Cambridge, MA, The Belknap Press of Harvard University Press, 2020.
3. Gaddis, *The United States and the Origins of the Cold War*. Gaddis generally explains US war and post-war policy with reference to the complexity of the domestic scene. For more critical takes on Roosevelt's (in)ability to act boldly at critical moments, even if he had strong ideas, see James MacGregor Burns, *Roosevelt: The soldier of freedom*, New York, Harcourt Brace, 1970; Robert A. Divine, *The Reluctant Belligerent: American entry into World War II*, New York, Wiley, 1979; Daniel Yergin, *Shattered Peace: The origins of the Cold War*, New York, Penguin Books, 1990. For an assessment placing Roosevelt on a par with George Washington and Abraham Lincoln as a great US president, see Patrick Renshaw, *Franklin D. Roosevelt*, New York, Routledge, 2016.
4. William H. McNeill, *America, Britain and Russia: Their co-operation and conflict, 1941–1946*, New York, Johnson Reprint Corporation, 1970.
5. H.V. Morton, *Atlantic Meeting*, London, Methuen & Co, 1944, 87.
6. Adolf A. Berle, Jr., "MEMORANDUM TO THE PRESIDENT: Peace Commitments," US Department of State, July 9, 1941, http://www.fdrlibrary.marist.edu/_resources/images/psf/psfa0498.pdf. The meeting between the two leaders had been on the cards for most of 1941, though also postponed on grounds of political difficulties: White House, "Memorandum of trip to meet Winston Churchill, August, 1941," August 23, 1941, http://www.fdrlibrary.marist.edu/_resources/images/psf/psfa0007.pdf.
7. Lloyd C. Gardner, "The Atlantic Charter: Idea and reality, 1942–1945," in Douglas Brinkley and David R. Facey-Crowther (eds), *The Atlantic Charter*, New York, St. Martin's Press, 1994, 51.
8. Franklin D. Roosevelt, "Telegram for: Winston Churchill," White House, July 14, 1941, http://www.fdrlibrary.marist.edu/_resources/images/psf/psfa0498.pdf.
9. Theodore A. Wilson, "The first summit: FDR and the riddle of personal diplomacy," in Douglas Brinkley and David R. Facey-Crowther (eds), *The Atlantic Charter*, New York, St. Martin's Press, 1994, 17.
10. Warren F. Kimball, "The Atlantic Charter: 'With all deliberate speed'," in Douglas Brinkley and David R. Facey-Crowther (eds), *The Atlantic Charter*, New York, St. Martin's Press, 1994, 104; Warren F. Kimball, *The Juggler: Franklin Roosevelt as wartime statesman*, Princeton, NJ, Princeton University Press, 1991; McNeill, *America, Britain and Russia*; Theodore A. Wilson, *The First Summit: Roosevelt and Churchill at Placentia Bay 1941*, Boston, MA, Houghton Mifflin Company, 1969.
11. Wilson, *The First Summit*, 200–202.
12. Ibid., 193–197.
13. David Reynolds, *The Creation of the Anglo-American Alliance 1937–1941: A study in competitive co-operation*, London, Europa Publications, 1981, 260.
14. Martin Gilbert, *Winston S. Churchill: Finest hour, 1939–1941*, New York, Rosetta Books, 2015.
15. The signatories were Belgium, Czechoslovakia, Greece, Luxembourg, the Netherlands, Norway, Poland, the Soviet Union, Yugoslavia, and Free France.

16. American and British Chiefs of Staff, "Memorandum by the United States and British Chiefs of Staff: American–British Grand Strategy," December 31, 1941, https://history.state.gov/historicaldocuments/frus1941-43/d115.

17. Warren F. Kimball, *Forged in War: Roosevelt, Churchill, and the Second World War*, New York, W. Morrow, 1997, 194.

18. Winston Churchill, "Address," March 21, 1943, http://www.cvce.eu/obj/address_given_by_winston_churchill_on_post_war_21_march_1943-en-831b4069-27e5-4cd7-a607-57d31278584d.html.

19. E.J. Hughes, "Winston Churchill and the formation of the United Nations Organization," *Journal of Contemporary History*, 9:4 (1974), 177–194; McNeill, *America, Britain and Russia*, 321.

20. David Dutton, *Anthony Eden: A life and reputation*, London, Arnold, 1997, 282.

21. Serhii Plokhy, *Yalta: The price of peace*, London, Penguin, 2011, 122; Hughes, "Winston Churchill and the formation of the United Nations Organization."

22. Kimball, *Forged in War*, 270.

23. United States, Britain, the Soviet Union, and China, "Four Nations Declaration," October 30, 1943, https://avalon.law.yale.edu/wwii/moscow.asp.

24. Neil Smith, *American Empire: Roosevelt's geographer and the prelude to globalization*, Berkeley, CA, University of California Press, 2004; Wertheim, *Tomorrow, the World*.

25. Robert L. Messer, *The End of an Alliance: James F. Byrnes, Roosevelt, Truman, and the origins of the Cold War*, Chapel Hill, NC, University of North Carolina Press, 1982.

26. Richard F. Fenno, *The Yalta Conference*, second edition, Lexington, MA, Heath, 1972.

27. Plokhy, *Yalta*, 124.

28. An affirmative vote is nine of fifteen Security Council members. The great powers also agreed that, if they were party to a conflict, they should abstain from voting on peaceful settlement recommendations.

29. Renshaw, *Franklin D. Roosevelt*, 152.

30. Inter-American Conference, "Act of Chapultepec," March 6, 1945, https://avalon.law.yale.edu/20th_century/chapul.asp.

31. James A. Gazell, "Arthur H. Vandenberg, internationalism, and the United Nations," *Political Science Quarterly*, 88:3 (1973), 389.

32. American States, "Inter-American Treaty of Reciprocal Assistance," September 2, 1947, http://www.oas.org/juridico/english/treaties/b-29.html.

33. George A. Finch, "The North Atlantic Pact in international law," *Proceedings of the American Society of International Law*, 43 (April 28–30, 1949), 90–102.

34. Lawrence S. Kaplan, *NATO and the UN: A peculiar relationship*, Columbia, MO, University of Missouri Press, 2010, 10. Italics in original.

35. John Lewis Gaddis, *George F. Kennan: An American life*, New York, Penguin Press, 2011, 321.

36. Peter Foot, "America and the origins of the Atlantic alliance: A reappraisal," in Joseph Smith (ed.), *The Origins of NATO*, Exeter, University of Exeter Press, 1990.

37. Ronald Steel, "How Europe became Atlantic: Walter Lippmann and the new geography of the Atlantic community," in Marco Mariano (ed.), *Defining the Atlantic Community*, London, Routledge, 2010, 21–35.

38. Klaus Schwabe, "The origins of the United States' engagement in Europe, 1946–1952," in Francis H. Heller and John R. Gillingham, *NATO: The founding of the*

Atlantic alliance and the integration of Europe, New York, St. Martin's, 1992, 161–192; Foot, "America and the origins of the Atlantic alliance"; Geir Lundestad, "Empire by invitation? The United States and Western Europe, 1945–1952," *Journal of Peace Research*, 23:3 (1986), 263–277.

39. Philip M. Coupland, "Western union, 'spiritual union,' and European integration, 1948–1951," *Journal of British Studies*, 43:3 (2004), 366–394.
40. Edward Fursdon, *The European Defence Community: A history*, London, Macmillan, 1980, 219.
41. Paul-Henri Spaak, *Combats Inachevés: De l'espoir Aux Déceptions*, Paris, Fayard, 1969, 33.
42. Lawrence S. Kaplan, *NATO 1948: The birth of the transatlantic alliance*, Lanham, MD, Rowman and Littlefield, 2007, 80.
43. Michael J. Hogan, *The Marshall Plan: America, Britain, and the reconstruction of Western Europe, 1947–1952*, Cambridge, Cambridge University Press, 2002, 218–220.
44. John Charmley, "Churchill and the American alliance," *Transactions of the Royal Historical Society*, 11 (2001), 353–371; John Charmley, *Churchill: The end of glory*, London, Hodder and Stoughton, 1993.
45. Sidney Aster, *Anthony Eden*, London, Weidenfeld and Nicolson, 1976, 77–82.
46. Dutton, *Anthony Eden*, 290.
47. Aster, *Anthony Eden*, 98; Dutton, *Anthony Eden*, 280.
48. Nicholas Henderson, *The Birth of NATO*, London, Weidenfeld and Nicolson, 1982; Richard D. McKinzie, "John D. Hickerson: Oral history interview" (Harry S. Truman Library, 1972/1973), https://www.trumanlibrary.gov/library/oral-histories/hickrson; Escott Reid, *Time of Fear and Hope: The making of the North Atlantic Treaty, 1947–1949*, Toronto, McClelland and Stewart, 1977.
49. Schwabe, "The origins of the United States' engagement in Europe."

Chapter 2 The North Atlantic Treaty

1. James Reston, "Alliance links countries in a common defense against aggressor," *New York Times*, April 5, 1949.
2. W.H. Lawrence, "President hopeful: Declares a similar pact would have prevented both world conflicts," *New York Times*, April 5, 1949.
3. Don Cook, *Forging the Alliance: NATO 1945–1950*, New York, Arbor House/ W. Morrow, 1989, 18–19.
4. Richard D. McKinzie, "John D. Hickerson: Oral history interview" (Harry S. Truman Library, 1972/1973), https://www.trumanlibrary.gov/library/oral-histories/hickrson.
5. Lawrence S. Kaplan and Sidney R. Snyder (eds), *Fingerprints on History: The NATO memoirs of Theodore C. Achilles*, Lyman L. Lemnitzer Center for NATO and European Community Studies Occasional Papers I, Kent State University, OH, 1992, 11–12.
6. Peter Foot, "America and the origins of the Atlantic Alliance: A reappraisal," in Joseph Smith (ed.), *The Origins of NATO*, Exeter, University of Exeter Press, 1990, 83.
7. Nicholas Henderson, *The Birth of NATO*, London, Weidenfeld and Nicolson, 1982.
8. Ibid., 3; Ernest Bevin, "Speech" (Hansard, January 22, 1948), https://api.parliament.uk/historic-hansard/commons/1948/jan/22/foreign-affairs.

9. Hubert Miles Gladwyn Jebb, Baron Gladwyn, *The Memoirs of Lord Gladwyn*, London, Weidenfeld and Nicolson, 1972, 210–211; Lawrence S. Kaplan, *NATO 1948: The birth of the transatlantic alliance*, Lanham, MD, Rowman and Littlefield, 2007, 26.

10. Theodore A. Achilles, "The Omaha milkman: The role of the United States," in Nicholas Sherwen (ed.), *NATO's Anxious Birth: The prophetic vision of the 1940s*, London, Hurst & Company, 1985, 30.

11. "The Brussels Treaty," March 17, 1948, https://www.nato.int/cps/en/natohq/official_texts_17072.htm.

12. Kaplan and Snyder, *Fingerprints on History*, 14–15.

13. Henderson, *The Birth of NATO*, 17.

14. Kaplan and Snyder, *Fingerprints on History*, 15.

15. US Senate, "US Senate Resolution 239 (Vandenberg Resolution)," June 11, 1948, https://www.nato.int/ebookshop/video/declassified/doc_files/Vandenberg%20resolution.pdf.

16. Daryl J. Hudson, "Vandenberg reconsidered: Senate Resolution 239 and American foreign policy," *Diplomatic History*, 1:1 (1977), 46–63.

17. George F. Kennan, "The sources of Soviet conduct," *Foreign Affairs*, 65:4 (1947), 566–582.

18. Escott Reid, *Time of Fear and Hope: The making of the North Atlantic Treaty, 1947–1949*, Toronto, McClelland and Stewart, 1977, 108–109. Canada's input into the thinking of George Kennan and others extended beyond the lunches offered by Ambassador Wrong, naturally. Widely noted is the impact of a speech made by Canadian Secretary of State for External Affairs Louis St. Laurent in late April 1948, in which he pleaded for the association of free nations in collective self-defense under UN Charter article 51. This emphasis was, as we have seen, paralleled by that of Senator Vandenberg. See Reid, *Time of Fear and Hope*, 109; Henderson, *The Birth of NATO*, 25.

19. Reid, *Time of Fear and Hope*, 112.

20. Kaplan, *NATO 1948*.

21. Sidney R. Snyder, "The role of the International Working Group in the creation of the North Atlantic Treaty: December 1947–April 1949," Kent State University, OH, 1992, 221.

22. Arthur Krock, "Ohio poll decides," *New York Times*, November 4, 1948.

23. Kaplan and Snyder, *Fingerprints on History*, 27.

24. Working Party, "Memorandum by the participants in the Washington Security Talks, July 6 to September 9, submitted to their respective governments for study and comment," Foreign Relations of the United States, September 9, 1948, https://history.state.gov/historicaldocuments/frus1948v03/d150.

25. Peter Boyle, "America's hesitant road to NATO," in Joseph Smith (ed.), *The Origins of NATO*, Exeter, University of Exeter Press, 1990.

26. F.H. Soward, "American foreign policy: Reflections, recollections, and recriminations," *International Journal*, 10:4 (1955), 282.

27. McKinzie, "John D. Hickerson: Oral history interview."

28. Henderson, *The Birth of NATO*, 91.

29. Ibid., 92–93.

30. Alexander Rendel, "The uncertain months: British anxieties over the outcome of the negotiations," in Sherwen (ed.), *NATO's Anxious Birth*, 55; Escott Reid, "The art of the almost impossible: Unwavering Canadian support for the emerging Atlantic Alliance," in Sherwen (ed.), *NATO's Anxious Birth*, 79.

31. Henderson, *The Birth of NATO*, 55.
32. Alex Danchev, "Taking the pledge: Oliver Franks and the negotiation of the North Atlantic Treaty," *Diplomatic History*, 15:2 (1991), 199–219.
33. Ibid., 208.
34. Henderson, *The Birth of NATO*, 95.
35. Martin H. Folly, "Britain and the issue of Italian membership of NATO, 1948–49," *Review of International Studies*, 13:3 (1987), 177–196.
36. Ibid., 190.
37. Kaplan and Snyder, *Fingerprints on History*, 27; Kaplan, *NATO 1948*, 207.
38. Working Party, "Report of the International Working Group to the Ambassadors' Committee," Foreign Relations of the United States, December 24, 1948, https://history.state.gov/historicaldocuments/frus1948v03/d199.
39. Achilles, "The Omaha milkman," 39.
40. Cook, *Forging the Alliance*, 224.
41. Reid, *Time of Fear and Hope*, 219.
42. Escott Reid, "The birth of the North Atlantic Alliance," *International Journal*, 22:3 (1967), 435–436.
43. McKinzie, "John D. Hickerson: Oral history interview."
44. John C. Milloy, *The North Atlantic Treaty Organization, 1948–1957: Community or alliance?* Montreal, McGill-Queen's University Press, 2006, 28–29.
45. Achilles, "The Omaha milkman," 39.
46. Milloy, *The North Atlantic Treaty Organization*, 25.
47. Reid, *Time of Fear and Hope*, 165.
48. Adam Chapnick, "Review: Escott Reid: Diplomat and scholar," *International Journal*, 61:2 (2006), 509–511.
49. Reid, *Time of Fear and Hope*, 229–230.
50. David G. Haglund and Stéphane Roussel, "Escott Reid, the North Atlantic Treaty, and Canadian strategic culture," in Stéphane Roussel and Greg Donaghy (eds), *Escott Reid: Diplomat and scholar*, Montreal, McGill-Queen's University Press, 2004, 44–64.
51. Ibid., 57.

Chapter 3 Aspiration Lost? The Emergence of Cold War NATO

1. North Atlantic Council, "Summary Record of the Third Meeting, September 16, 1950, 10:30 a.m.," September 16, 1950, https://archives.nato.int/uploads/r/null/1/9/19408/C_5-R_3_ENG.pdf.
2. NATO, "The Strategic Concept for the Defense of the North Atlantic Area," December 1, 1949, https://www.nato.int/docu/stratdoc/eng/a491201a.pdf.
3. NATO, "North Atlantic Council, First Session, Approved Summary Minutes," September 17, 1949, https://archives.nato.int/uploads/r/null/1/9/19139/C_1-R_1_ENG.pdf.
4. North Atlantic Council, "Summary Record of the Second Meeting Held at Lancaster House on the 26th July," July 26, 1950, https://archives.nato.int/uploads/r/null/3/4/34671/D-R_2_ENG.pdf.
5. Thomas J. Hamilton, "Action by council: Unit gives Washington authority to designate chief for its forces," *New York Times*, July 8, 1950.
6. Matthew B. Ridgway, *Soldier: The memoirs of Matthew B. Ridgway*, Westport, CT, Greenwood Press, 1974, 238–239.

7. NATO, "Final Communiqué, North Atlantic Council, Lisbon," February 20, 1952, https://www.nato.int/docu/comm/49-95/c520225a.htm; North Atlantic Military Committee, Standing Group, "Force Goals for 1952, 1953 and 1954," March 17, 1952, https://archives.nato.int/uploads/r/null/1/2/121172/SGM-0545-52_ENG_PDP.pdf; Michael L. Hoffmann, "US agrees to yearly review of military budget by Nato," *New York Times*, February 23, 1952.

8. This applied especially to the post of Commander in Chief, Center, which in the spring of 1952 was divided among three nations, and then also to a command organization suited to Turkish and Greek sensibilities. Ridgway, *Soldier*, 242–243.

9. Edward Fursdon, *The European Defence Community: A history*, London, Macmillan, 1980, 220.

10. Marc Trachtenberg and Christopher Gehrz, "America, Europe, and German rearmament, August–September 1950: A critique of a myth," in Marc Trachtenberg (ed.), *Between Empire and Alliance: America and Europe during the Cold War*, Lanham, MD, Rowman & Littlefield, 2003, 1–32.

11. Timothy Andrews Sayle, *Enduring Alliance: The history of NATO and the postwar global order*, Ithaca, NY, Cornell University Press, 2019, 18.

12. A.M. Rosenthal, "Pact council expected to set unified European command," *New York Times*, September 18, 1950.

13. "Allies announce decision on Bonn," *New York Times*, September 20, 1950.

14. Trachtenberg and Gehrz, "America, Europe, and German Rearmament," 17.

15. North Atlantic Council, "Summary Record of the Third Meeting, September 16, 1950, 10:30 a.m."

16. Hastings Lionel Pug Ismay, *NATO: The first five years*, Utrecht, Bosch-Utrecht, 1956; Suhnaz Yilmaz, "Turkey's quest for NATO membership: The institutionalization of the Turkish–American Alliance," *Journal of Southeast European and Black Sea Studies*, 12:4 (2012), 481–495.

17. Dean Acheson, *Present at the Creation: My years in the State Department*, New York, W.W. Norton & Co, 1987, 570.

18. Ibid., 440.

19. Lawrence S. Kaplan, "NATO and Adenauer's Germany: Uneasy partnership," *International Organization*, 15:4 (1961), 618–629.

20. Pierre Rouanet, *Mèndes France Au Pouvoir (18 Juin 1954-6 Février 1955)*, Paris, Robert Laffont, 1965, 270.

21. Marc Trachtenberg, *A Constructed Peace: The making of the European settlement, 1945–1963*, Princeton, NJ, Princeton University Press, 2020, 147.

22. Patrick M. Condray, "The new look of 1952–53," in Patrick M. Condray, *Charting the Nation's Course*, Maxwell, AB, Air University Press, 1999, 22, https://www.jstor.org/stable/resrep13803.9#metadata_info_tab_contents.

23. Gregory W. Pedlow, "NATO Strategy Documents, 1949–1969," NATO, n.d., 18, https://www.nato.int/docu/stratdoc/eng/intro.pdf. In parallel to US "New Look" policy planning, NATO's supreme commander, US General Alfred Gruenther, undertook matching "New Approach" planning. The NATO allies' military chiefs approved the new strategy in Military Committee document 48 (MC 48) some four weeks after the adoption of the new US strategy. It provided the guidance and concepts for NATO's later "massive retaliation" strategy contained in MC 14/2 of May 1957.

24. Robert Schuman, "Schuman Declaration," May 9, 1950, https://european-union.europa.eu/principles-countries-history/history-eu/1945-59/schuman-declaration-may-1950_en.

25. John Foster Dulles, "Statement by the secretary of state to the North Atlantic Council," December 14, 1953, https://history.state.gov/historicaldocuments/frus1952-54v05p1/d238. The record of the North Atlantic Council offers a polished version, whereby Dulles is recorded as saying that "the United States might reluctantly be compelled to reconsider its whole policy." NATO, "Summary record of a meeting of the Council," December 14, 1953, https://archives.nato.int/uploads/r/null/2/2/22936/C-R_53_54_ENG.pdf.

26. Kevin Ruane, "Agonizing reappraisals: Anthony Eden, John Foster Dulles and the crisis of European defence, 1953–54," *Diplomacy and Statecraft*, 13:4 (2002), 151–185.

27. Ibid., 166–172.

28. Nine-Power Conference, "Final Act of the Nine-Power Conference, London, 28 September–3 October, 1954" https://www.cvce.eu/en/collections/unit-content/-/unit/02bb76df-d066-4c08-a58a-d4686a3e68ff/9059327f-7f8a-4a74-ac7e-5a0f3247bcd3/Resources#9929e166-3f19-4768-94fd-74564959bc5a_en&overlay.

29. Gustav Schmidt, "Getting the balance right: NATO and the evolution of EC/EU integration, security and defence policy," in Gustav Schmidt (ed.), *A History of NATO: The first fifty years*, London, Palgrave, 2001, 11.

30. Peter James, "Franz Josef Strauß – Lasting legacy or transitory phenomenon?," *German Politics*, 7:2 (1998), 204.

31. Trachtenberg, *A Constructed Peace*.

32. Ibid., 234.

33. Ralph Dietl, "In defence of the West: General Lauris Norstad, NATO nuclear forces and transatlantic relations 1956–1963," *Diplomacy and Statecraft*, 17:2 (2006), 347–392; Trachtenberg, *A Constructed Peace*.

34. Robert S. Jordan, *Norstad: Cold-War NATO Supreme Commander: Airman, strategist, diplomat*, London, Palgrave Macmillan, 2000, 105–106.

35. Trachtenberg, *A Constructed Peace*, 230.

36. Robert S. McNamara, "Address by Secretary of Defense McNamara at the Ministerial Meeting of the North Atlantic Council," May 5, 1962, https://history.state.gov/historicaldocuments/frus1961-63v08/d82.

37. Jordan, *Norstad*, 8; Trachtenberg, *A Constructed Peace*, 302.

38. Paul-Henri Spaak, *Combats Inachevés: De l'espoir Aux Déceptions*, Paris, Fayard, 1969, 104; Paul-Henri Spaak, "The West in disarray," *Foreign Affairs*, 35:2 (1957), 184–190.

39. Harold Callender, "NATO talks open today, with pact on arms in doubt," *New York Times*, December 16, 1957.

40. Paul-Henri Spaak, "Problems facing the West," *University of Pennsylvania Law Review*, 107:8 (1959), 1085–1097.

41. Robert S. Jordan, *Political Leadership in NATO: A study in multinational diplomacy*, Boulder, CO, Westview Press, 1979, 69.

42. Ibid., 71.

43. Paul Van Campen, "The evolution of NATO political consultation 1949–1962," NATO, May 2, 1963, https://www.nato.int/archives/docu/d630502e.htm.

44. Ronald Wingate, *Lord Ismay: A biography*, London, Hutchinson, 1970, 192.

45. Ismay, *NATO*, 64–65.
46. Wingate, *Lord Ismay*, 209.
47. John C. Milloy, *The North Atlantic Treaty Organization, 1948–1957: Community or alliance?* Montreal, McGill-Queen's University Press, 2006, 84.
48. Ibid., 147.
49. NATO, "Report of the Committee of Three on non-military cooperation in NATO," December 13, 1956, https://www.nato.int/cps/en/natohq/official_texts_17481.htm.
50. Lawrence S. Kaplan, "Report of the 'Three Wise Men': 50 years on," NATO, November 4, 2008, https://www.nato.int/cps/en/natohq/opinions_22606.htm?selectedLocale=en.
51. Milloy, *The North Atlantic Treaty Organization*, 190.
52. Van Campen, "The evolution of NATO political consultation."
53. Harold Callender, "Dulles rules out consulting NATO in time of stress," *New York Times*, December 13, 1956.
54. Ryan C. Hendrickson, "NATO's secretaries-general: Organizational leadership in shaping alliance strategy," in Gulnur Aybet and Rebecca R. Moore (eds), *NATO in Search of a Vision*, Washington, DC, Georgetown University Press, 2010, 53.
55. Jordan, *Political Leadership in NATO*, 49.
56. Spaak, *Combats Inachevés*, 214–215.
57. Jordan, *Political Leadership in NATO*, 94.
58. Charles de Gaulle, "Lettre et Mémorandum Du Général de Gaulle Au Général Eisenhower," September 17, 1958, https://www.cvce.eu/en/obj/letter_and_memorandum_from_general_de_gaulle_to_general_eisenhower_17_september_1958-en-aebdd430-35cb-4bdd-9e56-87fce077ce70.html.
59. Spaak, *Combats Inachevés*, 182.
60. Milloy, *The North Atlantic Treaty Organization*, 177.
61. Myron A. Greenberg, "Kennedy's choice: The Skybolt crisis revisited," *Naval War College Review*, 53:4 (2000), 143–148; the commissioned study became a Skybolt case study in Richard E. Neustadt, *Alliance Politics*, New York, Columbia University Press, 1970.
62. Garret Martin, "The 1967 withdrawal from NATO – a cornerstone of de Gaulle's grand strategy?," *Journal of Transatlantic Studies*, 9:3 (2011), 232–243.
63. Harlan Cleveland, *NATO: The transatlantic bargain*, New York, Harper and Row, 1970, 53.
64. Lester Pearson, "NATO: Retrospect and prospects," *International Journal* (Toronto), 14:2 (1959), 82.
65. Spaak, *Combats Inachevés*, 421.

Chapter 4 Losing Its Luster: NATO without Atlanticism

1. Robert S. Jordan, *Political Leadership in NATO: A study in multinational diplomacy*, Boulder, CO, Westview Press, 1979, 200.
2. Edward Cowan, "Lemnitzer to rule soon on disputed Belgian site for NATO headquarters," *New York Times*, August 22, 1966; Jordan, *Political Leadership in NATO*, 200.
3. David P. Calleo, *The Atlantic Fantasy: The US, NATO, and Europe*, Baltimore, MD, Johns Hopkins University Press, 1970, 76.

4. Jeremy Suri, "Henry Kissinger and the reconceptualization of European security, 1969–1975," in Andreas Wenger, Vojtech Mastny, and Christian Nuenlist (eds), *Origins of the European Security System: The Helsinki process revisited, 1965–1975*, Abingdon, Routledge, 2008, 46–64.

5. White House, "Memorandum of conversation between Michel Jobert, Minister of Foreign Affairs, and Dr. Henry A. Kissinger, Assistant to the President for National Security Affairs," May 17, 1973.

6. Gregory W. Pedlow, "NATO Strategy Documents, 1949–1969," NATO, n.d., 24, https://www.nato.int/docu/stratdoc/eng/intro.pdf.

7. William Beecher, "Strategy change adopted by NATO," *New York Times*, December 13, 1967.

8. The Defence Planning Committee guided NATO's integrated military structure and force planning process for as long as France remained outside this integrated structure. When France in 2009 decided to rejoin the structure, NATO folded the DPC responsibilities back into the overarching North Atlantic Council and closed the DPC.

9. Kai-Uwe von Hassel, "Organizing Western Defense," *Foreign Affairs*, 43:2 (1965), 209–216.

10. Ibid., 211.

11. Helga Haftendorn, *NATO and the Nuclear Revolution: A crisis of credibility, 1966–67*, Oxford, Oxford University Press, 1996, 43.

12. "Seid eisern," *Der Spiegel*, August 28, 1966.

13. Haftendorn, *NATO and the Nuclear Revolution*, 38–39.

14. Sydney Gruson, "Britain disdains French atom bid," *New York Times*, September 25, 1963; Reuters, "Adenauer would join France in atom force," *New York Times*, October 5, 1963.

15. Dirk Stikker, "Annual Political Appraisal: Special Report by the Secretary General on NATO Defence Policy," NATO, April 17, 1962, Nuclear Planning Group (NATO Archives).

16. "NATO nuclear progress," *New York Times*, June 6, 1965.

17. Harlan Cleveland, *NATO: The transatlantic bargain*, New York, Harper and Row, 1970, 55.

18. Haftendorn, *NATO and the Nuclear Revolution*, 47; Michael O. Wheeler, "NATO nuclear strategy, 1949–90," in Gustav Schmidt (ed.), *A History of NATO: The first fifty years*, London, Palgrave, 2001, 121–139; Drew Middleton, "NATO preparing a report on when, how and where to use nuclear arms," *New York Times*, March 1, 1969.

19. Richard Lowenthal, "The Germans feel like Germans again," *New York Times*, March 6, 1966.

20. Cyrus L. Sulzberger, "A new kind of German(y)," *New York Times*, March 22, 1967.

21. Philip Bajon, "De Gaulle finds his 'master'. Gerhard Schröder's 'fairly audacious politics' in the European crisis of 1965–66," *Journal of European Integration History*, 17:2 (2011), 253–269.

22. David Tal, "The burden of alliance: The NPT negotiations and the NATO factor, 1960–1968," in Christian Nuenlist and Anna Locher (eds), *Transatlantic Relations at Stake: Aspects of NATO, 1956–1972*, Zurich, CSS/ETH, 2006, 97–124.

23. Cleveland, *NATO*; Seth A. Givens, "All part of the same struggle: Berlin's role in German–US relations during the Lyndon Johnson presidency," *Cold War History*, 22:3 (2022), 287–304.

24. Eugene Rostow, "A practical program for peace: The twentieth anniversary of the Harmel Report," *Atlantic Community Quarterly*, 25:3 (1987), 270–277.

25. Manlio Brosio, "Past and future tasks of the alliance: An analysis of the Harmel Report," *Atlantic Community Quarterly*, 6:2 (1968), 231–237; Sten Rynning, "The divide: France, Germany and political NATO," *International Affairs*, 93:2 (2017), 267–289, https://doi.org/10.1093/ia/iiw060.

26. NATO, "The future tasks of the alliance. Report of the Council—The Harmel Report," December 13, 1967, https://www.nato.int/cps/en/natohq/official_texts_26700.htm.

27. Ibid.

28. Rostow, "A practical program for peace," 274.

29. Vincent Dujardin, "Belgium, NATO, and détente, 1960–1973," in Christian Nuenlist and Anna Locher (eds), *Transatlantic Relations at Stake: Aspects of NATO, 1956–1972*, Zurich, ETH/CSS, 2006, 189–214.

30. Haftendorn, *NATO and the Nuclear Revolution*; Frédéric Bozo, "Détente versus Alliance: France, the United States and the politics of the Harmel Report (1964–1968)," *Contemporary European History*, 7:3 (1998), 343–360.

31. Rostow, "A practical program for peace," 272.

32. Haftendorn, *NATO and the Nuclear Revolution*, 323; Rostow, "A practical program for peace."

33. NATO Archives have since published the reports and associated documents: https://www.nato.int/cps/en/natohq/80830.htm.

34. Henry Tanner, "A changing alliance: Germans dominate NATO session, and talk is of detente with the East," *New York Times*, December 17, 1966.

35. "Brandt moved by visit to Warsaw Ghetto site," *New York Times*, December 8, 1970.

36. Henry A. Kissinger, "Memorial remarks for Egon Bahr," September 17, 2015, https://www.henryakissinger.com/remembrances/memorial-remarks-for-egon-bahr/; Henry A. Kissinger, *Leadership: Six studies in world strategy*, London, Allen Lane, 2022.

37. Judith Michel, "Willy Brandt's relations with the United States, 1933–1974," in Bernd Rother and Klaus Larres (eds), *Willy Brandt and International Relations*, London, Bloomsbury, 2019, 15–32.

38. Bruna Bagnato, "NATO in the mid-1960s: The view of Secretary-General Manlio Brosio," in Nuenlist and Locher (eds), *Transatlantic Relations at Stake*, 173.

39. NATO, "Final communiqué," November 15, 1968.

40. Susan Colbourn, *Euromissiles: The nuclear weapons that nearly destroyed NATO*, Ithaca, NY, Cornell University Press, 2022, 24.

41. NATO, "The Eurogroup," NATO Information Service, October 1975.

42. France, Iceland, and Portugal did not participate in the Eurogroup. Neither did the United States or Canada. The group thus comprised ten allies.

43. Phil Williams, "NATO and the Eurogroup," in Kenneth J. Twitchett (ed.), *European Co-operation Today*, London, Europa Publications, 1980, 40.

44. Denis Healey, "War and peace in the nuclear age: Interview with Denis Healey," October 27, 1986, https://openvault.wgbh.org/catalog/V_841B5BEC550448C381A8671A805C7AC4.

45. "Le 'rapport Davignon' Sur l'Europe Politique," *Le Monde*, November 3, 1970.

46. Suri, "Henry Kissinger and the Reconceptualization of European Security," 55.

47. Bernadette Marchal, "La Coopération Politique Des Six a Pris Un Départ Encourageant," *Le Monde*, November 21, 1970.
48. Max Frankel, "Moscow notes: Trust and doubt," *New York Times*, May 28, 1972.
49. Richard Nixon, *The Memoirs of Richard Nixon*, London, Arrow Books, 1978, 611.
50. Helga Haftendorn, "The link between CSCE and MBFR: Two sprouts from one bulb," in Andreas Wenger, Vojtech Mastny, and Christian Nuenlist (eds), *Origins of the European Security System: The Helsinki process revisited, 1965–1975*, Abingdon, Routledge, 2008, 250–251.
51. NATO, "Summary record of a meeting of the Council held at NATO headquarters, Brussels, 10th May, 1972," May 24, 1972.
52. NATO, "Summary record of a meeting of the Council held in Bonn, 30th May, 1972," 1972.
53. Nixon, *The Memoirs of Richard Nixon*, 281.
54. Drew Middleton, "NATO chief expects European security talks," *New York Times*, May 30, 1972.
55. Thomas Alan Schwartz, "'A Frankenstein monster': Henry Kissinger, Richard Nixon, and the year of Europe," *Journal of Transatlantic Studies*, 17:1 (2019), 116–117.
56. Henry A. Kissinger, "Speech on US relations with Europe," April 23, 1973, https://www.nytimes.com/1973/04/24/archives/text-of-kissingers-speech-at-ap-meeting-here-on-u-s-relations-with.html.
57. NATO, "Declaration on Atlantic relations," June 19, 1974, https://www.nato.int/cps/en/natohq/official_texts_26901.htm.
58. Matthew Jones, "'A man in a hurry': Henry Kissinger, transatlantic relations, and the British origins of the year of Europe dispute," *Diplomacy and Statecraft*, 24:1 (2013), 77–99.
59. Luke A. Nichter, *Richard Nixon and Europe: The reshaping of the postwar Atlantic world*, Cambridge, Cambridge University Press, 2015, 146–47.
60. Schwartz, "'A Frankenstein monster,'" 124–125; Michel Tatu, "Au Quai d'Orsay: Un an de 'Jobertisme,'" *Le Monde*, May 30, 1974.
61. Michel Tatu, "M. Kissinger Félicite M. Jobert Pour Son Projet de Déclaration Sur Les Relations Inter-Atlantiques," *Le Monde*, December 12, 1973; Timothy Andrews Sayle, *Enduring Alliance: The history of NATO and the postwar global order*, Ithaca, NY, Cornell University Press, 2019, 188.
62. Michel Tatu, "Le Conseil Ministériel de L'OTAN va Mettre Au Point La Déclaration Atlantique Qui Sera Signée à Bruxelles," *Le Monde*, June 18, 1974.
63. Kissinger, *Leadership: Six Studies in World Strategy*, 329.
64. Richard M. Nixon, "Asia after Viet Nam," *Foreign Affairs*, 46:1 (1967), 111–125; Richard M. Nixon, "Informal remarks in Guam with newsmen," July 25, 1969, https://www.presidency.ucsb.edu/documents/informal-remarks-guam-with-newsmen.
65. Flora Lewis, "European leaders turn NATO talk into summit meeting of their own," *New York Times*, June 27, 1974.

Chapter 5 Conserving NATO: The Dual-Track Decision

1. Flora Lewis, "NATO approves plan to install missiles and promote talks," *New York Times*, December 13, 1979.

2. Bernard Gwertzman, "Cyrus Vance plays it cool," *New York Times*, March 18, 1979.
3. Justin Vaïsse, *Zbigniew Brzezinski: America's grand strategist*, Cambridge, MA, Harvard University Press, 2018, 388; Stanley Hoffmann, "NATO and nuclear weapons: Reasons and unreason," *Foreign Affairs*, 60:2 (1981), 327–346.
4. Betty Glad, *An Outsider in the White House: Jimmy Carter, his advisors, and the making of American foreign policy*, Ithaca, NY, Cornell University Press, 2009, 26.
5. James Schlesinger, "Memorandum for the Assistant to the President for National Security Affairs: Response to NSSM 169," July 13, 1973, https://nsarchive2.gwu.edu/NSAEBB/NSAEBB173/SIOP-21.pdf.
6. Susan Colbourn, *Euromissiles: The nuclear weapons that nearly destroyed NATO*, Ithaca, NY, Cornell University Press, 2022, 44.
7. Gerhard Wettig, "The last Soviet offensive in the Cold War: Emergence and development of the campaign against NATO Euromissiles," *Cold War History*, 9:1 (2009), 79–110; Jonathan Haslam, *The Soviet Union and the Politics of Nuclear Weapons in Europe, 1969–1987*, Ithaca, NY, Cornell University Press, 1990.
8. Michael J. Brenner, "Tactical nuclear strategy and European defence: A critical appraisal," *International Affairs*, 51:1 (1975), 23–42.
9. Drew Middleton, "Carter facing a NATO issue: Nuclear force," *New York Times*, February 21, 1977.
10. Craig R. Whitney, "Schmidt says economic plight of world is a threat to NATO," *New York Times*, May 30, 1975.
11. Zbigniew Brzezinski, "Memorandum from the President's Assistant for National Security Affairs (Brzezinski) to President Carter," April 29, 1977, https://history.state.gov/historicaldocuments/frus1977-80v01/d36.
12. Vaïsse, *Zbigniew Brzezinski*.
13. Brzezinski, "Memorandum from the President's Assistant for National Security Affairs (Brzezinski) to President Carter."
14. Charles Mohr, "Carter hoping to rally US allies at summit conference in London," *New York Times*, May 4, 1977; Maurice Delarue, "Paris et Bonn resserrent leur coopération," *Le Monde*, February 5, 1977.
15. NATO, "Verbatim record of the meeting of the North Atlantic Council," May 10, 1977.
16. John Mashek, "Carter's triumph in Europe," *US News & World Report*, May 23, 1977.
17. Joseph Joffe, "The secret of Genscher's staying power: Memoirs of a 'slippery man'," *Foreign Affairs*, 77:1 (1998), 148–154.
18. NATO, "Summary record of a Restricted Meeting of the Defence Planning Committee held at the NATO headquarters, Brussels," May 17, 1977.
19. Timothy Andrews Sayle, *Enduring Alliance: The history of NATO and the postwar global order*, Ithaca, NY, Cornell University Press, 2019, 195–197; William Safire, "PRM-10 and Era-Two," *New York Times*, July 11, 1977.
20. Colbourn, *Euromissiles*, 61–62.
21. Raymond L. Garthoff, "The NATO decision on theater nuclear forces," *Political Science Quarterly*, 98:2 (1983), 198.
22. Helmut Schmidt, "War and peace in the nuclear age: Interview with Helmut Schmidt," GBH Archives, November 12, 1987, https://openvault.wgbh.org/catalog/V_55D8B7AC02BD4D7CA6D1E705F68A0604.

23. Garthoff, "The NATO decision on theater nuclear forces," 200.
24. Sayle, *Enduring Alliance*, 198.
25. Colbourn, *Euromissiles*, 72.
26. Cyrus R. Vance, *Hard Choices: Critical years in America's foreign policy*, New York, Simon & Schuster, 1983, 95.
27. Hans-Dietrich Genscher, *Rebuilding a House Divided: A memoir by the architect of Germany's unification*, New York, Broadway Books, 1997, 147.
28. Ibid., 149.
29. Jimmy Carter, *Keeping Faith: Memoirs of a president*, Fayetteville, AR, University of Arkansas Press, 1995, 13.
30. Kristina Spohr, *The Global Chancellor: Helmut Schmidt and the reshaping of international order*, Oxford, Oxford University Press, 2016, 7.
31. Vance, *Hard Choices*, 94–95.
32. NATO, "Summary record of a meeting with the participation of heads of state and government held in the State Department, Washington," May 30, 1978.
33. James Callaghan, *Time and Chance*, London, Collins, 1987, 482.
34. Raymond Carroll, Thomas M. DeFrank, and Scott Sullivan, "A swimsuit summit," *Newsweek*, January 15, 1979.
35. Garthoff, "The NATO decision on theater nuclear forces," 202.
36. Stephanie Freeman, "The making of an accidental crisis: The United States and the NATO dual-track decision of 1979," *Diplomacy and Statecraft*, 25:2 (2014), 337–338.
37. Mathias Haeussler, *Helmut Schmidt and British–German Relations: A European misunderstanding*, Cambridge, Cambridge University Press, 2019, 144.
38. Kristina Spohr Readman, "Conflict and cooperation in intra-alliance nuclear politics: Western Europe, the United States, and the genesis of NATO's dual-track decision, 1977–1979," *Journal of Cold War Studies*, 13:2 (2011), 56.
39. Ibid., 63.
40. Ivo H. Daalder, *The Nature and Practice of Flexible Response: NATO strategy and theater nuclear forces since 1967*, New York, Columbia University Press, 1991, 182; Freeman, "The making of an accidental crisis," 341.
41. Callaghan, *Time and Chance*, 549; Carter, *Keeping Faith*, 13.
42. Readman, "Conflict and cooperation in intra-alliance nuclear politics," 73–74.
43. Callaghan, *Time and Chance*, 544.
44. Flora Lewis, "Western summit with a difference," *New York Times*, January 5, 1979.
45. Georges-Henri Soutou, *L'alliance incertaine: Les rapports politico-stratégiques franco-allemands 1954–1996*, Paris, Fayard, 1996, 366–367.
46. Spohr, *The Global Chancellor*, 98.
47. Colbourn, *Euromissiles*.
48. Haeussler, *Helmut Schmidt and British–German Relations*, 150.
49. Ibid., 165.
50. Spohr, *The Global Chancellor*, 99.
51. Freeman, "The making of an accidental crisis," 345.
52. Readman, "Conflict and cooperation in intra-alliance nuclear politics," 81–83.
53. Edward C. Keefer, "Harold Brown: Offsetting the Soviet military challenge," Historical Office, Office of the Secretary of Defense, 2017, 470, https://history.defense.gov/Portals/70/Documents/secretaryofdefense/OSDSeries_Vol9.pdf.
54. William Safire, "Stumbling at the summit," *New York Times*, June 18, 1979.

55. Keefer, "Harold Brown," 470.
56. Ruud Van Dijk, "'A mass psychosis': The Netherlands and NATO's dual-track decision, 1978–1979," *Cold War History*, 12:3 (2012), 381–405; Colbourn, *Euromissiles*, 100.
57. NATO, "Special meeting of foreign and defence ministers," December 12, 1979, https://www.nato.int/docu/comm/49-95/c791212a.htm.
58. Aaron Donaghy, *The Second Cold War: Carter, Reagan, and the politics of foreign policy*, Cambridge, Cambridge University Press, 2021, 1.
59. Ibid.
60. James M. Markham, "Bonn parliament votes out Schmidt and elects Kohl," *New York Times*, October 2, 1982.
61. Henry A. Kissinger, *Leadership: Six studies in world strategy*, London, Allen Lane, 2022, 13–14.

Chapter 6 Prudence or Prophecy? NATO Confronts New Aspirations

1. Lech Walesa, *Håbets Vej*, Viborg, Gyldendal, 1987, 6.
2. Margaret Thatcher, *The Downing Street Years*, London, HarperCollins, 1993, 256.
3. NATO, "Summary record of a meeting of the Council held at NATO headquarters (C-R(81)28)," July 8, 1981.
4. NATO, "The situation in the Soviet Union and Eastern Europe (C-M(81)12)," April 8, 1981.
5. NATO, "Declaration on events in Poland," January 11, 1982, https://www.nato.int/docu/comm/49-95/c820111a.htm.
6. NATO, "Summary record of a restricted meeting of the Council (PR(82)2)," January 11, 1982, https://www.nato.int/nato_static_fl2014/assets/pdf/pdf_archives/20120105_21_19820119_PR_82_02-BIL.pdf.
7. NATO, "Summary record of private sessions of the Council held on Monday 15th, Tuesday 16th, Thursday 18th and Monday, 22nd December, 1980 (PR(80)74)," January 13, 1981, https://www.nato.int/nato_static_fl2014/assets/pdf/pdf_archives/20111213_11_19810113_PR_80_74-ENG.pdf.
8. Leslie H. Gelb, "NATO is facing paralysis of will, experts contend," *New York Times*, July 12, 1981.
9. John Vincour, "Allies moving out of step," *New York Times*, December 30, 1981.
10. Susan Colbourn, "An interpreter or two: Defusing NATO's Siberian pipeline dispute, 1981–1982," *Journal of Transatlantic Studies*, 18:2 (2020), 131–151.
11. Thatcher, *The Downing Street Years*, 255–256.
12. Jack F. Matlock, *Reagan and Gorbachev: How the Cold War ended*, New York, Random House, 2004, 33.
13. NATO, "Final communiqué," December 11, 1956, https://www.nato.int/cps/en/natolive/official_texts_17483.htm.
14. Charles A. Kupchan, "NATO and the Persian Gulf: Examining intra-alliance behavior," *International Organization*, 42:2 (1988), 320.
15. Sten Rynning, "NATO and the broader Middle East, 1949–2007: The history and lessons of controversial encounters," *Journal of Strategic Studies*, 30:6 (2007), 918.
16. Hubert Védrine, *Les Mondes de François Mitterrand*, Paris, Fayard, 1996, 243.
17. John M. Goshko, "From the allies: Patience," *Washington Post*, September 13, 1980.

18. Senem Aydin-Düzgit and Yaprak Gürsoy, "Turkey: The counterintuitive transition of 1983," in Kathryn Stoner and Michael McFaul (eds), *Transitions to Democracy: A comparative perspective*, Baltimore, MD, Johns Hopkins University Press, 2013, 299.

19. Office of the Historian, "Foreign relations of the United States, 1981–1988, Volume I: Foundations of foreign policy," US Department of State, 2022, https://history.state.gov/historicaldocuments/frus1981-88v01/d83.

20. Ruud van Dijk and Stanley R. Sloan, "NATO's inherent dilemma: Strategic imperatives vs. value foundations," *Journal of Strategic Studies*, 43:6–7 (2020), 1014–1038.

21. Constantine Melakopides, "The logic of Papandreou's foreign policy," *International Journal* (Toronto), 42:3 (1987), 559–584.

22. Mark Smith, *NATO Enlargement during the Cold War: Strategy and system in the Western Alliance*, Basingstoke, Palgrave, 2000; Anthony Gooch, "A surrealistic referendum: Spain and NATO," *Government and Opposition*, 21:3 (1986), 300–316.

23. George P. Shultz, *Turmoil and Triumph: My years as secretary of state*, New York, Charles Scribner's Sons, 1993, 151.

24. Aaron Donaghy, *The Second Cold War: Carter, Reagan, and the politics of foreign policy*, Cambridge, Cambridge University Press, 2021, 115.

25. Matlock, *Reagan and Gorbachev*.

26. Richard Reeves, *President Reagan: The triumph of imagination*, New York, Simon & Schuster, 2006.

27. Alexander Haig, *Caveat: Realism, Reagan, and foreign policy*, London, Weidenfeld and Nicolson, 1984, 356.

28. Peter Baker and Susan Glasser, *The Man Who Ran Washington: The life and times of James A. Baker III*, New York, Doubleday, 2020, 147.

29. Thatcher, *The Downing Street Years*, 180.

30. Haig, *Caveat*, 307.

31. Raymond L. Garthoff, *The Great Transition: American–Soviet relations and the end of the Cold War*, Washington, DC, Brookings Institution Press, 1994, 510; Strobe Talbott, *Deadly Gambits: The vivid inside story of arms control negotiations*, New York, Vintage Books, 1985, 81.

32. Matlock, *Reagan and Gorbachev*, 40.

33. Talbott, *Deadly Gambits*, 71.

34. Garthoff, *The Great Transition*, 509.

35. Talbott, *Deadly Gambits*, 263.

36. White House, "National Security Decision Directive 75: US relations with the USSR," January 17, 1983, https://irp.fas.org/offdocs/nsdd/nsdd-75.pdf.

37. Matlock, *Reagan and Gorbachev*, 53.

38. Paul Kengor, *The Crusader: Ronald Reagan and the fall of communism*, New York, Harper, 2006; Francis P. Sempa, "Richard Pipes: A neglected hero of the Cold War," *American Spectator*, November 1, 2022, https://spectator.org/richard-pipes-neglected-hero-cold-war/.

39. Ronald Reagan, "Speech on military spending and a new defense," *New York Times*, March 24, 1983.

40. William J. Broad, *Teller's War: The top-secret story behind the Star Wars deception*, New York, Simon & Schuster, 1992, 131.

41. Shultz, *Turmoil and Triumph*, 249.

42. Hans-Dietrich Genscher, *Rebuilding a House Divided: A memoir by the architect of Germany's unification*, New York, Broadway Books, 1997, 161.

43. François Mitterrand, "Discours de M. François Mitterrand, Président de La République, Devant Le Bundestag," January 20, 1983, https://www.elysee.fr/francois-mitterrand/1983/01/20/discours-de-m-francois-mitterrand-president-de-la-republique-devant-le-bundestag-a-loccasion-du-20eme-anniversaire-du-traite-de-lelysee-sur-la-cooperation-franco-allemande-la-securite-europeenne-et-la-cee-bonn-jeudi-20-janvier-1983.

44. Védrine, *Les Mondes de François Mitterrand*, 237.

45. R.-P. Paringaux, "La France s'est Opposée à Une Demande Japonaise d'association à l'OTAN," *Le Monde*, March 11, 1983.

46. Genscher, *Rebuilding a House Divided*, 165.

47. Susan Colbourn, "Debating détente: NATO's Tindemans initiative, or why the Harmel Report still mattered in the 1980s," *Journal of Strategic Studies*, 43:6–7 (2020), 897–919.

48. NATO, "Washington Statement on East–West Relations," May 31, 1984, https://www.nato.int/cps/en/natohq/official_texts_23262.htm.

49. Matlock, *Reagan and Gorbachev*, 104.

50. Ibid., 177; Garthoff, *The Great Transition*, 523.

51. Peter, Lord Carrington, *Reflecting on Things Past*, New York, Harper and Row, 1988, 392.

52. Bernard Gwertzman, "Reagan–Gorbachev talks end in stalemate as US rejects demand to curb 'Star Wars," *New York Times*, October 13, 1986.

53. Shultz, *Turmoil and Triumph*, 775–777.

54. James M. Markham, "Western allies grumble about Reykjavik plans," *New York Times*, October 22, 1986; Joseph Lelyveld, "Reykjavik was a shock at 10 Downing Street," *New York Times*, November 9, 1986; Timothy Andrews Sayle, *Enduring Alliance: The history of NATO and the postwar global order*, Ithaca, NY, Cornell University Press, 2019, 212.

55. Ivo H. Daalder, *The Nature and Practice of Flexible Response: NATO strategy and theater nuclear forces since 1967*, New York, Columbia University Press, 1991, 259–266.

56. Louis Deschamps, *The SDI and European Security Interests*, London, Atlantic Institute for International Affairs, 1987.

57. Shultz, *Turmoil and Triumph*, 777; Védrine, *Les Mondes de François Mitterrand*, 386.

58. Daalder, *The Nature and Practice of Flexible Response*, 258; Genscher, *Rebuilding a House Divided*, 231.

59. Western European Union, "Platform on European security interests," October 27, 1987, https://www.cvce.eu/content/publication/2002/1/29/444f642c-62ed-4fd9-8136-a129d2de3783/publishable_en.pdf.

60. Genscher, *Rebuilding a House Divided*, 237.

61. Sayle, *Enduring Alliance*, 214.

62. James M. Markham, "In NATO, brand new missile debate," *New York Times*, January 25, 1989; James M. Markham, "Bonn's dovish nuclear stand winning support in NATO," *New York Times*, April 26, 1989.

63. NATO, "Declaration of the heads of state and government participating in the meeting of the North Atlantic Council," May 29, 1989, https://www.nato.int/docu/comm/49-95/c890530a.htm.

64. George H.W. Bush, "A Europe whole and free," May 31, 1989, https://usa.usembassy.de/etexts/ga6-890531.htm.
65. John Tagliabue, "To his volatile young allies, Walesa preaches conciliation," *New York Times*, March 2, 1989.

Chapter 7 NATO's Search for New Atlanticism beyond the Cold War

1. Serge Schmemann, "NATO leaders try to keep lid on widespread disunity," *New York Times*, May 30, 1989.
2. Margaret Thatcher, *The Downing Street Years*, London, HarperCollins, 1993, 756.
3. Ibid., 309.
4. Hans Binnendijk, "NATO's nuclear modernization dilemma," *Survival*, 31:2 (1989), 137–155.
5. George Bush and Brent Scowcroft, *A World Transformed*, New York, Alfred A. Knopf, 1999, 67 (italics in original).
6. Timothy Andrews Sayle, *Enduring Alliance: The history of NATO and the postwar global order*, Ithaca, NY, Cornell University Press, 2019, 220.
7. Robert M. Gates, *From the Shadows: The ultimate insider's story of five presidents and how they won the Cold War*, London, Simon & Schuster, 1996, 463; Bush and Scowcroft, *A World Transformed*, 70.
8. Gates, *From the Shadows*, 464.
9. NATO, "Declaration of the heads of state and government participating in the meeting of the North Atlantic Council," May 29, 1989, https://www.nato.int/docu/comm/49-95/c890530a.htm; NATO, "The Alliance's comprehensive concept of arms control and disarmament," May 29, 1989, https://www.nato.int/cps/en/SID-E13A187D-D28E7D06/natolive/official_texts_23553.htm?selectedLocale=en; Michael R. Gordon, "Fast track on arms," *New York Times*, May 30, 1989.
10. NATO was asking the Soviet Union to reduce its Eastern European force presence by 325,000 troops, 35,000 tanks, and 30,000 artillery pieces. In return, NATO would withdraw 20,000 US troops from Europe and dismantle 2,000 tanks and 1,000 artillery pieces.
11. NATO, "Declaration of the heads of state and government participating in the meeting of the North Atlantic Council," 16.
12. Angela E. Stent, *Russia and Germany Reborn: Unification, the Soviet collapse, and the new Europe*, Princeton, NJ, Princeton University Press, 1999, 77.
13. NATO Expert Working Group, "The situation in the Soviet Union and Eastern Europe (C-M(89)13)," May 3, 1989, 8.
14. Serge Schmemann, "Bonn Declaration: 'heal the wounds,'" *New York Times*, June 14, 1989.
15. Stent, *Russia and Germany Reborn*, 88.
16. Alan Riding, "Western Europe pledges to aid East," *New York Times*, November 19, 1989.
17. Mary Elise Sarotte, *The struggle to create post-Cold War Europe*, Princeton, NJ, Princeton University Press, 2015, 64.
18. Helmut Kohl, "Zehn-Punkte-Plan: Erklärung von Bundeskanzler Helmut Kohl vor dem deutschen Bundestag am 28 November 1989," 1989, https://www.kas.de/c/document_library/get_file?uuid=eb8e3de0-bb1a-8a78-a08d-568bcbd0d677&groupId=252038.

19. Stent, *Russia and Germany Reborn*, 99.

20. Bush and Scowcroft, *A World Transformed*, 194–195; James A. Baker and Thomas M. DeFrank, *The Politics of Diplomacy: Revolution, war and peace 1989–1992*, New York, G.P. Putnam's Sons, 1995, 116.

21. The Warsaw Pact ceased to function in the course of 1989. It was formally disbanded in February 1991, ten months ahead of the dissolution of the Soviet Union.

22. Jeffrey A. Engel, *When the World Seemed New: George H.W. Bush and the end of the Cold War*, Boston, MA, Houghton Mifflin Harcourt, 2017.

23. Bush and Scowcroft, *A World Transformed*, 12.

24. Ibid., 200.

25. Sarotte, *1989*, 82.

26. Wilson Center, "Record of telephone conversation between Mikhail Gorbachev and President of France Francois Mitterrand," November 14, 1989, https://digitalarchive.wilsoncenter.org/document/record-telephone-conversation-between-mikhail-gorbachev-and-president-france-francois.

27. Wilson Center, "Record of conversation between M.S. Gorbachev and President of France F. Mitterrand," December 6, 1989, https://digitalarchive.wilsoncenter.org/document/record-conversation-between-m-s-gorbachev-and-president-france-f-mitterrand-0.

28. Frédéric Bozo, "The failure of a grand design: Mitterrand's European Confederation, 1989–1991," *Contemporary European History*, 17:3 (2008), 391–412.

29. Kristina Spohr, *Post Wall, Post Square: How Bush, Gorbachev, Kohl, and Deng shaped the world after 1989*, New Haven, CT, Yale University Press, 2020, 280–282; Stent, *Russia and Germany Reborn*, 103.

30. James A. Baker, "A new Europe, a new Atlanticism: Architecture for a new era," Current Policy No. 1233, US Department of State, Bureau of Public Affairs, December 12, 1989, http://aei.pitt.edu/101501/1/1.pdf; Thomas L. Friedman, "Baker, in Berlin, outlines a plan to make NATO a political group," *New York Times*, December 13, 1989.

31. Andrew Rosenthal, "President thinks he struck the right balance at Malta," *New York Times*, December 5, 1989.

32. Bush and Scowcroft, *A World Transformed*, 199.

33. Kristina Spohr, "Germany, America and the shaping of post-Cold War Europe: A story of German international emancipation through political unification, 1989–90," *Cold War History*, 15:2 (2015), 233.

34. George H.W. Bush, "Address before a joint session of the Congress on the state of the Union," January 31, 1990, https://bush41library.tamu.edu/archives/public-papers/1492.

35. Mary Elise Sarotte, "Not one inch eastward? Bush, Baker, Kohl, Genscher, Gorbachev, and the origin of Russian resentment toward NATO enlargement in February 1990," *Diplomatic History*, 34:1 (2010), 128; Mary Elise Sarotte, *Not One Inch: America, Russia, and the making of Post-Cold War stalemate*, New Haven, CT, Yale University Press, 2021.

36. Mark Kramer, "The myth of a no-NATO-enlargement pledge to Russia," *Washington Quarterly*, 32:2 (2009), 39–61; Joshua R. Itzkowitz Shifrinson, "Deal or no deal? The end of the Cold War and the US offer to limit NATO expansion," *International Security*, 40:4 (2016), 7–44; Mark Kramer, "NATO enlargement—Was there a promise?," *International Security*, 42:1 (2017), 186–192; Richard W. Maass,

"NATO non-expansion and German reunification," *International Security*, 41:3 (2017), 197–200. Soviet leader Mikhail Gorbachev later explained that at his meeting with James Baker the "topic of 'NATO expansion' was not discussed at all, and it wasn't brought up in those years." What the two did discuss, again in Gorbachev's recollection, was the non-deployment of NATO allies' forces "on the territory of the then-GDR after German reunification." Maxim Kórshunov, "Michael Gorbachev: I am against all walls," *Russia Beyond*, October 16, 2014, https://www.rbth.com/international/2014/10/16/mikhail_gorbachev_i_am_against_all_walls_40673.html.

37. Stent, *Russia and Germany Reborn*, 105.

38. Sayle, *Enduring Alliance*, 226.

39. Michael MccGwire and Michael Clarke, "NATO expansion: 'A policy error of historic importance,'" *International Affairs*, 84:6 (2008), 1281–1301; Shifrinson, "Deal or no deal?"; Sarotte, *Not One Inch*.

40. Peter Baker and Susan Glasser, Peter Baker and Susan Glasser, *The Man Who Ran Washington: The life and times of James A. Baker III*, New York, Doubleday, 2020, 381; Sarotte, *Not One Inch*, 74; Baker and DeFrank, *The Politics of Diplomacy*, 204–205.

41. Gates, *From the Shadows*, 490.

42. Bush and Scowcroft, *A World Transformed*, 237.

43. Hans-Dietrich Genscher, *Rebuilding a House Divided: A memoir by the architect of Germany's unification*, New York, Broadway Books, 1997, 345.

44. Sarotte, *1989*, 123.

45. Genscher, *Rebuilding a House Divided*, 348.

46. White House, "Memorandum of conversation between Helmut Kohl and George Bush at Camp David," February 24, 1990, https://nsarchive.gwu.edu/document/16127-document-13-memorandum-conversation-between.

47. Ibid.

48. Sayle, *Enduring Alliance*, 227.

49. George H.W. Bush, "Remarks at the Oklahoma State University commencement ceremony in Stillwater," May 4, 1990, https://www.presidency.ucsb.edu/documents/remarks-the-oklahoma-state-university-commencement-ceremony-stillwater.

50. Sarotte, *1989*, 162.

51. Bush and Scowcroft, *A World Transformed*, 275.

52. Ibid., 283.

53. Ibid., 293.

54. Andrew Rosenthal, "For Bush, life on the run catches up," *New York Times*, July 6, 1990.

55. NATO, "North Atlantic Council meeting with the participation of heads of state and government (C-VR(90)36, Part I)," July 5, 1990, 3, https://www.nato.int/nato_static_fl2014/assets/pdf/pdf_archives/20141218_C-VR-90-36-PART1.PDF.

56. Ibid., 18.

57. Thatcher, *The Downing Street Years*, 811.

58. NATO, "North Atlantic Council meeting with the participation of heads of state and government (C-VR(90)36, Part I)," 6.

59. Sarotte, *1989*, 161.

60. NATO, "North Atlantic Council meeting with the participation of heads of state and government (C-VR(90)36, Part I)," 13.

61. Ibid., 20.
62. NATO, "North Atlantic Council meeting with the participation of heads of state and government (C-VR(90)36, Part II)," July 6, 1990, https://www.nato.int/nato_static_fl2014/assets/pdf/pdf_archives/20141218_C-VR-90-36-PART2.PDF.
63. NATO, "Declaration on a transformed North Atlantic Alliance (The London Declaration)," July 6, 1990, https://www.nato.int/cps/en/natohq/official_texts_23693.htm.
64. Stent, *Russia and Germany Reborn*, 134.
65. Hanns Juergen Kuesters, "The Kohl–Gorbachev meetings in Moscow and in the Caucasus, 1990," *Cold War History*, 2:2 (2002), 198.
66. Sarotte, *Not One Inch*, 99–104.
67. Germany, France, the Soviet Union, Britain, and the United States, "Treaty on the final settlement with respect to Germany," September 12, 1990, https://treaties.un.org/doc/Publication/UNTS/Volume%201696/volume-1696-I-29226-English.pdf.
68. NATO Expert Working Group, "The situation in the Soviet Union and Eastern Europe, April 1990 to October 1990 (C-M(90)66)," November 20, 1990.
69. CSCE, "Charter of Paris for a New Europe," November 19, 1990, https://www.osce.org/files/f/documents/0/6/39516.pdf.
70. NATO, "Final communiqué," December 18, 1990, https://www.nato.int/cps/en/natohq/official_texts_23690.htm?selectedLocale=en.
71. NATO, "The Alliance's New Strategic Concept," November 7, 1991, https://www.nato.int/cps/en/natohq/official_texts_23847.htm.
72. NATO, "Declaration on peace and cooperation (The Rome Declaration)," November 8, 1991, https://www.nato.int/cps/en/natohq/official_texts_23846.htm?selectedLocale=en.
73. Gates, *From the Shadows*, 492.
74. Stent, *Russia and Germany Reborn*, 72.
75. Anatoly Dobrynin, *In Confidence: Moscow's ambassador to America's six cold war presidents (1962–1986)*, New York, Times Books, 1995, 630.
76. Thatcher, *The Downing Street Years*, 859.

Chapter 8 NATO Grows Bigger and Softer

1. George Joulwan, *Watchman at the Gates: A soldier's journey from Berlin to Bosnia*, Lexington, KY, University Press of Kentucky, 2021, Kindle edition: section 4135.
2. Ryan Hendrickson, "Leadership at NATO: Secretary General Manfred Woerner and the crisis in Bosnia," *Journal of Strategic Studies*, 27:3 (2004), 520.
3. Craig R. Whitney, "Manfred Wörner, 59, NATO leader, is dead," *New York Times*, August 14, 1994.
4. Manfred Wörner, "European security: Political will plus military might," in Hikmet Cetin et al. (eds) *What Is European Security after the Cold War?*, Brussels, Philip Morris Institute for Public Policy Research, 1993, 5.
5. NATO, "Dissolution of the Soviet Union announced at NATO meeting," n.d., https://www.nato.int/cps/en/natohq/declassified_136619.htm.
6. Alexander Vershbow, "Wales summit: The rollout of NATO 4.0," NATO, September 5, 2014, https://www.nato.int/cps/en/natohq/opinions_112977.htm?selectedLocale=en.

7. Jeffrey A. Engel, *When the World Seemed New: George H. W. Bush and the end of the Cold War*, Boston, MA, Houghton Mifflin Harcourt, 2017, 475.
8. Richard Holbrooke, *To End a War*, New York, The Modern Library, 1999.
9. Richard Caplan, *Europe and the Recognition of New States in Yugoslavia*, Cambridge, Cambridge University Press, 2007, 23.
10. William T. Johnsen, "NATO strategy in the 1990s: Reaping the peace dividend or the whirlwind?," Strategic Studies Institute, US Army War College, 1995, 15, https://press.armywarcollege.edu/cgi/viewcontent.cgi?article=1881&context=monographs.
11. Le Monde, "M. Kozyrev Assure La Serbie Du 'Soutien de La Grande Russie,'" December 16, 1992.
12. Derek Chollet and James Goldgeier, *America between the Wars: From 11/9 to 9/11*, New York, PublicAffairs, 2008, 42.
13. Mark Garnett, "Foreign and defence policy," in Kevin Hickson and Ben Williams (eds), *John Major: An Unsuccessful Prime Minister?*, London, Biteback, 2017, 280.
14. Ibid.
15. Robert E. Hunter, "Toward NATO enlargement: The role of USNATO," in Daniel S. Hamilton and Kristina Spohr (eds), *Open Door: NATO and Euro-Atlantic security after the Cold War*, Washington, DC, Johns Hopkins University Press, 2019, 301.
16. NATO, "Press statement: Meeting of NATO defence ministers, Travemünde 20th–21st October 1993 (M-DM-1(93)64)," October 21, 1993; NATO, "Declaration of the heads of state and government (M-1(94)003)," January 11, 1994, https://www.nato.int/cps/en/natohq/official_texts_24470.htm?mode=pressrelease.
17. Hunter, "Toward NATO enlargement," 308.
18. "L'OTAN sans Projet," *Le Monde*, October 22, 1993.
19. US Department of State, "Retranslation of Yeltsin letter on NATO expansion," October 9, 1993, https://nsarchive.gwu.edu/document/16376-document-04-retranslation-yeltsin-letter.
20. James M. Goldgeier, "NATO expansion: The anatomy of a decision," *Washington Quarterly*, 21:1 (1998), 85–102; James M. Goldgeier, *Not Whether but When: The US decision to enlarge NATO*, Washington, DC, Brookings Institution Press, 1999.
21. Stephen A. Oxman, "Your deputies' committee meeting on the NATO summit, September 15, 1993," September 14, 1993, https://nsarchive.gwu.edu/document/16375-document-03-your-deputies-committee-meeting.
22. Daniel S. Hamilton, "Piece of the puzzle: NATO and the Euro-Atlantic architecture after the Cold War," in Hamilton and Spohr (eds), *Open Door*, 12.
23. William Jefferson Clinton, "The president's news conference with Visegrad leaders in Prague," Government Information, January 12, 1994, https://www.govinfo.gov/content/pkg/WCPD-1994-01-17/pdf/WCPD-1994-01-17-Pg41.pdf.
24. National Security Archive, "NATO expansion: What Yeltsin heard," March 16, 2018, https://nsarchive.gwu.edu/briefing-book/russia-programs/2018-03-16/nato-expansion-what-yeltsin-heard.
25. Volker Rühe, "Opening NATO's door," in Hamilton and Spohr (eds), *Open Door*, 222.

26. Benoît d'Aboville, "Beyond NATO enlargement to Poland, the Czech Republic, and Hungary: A French reappraisal," in Hamilton and Spohr (eds), *Open Door*, 523–524.

27. "M Léotard Prône 'une Attitude Nouvelle de La France' Dans Une OTAN Rénovée," *Le Monde*, October 24, 1993.

28. Jane M.O. Sharp, "British views on NATO enlargement," NATO, October 7, 1997, https://www.nato.int/acad/conf/enlarg97/sharp.htm.

29. G. Wyn Rees, "Setting the parameters for European defence: The UK and the WEU," *Studia Diplomatica*, 51:1–2 (1998), 61–69; Alyson J.K. Bailes, "European defence and security: The role of NATO, WEU and EU," *Security Dialogue*, 27:1 (1996), 55–64; Stanley R. Sloan, "European proposals for a new Atlantic community (CRS 95-374 S)," Congressional Research Service, March 10, 1995.

30. Craig R. Whitney, "Clinton sizes up team: Summit, yes; Sumo, no," *New York Times*, January 11, 1994.

31. Steven Lee Myers, "Experienced player who shuns spotlight: Anthony Lake," *New York Times*, December 6, 1996.

32. Jenonne Walker, "Enlarging NATO: The initial Clinton years," in Hamilton and Spohr (eds), *Open Door*, 272.

33. Elizabeth Drew, *On the Edge: The Clinton presidency*, New York, Simon & Schuster, 1994.

34. Goldgeier, *Not Whether but When*, 49.

35. Alexander Vershbow, "Present at the transformation: An insider's reflection on NATO enlargement, NATO–Russia relations, and where we go from here," in Hamilton and Spohr (eds), *Open Door*, 432.

36. Roger Cohen, "As usual, Serbs call the shots," *New York Times*, July 12, 1995.

37. William Drozdiak, "Bulldozer heads for Halifax; French leader Chirac brings reputation for frank talk to summit," *Washington Post*, June 14, 1995.

38. "Paris et Londres affichent leur fermete face aux atermoiements de l'ONU en Bosnie," *Le Monde*, June 3, 1995.

39. John Major, *John Major: The autobiography*, London, HarperCollins, 2000, 542; Anthony Seldon and Lewis Baston, *Major: A political life*, London, Weidenfeld & Nicolson, 1997, 559.

40. Brendan Simms, *Unfinest Hour: Britain and the destruction of Bosnia*, London, Penguin, 2002, 326.

41. Drew, *On the Edge*.

42. Major, *John Major*, 616.

43. Seldon and Baston, *Major*, 561.

44. Ivo H. Daalder, "Decision to intervene: How the war in Bosnia ended," Brookings Institution, December 1, 1998, https://www.brookings.edu/articles/decision-to-intervene-how-the-war-in-bosnia-ended/.

45. United States Department of State, "The road to Dayton: US diplomacy and the Bosnia peace process, May–December 1995," May 1997 (declassified January 24, 2003), https://nsarchive2.gwu.edu/NSAEBB/NSAEBB171/intro.pdf (italics in original).

46. Holbrooke, *To End a War*, 67–68.

47. Craig R. Whitney, "France asks allied forces to help hold 'safe areas," *New York Times*, July 14, 1995.

48. United States Department of State, "The road to Dayton," chapter 1, https://nsarchive2.gwu.edu/NSAEBB/NSAEBB171/ch01.pdf, 23.

49. Craig R. Whitney, "NATO gives UN officials veto on air strikes in Bosnia," *New York Times*, July 26, 1995.

50. NATO, "Statement by the secretary general of NATO (Press Release (95)73)," August 30, 1995, https://www.nato.int/docu/pr/1995/p95-073.htm.

51. Craig R. Whitney, "Success has many fathers among allies," *New York Times*, November 23, 1995.

52. Cited in David S. Yost, *NATO Transformed: The alliance's new roles in international security*, Washington, DC, United States Institute of Peace Press, 2001, 300.

53. Strobe Talbott, "Why NATO should grow," *New York Review*, August 10, 1995, https://www.nybooks.com/articles/1995/08/10/why-nato-should-grow/; Goldgeier, *Not Whether but When*, 94.

54. NATO, "Study on NATO enlargement," September 3, 1995, https://www.nato.int/cps/en/natohq/official_texts_24733.htm.

55. Jonathan Eyal, "NATO's enlargement: Anatomy of a decision," *International Affairs*, 73:4 (1997), 695–719.

56. "M Chirac Propose 'un Véritable Dialogue' à M Eltsine," *Le Monde*, October 20, 1995.

57. United Nations, "Address by His Excellency Mr. Boris N. Yeltsin," October 22, 1995, 18, https://documents-dds-ny.un.org/doc/UNDOC/GEN/N95/863/89/PDF/N9586389.pdf?OpenElement.

58. Holbrooke, *To End a War*, 212.

59. John F. Harris, "Clinton, Yeltsin huddle on Bosnia," *Washington Post*, October 24, 1995.

60. Joulwan, *Watchman at the Gates*, Kindle 4607.

61. Holbrooke, *To End a War*, 212.

62. Goldgeier, *Not Whether but When*, 101.

63. Jacques Chirac, "Speech," C-SPAN, February 1, 1996, https://www.c-span.org/video/?69677-1/french-president-speech.

64. Mathieu Castagnet, "La France Revient à Petits Pas Vers l'Otan," *La Croix*, February 3, 1996.

65. Steven Erlanger, "Chirac offers a vision of NATO; Few in Congress come to listen," *New York Times*, February 2, 1996.

66. Ronald Tiersky, "A likely story: Chirac, France-NATO, European security, and American hegemony," *French Politics and Society*, 14:2 (1996), 5.

67. NATO, "Final communiqué," June 3, 1996, https://www.nato.int/docu/pr/1996/p96-063e.htm.

68. Charles Cogan, *Third Option: The emancipation of European defense, 1989–2000*, Westport, CT, Praeger, 2001, 87.

69. Hunter, "Toward NATO enlargement," 324.

70. Vershbow, "Present at the transformation," 434.

71. Hunter, "Toward NATO enlargement," 336.

72. Ronald D. Asmus, *Opening NATO's Door: How the alliance remade itself for a new era*, New York, Columbia University Press, 2002, 184–188.

73. NATO and Russia, "Founding Act on mutual relations, cooperation and security," May 27, 1997, https://www.nato.int/cps/su/natohq/official_texts_25468.htm.

74. NATO, "Madrid Declaration on Euro-Atlantic security and cooperation," July 8, 1997, https://www.nato.int/docu/pr/1997/p97-081e.htm.

75. Asmus, *Opening NATO's Door*, 241; Goldgeier, "NATO expansion," 121; Craig R. Whitney, "3 former members of Eastern Bloc invited into NATO," *New York Times*, July 9, 1997.

76. France and Britain, "Joint declaration on European defence," December 4, 1998, https://www.cvce.eu/content/publication/2008/3/31/f3cd16fb-fc37-4d52-936f-c8e9bc80f24f/publishable_en.pdf.

77. Ellen Hallams, "'War by committee': Operation Allied Force, Kosovo," in Ellen Hallams (ed.), *The United States and NATO since 9/11*, Abingdon, Routledge, 2010, 45–63.

78. Tom Bower, *Broken Vows. Tony Blair: The tragedy of power*, London, Faber & Faber, 2016, 129.

79. Tony Blair, "Doctrine of the international community," April 22, 1999, http://www.britishpoliticalspeech.org/speech-archive.htm?speech=279.

80. Lawrence Freedman, "Force and the international community: Blair's Chicago speech and the criteria for intervention," *International Relations*, 31:2 (2017), 107–124.

81. NATO, "The Alliance's Strategic Concept," April 24, 1999, https://www.nato.int/cps/on/natohq/official_texts_27433.htm.

82. Jane Perlez, "Kosovo now bellwether as well as battlefield," *New York Times*, April 25, 1999.

83. Ivo H. Daalder and Michael E. O'Hanlon. *Winning Ugly: NATO's war to save Kosovo*, Washington, DC, Brookings Institution Press, 2000, 45.

84. Adam Roberts, "NATO's 'humanitarian war' over Kosovo," *Survival*, 41:3 (1999), 102–123.

85. Celestine Bohlen, "View from Moscow: Success for its diplomacy," *New York Times*, May 8, 1999.

86. Mark Tran, "'I'm not going to start Third World War for you,' Jackson told Clark," *Guardian*, August 2, 1999.

87. White House, "Memorandum of conversation: Lake meeting with President Jacques Chirac of France," November 1, 1996, https://clinton.presidentiallibraries.us/collections/show/36.

Chapter 9 Runaway Aspiration

1. George Robertson, "Being NATO's secretary general on 9/11," *NATO Review*, September 4, 2011, https://www.nato.int/docu/review/articles/2011/09/04/being-nato-s-secretary-general-on-9-11/index.html; Edgar Buckley, "Invoking Article 5," *NATO Review*, June 1, 2006, https://www.nato.int/docu/review/articles/2006/06/01/invoking-article-5/index.html; Sten Rynning, *NATO in Afghanistan: The liberal disconnect*, Stanford, CA, Stanford University Press, 2012, 72–75.

2. Robertson, "Being NATO's secretary general on 9/11."

3. NATO, "Statement by the North Atlantic Council (Press Release (2001)124)," September 12, 2001, https://www.nato.int/docu/pr/2001/p01-124e.htm.

4. Interview with author, April 3, 2023.

5. Elizabeth Pond, *Friendly Fire: The near-death of the transatlantic alliance*, Pittsburgh, PA, European Union Studies Association, 2004.

6. George W. Bush, *Decision Points*, London, Virgin Books, 2010, 140.
7. Tom Raum, "Defense official presents evidence on terror attacks to NATO," Associated Press, September 27, 2001; Rynning, *NATO in Afghanistan*, 76.
8. "Rumsfeld's Pentagon news conference," *Washington Post*, October 18, 2001, https://www.washingtonpost.com/wp-srv/nation/specials/attacked/transcripts/rumsfeld_text101801.html; Donald Rumsfeld, *Known and Unknown: A memoir*, New York, Sentinel, 2011, 354.
9. Donald H. Rumsfeld, "Transforming the Military," *Foreign Affairs*, 81:3 (2002), 20–32, https://doi.org/10.2307/20033160.
10. Buckley, "Invoking Article 5."
11. Rynning, *NATO in Afghanistan*, 76.
12. Steven Erlanger, "US officials try to assure Europeans on NATO," *New York Times*, February 3, 2002; Thomas L. Friedman, "The end of NATO?," *New York Times*, February 3, 2002.
13. Tuomas Forsberg, "Russia's relationship with NATO: A qualitative change or old wine in new bottles?," *Journal of Communist Studies and Transition Politics*, 21:3 (2005), 332–353.
14. Interview with author, April 3, 2023.
15. Alan Friedman, *Berlusconi: The epic story of the billionaire who took over Italy*, New York, Hachette, 2015, 129.
16. NATO, "Final communiqué," NATO Press Release M-NAC-1(2002)59, May 14, 2002, https://www.nato.int/docu/pr/2002/p02-059e.htm.
17. NATO and Russia, "Rome Declaration," May 28, 2002, https://www.nato.int/nrc-website/media/59487/2002.05.28_nrc_rome_declaration.pdf.
18. John Tagliabue, "Rome journal; A faux treaty room, with missiles," *New York Times*, May 27, 2002.
19. Michael Wines, "Accord is near on giving Russia a limited role in NATO," *New York Times*, April 23, 2002.
20. "Rewriting history in Reykjavik," *New York Times*, May 15, 2002; Todd S. Purdum, "NATO strikes deal to accept Russia in a partnership," *New York Times*, May 15, 2002.
21. Friedman, *Berlusconi*, 131.
22. David S. Yost, *NATO's Balancing Act*, Washington, DC, United States Institute of Peace, 2014, 57.
23. Steven Erlanger, "German leader's warning: War plan is a huge mistake," *New York Times*, September 5, 2002.
24. Peter Ford, "NATO looks to retool itself," *Christian Science Monitor*, September 25, 2002.
25. Paal Sigurd Hilde, "Military change in NATO: The CJTF concept – a case study of military innovation in a multinational environment," in Jo Inge Bekkevold, Ian Bowers, and Michael Raska (eds), *Security, Strategy and Military Change in the 21st Century: Cross-regional perspectives*, Abingdon, Routledge, 2017, 221–240.
26. NATO, "Prague summit declaration," NATO Press Release (2002)127, November 21, 2002, https://www.nato.int/docu/pr/2002/p02-127e.htm.
27. Elisabeth Bumiller, "Bush, at NATO meeting, firms up his 'posse'," *New York Times*, November 22, 2002.
28. Robert Kagan, *Of Paradise and Power: America and Europe in the New World Order*, New York, Knopf, 2003.

29. Tony Blair, *A Journey*, London, Hutchinson, 2010, 429; Bob Woodward, *Plan of Attack*, London, Pocket Books, 2004, 347.
30. Michael Gordon and Bernard Trainor, *Cobra II: The inside story of the invasion and occupation of Iraq*, London, Atlantic, 2007, 129–130; Rynning, *NATO in Afghanistan*, 86–87.
31. Ari Fleischer, *Taking Heat: The president, the press, and my years in the White House*, New York, PerfectBound, 2005, 313.
32. Interview with author, April 3, 2023.
33. Rynning, *NATO in Afghanistan*, 88.
34. Jaap De Hoop Scheffer, "NATO: A bruised alliance marches on," *New York Times*, January 30, 2004.
35. Interview with author, March 22, 2023.
36. Theo Farrell, *Unwinnable: Britain's war in Afghanistan, 2001–2014*, London, The Bodley Head, 2017, 176.
37. ISAF, "ISAF placemat," January 29, 2007, https://www.nato.int/isaf/placemats_archive/2007-01-29-ISAF-Placemat.pdf.
38. Carlotta Gall, "Peacekeeper commander mired in Afghan combat," *New York Times*, October 15, 2006.
39. White House, "NSPD-44: Management of interagency efforts concerning reconstruction and stabilization," December 7, 2005, https://irp.fas.org/offdocs/nspd/nspd-44.html.
40. London Conference on Afghanistan, "The Afghanistan compact," February 1, 2006, https://www.diplomatie.gouv.fr/IMG/pdf/afghanistan_compact.pdf
41. Cedric de Coning and Karsten Friis, "Coherence and coordination: The limits of the comprehensive approach," *Journal of International Peacekeeping*, 15 (2011), 243–272.
42. Ahmed Rashid, *Descent into Chaos: The US and the disaster in Pakistan, Afghanistan, and Central Asia*, London, Penguin Books, 2009, 355.
43. NATO, "Riga summit declaration," November 29, 2006, https://www.nato.int/cps/en/natolive/official_texts_37920.htm; Judy Dempsey, "NATO chief urges overhaul of Afghanistan effort," *New York Times*, November 5, 2006.
44. Elizabeth Rubin, "Karzai in his labyrinth," *New York Times*, August 5, 2009; Rynning, *NATO in Afghanistan*.
45. F. Stephen Larrabee, "Turkey rediscovers the Middle East," *Foreign Affairs*, 86:4 (2007), 103–114.
46. President of Russia, "Speech and the following discussion at the Munich Conference on security policy," February 26, 2007, http://en.kremlin.ru/events/president/transcripts/24034.
47. Steven Lee Myers, "For now, a cold peace between Russia and the US," *International Herald Tribune*, February 19, 2007.
48. Interview with author, March 22, 2023.
49. Stefano Stefanini, interview with author, April 5, 2023.
50. John Vinocur, "Can NATO take a tough line when Putin shows up at its summit?," *New York Times*, February 25, 2008.
51. NATO, "Bucharest summit declaration – Issued by the heads of state and government participating in the meeting of the North Atlantic Council in Bucharest on 3 April 2008," April 3, 2008, http://www.nato.int/cps/en/natohq/official_texts_8443.htm.
52. Interview with author, March 22, 2023.

53. Bush, *Decision Points*, 431.
54. Scheffer, interview with author, March 22, 2023.
55. William J. Burns, "Your visit to Sochi," Department of State, April 1, 2008, https://carnegieendowment.org/pdf/back-channel/2008Moscow886.pdf.
56. Philip Zelikow, "US strategic planning in 2001–02," in Melvyn P. Leffler and Jeffrey W. Legro (eds), *In Uncertain Times: American foreign policy after the Berlin Wall and 9/11*, Ithaca, NY, Cornell University Press, 2011, 96–116. Two recent books critical of President Bush's decision-making, and notably the lack of coherent policy deliberation on Iraq, are Robert Draper, *To Start a War: How the Bush administration took America into Iraq*, New York, Penguin, 2022, and Melvyn Leffler, *Confronting Saddam Hussein: George W. Bush and the invasion of Iraq*, New York, Oxford University Press, 2023. For an assessment of the relative merits in the debate, see Melvyn P. Leffler, "An illuminating hand-off," in Stephen J. Hadley (ed.), *Hand-Off: The foreign policy George W. Bush handed to Barack Obama*, Washington, DC, Brookings Institution Press, 2023), 635–657; Hal Brands, "Reassessing Bush's legacy," in Hadley (ed.), *Hand-Off*, 658–675.
57. "Sarkozy et Merkel Affichent Leur Bonne Entente Retrouvée à Bucarest," Agence France Presse, April 3, 2008; Pierre Rousselin, "Sarkozy et Merkel Imposent la Voix de l'Europe," *Le Figaro*, April 4, 2008.
58. Benjamin Schreer, "A new 'pragmatism': Germany's NATO policy," *International Journal* (Toronto), 64:2 (2009), 383–398.
59. Background interview with author, June 2010.
60. ISAF, "ISAF's strategic vision," April 3, 2008, https://www.nato.int/cps/en/nato-live/official_texts_8444.htm; Rynning, *NATO in Afghanistan*, 152–153.
61. Michael Kofman, "The August War, ten years on: A retrospective on the Russo-Georgian war," *War on the Rocks*, August 17, 2018, https://warontherocks.com/2018/08/the-august-war-ten-years-on-a-retrospective-on-the-russo-georgian-war/.
62. Jaap de Hoop Scheffer and Ban Ki-Moon, "Joint declaration on UN/NATO Secretariat cooperation," September 23, 2008, http://streitcouncil.org/uploads/PDF/UN-NATO%20Joint%20Declaration.pdf; Rynning, *NATO in Afghanistan*, 131.
63. NATO, "Final communiqué (Press Release (2008) 153)," December 3, 2008, http://www.nato.int/cps/en/natohq/official_texts_46247.htm.
64. Paul D. Miller, "National Security Council memorandum: Afghanistan," in Hadley (ed.), *Hand-Off*, 116–123.
65. Rynning, *NATO in Afghanistan*; Bob Woodward, *Obama's Wars*, New York, Simon & Schuster, 2010.
66. NATO, "Statement on Afghanistan by ministers of foreign affairs of nations participating in the International Security Assistance Force (ISAF)," December 4, 2009, https://www.nato.int/cps/en/natohq/news_59701.htm.
67. David P. Auerswald and Stephen M. Saideman, *NATO in Afghanistan: Fighting together, fighting alone*, Princeton, NJ, Princeton University Press, 2014.
68. Barack Obama, "Speech on Afghanistan," *New York Times*, June 23, 2011, https://www.nytimes.com/2011/06/23/world/asia/23obama-afghanistan-speech-text.html; Mark Mazzetti and Scott Shane, "Petraeus says Afghan pullout is beyond what he advised," *New York Times*, June 23, 2011, https://www.nytimes.com/2011/06/24/world/asia/24petraeus.html.
69. NATO, "Summit declaration issued by the heads of state and government participating in the meeting of the North Atlantic Council in Strasbourg/Kehl," April 4, 2009, http://www.nato.int/cps/en/natohq/news_52837.htm.

70. Ryan C. Hendrickson, "NATO's first prime minister: Rasmussen's leadership surge," *RUSI Journal*, 155:5 (2010), 24–30.

71. NATO, "Strategic Concept for the defence and security of the members of the North Atlantic Treaty Organisation," 2010, 7, https://www.nato.int/lisbon2010/strategic-concept-2010-eng.pdf; Jens Ringsmose and Sten Rynning (eds), *NATO's New Strategic Concept: A comprehensive assessment*, Copenhagen: DIIS, 2011; Steven Erlanger, "NATO sees threats, but is reluctant to say just who the enemy might be," *New York Times*, November 2, 2010.

72. Nabi Adbullaev, "Medvedev shows he's his own man," *Moscow Times*, September 28, 2010.

73. Julie Pace, "Ray's Hell Burger: Obama and Medvedev have 'historic' hamburger summit," *Christian Science Monitor*, June 24, 2010, https://www.csmonitor.com/From-the-news-wires/2010/0624/Ray-s-Hell-Burger-Obama-and-Medvedev-have-historic-hamburger-summit.

74. Richard Weitz, "Illusive visions and practical realities: Russia, NATO and missile defence," *Survival*, 52:4 (2010), 99–120.

75. NATO, "Lisbon summit declaration issued by the heads of state and government participating in the meeting of the North Atlantic Council in Lisbon," November 20, 2010, 38, https://www.nato.int/cps/en/natohq/official_texts_68828.htm; Judy Dempsey, "NATO leaders agree to new start with Russia," *New York Times*, November 22, 2010, https://www.nytimes.com/2010/11/22/world/europe/22iht-allies.html.

76. Volker Rühe et al., "Open letter: It's time to invite Russia to join NATO," *Der Spiegel*, March 8, 2010, https://www.spiegel.de/international/world/open-letter-it-s-time-to-invite-russia-to-join-nato-a-682287.html.

77. James Joyner, "Russia: NATO member?," Atlantic Council (blog), March 8, 2010, https://www.atlanticcouncil.org/blogs/new-atlanticist/russia-nato-member/.

78. Oksana Antonenko and Igor Yurgens, "Towards a NATO-Russia strategic concept: Ending Cold War legacies; Facing new threats together," INSOR & IISS, November 1, 2010, http://www.insor-russia.ru/files/IISS-INSOR.PDF (website active at the time of writing in March 2023); also see https://www.nytimes.com/2010/11/19/opinion/19iht-edantonenko.html.

79. Oksana Antonenko, "5 ways to bring NATO and Russia together," *Moscow Times*, November 16, 2010; Michael Bohm, "5 reasons why Russia will never join NATO," *Moscow Times*, November 18, 2010; Alexander Kramarenko, "5 reasons why Russia could join NATO," *Moscow Times*, December 8, 2010. Oksana Antonenko and Igor Yurgens, "Towards a NATO–Russia strategic concept," *Survival*, 52:6 (2010), 5–11, https://doi.org/10.1080/00396338.2010.540780; Dmitry Trenin, "Turning a Happy Hour into a Happy Alliance," *Moscow Times*, November 21, 2010; John Vinocur, "Partners for peace? Just possibly," *New York Times*, November 29, 2010, https://www.nytimes.com/2010/11/30/world/europe/30iht-politicus.html; Roberto Zadra, "NATO, Russia and missile defence: Towards the Lisbon summit," *RUSI Journal*, 155:5 (2010), 12–16; Jakub Kulhanek, "Russia's uncertain rapprochement with NATO," *RUSI Journal*, 156:1 (2011), 40–45.

80. Group of Experts, "NATO 2020: Assured security; dynamic engagement," NATO, May 17, 2010, 16, https://www.nato.int/nato_static_fl2014/assets/pdf/pdf_2010_05/20100517_100517_expertsreport.pdf; Judy Dempsey, "East Europe feels ignored by NATO, report says," *New York Times*, May 17, 2010, https://www.nytimes.com/2010/05/17/world/europe/17iht-nato.html.

81. NATO, "Strategic concept for the defence and security of the members of the North Atlantic Treaty Organisation," 29.
82. Ellen Hallams and Benjamin Schreer, "Towards a 'post-American' alliance? NATO burden-sharing after Libya," *International Affairs*, 88:2 (2012), 313–327; Jeffrey H. Michaels, "Able but not willing: A critical assessment of NATO's Libya intervention," in Kjell Engelbrekt, Marcus Mohlin, and Charlotte Wagnsson (eds), *The NATO Intervention in Libya: Lessons learned from the campaign*, Abingdon, Routledge, 2013, 17–40; Stéfanie von Hlatky and Thomas Juneau, "When the coalition determines the mission: NATO's detour in Libya," *Journal of Strategic Studies*, 45:2 (2022), 258–279.
83. "Putin defers to Medvedev on Libya," Radio Free Europe, March 22, 2011.
84. Friedman, *Berlusconi*, 192.
85. Robert M. Gates, "Reflections on the status and future of the transatlantic alliance," June 10, 2011.
86. Barack Obama, "Osama Bin Laden dead," May 2, 2011, https://obamawhitehouse.archives.gov/blog/2011/05/02/osama-bin-laden-dead.

Chapter 10 NATO's Nationalization

1. Ryan J. Foley and Nomaan Merchant, "A mixed message: Sparkling city, world leaders, clashes with police," Associated Press, May 21, 2012.
2. Anders Fogh Rasmussen, "Doorstep statement by NATO Secretary General Anders Fogh Rasmussen at the beginning of the summit meetings of heads of state and government in Chicago," NATO, May 20, 2012, http://www.nato.int/cps/en/natohq/opinions_87571.htm.
3. Department of Defense, "Sustaining US global leadership: Priorities for 21st century defense," January 2012, https://www.globalsecurity.org/military/library/policy/dod/defense_guidance-201201.pdf; Elisabeth Bumiller and Thom Shanker, "Obama puts his stamp on strategy for a leaner military," *New York Times*, January 5, 2012, https://www.nytimes.com/2012/01/06/us/obama-at-pentagon-to-outline-cuts-and-strategic-shifts.html.
4. NATO, "Chicago summit declaration issued by NATO heads of state and government (2012)," May 20, 2012, 6, https://www.nato.int/cps/en/natohq/official_texts_87593.htm.
5. Robert Michael Gates, *Duty: Memoirs of a secretary at war*, New York, Vintage Books, 2015, 530–531.
6. Author's interview with Alexander Vershbow, former US ambassador to Russia and former NATO deputy secretary general (2012–2014), April 11, 2023.
7. Karl-Heinz Kamp, "NATO's strategy after the Lisbon summit," *Atlantisch Perspectief*, 34:8 (2010), 4–7; Paul Zajac, "NATO's defense and deterrence posture review: A French perspective on nuclear issues," *Nuclear Policy Paper* No. 7, British American Security Information Council, April 27, 2011; Oliver Thränert, "NATO's deterrence and defense posture review," *SWP Comments*, 34 (November 2011), https://www.swp-berlin.org/publications/products/comments/2011C34_trt_ks.pdf; David Stamp, "Merkel's German nuclear policy switch draws fire," Reuters, March 15, 2011, https://www.reuters.com/article/uk-germany-nuclear-idUKTRE72E2SI20110315; Helmut Schmidt and Sam Nunn, "Toward a world without nukes," *New York Times*, April 13, 2012, https://www.nytimes.com/2012/04/14/opinion/toward-a-world-without-nukes.html.

8. NATO, "Deterrence and defence posture review," May 20, 2012, https://www.nato.int/cps/en/natohq/official_texts_87597.htm

9. Mark Landler, "Obama threatens force against Syria," *New York Times*, August 21, 2012, https://www.nytimes.com/2012/08/21/world/middleeast/obama-threatens-force-against-syria.html.

10. Jeffrey Goldberg, "The Obama doctrine," *The Atlantic*, March 10, 2016, https://www.theatlantic.com/magazine/archive/2016/04/the-obama-doctrine/471525/.

11. Charles Krauthammer, "Decline is a choice," *Weekly Standard*, October 19, 2009.

12. Adam Quinn, "The art of declining politely: Obama's prudent presidency and the waning of American power," *International Affairs*, 87:4 (2011), 803–824; Nicholas Kitchen, "The Obama doctrine—détente or decline?," *European Political Science*, 10:1 (2011), 27–35; James Mann, *The Obamians*, New York, Penguin, 2012; Ben Rhodes, "Inside the White House during the Syrian 'Red Line' crisis," *The Atlantic*, June 3, 2018, https://www.theatlantic.com/international/archive/2018/06/inside-the-white-house-during-the-syrian-red-line-crisis/561887/.

13. Claudia Major and Christian Mölling, "The framework nations concept. Germany's contribution to a capable European defence," *SWP Comments*, 52 (December 2014), https://www.swp-berlin.org/publications/products/comments/2014C52_mjr_mlg.pdf.

14. NATO, "Summit declaration on defence capabilities: Toward NATO forces 2020," May 20, 2012, https://www.nato.int/cps/en/natohq/official_texts_87594.htm.

15. Interview with author, April 11, 2023.

16. John Irish and Elizabeth Pineau, "Despite pressure, France won't cancel warship deal with Russia," Reuters, May 12, 2014, https://www.reuters.com/article/us-france-russia-mistral-idUSBREA4B08V20140512; "France suspends Mistral warship delivery to Russia," France 24, September 3, 2014, 2, https://www.france24.com/en/20140903-france-suspends-plans-deliver-first-mistral-helicopter-carrier-russia.

17. NATO, "Wales summit declaration issued by the heads of state and government participating in the meeting of the North Atlantic Council in Wales," September 5, 2014, 5–13, http://www.nato.int/cps/en/natohq/official_texts_112964.htm.

18. Ibid., 14–15.

19. Ibid., 16–23.

20. White House, "Statement by the president on ISIL," September 10, 2014, https://obamawhitehouse.archives.gov/the-press-office/2014/09/10/statement-president-Isil-1; Helene Cooper, "Obama enlists 9 allies to help in the battle against ISIS," *New York Times*, September 5, 2014, https://www.nytimes.com/2014/09/06/world/middleeast/us-and-allies-form-coalition-against-isis.html.

21. Kristian Atland, "Destined for deadlock? Russia, Ukraine, and the unfulfilled Minsk agreements," *Post-Soviet Affairs*, 36:2 (2020), 122–139; Duncan Allan and Kataryna Wolczuk, "Why Minsk-2 cannot solve the Ukraine crisis," Chatham House, February 16, 2022, https://www.chathamhouse.org/2022/02/why-minsk-2-cannot-solve-ukraine-crisis.

22. Based on author's interviews in NATO headquarters with both NATO and national officials in June and November 2015.

23. Adrian Croft, "Ministers let their hair down at NATO meeting," Reuters, May 14, 2015, https://www.reuters.com/article/nato-ministers-song-idINK-BN0NZ21G20150514. The scene can be viewed on YouTube: https://www.youtube.com/watch?v=0y7vs9cV3iA.
24. Krishnadev Calamur, "What NATO diplomats do on their downtime: Sing 'We Are the World'," NPR, May 14, 2015, https://www.npr.org/sections/thetwo-way/2015/05/14/406757515/what-nato-diplomats-do-on-their-downtime-sing-we-are-the-world.
25. Stephen F. Szabo, "Germany: From civilian power to a geo-economic shaping power," *German Politics and Society*, 35:3 (2017), 38–54; Tuomas Forsberg, "From 'Ostpolitik' to 'Forstpolitik'? Merkel, Putin and German foreign policy towards Russia," *International Affairs*, 92:1 (2016), 21–42.
26. Auswärtiges Amt, "Speech by Federal Foreign Minister Frank-Walter Steinmeier at the 51st Munich security conference," German Federal Foreign Office, February 8, 2015, https://www.auswaertiges-amt.de/en/newsroom/news/150208-muesiko/269034.
27. Euan MacDonald, "Poroshenko tells Germany Nord Stream 2 gas pipeline is a 'political bribe'," *Kyiv Post*, April 10, 2018, https://archive.kyivpost.com/ukraine-politics/poroshenko-tells-germany-nord-stream-2-gas-pipeline-political-bribe.html; Agnieszka Barteczko, "Poland and Ukraine to jointly oppose EU over Nord Stream 2, Opal," Reuters, December 2, 2016, https://www.reuters.com/article/eu-energy-ukraine-poland-idAFL8N1DX2OZ; Andrius Sytas, "EU leaders sign letter objecting to Nord Stream-2 gas link," Reuters, March 16, 2016, https://www.reuters.com/article/uk-eu-energy-nordstream-idUKKCN0WI1YV.
28. Jim Yardley and David M. Herszenhorn, "Making Merkel wait, finding time for truffles," *New York Times*, October 18, 2014, https://www.nytimes.com/2014/10/18/world/unbowed-putin-chews-the-scenery-in-milan.html.
29. Soner Cagaptay, "Erdogan's failure on the Nile," Washington Institute, May 28, 2019, https://www.washingtoninstitute.org/policy-analysis/erdogans-failure-nile.
30. Emre Ersen, "Evaluating the fighter jet crisis in Turkish–Russian relations," *Insight* (Turkey), 19:4 (2017), 85–104.
31. Adam Thomson, "NATO and unconventional threats," November 11, 2015, https://www.gov.uk/government/news/speech-nato-and-unconventional-threats.
32. Author's interview with NATO official, November 2015.
33. NATO, "Warsaw summit communiqué—issued by the heads of state and government participating in the meeting of the North Atlantic Council in Warsaw, 8–9 July 2016," July 9, 2016, 94–96, http://www.nato.int/cps/en/natohq/official_texts_133169.htm.
34. Ibid., 15.
35. Fabrice Pothier, "An area-access strategy for NATO," *Survival*, 59:3 (2017), 73–80; Martin Zapfe, "Deterrence from the ground up: Understanding NATO's enhanced forward presence," *Survival*, 59:3 (2017), 147–160.
36. Author's interview with Alexander Vershbow, April 11, 2023.
37. Philip Bump, "Analysis: Trump's NATO isolationism is at least 30 years old," *Washington Post*, January 15, 2019, https://www.washingtonpost.com/politics/2019/01/15/trumps-nato-isolationism-is-least-years-old/.

38. Cyra Master, "Trump tells German paper: NATO is 'obsolete'," The Hill (blog), January 16, 2017, https://thehill.com/homenews/administration/314432-trump-nato-is-obsolete/.

39. Jenna Johnson, "Trump on NATO: 'I said it was obsolete. It's no longer obsolete'," Washington Post, April 12, 2017, https://www.washingtonpost.com/news/post-politics/wp/2017/04/12/trump-on-nato-i-said-it-was-obsolete-its-no-longer-obsolete/.

40. Jens Stoltenberg, "Doorstep statement by NATO Secretary General Jens Stoltenberg ahead of the meeting of NATO heads of state and/or government," NATO, May 25, 2017, http://www.nato.int/cps/en/natohq/opinions_144083.htm; Gilles Paris, Jean-Pierre Stroobants, and Nathalie Guibert, "La Visite de Trump à l'OTAN Dominée Par Le Terrorisme," Le Monde, May 24, 2017, https://www.lemonde.fr/europe/article/2017/05/24/la-visite-de-trump-a-l-otan-dominee-par-le-terrorisme_5133180_3214.html.

41. Peter Baker and Susan Glasser, The Divider: Trump in the White House, 2017–2021, New York, Doubleday, 2022, 76–77; Susan B. Glasser, "Trump national security team blindsided by NATO speech," Politico Magazine, June 5, 2017, https://www.politico.com/magazine/story/2017/06/05/trump-nato-speech-national-security-team-215227.

42. Baker and Glasser, The Divider, 77.

43. Donald J. Trump, "Remarks by President Trump at NATO," US Embassy and Consulates in Russia, May 26, 2017, https://ru.usembassy.gov/remarks-president-trump-nato/.

44. Interview with author, April 28, 2023.

45. Julian E. Barnes and Helene Cooper, "Trump discussed pulling US From NATO, aides say amid new concerns over Russia," New York Times, January 14, 2019.

46. John Bolton, The Room Where It Happened: A White House memoir, New York, Simon & Schuster, 2020, 136–146.

47. US Mission to NATO, "Remarks by President Trump at press conference after 2018 NATO summit in Brussels," July 12, 2018, https://nato.usmission.gov/july-12-2018-remarks-by-president-trump-at-press-conference-after-2018-nato-summit-in-brussels/.

48. Julie Hirschfeld Davis, "Trump warns NATO allies to spend more on defense, or else," New York Times, July 2, 2018, https://www.nytimes.com/2018/07/02/world/europe/trump-nato.html.

49. Ron Elving, "Trump's Helsinki bow to Putin leaves world wondering: Why?," NPR, July 17, 2018, https://www.npr.org/2018/07/17/629601233/trumps-helsinki-bow-to-putin-leaves-world-wondering-whats-up; Brian Bennett, "A crisis of his own making," Time, July 30, 2018, 22–29; "Humiliation in Helsinki; Donald Trump's European tour," The Economist, 428:9101 (2018), 10.

50. NATO, "Brussels summit declaration issued by NATO heads of state and government," July 11, 2018, https://www.nato.int/cps/en/natohq/official_texts_156624.htm; Paul Belkin, "CRS insight: NATO's 2018 Brussels summit," Congressional Research Service, July 5, 2018, https://sgp.fas.org/crs/row/IN10926.pdf.

51. Gjert Lage Dyndal and Paal Sigurd Hilde, "Strategic thinking in NATO and the new 'military strategy' of 2019," in Janne Haaland Matlary and Rob Johnson (eds), Military Strategy in the 21st Century. The challenge for NATO, London, Hurst & Company, 2020, 320.

52. This paragraph is based on background interviews conducted in March 2021 and April 2023.
53. Jens Ringsmose and Sten Rynning, "NATO's next strategic concept: Prioritise or perish," *Survival*, 63:5 (2021), 147–168.
54. David Vergun, "NATO's new strategy will better protect Europe, top commander says," US Department of Defense, October 4, 2019, https://www.defense.gov/ Explore/News/Article/Article/1981374/natos-new-strategy-will-better-protect-europe-top-commander-says/.
55. Interview by author and Jens Ringsmose, March 9, 2021.
56. "Emmanuel Macron warns Europe: NATO is becoming brain dead," *The Economist*, November 7, 2019, https://www.economist.com/europe/2019/11/07/ emmanuel-macron-warns-europe-nato-is-becoming-brain-dead.
57. Jeffrey Goldberg, "The man who couldn't take it anymore," *The Atlantic*, 2019, https://www.theatlantic.com/magazine/archive/2019/10/james-mattis-trump/ 596665/.
58. David E. Sanger, "As NATO envoys celebrate, signs of fracturing from within," *New York Times*, April 4, 2019, https://www.nytimes.com/2019/04/04/us/poli-tics/nato-anniversary.html; Nicholas Burns and Douglas Lute, "NATO's biggest problem is President Trump," *Washington Post*, April 3, 2019, https://www. washingtonpost.com/opinions/natos-biggest-problem-is-president-trump/ 2019/04/02/6991bc9c-5570-11e9-9136-f8e636f1f6df_story.html.
59. Angelique Chrisafis, "Macron criticised by US and Germany over Nato 'brain death' claims," *Guardian*, November 7, 2019, https://www.theguardian.com/ world/2019/nov/07/macron-warns-of-nato-brain-death-as-us-turns-its-back-on-allies.
60. NATO, "London declaration," December 4, 2019, http://www.nato.int/cps/en/ natohq/official_texts_171584.htm.
61. This paragraph and the next are based on the author's background interviews at NATO headquarters, September 2022.
62. Reflection Group, "NATO 2030: United for a new era," NATO, November 25, 2020, https://www.nato.int/nato_static_fl2014/assets/pdf/2020/12/pdf/201201-Reflection-Group-Final-Report-Uni.pdf.
63. Jens Stoltenberg, "Food for thought paper: NATO 2030—A transatlantic agenda for the future," NATO unclassified PO(2021)0053, February 11, 2021.
64. NATO, "Brussels summit communiqué," NATO Press Release 086, June 14, 2021, 6–7.
65. NATO, "London declaration," 5.
66. Jens Ringsmose and Sten Rynning, "China brought NATO closer together," *War on the Rocks*, February 5, 2020, https://warontherocks.com/2020/02/ china-brought-nato-closer-together/; Sten Rynning, "Nato's struggle for a China policy: Alliance, alignment, or abdication?," *Asian Affairs*, 53:3 (2022), 481–499.
67. Steven Erlanger, "Blinken's welcome by NATO doesn't hide differences on key issues," *New York Times*, March 24, 2021, https://www.nytimes.com/2021/03/24/ world/europe/Blinken-Biden-NATO-Europe.html.
68. "Les Trois Leçons de l'alliance Entre l'Australie, Les Etats-Unis et Le Royaume-Uni," *Le Monde*, September 17, 2021, https://www.lemonde.fr/idees/article/ 2021/09/17/les-trois-lecons-de-l-alliance-entre-l-australie-les-etats-unis-et-le-royaume-uni_6095013_3232.html.

69. White House, "US withdrawal from Afghanistan," April 6, 2023, https://www.whitehouse.gov/wp-content/uploads/2023/04/US-Withdrawal-from-Afghanistan.pdf.

70. NATO, "Afghanistan lessons learned process," November 2021, https://www.nato.int/nato_static_fl2014/assets/pdf/2021/12/pdf/2112-factsheet-afgh-lessons-en.pdf; Sten Rynning and Paal Sigurd Hilde, "Operationally agile but strategically lacking: NATO's bruising years in Afghanistan," *LSE Public Policy Review*, 2:3 (2022).

71. Steven Erlanger and Michael D. Shear, "Shifting focus, NATO views China as a global security challenge," *New York Times*, June 14, 2021, https://www.nytimes.com/2021/06/14/world/europe/biden-nato-china-russia.html.

72. Ibid.

Chapter 11 Comeback? Classical NATO for a New Era

1. Joe Biden, "Remarks by President Biden on the united efforts of the free world to support the people of Ukraine," White House, March 26, 2022, https://www.whitehouse.gov/briefing-room/speeches-remarks/2022/03/26/remarks-by-president-biden-on-the-united-efforts-of-the-free-world-to-support-the-people-of-ukraine/.

2. Serhii Plokhy, *The Russo-Ukrainian War: The return of history*, New York, Norton, 2023, 246.

3. David Remnick, "How the war in Ukraine ends," *New Yorker*, February 17, 2023, https://www.newyorker.com/news/the-new-yorker-interview/how-the-war-in-ukraine-ends.

4. NATO, "Press conference by NATO Secretary General Jens Stoltenberg with President of Ukraine Volodymyr Zelenskyy in Kyiv," April 20, 2023, https://www.nato.int/cps/en/natohq/opinions_214039.htm.

5. Miriam Berger, "Putin says he will 'denazify' Ukraine. Here's the history behind that claim," *Washington Post*, March 1, 2022, https://www.washingtonpost.com/world/2022/02/24/putin-denazify-ukraine/.

6. Steven Erlanger, "With the Ukraine invasion, NATO is suddenly vulnerable," *New York Times*, February 24, 2022, https://www.nytimes.com/2022/02/24/world/europe/ukraine-russia-nato-europe.html.

7. Isaac Chotiner, "John Mearsheimer on Putin's ambitions after nine months of war," *New Yorker*, November 17, 2022, https://www.newyorker.com/news/q-and-a/john-mearsheimer-on-putins-ambitions-after-nine-months-of-war.

8. Russian Ministry of Foreign Affairs, "Agreement on measures to ensure the security of the Russian Federation and member states of the North Atlantic Treaty Organization," December 17, 2021, https://mid.ru/ru/foreign_policy/rso/nato/1790803/?lang=en&TSPD_101_R0=08765fb817ab20001c3a5fd477e6f646cb2da0301fb1069911ea6dc3b60cf58bfe473c604aee364d-08b1aa6b841430003456e50dd5740336313343cc99209bb77aaf-34264a8ab2791d08d9c14ae29d3b9b5e7420a7fb573956818038f279118f; Russian Ministry of Foreign Affairs, "Treaty between the United States of America and the Russian Federation on security guarantees," December 17, 2021, https://mid.ru/ru/foreign_policy/rso/nato/1790818/?lang=en&TSPD_101_R0=08765fb817ab20005c61e329a02e900c8dc723d1cfd2e7338be76f062a5f632ec69c848b10cdeaa408920aa26c143000636e58aa8f1628719098a

36eada1605286eae99001f88e6fc0b867fd090a99a691dae0bfc2f37009 cc48225c6e2ae83d (both websites available at the time of writing, in June 2023).

9. William Alberque, "Russia's new draft treaties: Like 2009, but worse," IISS, January 25, 2022, https://www.iiss.org/online-analysis/online-analysis/2022/01/russias-new-draft-treaties-like-2009-but-worse/.

10. Audrey Tolstoy and Edmund McCaffray, "Mind games: Alexander Dugin and Russia's war of ideas," *World Affairs*, 177:6 (2015), 25–30; Anton Barbashin and Hannah Thoburn, "Putin's brain," *Foreign Affairs*, March 31, 2014, https://www.foreignaffairs.com/articles/russia-fsu/2014-03-31/putins-brain; Charles Clover, *Black Wind, White Snow: The rise of Russia's new nationalism*, New Haven, CT, Yale University Press, 2016.

11. Fiona Hill and Clifford G. Gaddy, *The Siberian Curse: How communist planners left Russia out in the cold*, Washington, DC, Brookings Institution Press, 2003; Walter Laqueur, *Putinism: Russia and its future with the West*, New York, Thomas Dunne Books, 2015.

12. NATO, "Statement by the North Atlantic Council on the situation in and around Ukraine," December 16, 2021, https://www.nato.int/cps/en/natohq/news_190373.htm.

13. " 'We knew': NATO chief looks back at Russia's Ukraine invasion," France 24, February 16, 2023, https://www.france24.com/en/live-news/20230216-we-knew-nato-chief-looks-back-at-russia-s-ukraine-invasion.

14. Suzanne Lynch, Lili Bayer, and Jacopo Barigazzi, " 'Oh my God, it's really happening,' " Politico (blog), February 24, 2023, https://www.politico.eu/article/ukraine-invasion-war-russia-zelenskyy-putin-one-year-on-michel-stoltenberg/.

15. John Ismay, "A new US-led international group will meet monthly to focus on aiding Ukraine," *New York Times*, April 26, 2022, https://www.nytimes.com/2022/04/26/world/europe/lloyd-austin-ukraine-contact-group.html.

16. NATO, "Madrid summit declaration issued by NATO heads of state and government," June 29, 2022, https://www.nato.int/cps/en/natohq/official_texts_196951.htm; NATO, "NATO 2022 strategic concept," June 29, 2022, https://www.nato.int/nato_static_fl2014/assets/pdf/2022/6/pdf/290622-strategic-concept.pdf.

17. Author's interviews at NATO headquarters, September 2022.

18. NATO, "NATO 2022 strategic concept."

19. Henry A. Kissinger, *World Order: Reflections on the character of nations and the course of history*, London, Allen Lane, 2014.

20. Steven Erlanger, "Arctic risks loom large as Blinken tours NATO's north," *New York Times*, May 31, 2023, https://www.nytimes.com/2023/05/31/world/europe/blinken-arctic-nato-russia.html; Liselotte Odgaard, "Russia's Arctic designs and NATO," *Survival*, 64:4 (2022), 89–104.

21. Philippe Ricard, Piotr Smolar, and Bruno Philip, "Macron's Taiwan statements upset France's allies," *Le Monde*, April 11, 2023, https://www.lemonde.fr/en/international/article/2023/04/11/macron-taiwan-statements-upset-france-s-allies_6022513_4.html; Emily Rauhala, "Macron's Taiwan comments anger allies, delight Beijing," *Washington Post*, April 11, 2023, https://www.washingtonpost.com/world/2023/04/11/macron-taiwan-china/; Jamil Anderlini and Clea Caulcutt, "Europe must resist pressure to become 'America's followers,' says Macron," *Politico*

(blog), April 9, 2023, https://www.politico.eu/article/emmanuel-macron-china-america-pressure-interview/.

22. German Federal Government, "Integrated security for Germany: National security strategy," June 2023, https://www.nationalesicherheitsstrategie.de/National-Security-Strategy-EN.pdf.

23. Karl-Heinz Kamp, "The Zeitenwende at work: Germany's national security strategy," *Survival*, 65:3 (2023), 73–80.

24. Hans Binnendijk and Sarah Kirchberger, "The China plan: A transatlantic blueprint for strategic competition," Atlantic Council (blog), March 22, 2021, https://www.atlanticcouncil.org/in-depth-research-reports/report/china-plan-transatlantic-blueprint/.

25. John K. Culver and Sarah Kirchberger, "US-China lessons from Ukraine: Fueling more dangerous Taiwan tensions," Atlantic Council (blog), June 15, 2023, https://www.atlanticcouncil.org/in-depth-research-reports/report/us-china-lessons-from-ukraine/.

26. Kurt Volker, "Nine lessons for the West about ending Russia's war on Ukraine in 2023," SCEEUS, January 16, 2023, https://sceeus.se/en/publications/nine-lessons-for-the-west-about-ending-russias-war-on-ukraine-in-2023/.

27. Emmanuel Macron, "Discours de Clôture Du Président de La République," elysee.fr, June 1, 2023, https://www.elysee.fr/emmanuel-macron/2023/06/01/sommet-globsec-a-bratislava.

28. Sten Rynning, "The treadmill of NATO summitry," UK in a Changing Europe, August 22, 2023, https://ukandeu.ac.uk/the-treadmill-of-nato-summitry/.

29. NATO, "Defence expenditure of NATO countries (2014–2022)," 2023, https://www.nato.int/nato_static_fl2014/assets/pdf/2023/3/pdf/230321-def-exp-2022-en.pdf.

30. André de Staercke, "An alliance clamouring to be born—Anxious to survive," in Nicholas Sherwen (ed.), *NATO's Anxious Birth: The prophetic vision of the 1940s*, London, Hurst & Company, 1985, 158–159.

31. NATO, "Summary record of a meeting of the Council held at the NATO headquarters, Brussels (C-R(76)4)," January 29, 1976, https://www.nato.int/nato_static_fl2014/assets/pdf/pdf_history/20161027_E1-Symbols-NATOMotto-c-r764.pdf.

32. André de Staercke, Jean Stengers, and Ginette Kurgan-van Hentenryk, *Tout Cela a Passé Comme Une Ombre: Mémoires Sur La Régence et La Question Royale*, Brussels, Éditions Racine, 2003, 272.

33. de Staercke, "An alliance clamouring to be born," 168.

Appendix: The North Atlantic Treaty

1. The definition of the territories to which Article 5 applies was revised by Article 2 of the Protocol to the North Atlantic Treaty on the accession of Greece and Turkey signed on 22 October 1951.

2. On January 16, 1963, the North Atlantic Council noted that insofar as the former Algerian Departments of France were concerned, the relevant clauses of this Treaty had become inapplicable as from July 3, 1962.

3. The Treaty came into force on 24 August 1949, after the deposition of the ratifications of all signatory states.

Select Bibliography

Overviews of NATO

Hendrickson, Ryan C. *Diplomacy and War at NATO: The secretary general and military action after the Cold War*, Columbia, MO, University of Missouri Press, 2006.

Johnston, Seth A. *How NATO Adapts: Strategy and organization in the Atlantic Alliance since 1950*, Baltimore, MD, Johns Hopkins University Press, 2017.

Jordan, Robert S. *Political Leadership in NATO: A study in multinational diplomacy*, Boulder, CO, Westview Press, 1979.

Kaplan, Lawrence S. *NATO Divided, NATO United: The evolution of an alliance*, Westport, CT, Praeger, 2004.

Kaplan, Lawrence S. *NATO and the UN: A peculiar relationship*, Columbia, MO, University of Missouri Press, 2010.

Lindley-French, Julian. *The North Atlantic Treaty Organization: The enduring alliance*, Abingdon, Routledge, 2023.

Mayer, Sebastian (ed.). *NATO's Post-Cold War Politics: The changing provision of security*, London, Palgrave, 2014.

Schmidt, Gustav (ed.). *A History of NATO: The first fifty years*, London, Palgrave, 2001.

Sloan, Stanley R. *Defense of the West: Transatlantic security from Truman to Trump*, Manchester, Manchester University Press, 2020.

Thies, Wallace J. *Why NATO Endures*, Cambridge, Cambridge University Press, 2009.

Western community and ideals

Anderson, Jeffrey J., G. John Ikenberry, and Thomas Risse-Kappen. *The End of the West?: Crisis and change in the Atlantic order*, Ithaca, NY, Cornell University Press, 2008.

Burnham, James. *Suicide of the West: An essay on the meaning and destiny of liberalism*, New York, John Day, 1964.

Deutsch, Karl Wolfgang. *Political Community and the North American Area: International organization in the light of historical experience*, Princeton, NJ, Princeton University Press, 1957.

Gress, David. *From Plato to NATO: The idea of the west and its opponents*, New York, Free Press, 1998.

Jackson, Patrick Thaddeus. *Civilizing the Enemy: German reconstruction and the invention of the west*, Ann Arbor, MI, University of Michigan Press, 2009.

Kagan, Robert. *Of Paradise and Power: America and Europe in the New World Order*, New York, Knopf, 2003.

Kaplan, Robert D. *Earning the Rockies: How geography shapes America's role in the world*, New York, Random House, 2017.

Kimmage, Michael. *The Abandonment of the West: The history of an idea in American foreign policy*, New York, Basic Books, 2020.

Kissinger, Henry A. *World Order: Reflections on the character of nations and the course of history*, London, Allen Lane, 2014.

Lundestad, Geir. *The United States and Europe Since 1945: From "empire" by invitation to transatlantic drift*, Oxford, Oxford University Press, 2005.

McNeill, William H. *The Rise of the West: A history of the human community*, Chicago, IL, University of Chicago Press, 1963.

Risse-Kappen, Thomas. *Cooperation among Democracies: The European influence on US foreign policy*, Princeton, NJ, Princeton University Press, 1995.

Rynning, Sten, Olivier Schmitt, and Amelie Theussen (eds). *War Time: Temporality and the decline of western military power*, Washington, DC, Brookings Institution Press, 2021.

Founding and early Cold War

Brinkley, Douglas, and David R. Facey-Crowther (eds). *The Atlantic Charter*, New York, St. Martin's Press, 1994.

Cook, Don. *Forging the Alliance: NATO 1945–1950*, New York, Arbor House/W. Morrow, 1989.

De Porte, Anton W. *Europe between the Superpowers: The enduring balance*, New Haven, CT, Yale University Press, 1979.

Dietl, Ralph. "In defence of the west: General Lauris Norstad, NATO nuclear forces and transatlantic relations 1956–1963," *Diplomacy and Statecraft*, 17:2 (2006), 347–392.

Divine, Robert A. *The Reluctant Belligerent: American entry into World War II*, New York, Wiley, 1979.

Finch, George A. "The North Atlantic Pact in international law," *Proceedings of the American Society of International Law*, 43 (April 28–30, 1949), 90–102.

Gaddis, John Lewis. *The United States and the Origins of the Cold War, 1941–1947*, New York, Columbia University Press, 2000.

Heller, Francis H., and John R. Gillingham (eds). *NATO: The founding of the Atlantic Alliance and the integration of Europe*, New York, St. Martin's Press, 1992.

Henderson, Nicholas. *The Birth of NATO*, London, Weidenfeld and Nicolson, 1982.

Ismay, Hastings Lionel Pug. *NATO: The first five years*, Utrecht, Netherlands, Bosch-Utrecht, 1956.

Kaplan, Lawrence S. *The United States and NATO: The formative years*, Lexington, KY, University Press of Kentucky, 1984.

Kaplan, Lawrence S. *NATO 1948: The birth of the transatlantic alliance*, Lanham, MD, Rowman and Littlefield, 2007.

Kaplan, Lawrence S., and Sidney R. Snyder (eds). *Fingerprints on History: The NATO memoirs of Theodore C. Achilles*, Lyman L. Lemnitzer Center for NATO and European Community Studies Occasional Papers I, Kent State University, OH, 1992.

Kimball, Warren F. *Forged in War: Roosevelt, Churchill, and the Second World War*, New York, W. Morrow, 1997.

Leffler, Melvyn P. *A Preponderance of Power: National security, the Truman administration, and the Cold War*, Stanford, CA, Stanford University Press, 1992.

Lundestad, Geir. "Empire by invitation? The United States and Western Europe, 1945–1952," *Journal of Peace Research*, 23:3 (1986), 263–277.

Mariano, Marco (ed.). *Defining the Atlantic Community*, London, Routledge, 2010.

Milloy, John C. *The North Atlantic Treaty Organization, 1948–1957: Community or alliance?* Montreal, McGill-Queen's University Press, 2006.

Plokhy, Serhii. *Yalta: The price of peace*, London, Penguin, 2011.

Reid, Escott. *Time of Fear and Hope: The making of the North Atlantic Treaty, 1947–1949*, Toronto, McClelland and Stewart, 1977.

Sayle, Timothy Andrews. *Enduring Alliance: The history of NATO and the postwar global order*, Ithaca, NY, Cornell University Press, 2019.

Sherwen, Nicholas (ed.). *NATO's Anxious Birth: The prophetic vision of the 1940s*, London, Hurst & Company, 1985.

Smith, Joseph (ed.). *The Origins of NATO*, Exeter, University of Exeter Press, 1990.

Smith, Mark. *NATO Enlargement during the Cold War: Strategy and system in the Western Alliance*, Basingstoke, Palgrave, 2000.

Trachtenberg, Marc (ed.). *Between Empire and Alliance: America and Europe during the Cold War*, Lanham, MD, Rowman & Littlefield, 2003.

Trachtenberg, Marc. *A Constructed Peace: The making of the European settlement, 1945–1963*, Princeton, NJ, Princeton University Press, 2020.

Wertheim, Stephen. *Tomorrow, the World: The birth of US global supremacy*, Cambridge, MA, The Belknap Press of Harvard University Press, 2020.

Yergin, Daniel. *Shattered Peace: The origins of the Cold War*, New York, Penguin Books, 1990.

Cold War détente, crisis, and ending

Binnendijk, Hans. "NATO's nuclear modernization dilemma," *Survival*, 31:2 (1989), 137–155.

Calleo, David P. *The Atlantic Fantasy: The US, NATO, and Europe*, Baltimore, MD, Johns Hopkins University Press, 1970.

Cleveland, Harlan. *NATO: The transatlantic bargain*, New York, Harper and Row, 1970.

Colbourn, Susan. *Euromissiles: The nuclear weapons that nearly destroyed NATO*, Ithaca, NY, Cornell University Press, 2022.

Daalder, Ivo H. *The Nature and Practice of Flexible Response: NATO strategy and theater nuclear forces since 1967*, New York, Columbia University Press, 1991.

Donaghy, Aaron. *The Second Cold War: Carter, Reagan, and the politics of foreign policy*, Cambridge, Cambridge University Press, 2021.

Freeman, Stephanie. "The making of an accidental crisis: The United States and the NATO dual-track decision of 1979," *Diplomacy and Statecraft*, 25:2 (2014), 337–338.

Garthoff, Raymond L. *The Great Transition: American–Soviet relations and the end of the Cold War*, Washington, DC, Brookings Institution Press, 1994.

Gates, Robert M. *From the Shadows: The ultimate insider's story of five presidents and how they won the Cold War*, London, Simon & Schuster, 1996.

Haftendorn, Helga. *NATO and the Nuclear Revolution: A crisis of credibility, 1966–67*, Oxford, Oxford University Press, 1996.

Haslam, Jonathan. *The Soviet Union and the Politics of Nuclear Weapons in Europe, 1969–1987*, Ithaca, NY, Cornell University Press, 1990.

Larres, Klaus. *Uncertain Allies: Nixon, Kissinger, and the threat of a united Europe*, New Haven, CT, Yale University Press, 2021.

Matlock, Jack F. *Reagan and Gorbachev: How the Cold War ended*, New York, Random House, 2004.

Neustadt, Richard E. *Alliance Politics*, New York, Columbia University Press, 1970.

Nichter, Luke A. *Richard Nixon and Europe: The reshaping of the postwar Atlantic world*, Cambridge, Cambridge University Press, 2015.

Sayle, Timothy Andrews. *Enduring Alliance: The history of NATO and the postwar global order*, Ithaca, NY, Cornell University Press, 2019.

Soutou, Georges-Henri. *L'alliance incertaine: Les rapports politico-stratégiques franco-allemands 1954–1996*, Paris, Fayard, 1996.

Spohr, Kristina. "Conflict and cooperation in intra-alliance nuclear politics: Western Europe, the United States, and the genesis of NATO's dual-track decision, 1977–1979," *Journal of Cold War Studies*, 13:2 (2011), 39–89.

Spohr, Kristina. *The Global Chancellor: Helmut Schmidt and the reshaping of international order*, Oxford, Oxford University Press, 2016.

Vaïsse, Justin. *Zbigniew Brzezinski: America's grand strategist*, Cambridge, MA, Harvard University Press, 2018.

Wenger, Andreas, Vojtech Mastny, and Christian Nuenlist (eds). *Origins of the European Security System: The Helsinki process revisited, 1965–1975*, Abingdon, Routledge, 2008.

Wenger, Andreas, and Victor Mauer (eds). *Transatlantic Relations at Stake: Aspects of NATO, 1956–1972*, Zurich, CSS/ETH, 2006.

Zubok, Vladislav M. *Collapse: The fall of the Soviet Union*, New Haven, CT, Yale University Press, 2021.

Post-Cold War Europe and NATO enlargement

Asmus, Ronald D. *Opening NATO's Door: How the alliance remade itself for a new era*, New York, Columbia University Press, 2002.

Ball, Christopher L. "Nattering NATO negativism? Reasons why expansion may be a good thing," *Review of International Studies*, 24:1 (1998), 43–67.

Bush, George, and Brent Scowcroft. *A World Transformed*, New York, Alfred A. Knopf, 1999.

Calleo, David P. *Rethinking Europe's Future*, Princeton, NJ, Princeton University Press, 2001.

Chollet, Derek, and James Goldgeier. *America between the Wars: From 11/9 to 9/11*, New York, PublicAffairs, 2008.

Cogan, Charles. *Third Option: The emancipation of European Defense, 1989–2000*, Westport, CT, Praeger, 2001.

Daalder, Ivo H., and Michael E. O'Hanlon. *Winning Ugly: NATO's war to save Kosovo*, Washington, DC, Brookings Institution Press, 2000.

Engel, Jeffrey A. *When the World Seemed New: George H. W. Bush and the end of the Cold War*, Boston, MA, Houghton Mifflin Harcourt, 2017.

Eyal, Jonathan. "NATO's enlargement: Anatomy of a decision," *International Affairs*, 73:4 (1997), 695–719.

Gaddis, John Lewis. "History, grand strategy and NATO enlargement," *Survival*, 40:1 (1998), 145–151.

Goldgeier, James M. *Not Whether but When: The US decision to enlarge NATO*, Washington, DC, Brookings Institution Press, 1999.

Goldgeier, James, and Joshua R. Itzkowitz Shifrinson. *Evaluating NATO Enlargement: From Cold War victory to the Russia–Ukraine War*, London, Palgrave, 2023.

Hamilton, Daniel S., and Kristina Spohr (eds). *Open Door: NATO and Euro-Atlantic security after the Cold War*, Washington, DC, Johns Hopkins University Press, 2019.

Hooft, Paul van. "Land rush: American grand strategy, NATO enlargement, and European fragmentation," *International Politics*, 57:3 (2020), 530–553.

Kramer, Mark. "The myth of a no-NATO-enlargement pledge to Russia," *Washington Quarterly*, 32:2 (2009), 39–61.

Kramer, Mark. "NATO enlargement—Was there a promise?," *International Security*, 42:1 (2017), 186–192.

Kupchan, Charles A. "The origins and future of NATO enlargement," *Contemporary Security Policy*, 21:2 (2000), 127–148.

Layne, Christopher. "The US foreign policy establishment and grand strategy: How American elites obstruct strategic adjustment," *International Politics*, 54:3 (2017), 260–275.

Maass, Richard W. "NATO non-expansion and German reunification," *International Security*, 41:3 (2017), 197–200.

Mandelbaum, Michael. "Preserving the peace: The case against NATO expansion," *Foreign Affairs*, 74:3 (1995), 9–13.

MccGwire, Michael, and Michael Clarke. "NATO expansion: 'A policy error of historic importance,'" *International Affairs*, 84:6 (2008), 1281–1301.

Mearsheimer, John J. "Why the Ukraine crisis is the west's fault: The liberal delusions that provoked Putin," *Foreign Affairs*, 93:5 (2014), 1–12.

Rynning, Sten. *NATO Renewed: The power and purpose of transatlantic security cooperation*, New York, Palgrave, 2005.

Sakwa, Richard. *Russia and the Rest: The post-Cold War crisis of world order*, Cambridge, Cambridge University Press, 2017.

Sarotte, Mary Elise. *1989: The struggle to create post-Cold War Europe*, Princeton, NJ, Princeton University Press, 2015.

Sarotte, Mary Elise. *Not One Inch: America, Russia, and the making of post-Cold War stalemate*, New Haven, CT, Yale University Press, 2021.

Shifrinson, Joshua R. Itzkowitz. "Deal or no deal? The end of the Cold War and the US offer to limit NATO expansion," *International Security*, 40:4 (2016), 7–44.

Shifrinson, Joshua R. Itzkowitz. "Eastbound and down: The United States, NATO enlargement, and suppressing the Soviet and Western European alternatives, 1990–1992," *Journal of Strategic Studies*, 43:6–7 (2020), 816–846.

Spohr, Kristina. "Germany, America and the shaping of post-Cold War Europe: A story of German international emancipation through political unification, 1989–90," *Cold War History*, 15:2 (2015), 221–243.

Spohr, Kristina. *Post Wall, Post Square: How Bush, Gorbachev, Kohl, and Deng shaped the world after 1989*, New Haven, CT, Yale University Press, 2020.

Stent, Angela. *Russia and Germany Reborn: Unification, the Soviet collapse, and the new Europe*, Princeton, NJ, Princeton University Press, 1999.

Yost, David. *NATO Transformed: The alliance's new roles in international security*, Washington, DC, United States Institute of Peace, 2001.

War on terror and global NATO

Alexander, Yonah, and Richard Prosen. *NATO: From regional to global security provider*, Lanham, MD, Lexington Books, 2015.

Antonenko, Oksana, and Igor Yurgens. "Towards a NATO–Russia strategic concept," *Survival*, 52:6 (2010), 5–11.

Auerswald, David P., and Stephen M. Saideman. *NATO in Afghanistan: Fighting together, fighting alone*, Princeton, NJ, Princeton University Press, 2014.

Brzezinski, Zbigniew. "An agenda for NATO," *Foreign Affairs*, 88:5 (2009), 2–20.

Calleo, David P. *Follies of Power: America's unipolar fantasy*, Cambridge, Cambridge University Press, 2009.

Daalder, Ivo, and James Goldgeier. "Global NATO," *Foreign Affairs*, 85:5 (2006), 105–113.

Farrell, Theo. *Unwinnable: Britain's war in Afghanistan, 2001–2014*, London, The Bodley Head, 2017.

Hadley, Stephen J. *Hand-Off: The foreign policy George W. Bush handed to Barack Obama*, Washington, DC, Brookings Institution Press, 2023.

Hallams, Ellen (ed.). *The United States and NATO since 9/11*, Abingdon, Routledge, 2010.

Hardt, Heidi. *NATO's Lessons in Crisis: Institutional memory in international organizations*, Oxford, Oxford University Press, 2018.

Hendrickson, Ryan C. "NATO's first prime minister: Rasmussen's leadership surge," *RUSI Journal*, 155:5 (2010), 24–30.

Hlatky, Stéfanie von, and Thomas Juneau. "When the coalition determines the mission: NATO's detour in Libya," *Journal of Strategic Studies*, 45:2 (2022), 258–279.

Leffler, Melvyn P., and Jeffrey W. Legro. *In Uncertain Times: American foreign policy after the Berlin Wall and 9/11*, Ithaca, NY, Cornell University Press, 2011.

Rashid, Ahmed. *Descent into Chaos: The US and the disaster in Pakistan, Afghanistan, and Central Asia*, London, Penguin Books, 2009.

Robertson, George. "Being NATO's secretary general on 9/11," *NATO Review*, September 4, 2011. https://www.nato.int/docu/review/articles/2011/09/04/being-nato-s-secretary-general-on-9-11/index.html

Rynning, Sten. *NATO in Afghanistan: The liberal disconnect*, Stanford, CA, Stanford University Press, 2012.

Rynning, Sten, and Paal Sigurd Hilde. "Operationally agile but strategically lacking: NATO's bruising years in Afghanistan," *LSE Public Policy Review*, 2:3 (2022), 1–11.

Slobodchikoff, Michael O., G. Doug Davis, and Brandon Stewart. *The Challenge to NATO: Global security and the Atlantic Alliance*, Lincoln, NE, Potomac Books, 2021.

Williams, Michael J. *The Good War: NATO and the liberal conscience in Afghanistan*, London, Palgrave, 2011.

Yost, David. *NATO's Balancing Act*, Washington, DC, United States Institute of Peace, 2014.

Strategic competition in the twenty-first century

Ash, Timothy Garton. "Postimperial Europe: How the war in Ukraine is transforming Europe," *Foreign Affairs*, 102:3 (2023), 64–75.

Baker, Peter, and Susan Glasser. *The Divider: Trump in the White House, 2017–2021*, New York, Doubleday, 2022.

Belton, Catherine. *Putin's People: How the KGB took back Russia and then took on the West*, London, William Collins, 2020.

Biscop, Sven. *European Strategy in the 21st Century: New future for old power*, London, Routledge, 2019.

Blackwill, Robert D. *Trump's Foreign Policies are Better than they Seem*, New York, Council on Foreign Relations, 2019.

Carpenter, Ted Galen. *NATO: The dangerous dinosaur*, Washington, DC, Cato, 2019.

Fazal, Tanisha M. "The return of conquest? Why the future of global order hinges on Ukraine," *Foreign Affairs*, 101:3 (2022), 20–27.

Giles, Keir. *Moscow Rules: What drives Russia to confront the West*, Washington, DC, Brookings Institution Press, 2019.

Giles, Keir. *Russia's War on Everybody – And what it means for you*, London, Bloomsbury, 2023.

Haroche, Pierre, and Martin Quencez. "NATO facing China: Responses and adaptations," *Survival*, 64:3 (2022), 73–86.

Hooker, Richard D. "The state of NATO: An American view," *Survival*, 64:3 (2022), 103–113.

Ikenberry, G. John. "Why American power endures: The US-led order isn't in decline," *Foreign Affairs*, 101:6 (2022), 56–73.

Kauffmann, Sylvie. *Les aveuglés*, Paris, Stock, 2023.

Layne, Christopher. "Hyping the China threat," *National Interest*, 169 (2020), 21–31.

Lee, Sheryn, and Benjamin Schreer. "Will Europe defend Taiwan?," *Washington Quarterly*, 45:3 (2022), 163–182.

Mankoff, Jeffrey. *Empires of Eurasia: How imperial legacies shape international security*, New Haven, CT, Yale University Press, 2022.

Matlary, Janne Haaland, and Rob Johnson (eds). *Military Strategy in the 21st Century: The challenge for NATO*, London, Hurst & Company, 2020.

McMaster, Harold R. *Battlegrounds: The fight to defend the free world*, New York, Harper, 2020.

Plokhy, Serhii. *The Russo-Ukrainian War: The return of history*, New York, Norton, 2023.

Posen, Barry. *Restraint: A new foundation for US grand strategy*, Ithaca, NY, Cornell University Press, 2015.

Ringsmose, Jens, and Sten Rynning. "Now for the hard part: NATO's strategic adaptation to Russia," *Survival*, 59:3 (2017), 129–146.

Ringsmose, Jens, and Sten Rynning. "China brought NATO closer together," *War on the Rocks*, February 5, 2020. https://warontherocks.com/2020/02/china-brought-nato-closer-together/

Ringsmose, Jens, and Sten Rynning. "NATO's next strategic concept: Prioritise or perish," *Survival*, 63:5 (2021), 147–168.

Rynning, Sten. "Nato's struggle for a China policy: Alliance, alignment, or abdication?," *Asian Affairs*, 53:3 (2022), 481–499.

Staunton, Eglantine. "A useful failure: Macron's overture to Russia," *Survival*, 64:2 (2022), 17–24.

Stent, Angela E. *Putin's World: Russia against the West and with the rest*, New York, Twelve, 2020.

Truitt, Wesley B. *NATO Reconsidered: Is the Atlantic Alliance still in America's interest?* Santa Barbara, CA, Praeger, 2020.

Index

337

INDEX

INDEX